SPORT MANAGEMENT SERIES
Series editor: Professor David Shilbury

Strategic Sport Marketing

2nd edition

David Shilbury
Shayne Quick
and Hans Westerbeek

ALLEN&UNWIN

First published in 1998
This edition first published in 2003

Allen & Unwin
83 Alexander Street
Crows Nest, NSW 2065
Australia
Phone: (61 2) 8425 0100
Fax: (61 2) 9906 2218
E-mail: info@allenandunwin.com
Web: www.allenandunwin.com

National Library of Australia
Cataloguing-in-Publication entry:

Shilbury, David, 1958- .
Strategic sport marketing.

2nd ed,
Bibliography.
Includes index.
ISBN 978 1 86508 918 8
ISBN 1 86508 918 4.

1. Sports—Marketing. 2. Sports sponsorship. 3. Sports—Economic aspects.
I. Quick, Shayne P. (Shayne Pearce).
II. Westerbeek, Hans, 1965– . III. Title.

796.0698

Set in 10/12 pt Savoy by Bookhouse, Sydney
Printed and bound in Singapore by CMO Image Printing Enterprise

10 9 8 7 6 5 4 3

Contents

Preface

The face of sport has changed radically over the last 30 years. What was once just a local Saturday afternoon activity for both participants and spectators now takes place on any night of the week, and can be intrastate or interstate, with the fan experience live or mediated. In increasing numbers, supporters are demonstrating their allegiance to sport via the merchandise they buy, the literature they read and the television they watch. Sport in the 2000s is a multifaceted, multimedia industry, with growing appeal to an ever-increasing number of stakeholders and supporters. What was once a clearly defined, stable activity is now a highly complex, constantly changing industry. This is the environment in which the current generation of sport marketing practitioners must operate.

The sport experience can present a host of problematic consumer preferences for the sport marketer to target–compounded by the fact that sport no longer faces competition merely from within its own ranks. With decreasing amounts of leisure time, and discretionary income being judiciously allocated, sport now has to compete for the consumer dollar with a vast array of both sport and non-sport activities. The various branches of the arts, the increasing proclivity toward short-term tourist activities and the growth of passive recreation all provide viable alternatives to the sport experience for the modern consumer. Sport is now just one component, albeit a very important one, of the entertainment milieu.

Given this cluttered environment, sport attracts consumers not through serendipity, but rather through carefully structured planning, creativity and perseverance. Successful sport marketing is the implementation of clearly defined strategies which are rooted in both perspiration and inspiration. The notion 'if we build it they will come' is no longer appropriate. Planning processes are now required that view sport not merely as an athletic endeavour, but as an activity in which multiple individuals and groups can engage.

There is little doubt that sport is changing both on and off the field. While athletes have become fitter, stronger and faster to cope with the demands of the modern game, the management of sport has, at the same time, become a highly professional endeavour. To facilitate this process, and enhance the expertise of those charged with its effective management, education and training are now vital components of the sport environment. Increasingly, both the sport industry and educational institutions have realised that sport can no longer be managed by individuals or groups who do not come equipped with certain skills.

It is important to recognise the range of skills required to manage the modern sporting organisation when preparing the educational framework for future sports managers. The growth in sport marketing teaching and practice is accompanied by a growth in sport management education generally. Sport marketing remains a popular area of study, viewed as exciting and attractive to the next generation of sport managers. The challenge of preparing graduates and practitioners for the rigours of sport management lies in balancing the emotion and tribal character of sport with the need for an objective application of business principles. Modern management of sport is more than just a response to traditional actions or present realities. It encompasses a vision for the future and the strategies and implementations required for bringing about that vision. This vision is based on a well-rounded curriculum cognisant of the need to integrate sport industry knowledge with the fundamentals of management, marketing, accounting and finance, and other business studies. Texts such as this one play an important part in assisting in this process. They are constructed by individuals and groups who understand the sport experience and what it means to play, spectate and officiate, and who understand the meaning of management. In many instances they have moved beyond sport and have appropriated from other fields of endeavour those theories and strategies which, when used appropriately, result in a successful sport experience for all concerned.

The ability to translate theory into effective strategic practice is the result of management education programs that utilise business practice to comprehend contemporary sport while simultaneously remaining cognisant of what sport means to the end consumer or fan. The modern consumer is discerning and needs to be treated as such. This text, through the provision of theory and example, will result in future generations of sport marketers having the skills critical to the successful promotion of their sport.

Strategic Sport Marketing is unique from two perspectives. It is the first sport marketing text to truly integrate international examples. Case studies, sportviews and examples from a myriad of national and international sports and events have been used to reinforce theoretical positions and key points. From Australian Rules Football to European Soccer, from the Sydney Kings to the Chicago Bulls, a concerted effort has been made to include as many popular sports and events as possible.

While this is important, more significant is the fact that there has been a conscious decision to place the text within a framework of strategic decision making. The three major components of the text underscore this commitment. Part I of *Strategic Sport Marketing* concentrates on identifying market opportunities, focusing on the consumer and the way in which information can be gathered, collated and utilised in order to establish an effective marketing management process. In this new edition, Part II delves into determining the best strategies to use when dealing with a particular component of the sport experience. Included in this section is the recognition that sporting organisations provide a service. New chapters have been added to expand the focus on service provision and emphasise service quality and customer satisfaction. Linda van Leeuwen has written the newly added chapter 8 focusing on customer satisfaction and service quality. Technology and its implications on the selection of marketing mix variables are also considered in a new chapter, written by Daniel Evans, exploring sport and the Internet. Sponsorship and its importance in the promotions mix have been expanded into two chapters: chapter 13 focusing on how to attract sponsorship and chapter 14 on measuring sponsorship effectiveness. Thus, Part II develops in some detail the theoretical and practical significance of marketing the sport service. Finally, Part III establishes mechanisms for the ongoing evaluation, adjustment and maintenance of the strategic marketing process. Collectively, the three sections provide a seamless comprehension of the integration of consumer, activity and process. In addition, the second edition of *Strategic Sport Marketing* gathers together a new set of sportviews, case studies and examples to illustrate sport marketing in action.

Strategic Sport Marketing is aimed at senior undergraduates and entry-level graduate sport marketing students. It is also a useful resource for the practitioner engaged in sport marketing. While the case studies provide obvious examples of how the text can be used, we hope that this text will be used by sport marketing teachers and practitioners not only to stimulate the thought processes, but to engage with and improve the sport experience for the benefit of all concerned. Finally, it is hoped that the utility of this text will result in calls for ongoing literary contributions to the field of sport management.

David Shilbury
Shayne Quick
Hans Westerbeek

About the authors

David Shilbury is Head of the Bowater School of Management and Marketing and Professor of Sport Management at Deakin University. In 1990 he was responsible for the implementation of the first business-based programs in sport management in Australia, establishing the Bachelor of Commerce (Sport Management) and the Master of Business (Sport Management).

Prior to commencing at Deakin University, David worked for the Australian Cricket Board in Perth, the City of Stirling and the Western Australian Golf Association. He was a member of the Victorian Sports Council in 1995 and has been a member of the AFL Tribunal since 1992. In 1999/2000 David won the Eunice Gill Award for Sport Management presented by the Victorian Sports Federation. He was also the Foundation President of the Sport Management Association of Australia and New Zealand between 1995 and 2001.

David is the editor of *Sport Management Review* and a member of the editorial board for the *International Journal of Sport Management*. His most recent textbook, *Sport Management in Australia* (2001), serves as the introductory text to many sport management courses in Australia. David has been published widely in various journals and has presented papers at conferences in Australia, New Zealand, North America and Europe.

David received a Diploma of Teaching and a BAppSc (Recreation) from Edith Cowan University in 1976 and 1984 respectively, a MSc (Sport Management) from the University of Massachusetts/Amherst in 1989, and PhD from Monash University in 1995. His principal research interests lie in the areas of sports development, strategy, marketing and organisational effectiveness in sporting organisations.

Shayne Quick is the Director for Project Development at the University of Technology, Sydney and Coordinator of the Sport Management program. He has taught undergraduate and postgraduate subjects in sport management and sport marketing at universities in both Australia and North America and is an adjunct professor at the Democritus University of Thrace in Greece. He is also the President of the Sport Management Association of Australia and New Zealand.

Shayne obtained a BAppSci (PE) from Victoria University of Technology, a BEd from Monash University, a MA from the University of Western Ontario, Canada, and a PhD from the Ohio State University, USA. He has been a consultant to the Houston Rockets, Sydney Kings, the Australian Motorcycle Grand Prix, the NSW Waratahs and the Australian Rugby Union.

Shayne's research has focused on the management of professional sporting organisations in Australia, sport and consumer behaviour and sport management education. He has published widely on these topics and presented papers at both domestic and international forums.

Hans Westerbeek is Senior Lecturer in Deakin University's (Melbourne) Sport Management program and Senior Associate with the Centre for Business Research, specialising in international (sport) marketing and quantitative research. He also is a visiting Professor in Sports Marketing with the VLEKHO Business School in Brussels, Belgium.

Hans is a founding Board member of the Dutch Society for Managers in Sport (NVMS), the European Association for Sport Management (EASM) and the Sport Management Association of Australia and New Zealand (SMAANZ). Currently Vice President of SMAANZ, he also holds an executive position on the Board of the Australian Netherlands Chamber of Commerce (Holland Trade) and is a director of the Dutch–Australian consulting company Manage to Manage.

Before moving to Australia in 1994, Hans worked throughout Europe as a member of the sport management committee of the European Union's Network of Sport Science Institutes, creating the European Masters of Sport Management.

As a consultant, Hans has worked with a range of corporate clients including Philips, Australia Post, Coles Myer and the Western Mining Company. Among the organisations he has worked with in the sport industry are the International Management Group, FIFA, Tennis Australia, the Giro d'Italia, the Australian Cricket Board and the Australian Football League.

Hans has authored numerous articles in academic journals such as the *International Marketing Review*, the *Journal of Marketing Communications*, the *Sport Marketing Quarterly* and the *Sport Management Review*. He is a regular contributor to a number of professional publications including the *SportBusiness International* magazine and he is co-author of *Sport Business in the Global Marketplace* (Palgrave Macmillan, 2003). Hans holds a Bachelors degree in Physical Education, Masters degrees in Human Movement Sciences (MSc) and Business Administration (MBA) and a PhD in International Marketing.

1

An overview of sport marketing

CHAPTER OBJECTIVES

After studying this chapter you should be able to:

1. Discuss the role of marketing in organisations.
2. Identify the marketing mix.
3. Describe the importance of marketing in sport organisations.
4. Describe the unique product features of sport and their impact on sport marketing.
5. Define sport marketing.

HEADLINE STORY

Promoters breathless as Woods beats cut

As Tiger Woods tapped in the shortest of birdie putts on the 18th green last night, you could almost hear the sighs of relief from the promoters of the New Zealand Open. For almost five hours, their multi-million-dollar investment in the world No. 1 had hung on a knife edge. Where a week ago the bookies would only talk of Woods winning, yesterday the unthinkable loomed. Fears of him missing his first cut anywhere in the world since 1997. With his putter still out of sync and his long game becoming a co-conspirator, the promoters were having nightmares about a mile-long of angry spectators demanding their money back for a weekend without the star attraction. But the sight of him not putting one of his drives within 15 yards of a fairway over the first seven holes and then missing twice from four feet as he dropped three successive shots on the back nine called for a rethink. (Otway 2002: 43)

'Woods' flat fee of $NZ5 million ($A4.16 million) to appear in the tournament dwarfs the $NZ1 million total prizemoney' (Carroll 2002: 8), but was seen by promoters as worth the risk in order to highlight golf for a New Zealand and global golfing public. Golf's dilemma is indicative of the challenges confronting sports in an increasingly competitive and commercial environment—that is, how to obtain a competitive advantage over other sports by maximising the promotional potential of its star players. The risk for promoters was financial. Would the drawing power of Tiger Woods, and the subsequent rise in ticket prices, ensure at least break-even or better for the tournament promoters? As Carroll noted (2002: 8), the 'local golf association that normally stages the tournament was out of its financial league and had to contract the event to a private corporation'. By contracting the event out, the local golf association divorced itself from the financial risk yet encouraged the potential for a promotional windfall for golf in New Zealand. Globally, television was the vehicle used to promote golf, New Zealand and the star attraction, Tiger Woods.

In the technological world of the 1990s and 2000s, many sports have emerged via the media to challenge for the position of global dominance. Soccer has long remained unchallenged as the world's most globalised sport. This competitive advantage has been based on high levels of participation and interest in so many countries throughout the world. For example, the 1998 World Cup drew a cumulative television audience of nearly 40 billion for the 64 matches (Dauncey & Hare 2000). Basketball, via the National Basketball Association (NBA), is another example, as is tennis. Golf, a genuinely global game but generally targeting different demographic groups from basketball or soccer, nicely expounds the conundrum confronting sport marketers. The challenge is how to maintain the integrity of golf's traditions, yet ensure that sophisticated marketing strategies are devised to position and expand the sport globally.

Major changes to the competitive positions of a variety of sports have occurred as a consequence of the media's ability to show sporting competitions played in all parts of the world. Domestic competitions also have increased in familiarity through the media. For example, the former Victorian Football League (VFL) has expanded from a 12-team state-based competition to become a 16-team national competition played in five states. Basketball also has capitalised on its increased exposure, creating the National Basketball League (NBL).

> Television has contributed to the emergence of new and restructured competitions. Changing environmental conditions have forced sport managers to develop marketing strategies for their sports, leading to the creation of sport-marketing departments and the employment of marketing specialists in sporting organisations.

The purpose of this book is to examine the role of marketing within the sports context. More specifically, it will consider the role of marketing from a strategic perspective, highlighting the ways in which marketing contributes to the growth and development of sports. Marketing assumes greater significance than other management functions in sporting organisations, as it remains the principal means by which sports compete off the field. For instance, large firms such as BHP, PepsiCo and Pacific Dunlop have the option to pursue acquisition-type strategies to build market share, or to engage in product development or diversification. These strategies are generally not available to sporting organisations, whose principal responsibility is as a national governing body, such as the Australian Soccer Federation, Australian Softball Federation or Women's Cricket Australia. In the broader context of the sport industry, major manufacturing firms such as Nike, Adidas, Puma and Spalding are large firms that do have the capacity to pursue acquisition-based strategies. In sport, each governing body is responsible for a specific code, and its charter is to develop and enhance that particular sport. Minor game modifications may occur, but sport-governing bodies rarely use strategies based on product diversification or acquisition. This is particularly evident for club-based sport systems.

New Zealand golf's desire to make the game more appealing by attracting Tiger Woods is an example of a sport embarking on a market penetration strategy designed to capture a larger share of the existing market. It could also be argued that this strategy was designed to create a new market for an existing product, largely based on the aura and ability of 'Tiger Woods' to crash through the media clutter. The importance of marketing strategy in sport management is illustrated by golf and is further discussed later in this chapter.

Marketing defined

Marketing, as defined by Kotler et al. (1994: 5), is 'a social and managerial process by which individuals and groups obtain what they need and want through creating and exchanging products and value with others'. The identification of consumer needs and wants is a critical aspect of the marketer's role. Marketing strategies must be based on known consumer needs.

In sport, it has been assumed that the original form of the game is naturally attractive and therefore satisfies consumer needs. An analysis of sporting organisations in Australia shows this to be an outdated view. Many sports have modified rules to make their games more attractive, and in the case of cricket one-day matches have become an important part of the range of product offerings. One-day international matches played throughout an Australian summer have more readily satisfied consumer need for compressed entertainment and a quick result. At junior levels, many sports have been significantly modified to satisfy the desire of many more young people to participate in the game. Inherent in this change has been the recognition that juniors wish to develop game skills through actual participation, to have fun, and in general to be with their friends through the sport setting.

The sport marketer must identify what needs and wants are being satisfied through the exchange process. Kotler et al. (1994: 7) identify the process of exchange 'as the act of obtaining a desired object from someone by offering something in return'. What is offered in return for the sport consumer's membership fees or entry fee may include social interaction, physical activity, an avenue for competition, health and fitness, as well as entertainment. Identifying the needs of various segments of population is the challenge inherent in the early phase of the marketing process. Obtaining this information will allow the sport product benefits to be communicated in such a way as to define the sport's positioning. For example, the product attributes of one-day cricket matches and five-day Test match cricket are different, and are likely to attract different segments of the market.

Having established the range of product attributes in relation to needs and wants, the sport marketer embarks on the challenge of effecting the exchange. Sporting organisations must develop a mix of marketing strategies to influence consumers to buy their products, via either attendance or participation. Combined, the four variables of product, price, promotion and place are known as the traditional four Ps of marketing.

Defining the sport marketing mix

Figure 1.1 depicts the seven component strategies of the marketing mix, composed of the traditional 4Ps of marketing plus the 3Ps of service–process, people and physical evidence. These 7Ps form the nucleus of this book, and each will be described in more detail in later chapters. A brief description of the 7Ps is as follows:

- *Product*–ensures that product characteristics provide benefits to the consumer (includes identifying the actual product).
- *Price*–ensures that the product is priced at a level that reflects consumer value.
- *Place*–distributes the product to the right place at the right time to allow ease of purchase.
- *Physical evidence*–is the visual and/or tangible clues of the service product, such as the design and construction of the facility, and in general the aesthetic appeal.
- *Process*–represents the convergence of the marketing and operations functions and therefore affects real-time service delivery and quality.
- *People*–are responsible for delivering the event and are a major distinguishing quality factor in the consumption process.
- *Promotion*–communicates the product's ability to satisfy the customer through advertising, personal selling, sales promotions, sponsorship, public relations and promotional licensing.

In sport, the combination and implementation of these marketing mix variables change due to the unique characteristics of the sport product. The most notable change from the traditional 4Ps of marketing is not only in its expansion to 7Ps, but in the order we recommend in determining marketing strategies for sporting organisations, particularly those reliant on facilities to host the sporting contest. This expansion and reordering also take account of the special features of sport, and are described in the next section.

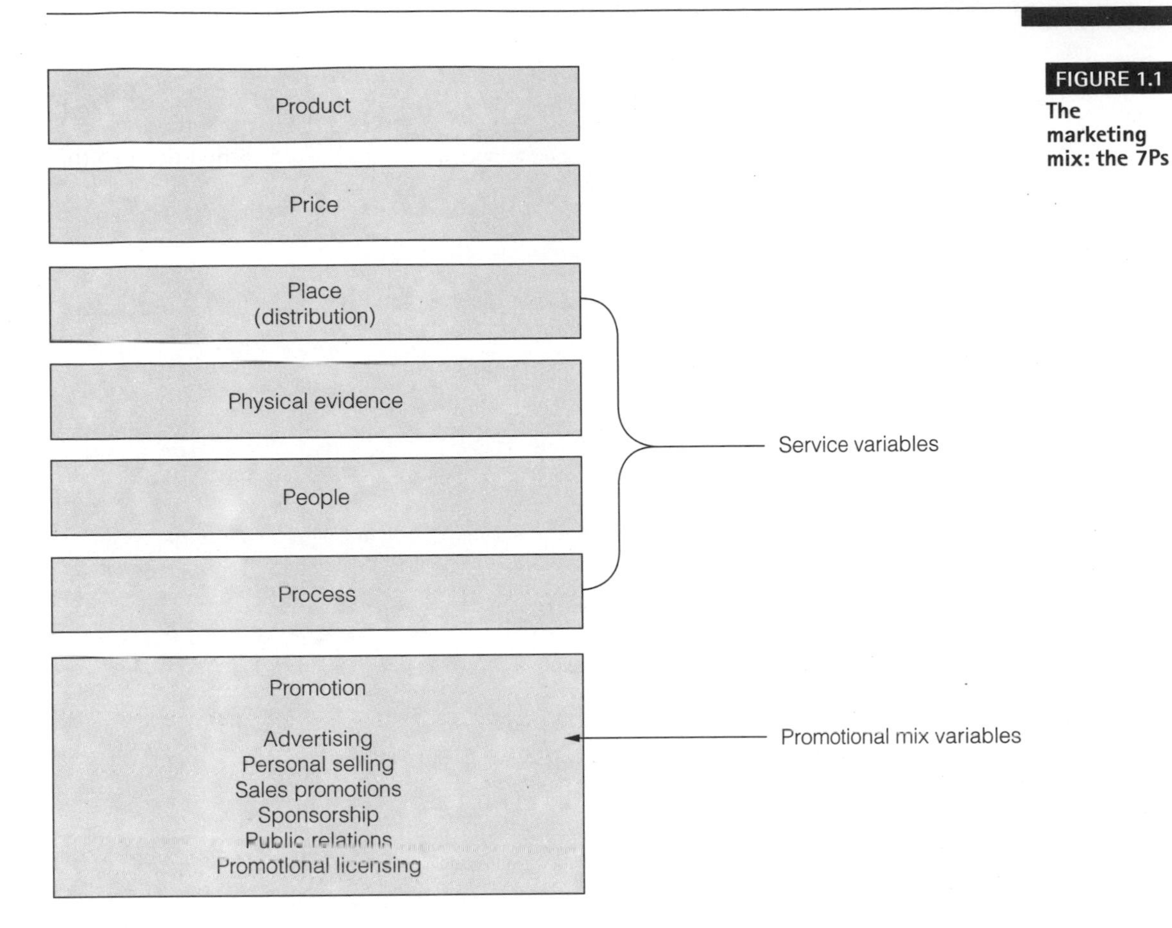

FIGURE 1.1 The marketing mix: the 7Ps

Unique characteristics of sport and sport marketing

In 1980 Mullin identified, for the first time, a series of characteristics of the sport product that affect the marketing process. Mullin argued that sport had progressed from a form of institution that was simply 'administered' to a form of organisation that required 'managing'. In making this distinction, he noted that sport had reached a phase in its development where it was incumbent on the sport manager to be actively seeking ways to expand the revenue base of the organisation. Typically, the administrator is responsible for maintaining the status quo within the sporting organisation. The manager, on the other hand, is responsible for assessing and evaluating environmental trends likely to affect the organisation's survival and, ultimately, its success. The modern sport marketer is charged with one simple responsibility: to increase the sources of revenue for the sport. The tools to achieve this will be discussed in later chapters.

Mullin identified five special characteristics of sport marketing. In examining these characteristics, he noted (1985: 106):

TABLE 1.1
Unique characteristics of sport marketing

Market for sport products and services
- Sport organisations simultaneously compete and cooperate.
- Partly due to the unpredictability of sport, and partly due to strong personal identification, sport consumers often consider themselves 'experts'.

Sport product
- Sport is invariably intangible and subjective.
- Sport is inconsistent and unpredictable.
- Marketing emphasis must be placed on product extensions rather than the core product.
- Sport is generally publicly consumed, and consumer satisfaction is invariably affected by social facilitation.
- Sport is both a consumer and an industrial product.
- Sport evokes powerful personal identification and emotional attachment.
- Sport has almost universal appeal and pervades all elements of life, i.e. geographically, demographically and socioculturally.

Price of sport
- The price of sport paid by the consumer is invariably quite small in comparison to the total cost.
- Indirect revenues (e.g. from television) are often greater than direct operating revenues (e.g. gate receipts).
- Sport programs have rarely been required to operate on a for-profit basis.
- Pricing is often decided by what the consumer will bear rather than by full cost recovery.

Promotion of sport
- Widespread exposure afforded to sport by the media has resulted in a low emphasis on sport marketing and, often, complacency.
- Due to the high visibility of sport, many businesses wish to associate with sport.

Sport distribution system
- Sports generally do not physically distribute their product. Most sport products are produced, delivered and consumed simultaneously at the one location. The exceptions are sporting goods and retail and broadcast sport.

Source: Adjusted from Mullin (1985).

> Almost every element of marketing requires significantly different approaches when the product being marketed is sport. Predictably, the critical differences lie in the unique aspects of the sport product, and the unusual market conditions facing sport marketers.

The five characteristics noted by Mullin are summarised in Table 1.1, with supporting examples. Interestingly, some of these characteristics reflect attributes associated with marketing services. Whether this was intentional is uncertain; clearly sport is a service product. Service-marketing implications for sport marketing will be further developed and integrated throughout this text.

Consumer involvement

Perhaps the most readily identifiable characteristic is the 'expertise' demonstrated by the sport consumer. On the one hand this is a disadvantage, as every move made by the sport manager and coaching staff is critically examined and dissected. The 'armchair selector' syndrome is an issue within sport. It is, however, one reason why sport is so popular. The pervasiveness and universal nature of sport, and the ease with which the consumer identifies with the sport product, compensate for the intensity with which the consumer follows sport. Very few businesses in the world are viewed with such simplicity and such personal identification by the consumer.

Unpredictability

As with most service products, the consumer's interpretation and enjoyment of the sport product are open to considerable subjectivity. Participation in, and attendance at, sporting contests allow the consumer to gain varying forms of gratification. For example, some spectators may enjoy the closeness of the game, others the entertainment surrounding the game, and yet others the inherent strategies of the contest. This makes it difficult for the sport marketer to ensure a high probability of satisfaction and hence repeat-attendance. The intangibility and subjective nature of sport spectating and sport attending clearly align sport with the service industry. No tangible product is taken from the sporting contest–as opposed, for example, to the purchase of a washing machine or similar goods. These characteristics of the service experience are further examined and extended in chapters 5, 7 and 8, which cover service quality, facility management in the context of service delivery, and customer satisfaction in sport.

Equally unpredictable is the actual sporting contest, which varies week by week. This heterogeneity is a feature of sport. It is the unpredictability of the result, and the quality of the contest, that consumers find attractive. For the sport marketer this is problematic, as the quality of the contest cannot be guaranteed, no promises can be made in relation to the result, and no assurances can be given in respect of the performance of star players. Unlike consumer products, sport cannot and does not display consistency as a key feature of marketing strategies. The sport marketer therefore must avoid marketing strategies based solely on winning, and must focus on developing product extensions rather than on the core product (i.e. the game itself). Product extensions include the facility, parking, merchandise, souvenirs, food and beverages–in general, anything that affects spectators' enjoyment of the event. In chapters 5, 7 and 8 we discuss the methods by which sport marketers can develop and improve the quality of product extensions.

Competition and cooperation

Another feature of the sportscape is the peculiar economy that dictates, in professional leagues at least, that clubs must both engage in fierce competition and at the same time cooperate. This is necessary to ensure that each club's contribution to the league enhances the strength of the league. An unusual blend of politics and competition emerges in sports leagues, often amplifying the importance of the public relations function, to be further explored in chapter 15.

Sponsorship

Sponsorship of sport is also a unique feature of the sports economy. While not necessarily specific to sport, sponsorship has provided, and continues to provide, an opportunity for commercial advertising by corporations and businesses. Sponsorship represents the 'industrial' component of the sport product, and is manifested through commercial advertising of its industrial aspect.

Publicity

Complacency in developing adequate marketing strategies has resulted from an almost unlimited amount of media exposure for sporting clubs, leagues and associations. Sport has traditionally been able to rely on publicity as its principal form of marketing and promotion. The disadvantage of relying on publicity is the amount of negative press that occurs during a season or major event. More recently, major leagues, clubs and associations have become cognisant of the need to develop an effective public relations strategy to counter the issues that typically occur during a season or event. This book views the public relations function as a very important aspect of the promotional mix.

Distribution

The final characteristic relates to the distribution system used by sport. As with most service providers, sports participation and spectating revolve around specific facilities for specific sports. To attend a sporting contest, spectators must travel to the venue, usually a major facility within a city. The actual facility becomes an integrated component of the marketing function, as the sport product is produced, consumed and delivered at the same time at the same venue. Many facilities, such as the Melbourne Cricket Ground (MCG), the Royal Melbourne Golf Club, Fenway Park in Boston and Wembley Stadium in London, have developed an aura and mystique as a result of heroic performances on the ground over the years.

As a consequence of developments in television networks, the distribution system for sport has undergone radical change during the past decade. It is now possible to distribute a game to all parts of the country and the world via the networks. The introduction of pay-television in Australia has further enhanced the distribution network for sport, as well as increasing the number and levels of different sport competitions shown. In general, however, the televised sport product is different from the live event. The mix of benefits is slightly different in each mode of consumption.

Due to the relatively stable nature of distribution (i.e. one major stadium per sport per city), it is vitally important to locate teams and facilities so that they are able to compete effectively in the market. In Australia, product distribution has been the focus of intense debate during the past decade. This is particularly evident in the move to expand the Victorian Football League (VFL) to become the Australian Football League (AFL). In the early 1980s, the VFL was a 12-team, state-based competition primarily located in Melbourne. By 1991 the league had changed its name to the AFL, as it had relocated the South Melbourne Football Club to Sydney and admitted the Brisbane Football Club and West Coast Football Club in 1987, followed by the Adelaide Crows in 1991. By 1995 a second team from Western Australia (Fremantle) had joined the competition, and a second team from South Australia (Port Adelaide) entered in 1997. Nine teams, however, remain in Melbourne, a city of approximately 3.7 million people. While this is an example of a league reconfiguring its distribution, once established it should remain relatively stable.

A comparison between the United States and Australia illustrates how important location of the product is in terms of developing appropriate marketing strategies, particularly in view of the substantial population differences between the two countries. The United States, for example, has a population in excess of 280 million, compared to Australia's 19 million. The US national competitions of basketball (National Basketball Association, NBA), football (National Football League, NFL), baseball (Major League Baseball, MLB) and ice hockey (National Hockey League, NHL) have evolved past the point of overcapacity in any one city. Significantly, the three major markets of New York, Los Angeles and Chicago (all with a population of 10–14 million) all host professional franchises. However, not one of these markets hosts more than two teams of any one code. The importance of marketing as a revenue-generating activity for the clubs is important in this issue of location. Overcapacity intensifies competition and reduces the available income for each of the teams located in any one common market.

Importance of marketing in sport management

As indicated earlier in this chapter, marketing plays a key role in the sporting organisation's overall planning efforts. This has not always been the case. The professionalisation of sport during the past 20–30 years has raised the level of importance of the marketing function.

For much of sport history, volunteers have administered organisations in the true spirit of amateur participation. As sport systems founded on club-based models evolved from amateur to professional clubs, leagues and associations, there was a lengthy transition period between what is described as 'kitchen table' administration and professional management. In Australia, this was the period pre-1970. As Figure 1.2(a) illustrates, during this period of voluntary administration the marketing function was non-existent. The predominant tasks were to ensure the ongoing operation of the club, league or association. Administrators adopted a very narrow view of their organisation, preferring to concentrate on internal operations. Typically, administrators dealt with only half of the accounting and budgetary process–the allocation and control of expenditures. Even as sporting organisations began to professionalise, the administrator 'culture' lingered for some years.

Figure 1.2(b) displays the progressive movement away from administration to management of organisations. One of the manager's main tasks is to monitor environmental trends and plan for the organisation's ongoing growth. Sport was very reluctant to embrace proactive growth. The Australian Cricket Board's (ACB) dispute with Kerry Packer over television rights, and the players' push for improved remuneration and playing conditions in 1977, are examples of a major sport adopting narrow internal perspectives. The introduction of colour television was an example of a technological change ignored by the ACB. World Series Cricket (WSC) subsequently proved to be the catalyst that forced sporting organisations in Australia to embrace a greater range of business functions. This view is supported by Halbish (1995: 3), noting that 'looking back traditional cricket had grown out of touch with the fast emerging professionalism of sport in Australia'. By 1980, WSC and the ACB had reconciled their differences; however, from that point marketing was to become an important element of business activity in sport.

Initially, marketing activities were outsourced by a number of sports. The ACB, for example, granted marketing rights to a company known as PBL Marketing. Taylor (1984: 13), managing director of PBL at the time, made the following observations about the status of marketing and sponsorship in sport following the reconciliation:

> Five years ago the Australian Cricket Board did not have a published program... Last year more than 300 000 copies of the ACB program were sold and this year almost 20 publications will be on sale. Work has also been put into merchandising... it has taken five years to develop

FIGURE 1.2
Importance of sport marketing

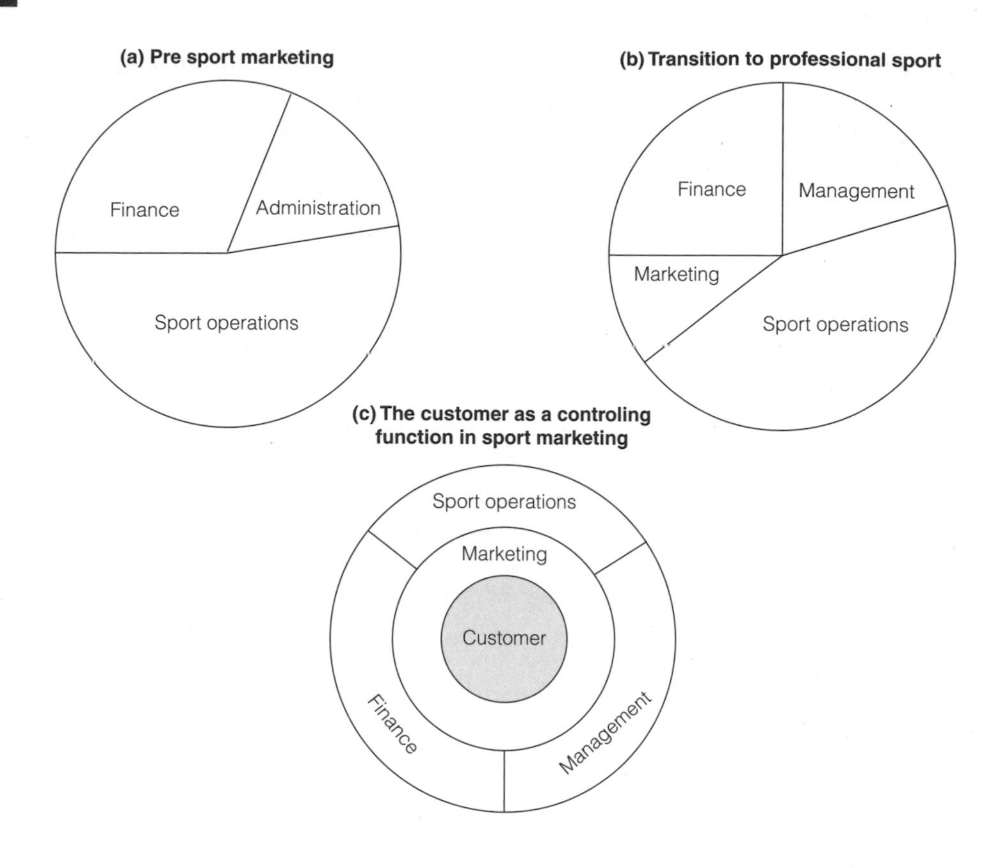

> 29 licensees, but this season we expect cricket merchandise to top $5 million in retail turnover and to start producing a satisfactory level of return.

Figure 1.2(c) demonstrates the importance that marketing has gained, despite a long period of resisting the need to promote and nurture new and fertile markets. For the first time, the identification and nurturing of new markets brought recognition that the customer is central to ongoing organisational survival. Sports had to find ways of generating revenue to sustain the growing costs of professional competitions. One-day cricket is an example of modifying the product to increase market share for the sport. Together with sport operations (i.e. all that surrounds the management of fielding a team), marketing is a sporting organisation's principal ground for identifying and creating a competitive advantage. Normal acquisitional strategies associated with for-profit firms are not so readily applicable to sport. Internal growth strategies tend to be the major ground on which sport competes. These strategies are further developed in chapter 2.

Ethical behaviour

Increasingly, commercial pressures create tension for the sport marketer. That is, sport-marketing executives often find themselves caught between an opportunity to generate revenue for their sport and the consequences of changes that might accompany these revenues. Consider, for example, the staging of an Olympic marathon during the middle and hottest part of the day because a television network asks for it to be staged at that time to maximise ratings. What do you do? Clearly, scheduling the marathon at this time will not be in the best interests of the athletes. Alternatively, what do you do if you work with the NRL and the strategic goal is to reduce the number of clubs in the competition? This was a real-life dilemma, as the South Sydney Rugby League club was removed from the competition as part of a rationalisation strategy. The club subsequently won the right, through a protracted legal battle, for readmission to the NRL competition from 2002. As a sport-marketing manager, with the goal of maximising revenues for the competition, how do you balance the commercial interests against social and community interests in the South Sydney club? These two examples illustrate ethical dilemmas, which are practical problems requiring solutions, often involving equally compelling reasons to act one way or the other. In essence, the sport manager must determine what is the right thing to do without a definitive 'rule book' available to guide decision making.

Although space precludes a detailed analysis of ethics and corporate social responsibility, sport managers must consider their actions within a broader societal framework. De Sensi and Rosenberg (1996: 115) note that social responsibility 'involves a moral and legal accountability on the part of individuals for self and others... Questions regarding the nature of the complex relationship between society, sport and the formal organisations of sport are raised within social responsibility'. Given the significant standing of sport in Australian culture and as a social institution, community expectations in relation to the behaviour of sport managers are often high. There are many examples of sport-marketing decisions that create ethical tensions for individuals, and collectively for organisations, wishing to be good corporate citizens. Some of these are explored during this book–in particular in the chapters on sponsorship, where ambush marketing is a source of considerable ethical frustration for managers.

Sport marketing defined

The term 'sport marketing' was first used in the United States by the *Advertising Age* in 1978. Since then it has been used to describe a variety of activities associated with sport promotion. Two distinct streams exist within the broad concept of sport marketing–marketing 'of' sport, and marketing 'through' sport.

Marketing 'of' sport

This refers to the use of marketing mix variables to communicate the benefits of sport participation and spectatorship to potential consumers. Ultimately, the goal is to ensure the ongoing survival of the sport in rapidly changing environmental circumstances. It is this aspect of marketing that has only recently developed in sporting organisations. Survival depends largely on the principal purpose of the sporting organisation. National sporting organisations predominantly associated with elite-level professional sporting competitions will be striving to develop their marketing mix to ensure that the sport product is attractive as a form of live entertainment and live television. Sports-governing bodies will also be responsible for ensuring that participation in their sport remains healthy. Participants are the lifeblood of sports, as they become the next generation of champions and spectators.

We do not make any notable distinctions in this book between marketing strategies specifically pursued for either spectator or participant sport. The theories posited are equally applicable, regardless of the principal objective of the marketing strategy. As with all marketing strategies, when the objectives change, the actions or strategies used to achieve the objectives also change. The application of the marketing mix does not, although various components of the mix may assume more importance in the two different scenarios. For example, the outlets used to advertise a junior sporting competition would be different from those used to advertise a major sporting event. Students of sport marketing should adapt the concepts of sport marketing to either situation, because each is vital to the ongoing survival and financial wellbeing of individual sporting organisations.

Marketing 'through' sport

Sponsorship of sport by firms is an example of marketing 'through' sport. Large corporations use sport as a vehicle to promote and advertise their products, usually to specifically identifiable demographic markets known to follow a particular sport. Sports with significant television time are very attractive to firms seeking to promote their products through an association with sport. Developing licensing programs is another example of marketing through sport. Typically, major companies such as Tip Top (bread) or Coca-Cola pay for the right to use a sport logo to place on their products to stimulate sales.

Although the main emphasis of this book is on marketing 'of' sport, the role of corporate sponsorship and licensing in sport marketing is also examined.

Definition

Given these perspectives, and information pertaining to marketing in general, the following definition of sport marketing is offered:

> Sport marketing is a social and managerial process by which the sport manager seeks to obtain what sporting organisations need and want through creating and exchanging products and value with others.

The exchange of value with others recognises the importance of the sport consumer. The many different types of sport consumer are discussed in more detail in Part I of this book.

Overview of this book

The ability to recognise the needs and wants of consumers does not necessarily imply action. It is the action associated with the marketing process in sport that is the focus of this text. This is known as the marketing management process, which is described by Kotler et al. (1994: 9) as 'the analysis, planning, implementing and control of programs designed to create, build and maintain beneficial exchanges with target buyers for the purpose of achieving organisational objectives'.

Chapter 1 has defined marketing and sport marketing, as well as introducing the unique characteristics of sport and how they impinge on the marketing process. Hereafter this book is divided into three parts.

Part I examines how the sport marketer identifies marketing opportunities. Chapter 2 examines the place of marketing in the planning process and specifically reviews the strategic sport-marketing planning process. Chapter 3 concentrates on understanding the sport consumer, and chapter 4 on the market research and information systems, and the implications this information has for segmenting the sport marketplace.

Part II covers the strategy determination stage. It examines the sport marketing mix and the way in which the organisation is positioned in relation to target markets. Selection of the core marketing strategy is significant in this stage, and the contribution of the 7Ps–product, price, place, physical evidence, process, people and promotion–to strategy determination are examined. The issues specific to sport marketing contained in these chapters include the place of the facility in service provision, service quality and customer satisfaction, sponsorship, public relations, television and its impact on sport marketing, and promotional licensing.

Finally, Part III returns to the important marketing management process of implementation and evaluation. This part comprises only one chapter, which examines how the sport marketer evaluates the success of marketing strategies and the coordinating function between the sport marketer and the rest of the organisation. Of interest to students in particular is a section on careers related to sport marketing.

PART I

Identification of marketing opportunities

2

The strategic sport-marketing planning process

Stage 1—Identification of marketing opportunities

Step 1—Analyse external environment (forces, competition, publics)

Step 2—Analyse organisation (mission, objectives, SWOT)

Step 3—Examine market research and marketing information systems

Step 4—Determine marketing mission and objectives

▼

Stage 2—Strategy determination

▼

Stage 3—Strategy implemention, evaluation and adjustment

CHAPTER OBJECTIVES

Chapter 2 identifies three stages comprising the strategic sport-marketing planning process. Within these stages, eight steps are isolated as constituting the marketing planning sequence for sporting organisations. Steps 1–4 are reviewed in this chapter, with the remaining steps covered in Parts II and III. In sporting organisations, the strategic sport-marketing planning process (SSMPP) assumes great significance because these organisations are often one-product entities, and therefore organisation-wide planning and marketing planning become the same process.

After studying this chapter you should be able to:

1 Understand the strategic sport-marketing planning process.
2 Recognise the role of strategic sport-marketing planning in sport.
3 Analyse the forces driving industry competition.
4 Conduct a SWOT analysis.
5 Recognise the principal strategies available in sport marketing.

HEADLINE STORY

Rugby's dream run

When the rugby world cup final is played at Stadium Australia in Sydney in 2003, sports lovers will be watching from all across the nation. A decade ago, the event would have produced very little interest outside New South Wales and Queensland. But thanks to the success of the Wallabies, the national rugby union team, which won the world cup for the first time in 1991 and again in 1999, the sport is enjoying a boom. Last year the Australian Rugby Union (ARU) received its highest-ever net revenue: $75 million, up 25.5% from $42.8 million in 2000 thanks to record crowds at matches, sponsorship revenue and television broadcasting rights. In 1987, when Australia co-hosted the world cup with New Zealand, just 17,000 people watched Australia play the semi-final against France. In 2001, the Wallabies played the British lions in a Test match in front of 85,000 fans at Stadium Australia. About 1.8 million TV viewers watched the match, which was broadcast nationally in prime time by the Seven Network. Last year, attendance figures at rugby union Test matches held in Australia jumped 22%, and the total TV audience for rugby union matches increased 38%. (Stensholt 2002: 70)

The ARU's goal of becoming Australia's main winter sport is ambitious, but it is also an example of how sporting organisations need to map out their strategies and adopt a systematic approach to achieve their stated goals. Consider the competitive marketplace for the football codes, which includes the AFL and NRL, and it is apparent that the ARU will have to know its market. It is clear, however, that rugby's dream run has commenced. Already, as indicated in the headline story, rugby in Australia has made considerable progress. With competition intensifying due to the move by both the NRL and AFL to national competitions during the 1990s, rugby's response has been to capitalise on its international prominence through the Tri-nations series and Bledisloe Cup matches against New Zealand. Test matches, with the advent of Stadium Australia and its (former) 100 000-plus capacity, boosted rugby's ability to stage mega-events. In addition, the advent of the Super 12s has been the key strategy that has lifted the profile and image of rugby in Australia. The Super 12 competition is an alliance between Australia, South Africa and New Zealand that has seen club rugby played internationally. Moreover, it has meant that there exists a constant product for the respective rugby-governing bodies to market, which provides more games to boost attendances, sponsorship revenues and, significantly, revenue from television rights.

The strategies used to move the code from an amateur to a professional structure have been carefully crafted and done so cognisant of the importance of marketing strategy. The ARU's dream run has continued with the staging of the 2003 World Cup being granted solely to Australia, after New Zealand was not able to fulfil International Rugby Union conditions in relation to the provision of clean stadiums (stadiums free of existing advertising). This hallmark event provides another important opportunity to market the game throughout Australia and beyond. Given that marketing is primarily concerned with consumer needs, it is the responsibility of the company to satisfy these needs. The ARU, for example, must satisfy multiple demands from:

- *the players*, who need matches and tournaments with attractive financial rewards;
- *the sponsors*, who require star players and close quality contests to ensure that their financial investment in rugby attracts maximum exposure via the media;
- *the paying public*, which wants to see rugby played at the optimum level.

Recognising and satisfying consumer needs ensures maximum market share, market development opportunities and growth. The ARU's challenge has been to develop its product by identifying opportunities for growth. To some extent there existed latent demand for rugby union, as its former amateur structure did not aim to harness the potential of the sport by maximising playing opportunities. Spectators and players now have ample opportunity to watch or play at the elite level. Kotler and Andreasen (1991: 68) noted that, 'just as "customer centredness" is the advocated way of thinking about marketing, the strategic marketing planning process is the advocated way of doing marketing'. In this book, the strategic marketing planning process is specific in its reference to sport and is labelled the strategic sport-marketing planning process (SSMPP). Figure 2.1 illustrates the SSMPP, which includes the following eight steps.

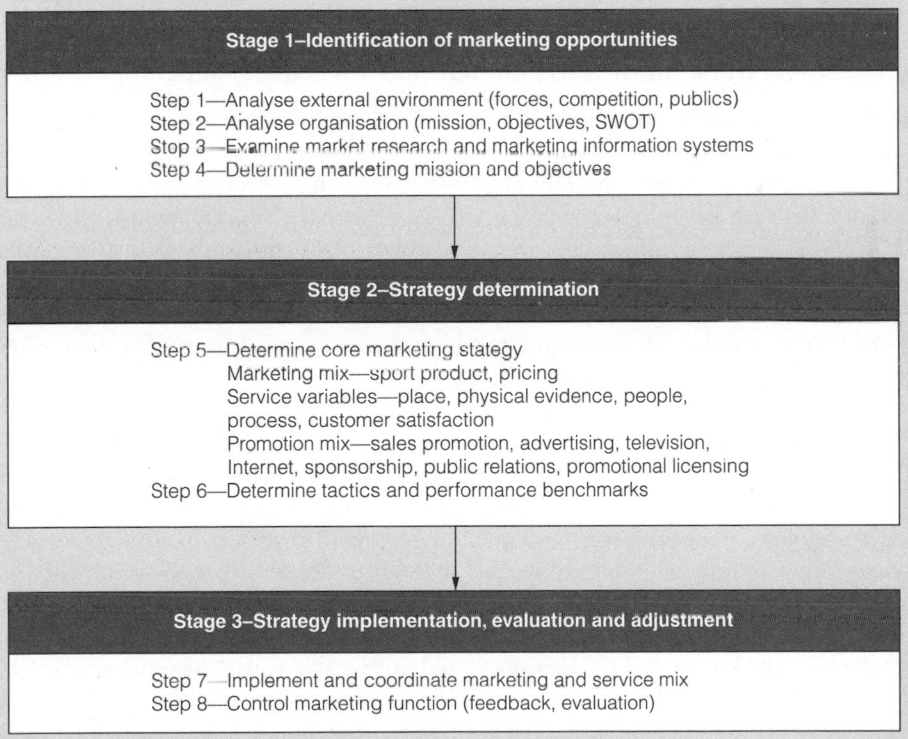

Stage 1–Identification of marketing opportunities

Step 1—Analyse external environment (forces, competition, publics)
Step 2—Analyse organisation (mission, objectives, SWOT)
Step 3—Examine market research and marketing information systems
Step 4—Determine marketing mission and objectives

↓

Stage 2–Strategy determination

Step 5—Determine core marketing stategy
Marketing mix—sport product, pricing
Service variables—place, physical evidence, people, process, customer satisfaction
Promotion mix—sales promotion, advertising, television, Internet, sponsorship, public relations, promotional licensing
Step 6—Determine tactics and performance benchmarks

↓

Stage 3–Strategy implementation, evaluation and adjustment

Step 7—Implement and coordinate marketing and service mix
Step 8—Control marketing function (feedback, evaluation)

FIGURE 2.1
Strategic sport-marketing planning process

The strategic sport-marketing planning process

1. Analyse the external environment, the forces driving industry competition and the publics to be served.
2. Analyse the sporting organisation internally, to determine mission, goals and objectives, and to assess strengths, weaknesses, opportunities and threats (SWOT).
3. Examine market intelligence data in relation to the existing product range.
4. Determine the specific marketing mission and objectives for the prescribed period of the plan.
5. Determine the core marketing strategy using marketing mix variables, identifying and selecting the desired competitive position in relation to an identified sustainable competitive advantage.
6. Establish tactics to achieve objectives, and formulate benchmarks to measure progress.
7. Implement and operationalise the planned strategies.
8. Measure the success of core strategies, and adjust strategies where necessary.

This chapter examines Steps 1–4 of the SSMPP. Later chapters deal with individual aspects of the marketing and service mix variables, detailing the factors to consider in selecting a core marketing strategy, and Steps 7 and 8 are encapsulated in the final chapter. First we examine both the external and internal environments and the forces driving competition.

Step 1: Understanding the environment in which the sport competes

A marketing program is not delivered in isolation of the organisation-wide planning process. In normal circumstances, the marketing planning process must reflect the overall plans for the organisation. In sport, as indicated by the rugby union example, there is often little difference between organisation-wide planning and the marketing planning process. The ARU's overall direction and success are based solely on its major product offerings: Test match and club rugby. Determining the difference between organisation-wide planning and marketing planning requires careful attention by sport marketers.

The first step of the SSMPP is equivalent to conducting an inventory. The data collected form the basis of decisions made later in the process.

External forces

Figure 2.2 shows the environmental factors requiring consideration, which are the forces that affect an organisation indirectly. They include government legislation, economic climate, technology, political forces, and demographic and social trends. It is important for sporting organisations to monitor changes in each of these forces. Government legislation, for example, can alter the economic infrastructure of an industry through legislative changes. For instance, when pay-TV was introduced to Australia in the 1990s, government legislation dictated that pay-TV operators would not be able to sell advertising time for the first five years. This was designed to protect the free-to-air networks and, given the importance of sports programming to television revenues, this policy reduced pay-TV's capacity to generate revenue and, in turn, its capacity to pay for rights to broadcast sport. Technology can also change the way businesses operate. The Internet, through World Wide Web

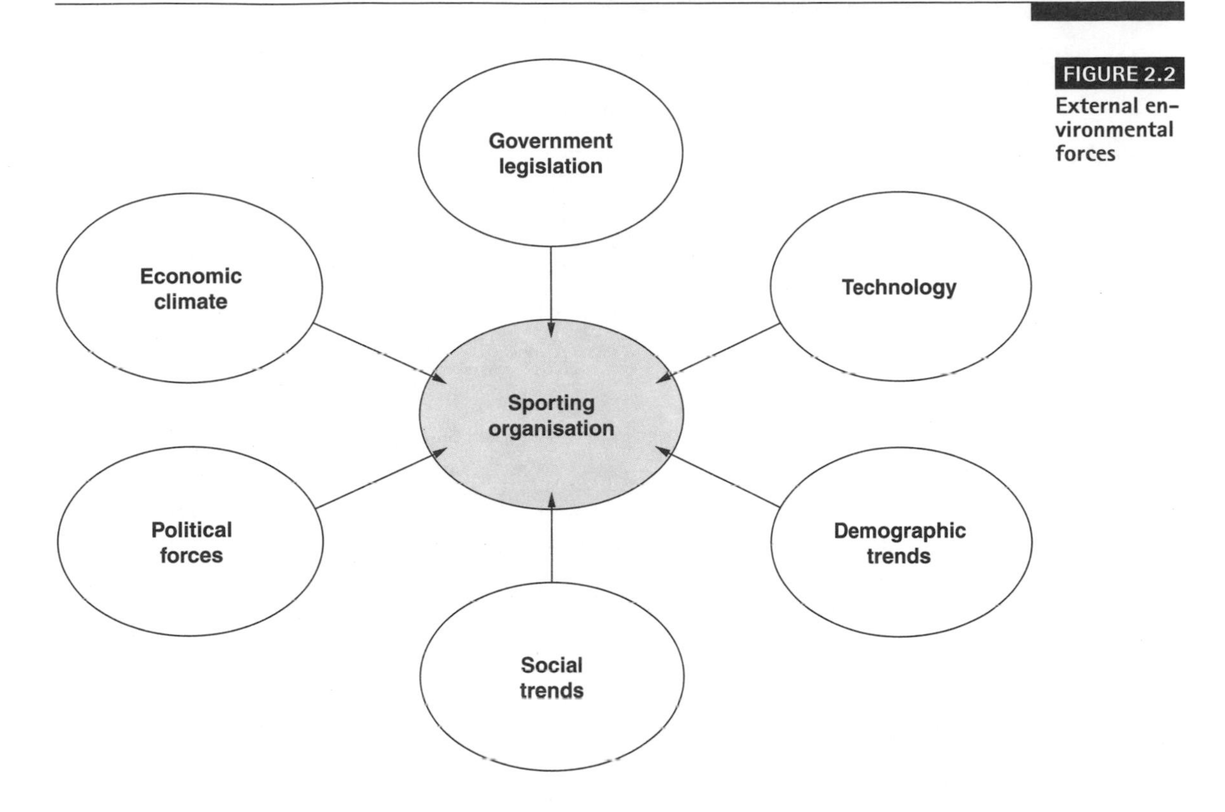

FIGURE 2.2
External environmental forces

pages and e-mail, has altered the means through which organisations can communicate with members, players, coaches and officials. It is also an important source of information for fans. The role of the Internet in the marketing mix, and specifically the promotions mix, is considered in detail in chapter 12.

Political forces, at a macro-level, might involve government policy directly affecting an industry. In Australian sport, the Australian Sports Commission is the agency responsible for implementing government policy. A change of government often leads to new policies. The most obvious and important policy for many sports is government policy in relation to funding support. Most national and state sporting organisations are non-profit, with limited sources of revenue. Government funding is critical for ongoing development. One simple example of government policy is the focus of funding and programs for the elite or for mass participatory programs. Demographic and social trends refer to the changing population makeup of Australia. For example, the increasingly multicultural composition of Australian communities will affect when, why and how sport marketers communicate with the community. It cannot be assumed that all sports consumers in a diversified society will respond in the same way to all marketing strategies, or that everyone will respond to the same sports. For many years, sporting organisations neglected to examine these forces and the impact that a changing environment might have on their sport. The example of the Australian Cricket Board (ACB) cited in chapter 1 indicates this past neglect.

FIGURE 2.3
Forces driving industry competition

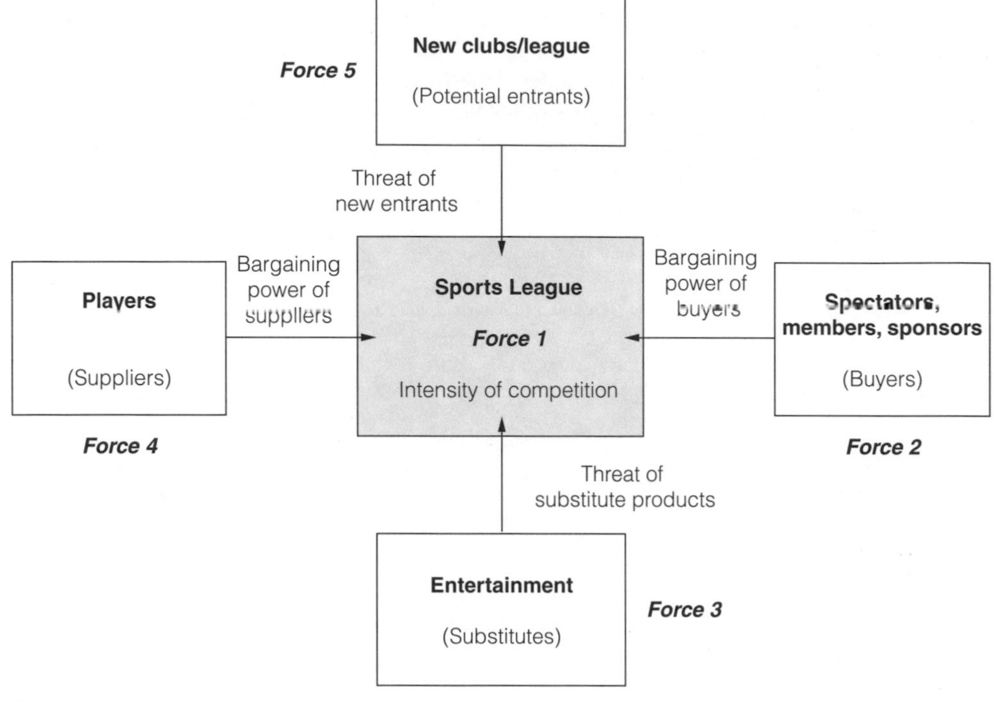

Source: Adjusted from Porter (1985).

Industry competition

On a more direct level, sporting organisations need to monitor the industry in which they compete. Figure 2.3 incorporates an adapted version of Porter's (1980) competitive forces model. Porter described five forces that managers should review when examining competition and the attractiveness of an industry:

1 the intensity of competition between existing firms within an industry;
2 the bargaining power of buyers;
3 the threat of substitute products;
4 the bargaining power of suppliers; and
5 the threat of new entrants.

The attractiveness of an industry is typically measured by profitability, which is not always the principal goal of non-profit and sporting organisations. Viability and winning games are important outcomes and become the primary measure of attractiveness for sporting organisations. In professional sports leagues, for example, the number and location of teams in respective markets require the league to assess the attractiveness of a market in terms of viability. Other questions indicative of industry attractiveness may include: Is the economic base of a city or region large enough to sustain just one or more than one team? How many other professional sports already exist in this market? What other recreation and leisure pursuits are potentially competing for disposable income? A brief review of Porter's five forces follows.

Professional sport leagues for football will be used to illustrate the applicability of Porter's model. The model in this instance assumes that a professional sport league can be considered an industry, although this industry is subject to the broader market and competitive pressures of the entertainment and leisure sectors. The Australian Football League (AFL) and its member clubs, for example, turns over in excess of $300 million, making it a large and significant economic entity.

Force 1: Intensity of competition

The first force is the intensity of competition within the industry. In the case of a sport league, the number of teams and their location are the first indicators of the intensity of competition. Obviously, nine AFL clubs based in Melbourne and ten professional rugby league clubs based in Sydney intensify competition in these markets. This competition is further heightened by the presence of other sporting codes seeking sponsor dollars, spectators and members. In both codes, despite the large number of teams in each market, exit barriers have remained very high. This highlights the peculiar economics associated with sport leagues. Tradition, emotion and club loyalties often override the economic deficiencies experienced by some clubs, explaining why it has not been so easy to achieve a better geographical balance of teams competing in these national leagues.

Force 2: Bargaining power of buyers

The second force, the buyers or consumers of sport, is finite in relation to the number of teams located in one market—hence the intensity of competition to attract spectators, members and sponsors by clubs. Attendance, membership and sponsorship revenues are the main sources of income generated by sporting clubs. Typically, customers can force prices down, demand higher quality and play competitors off against each other. Too many teams located in one market exacerbates the leverage of consumers, although sports consumers in some sport leagues have less leverage in this regard, as club membership tends to be price-standardised throughout a league and the cost of attendance common to all games. Most bargaining power lies with sponsors seeking to choose the best range of benefits from clubs. Sponsor bargaining power strengthens as the number of clubs based in a market grows.

Force 3: Threat of substitute products

Another major force comes from the substitutability of products—that is, other recreation and leisure activities offering similar benefits to those provided by participation in sport. It is this force that provides the greatest range of competitive forces for a sport league. Under the broad heading of 'entertainment', a variety of products have the potential to attract the consumer's money normally available for leisure pursuits. These may include other sports, the movies, videos and the theatre. A major determinant of the strength of these potential substitutes is the switching cost associated with each product. Switching cost refers to the cost of changing brands or products. If the cost is low, both financially and psychologically, then consumers are more likely to switch, and a product becomes susceptible to substitution. This of course has the potential to erode profits. A major advantage possessed by various sports is that brand loyalty (to the sport or club) is very high. Psychological association with a sport or club is often far more important than economic considerations. In part, this explains the fanatical support for some sports and clubs, such as for soccer clubs worldwide and for AFL clubs in Australia.

Force 4: Bargaining power of suppliers
Suppliers can exert bargaining power on participants in an industry by raising or reducing the quality of purchased goods and services. In a sport league the major supply required to operate successfully is the players. No one source has exclusive control over player supply and, with the exception of some sports like soccer, it no longer costs clubs to buy players. This is also the area that the sport marketer has least control over in terms of product quality. The bargaining power of the players has the potential to erode industry profits via their salary demands, rather than through what it costs to procure players from specific suppliers. In their quest for the ultimate prize, a premiership or championship, clubs often accede to the demands of high-priced athletes, explaining why the sport economy is often regulated by the use of salary caps.

Force 5: Threat of new entrants
New clubs or a new rival league can reduce industry profits and specific market share for the existing clubs and/or league. The commencement of the Superleague competition in rugby league is an example of a rival league's entry. Superleague, owned by News Ltd, was established to form a breakaway league, enticing existing clubs and players in the Australian Rugby League's (ARL) New South Wales competition to defect to Superleague. In the process, contractual obligations of both players and clubs were displaced, ultimately

FIGURE 2.4
Publics impacting on a professional club

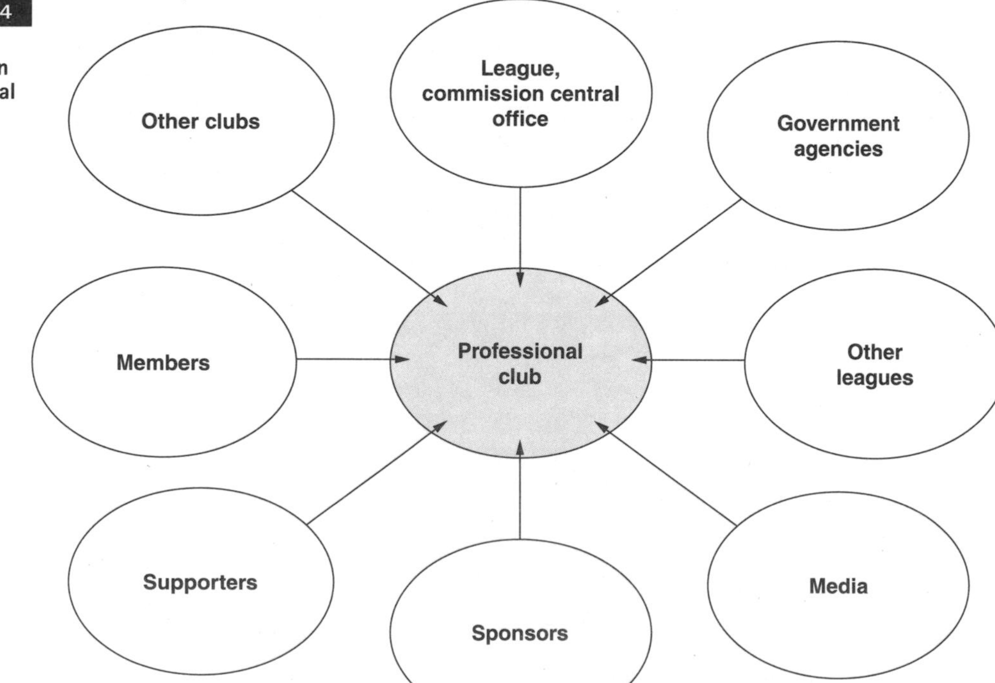

creating serious divisions within the league. In attempting to overcome the barriers to entry, the structure and product offerings of the ARL competition were seriously threatened. The gravity of this threat largely depended on the barriers to entry. The major barrier in this case was provided by the established and recognised keeper of the code–the ARL through the New South Wales Rugby League competition. Access to a supply of talented players is usually a major barrier to entry.

Publics

Examination of the external environment can be concluded by identifying the publics to which the sport is responsible. To an extent, some of these will have been identified from the competitive analysis conducted using the Porter framework. Kotler and Andreasen (1991: 89) define a public as 'a distinct group of people, organisations, or both whose actual or potential needs must in some sense be served'. The competitive forces model has already shown that diverse publics exist for a club competing in a professional league. Figure 2.4 illustrates the publics that may exist for a professional sport club.

Another group of publics exists within the organisation. This leads us to consider Step 2 in the SSMPP.

Step 2: Understanding the internal capabilities of the organisation

Sport managers gauge the significance of a sport's internal competencies on the basis of the opportunities and threats present in the sport's competitive environment. For example, the arrival of colour television in Australia in 1974 represented an opportunity for sport. The ACB, as previously discussed, did not possess the internal capabilities at the time to capitalise on this development. Similarly, the globalisation of sporting competitions via the media has opened a window of opportunity for the professionalisation of rugby union.

SWOT analysis

An important foundation for understanding the internal capabilities of a sport is the ability of the sport manager or marketer to match strengths and weaknesses with industry opportunities and threats. The international rugby union community clearly identified the threat of being overrun by the larger and more powerful professional football codes. The choice of the ARU to engage in an alliance with New Zealand and South Africa is evidence of a sport recognising an opportunity to share the production and professionalisation of rugby union, rather than be forced to expand the code in limited markets in each country. The strengths, weaknesses, opportunities and threats (SWOT) analysis is a commonly accepted tool used by managers to assess the current capabilities of their organisations. In essence, it provides a structure for their analysis:

- Strengths are resources, skills or other advantages relative to competitors.
- Weaknesses are limitations or deficiencies in resources, skills and capabilities that inhibit a sport's effectiveness in relation to competitors.
- Opportunities are major favourable situations in a sport's environment.
- Threats are major unfavourable situations in a sport's environment.

Mission, objectives and goals

Having established the internal capabilities, it is necessary to ascertain the mission of the organisation, followed by a review of the organisation's principal goals and objectives. The mission statement provides direction for the sport, defining and clarifying its meaning and reason for existence. To be unambiguous, a mission statement should clearly answer 'What is our business?' For example, the Australian Sports Commission's mission statement is deceptively simple: 'To enrich the lives of all Australians through sport'. The key to defining a mission for a sporting organisation is to ensure that the mission statement is not so narrow that it limits its scope of operations or is simply a list of services provided.

In the context of sport, another factor impinges on formulating mission statements. Most sports are non-profit entities, and as such exist to achieve a common group of objectives by a relatively homogeneous group of people. Non-profits by definition exist to fight a cause. This cause becomes the operating charter, which is generally less flexible than the mission statement of a for-profit firm. If the cause ceases to exist, so too will the organisation. If profits cease to exist, the for-profit firm has the choice of redefining the business it wishes to be in and hence its range of product offerings. If, for instance, the ARU's alliance with other countries is not successful, professional rugby union could disappear and with it the Super 12s. Defining the mission implicitly defines the broad goals to be pursued by an organisation.

Organisational goals refer to the broad aims that organisations strive to achieve. In sport, these may include ensuring financial viability, increasing participation, raising the number of members, and stimulating public interest in the sport. Examples of organisational goals, or key result areas, are shown in Table 2.1 using the Tennis Australia strategic plan 2002–04. Broad goals become the focus for devising more specific objectives, which are shown also for each key result area. Key result area 1, for example, is important, as the Australian Open in its own right is an important marketing and promotional tool used to lift the profile of tennis. Note the objectives aimed at ensuring size and quality in defined target groups, including the Asia-Pacific region, the tennis fan and the media. These organisational objectives should provide the necessary detail to achieving key result areas. Objectives should be SMART, that is:

S–Specific
M–Measurable
A–Achievable
R–Realistic
T–Timebound.

Key result area 2, for example, is specific in terms of competition players, non-registered players and participation frequency, and in each case a measurable target and time period are defined. Key result area 8, while a separate area, is in essence an aggregation of the other key result areas. The various products, including social and competitive tennis, major events and Grand Slam events for example, naturally promote and market the sport. The more successful these events and programs, the greater the marketing-related benefits and the easier it will be to develop a coherent marketing strategy to promote and develop tennis at all levels.

TABLE 2.1
Tennis Australia Goals, 2002–04

Key result area	Objectives
1. Australian Open	• To become the biggest sporting event and number 1 tennis brand in the Asia-Pacific region • To meet the challenge of retaining recognition as the 'People's Grand Slam' • To be recognised as a world leader in event presentation • To maximise our electronic media appeal • To develop an internationally recognised brand
2. Participation	• To increase registered and competition players by 10% per annum • To increase non-registered and social players by 5% per annum • To increase the participation rate (frequency of play) by 10% per annum
3. Player development	• To work closely with member associations, the Australian Institute of Sport and state Institutes of Sport to provide a world-class player development program • To have, for both men and women, three players in the top 20 and ten in the top 100 by 2004
4. Representative teams	• To stay permanently in the World Group of both Davis and Fed Cups and be extremely competitive therein • To at least maintain our achievements of winning one medal at every Olympic Games since the reintroduction of tennis in 1998 • To participate regularly in International Junior Tennis events, but view them as part of longer-term development opportunity
5. Event management	• To retain international and domestic recognition for excellence in event management by continuing to outstandingly manage, coordinate and conduct these events to showcase the sport of tennis
6. Tennis for people with a disability	• To maintain world leadership in wheelchair tennis • To continue to promote the programs and support available to people with a disability • To increase participation in programs and events by a minimum of 10% per annum
7. Partnership with member associations	• To recognise that communication and consultation over matters requiring change is the basis of teamwork • To provide member associations with sufficient funding and resources to meet their service and program needs • To continue to recognise that both professional and staff volunteers have a significant role to play in the ongoing development of the game
8. Marketing the sport	• To continue to develop, implement and monitor a uniform image for the sport of tennis throughout Australia • To brand, advertise and promote existing Tennis Australia products, programs and services to identified target market groups to increase participation • To boldly promote Tennis Australia events and the Summer Circuit with the aim of achieving capacity crowds • To develop the Melbourne Park tennis brand and its leadership role as a centre of excellence

Source: Tennis Australia (2001).

Step 3: Examining market research and utilising information systems

Step 3 recognises that the important phase of marketing research is undertaken to ensure that decisions made in relation to marketing missions and objectives are based on a sound understanding of the marketplace. Basically, market research in sporting organisations seeks to answer six questions about consumers in relation to their consumption of the product. Initially, sporting organisations need to know WHO their consumers are, but this is only the tip of the iceberg. WHY they choose the particular sport product and WHEN and WHERE that consumption takes place are equally important. WHAT that consumption entails in terms of pre- and post-event activities, and HOW the product is used also are critical in terms of establishing a complete consumer profile.

To make informed decisions, organisations need information, and lots of it. Yet the collection of this material is only a starting point for the construction of a management information system (MIS). Once compiled, this information must be integrated, analysed and used to guide the direction of the organisation. Stanton et al. (1995: 48) believe that an MIS is an 'ongoing, organised set of procedures and methods designed to generate, analyse, disseminate, store and later retrieve information for use in decision making'. Nevertheless, they also acknowledge that, for the MIS to be successful, the data should be not only of high quality but also used in a realistic manner and adopted as a source of decision making by the organisation. Information collated through market research and organised into meaningful data sets provides the foundation for sport marketers to determine marketing strategies. In other words, this information helps sport marketers refine and develop their sports, to know where and when to offer them and to what age groups and at what times. These are just a few examples of how this information underpins marketing strategy decisions.

Step 4: Determining the marketing mission and objectives

Marketing must devise its own specific plans complementary to the organisation's overall mission, goals and objectives. The purpose of the planning process is to establish a competitive advantage over rival firms. The mission of marketing is to develop a range of product offerings that reflect a firm's organisation-wide mission statement. These products may be in the form of goods or services or both, depending on the nature of the business. In sport, the product offerings tend to be limited, although they are clearly in the service domain. Inherent in the challenge confronting the sport marketer is designing this portfolio of product offerings to achieve a competitive advantage.

Competitive advantage

Porter (1985: 26) describes competitive advantage as 'the way a firm can choose and implement a generic strategy to achieve and sustain a competitive advantage'. This definition is specific to three generic strategies that he describes, which will be discussed later in this chapter. The concept of competitive advantage, however, is broader than Porter's direct application to his theories. Implicit in this concept is the notion of sustainability. Without sustainability a competitive advantage becomes elusive. Coyne (1986: 55) posits three conditions that must be met for a firm to have achieved a sustainable competitive advantage:

- Customers perceive a consistent difference in important attributes between the producer's products or services and those of competitors.
- That difference is the direct consequence of a capability gap between the producer and competitors.
- Both the difference in important attributes and the capability gap can be expected to endure over time.

The key to sustainability is differentiation among competitor products. Coyne (1986: 55) further notes that:

> for a producer to enjoy a competitive advantage in a product/market segment, the difference or differences between him and his competitors must be felt in the marketplace: that is, they must be reflected in some product/delivery attribute that is the key buying criterion for the market.

Each individual sport has its own unique set of product attributes, via the special nature of each sport. In this regard, some sports are inherently more appealing to some segments of the population. For many years sports believed that these unique features of their game would remain popular forever. In Australian sport, this was proven not to be the case. The traditional sports of cricket, Australian rules football, netball and softball suddenly found that their competitive advantage was being eroded by changing attitudes towards leisure options. Increasing diversity of recreational and sporting opportunities saw these sports struggling in the late 1970s and early 1980s, and as a consequence they had to re-examine their key buying criterion and look to repositioning themselves. One technique that these sports could have used to examine their range of product offerings is covered in the next section.

Product market expansion

Ansoff (1957) devised the product/market expansion grid, shown in Figure 2.5, to help managers to balance their product offerings.

Market penetration

Market penetration (or concentration) refers to making more sales to existing customers without changing the product. Typically, this involves intensifying the advertising and promotions campaign to attract consumer attention. Often this strategy involves also a price reduction aimed at moving consumers away from competitor products.

The former New South Wales Rugby League (NSWRL) advertising and promotional campaign 'Simply the best', featuring Tina Turner, is an example of a market penetration strategy in sport. Although there were some minor adjustments to the game in terms of

FIGURE 2.5 **Product/market expansion grid**

	Existing products	New products
Existing markets	1 Marketing penetration	3 Product development
New markets	2 Market development	4 Diversification

Source: Adjusted from Ansoff (1975).

a crackdown on excessive on-field violence during the 1980s, the game itself remained unchanged. The NSWRL was successful in stimulating interest in the game, which translated into flourishing attendances and television viewership. The 'Simply the best' advertising campaign is considered to be one of the most sophisticated, inspiring, modern promotional campaigns seen in Australian sport, as will be shown when this campaign is examined in chapter 10.

Market development

A market development strategy is a relatively inexpensive way of creating new markets for existing products. It typically involves few risks and requires only minor modification to the product. It depends on sound research indicating new segments of the population willing to buy the product.

Product development

A product development strategy involves offering a modified or new product to current markets. Australian cricket's introduction of one-day cricket is an example of a sport exhibiting aspects of both market development and product development. One-day cricket can be considered to be the same product as four- and five-day cricket. Notably, the condensed version of the game has attracted a large following among women, which Test match cricket did not. On the other hand, one-day cricket can be considered to be a modified form of the game and better described as a product development strategy by the ACB. The weakness in this view is that one-day cricket has obviously had the capacity to expand the market interest in cricket. The traditional form of the game was not creating this expansion, although in recent times an exciting brand of cricket has been a feature of Test matches. This has largely been the result of rule changes that allow for extended hours to make up for time lost due to rain and the need to bowl a minimum number of overs in a day's play. Combined with an aggressive and relentless approach by the Australian cricket team, Test match cricket has undergone a resurgence of interest. It also illustrates the impact sport managers can have on the product through rule changes, such as those shown in cricket.

Regardless of the final distinction and product form responsible for growing cricket, it raises an interesting dilemma in sport marketing: namely, the point at which the game has been modified to such an extent that it is in effect a new product offering. In one-day cricket, for example, the basic elements of the game are still apparent: batting, bowling and fielding. The condensed version of the game forces more action, but whether this constitutes a new or different product is debatable, and illustrates the conflict that can exist between the 'purists' and those who prefer non-stop excitement in sport. This conflict is also central to soccer's dilemma regarding the number of goals, described in chapter 1.

Another example of sports having to modify their range of product offerings has been seen in junior sports. For many years juniors played the adult form of the game, complete with all the rules and traditions associated with that particular sport. As research began to show that this was not providing a satisfactory sport environment for juniors, many sports were modified to make them more attractive to juniors. In essence, sports have been modified to encourage more success in game elements, increasing the likelihood of juniors continuing to participate. Although sports initially did not see this as a marketing-related issue, this has now changed. The long-term fortunes of a sport, from both an elite performance and an ongoing interest and spectatorship perspective, are founded on the success of its junior programs. Market development and product development strategies therefore assume a heightened level of importance, with sports carefully considering their range of sport offerings for juniors in various age groups.

Product diversification

The final category of product diversification requires a firm to develop an entirely new product for a new market. This can be achieved internally through a strong research and development function or via the external acquisition of a new firm with a new range of product offerings. In terms of the core sport product, this strategy is not common in sport. Sporting organisations in the main do not seek to buy other sporting organisations, although it remains an option, as demonstrated by the Western Bulldogs Football Club. In 1991 the Western Bulldogs (formerly Footscray Football Club) purchased a half-share in the Melbourne Monarch's Baseball Club. This is an example of product diversification in sport, in this case developing or acquiring a new but related (in terms of sport) product. The objective was to provide Western Bulldogs club members and supporters with added value via the provision of another sport, as well as to attract new consumers to the club and associated facilities.

The product/market expansion grid provides a framework for the sport marketer to consider the balance of product offerings. This balance of product offerings should reflect the marketing mission, which in turn should mirror the overall mission, goals and objectives of the organisation. Sportview 2.1 describes the National Hockey League's (NHL) competitive positioning and attempts to broaden its appeal. Also note that the NHL needs to know its fans better, illustrating the importance of the market research function in guiding strategic decisions.

SPORTVIEW 2.1

Hockey comeback tied to engaging its core audience

Sporting differences

While the NHL hasn't sufficiently leveraged its star power for more sponsorships and ratings, the PGA Tour continues to bask in the phenomenon that is Tiger Woods. The National Hockey League isn't yet skating on thin ice—but it needs more than a Zamboni to smooth its uneven surface. In the early 1990s, the NHL seemed poised to reach the same heights as the National Basketball Association, National Football League and Major League Baseball. By 1994, the sport had scored its the first network TV coverage in years.

Fox tried to broaden hockey's appeal with cool on-air promos to foster NHL's core 18–34 male demographic. The network also tried to address the age-old complaint that hockey's presentation on TV has been lackluster, jazzing up the sport with a 'glowing' puck to help the viewer follow the game. The league then stepped in, with expansion teams in the West and the South, and by 1999 the NHL had lured a total $300 million in annual sponsorships, up from $25 million five years earlier. Ratings also started to rise, albeit slowly. In the network's first year broadcasting hockey, the 1994/95 regular season, NHL games averaged a 2.0 rating and inched up to a 2.1 in 1995/96. At the time, the NHL 'went through a phase where they looked as though they were going to take off', said Steve Grubbs, exec VP–national broadcast at BBDO Worldwide, New York.

Momentum fades

But the momentum didn't last. By 1999 ratings had fallen to an average 1.5. Worse still, last season's Stanley Cup championship round witnessed a 13% drop in its key demographic. ABC and ESPN this season start a new contract, whose approach is to tone down broad-based marketing attempts and instead target hockey's existing core audience. 'We have found in our research that the fans really don't know the game that well', said Artie Bulgrin, VP–research and sales development for ESPN. So the ABC–ESPN partnership started running a series of vignettes called 'The Rules', explaining face-offs, penalties and other details of the game. But analysts believe the NHL also needs to use its sponsors to help market its players.

'With the exception of Anheuser-Busch, Dodge and, to some extent, Wendy's, I don't see NHL sponsors implementing into their advertising any national creative, as well as doing some sweepstakes and promotion', said Eric Bechtel, VP–marketing for SFX Sports, a sports marketing company.

Attracting kids

Reaching young fans and potential young NHL viewers is another hurdle for the league. 'People don't grow up with [hockey] in this country', said one TV programming executive. In recent years, the NHL has been trying to address that issue by running in-line skating street hockey tournaments as well as donating hockey sticks and balls and providing instruction in floor hockey to kids. The NHL already has seen hints of better days to come. Attendance at games is running 2% higher than last year. ABC's recent broadcast of the league's all-star game posted a Nielsen Media Research rating of 2.7—up 19% from a year ago. An ESPN Sunday-night game 13 February pulled a 1.0, the highest-rated telecast of the season so far. But that's still well below the typical 3–4 rating an NBA game draws on cable.

Ed Horne, group VP–marketing for NHL Enterprises, said the ABC–ESPN partnership is better for the league's future than the Fox deal: 'ABC promoted the all-star game in prime time, on "Who Wants to Be a Millionaire", "NYPD Blue", and even on "The View". Cross-promotion is a big issue for us', he said, adding that Fox hadn't promoted the NHL in its prime-time programming.

Source: Adapted from Friedman (2000: 40). Reprinted by permission *Advertising Age*, 28 February 2000. Copyright, Crain Communications Inc.

Generic strategies

As indicated earlier, Porter (1985) describes three generic strategies that firms can use as an alternative framework to achieve competitive advantage:

- cost leadership;
- differentiation; and
- focus.

Both the *cost leadership* and *differentiation* strategies aim to seek a competitive advantage in a broad range of markets. The *focus* strategy aims to seek a competitive advantage by using either a cost leadership or differentiation strategy in a narrow or niche market segment. Cost leadership is perhaps the simplest of the three options. The organisation's principal objective is to distribute its products to the widest possible market at a lower cost than competitors. Achieving lower cost may be the result of internal economies of scale, innovative technologies or lower distribution costs. In the end, it is the consumer who decides whether the cost differential is significant enough to warrant the purchase of one product over that of competitors.

Differentiation is typically more expensive. It involves an advantage based on distinctive product attributes. Products may, for instance, offer benefits that others do not, or they might be new and innovative products not currently available. Again, differentiation is seeking to establish its product prominence in as wide a market as possible. In sport, cost leadership strategies are difficult to achieve. In a sporting league, the clubs generally compete on equal terms in terms of cost. Standardised prices for attendance and membership reduce the significance of cost as a source of competitive advantage. For example, in 2002 AFL club memberships cost approximately $88, and ground entry to all matches was $16.50. Although there is league-wide price regulation, the restriction is the same for all competing clubs. As will be examined in chapter 6, clubs and leagues cannot always achieve full cost recovery on ticket prices. If full cost recovery (in terms of covering event costs) were an objective, most sports would become too expensive for regular attendance.

Differentiation strategy provides scope for application in the sport setting. Although all the clubs in a league appear the same in terms of production, they do offer distinct brand images. These are of course the clubs themselves, with their distinctive colours, heritage and traditions, with which supporters identify with a good degree of emotional intensity. On a macro-level, each sport is a differentiated product in its own right, each offering similar benefits to consumers. The choice for consumers, in terms of physical activity, competing or spectating, is which of the myriad sports offer the best outlet to satisfy their needs and wants. This is equally applicable for juniors when choosing the sports in which to participate. Some sports, such as cricket, golf, softball, swimming and netball, offer the challenge of special skill development without any excessive body contact. Football codes, basketball and wrestling offer a different range of skills, to be mastered in the context of body contact. The challenge for the sport marketer is to accentuate the differentiated product benefits to potential participants, and this sometimes means changing the fundamental rules and traditions of a sport. Although this is obviously an option, sport managers and marketers need to carefully consider the impact of proposed changes before implementation.

Summary

This chapter introduced the SSMPP and reviewed the first four steps in this process. These four steps constitute the data collection and review phase of the planning process. Organisation-wide data are required to place into context the role that marketing strategy plays in ensuring that a sport creates a sustainable competitive advantage.

In the first instance, a sporting organisation needs to review the external environmental factors impinging on its existence. These factors are best described as the set of societal influences that encroach on all organisations, which include government legislation, economic environment, technology, political forces, and social and demographic trends. A more direct form of analysis involves a review of industry characteristics specific to a sport. Porter's five-forces model provides sport managers with a structured framework to scan the competitive environment, and is the precursor to a review of the internal capabilities of a sporting organisation. SWOT analysis was described in this chapter as a useful tool to assist with this internal examination.

Review of the external and internal environments is an important precursor to determining the best strategies to create a competitive advantage. In essence, marketing personnel are responsible for developing an array of product offerings that assist an organisation to achieve a competitive advantage. In predominantly single-product organisations such as sports, marketing's contribution to creating a competitive advantage is considerable.

Sport and marketing, in many ways, are still becoming accustomed to each other. For many years most sport administrators did not believe that the role of marketing was important. However, as the sport landscape became increasingly competitive, sport managers began to adjust their thinking. Most large sporting entities have now created marketing departments, and many smaller sporting organisations are beginning to employ marketing specialists to manage the contribution of marketing in the planning process. As indicated in chapter 1, sporting organisations have been guilty of complacency in the past in relation to marketing and promoting their sport. This is clearly changing, as is exemplified by the case study at the end of this chapter.

This chapter discussed the steps in the SSMPP and specifically outlined four of the eight steps shown in Figure 2.1. Such is the significance of understanding the sport consumer, conducting market research and defining market segments that it is incorporated in Part I of this book. Part II of this book examines in detail the sport marketing mix variables that combine to form the nucleus of a core marketing strategy—a strategy based on the environmental scanning and data intelligence phase described in Steps 1–4 of the SSMPP in this chapter.

CASE STUDY

Marketing to build up British sport

As the England & Wales Cricket Board unveils its plans to breathe life into kids' teams, Mark Kleinman looks into British sport's new mission to market effectively to young people. It may have come too late to help this year's England Ashes team, but last week's launch of 'The Pride Side', a new initiative to get youngsters involved in cricket, was potentially of great significance for the future of British sport.

Developed by the England & Wales Cricket Board (ECB) in conjunction with Interfocus and Raymedia, 'The Pride Side' is a quartet of animated lion characters that will spearhead the ECB's marketing and educational messages. The project, which forms part of the ECB's five-year strategy for the revitalisation of youth cricket by promoting values such as teamwork, sporting excellence and participation, underlines the value that UK sport's governing bodies attach to marketing.

Grassroots support

ECB chief executive Tim Lamb suggests that 'The Pride Side' represents the ideal vehicle to help the body achieve its aim of introducing young people to cricket. As the initiative's strapline, 'Cricket to the Roots', indicates, the objective is to help county boards and cricket development officers around the country communicate their message in an attractive way.

'This has been an exciting project for us to work on', says Interfocus head of strategic planning Stuart Leach: 'The characters will become integral to the ECB's marketing strategy because they are the personification of everything the sport should be about.' 'The Pride Side' is backed by the ECB's commercial partners, which include Npower, NatWest, Norwich Union and Vodafone. The theme will be used in an animated film, Channel 4 *Howzat!* Educational packs, an internet portal and a mobile roadshow. Importantly, half of the money raised by consumers switching to Npower will be donated to 'The Pride Side' for investment in grassroots cricket.

'Our plan for the Test series is to inject as much fun into cricket as we can and attract a wider audience to the sport', says Npower head of brand Kevin Peake: '"The Pride Side" represents everything in cricket that attracted Npower to the sponsorship and looks to be a fantastic vehicle that will engage and inspire young players.' It is not only cricket that is getting its marketing act together. Interfocus has worked with the Football Association on developing its 'Three Lions' characters, though the agency and the FA are now involved in a legal dispute regarding their use.

Hitting the target

The 'Three Lions' were launched to the public earlier this year, for use on a range of marketing, merchandise and educational programs. FA marketing chief Paul Barber has stressed the importance of reaching all audiences, a philosophy reflected in the FA's new commercial partnership strategy.

Steve Curzon, marketing director of the Lawn Tennis Association and a former Nestlé marketer, has introduced a range of children-friendly projects, including 'Mini Tennis', in a bid to find Britain's next Grand Slam champion. A trio of characters will accompany the launch of 400 Mini Tennis centres over the next year, backed by an advertising and promotional campaign created by Volcano.

'Our priority is getting kids into tennis, to build the playing base from a young age. The fundamental difference between us and the ECB and FA is that we do not have a national team that plays regularly with which kids can identify', says Curzon. Perhaps Tim Henman's lack of success at this year's Wimbledon has driven home the message that something has to be done to revitalise British sport. As Curzon says: 'The whole industry now is becoming more marketing-literate because young people are the future of our sports.'

Source: Kleinman (2001: 26). Reproduced from *Marketing* magazine with the permission of the copyright owner, Haymarket Business Publications.

Questions

1. Why is it important for English cricket to breathe life into kids' teams?
2. Why is 'The Pride Side' initiative an important element of the ECB's overall strategy?
3. Identify the key marketing strategies used by the ECB to develop its grassroots strategy.

4. Identify the goals that might drive, or explain why and how the ECB and other sports might communicate with children and adolescents.
5. Can you identify special challenges confronting sport marketing strategists when marketing their sport to children and adolescents?
6. Are sport marketing strategies designed to encourage participation different from those formulated to encourage attendance at professional sporting competitions? If so, describe the differences.

3

Understanding the sport consumer

Stage 1—Identification of marketing opportunities

Step 1—Analyse external environment (forces, competition, **publics**)

Step 2—Analyse organisation (mission, objectives, SWOT)

Step 3—Examine market research and marketing information systems

Step 4—Determine marketing mission and objectives

▼

Stage 2—Strategy determination

▼

Stage 3—Strategy implemention, evaluation and adjustment

CHAPTER OBJECTIVES

Chapter 3 is the first of two chapters relating to understanding the sport consumer. It explores how marketing influences consumer behaviour and then determines what makes the sport consumption process special. It explains the various predispositions that consumers have towards product purchase, including the decision-making process undertaken prior to the sport purchase.

After studying this chapter you should be able to:

1 Define consumer behaviour.
2 Identify the key components in the consumer behaviour process.
3 Describe the steps in consumer decision making.
4 Understand the sport consumption process.

HEADLINE STORY

Understanding consumer behaviour

In the 12-month period ending April 1999, the Australian Bureau of Statistics determined that 2.5 million people over the age of 15 had attended an Australian rules match in the preceding 12 months. This figure was up 600000 on the previous 1995 survey. However, this was not the only sport to illustrate variance in attendance patterns between the two survey periods. Table 3.1 compares the 1995 figures with those of 1999 and provides the percentage change. (ABS 1996, 2000)

TABLE 3.1

Comparison between 1995 and 1999 ABS sports attendance

Sport	1995	1999	% change
Australian rules	1.9 million	2.5 million	+31.6
Horseracing	1.7 million	1.75 million	+.29
Rugby league	1.4 million	1.5 million	+.71
Cricket	1.1 million	.95 million	-13.6
Basketball	.7 million	.52 million	-25.7
Harness racing	.6 million	.53 million	-11.7
Soccer	.55 million	.62 million	+12.7
Motor sports	.45 million	1.5 million	+333
Tennis	.43 million	.44 million	+2.3
Rugby union	.35 million	.44 million	+26
Netball	.3 million	.24 million	-20

Source: Australian Bureau of Statistics (1996, 2000).

As Table 3.1 exemplifies, sport attendance, and diversity of choice, is very important to a large percentage of the Australian public. Hence it is becoming increasingly important to ascertain why fans turn up to the game week in and week out. Is it for team loyalty, stadium preference, clashes between traditional rivals, star appeal, or reasons we have yet to discern? Over the past decade an increasing amount of research has been conducted on the sport consumption process, with sport marketers now better prepared than at any stage in the past to make informed decisions based on their understanding of the consumer. Increasingly sport marketers understand the process and how and at what level distinctive variables interact to influence individual choice. These variables may be person-specific, they may be psychological or they may be social. Furthermore, they may be internal or external to the product or service choice. However, this is an ongoing process. It should never be questioned that the better we know and understand our consumers, the more prepared we will be to deliver a satisfactory product or service.

A model of consumer behaviour

Mullin et al. (2000) suggest that models of consumer behaviour are a process rather than a prescriptive formula, and the model provided in Figure 3.1 is no exception to that philosophy. To suggest that it is possible to construct a blueprint that is capable of determining behaviour is foolhardy, as the information sources for such models are both diverse and all-inclusive.

The research on sport consumption is voluminous and in many instances emanates from disciplines beyond sport, although early works by Nowell (1995), Stotlar (1995) and Shoham and Kahle (1996), and more recently Hunt, Bristol and Bashaw (1999), Fink, Trail and Anderson (2002), Funk, Mahony and Ridinger (2002) and Mahony et al. (2002) indicate that it is being given increasing attention in the sport marketing literature. However, Kates (1998) suggested that while the fields of sport marketing, sociology and consumer research had much in common, the utilisation of each other's theories was minimal. He reasoned that by bringing such discourses together new marketing insights could result. Whatever the perception, there is little doubt that disciplines such as psychology, sociology, communication and anthropology have all contributed to our understanding of consumer behaviour.

The study of individual human behaviour is important and is the reason why the discipline of psychology has so much to offer our research efforts in understanding sport consumers. One important principle of psychology is that each individual is different and therefore each individual has a unique personality, different perceptions, life experiences, capabilities and interests, and importantly different attitudes, beliefs and values. Most but not all sport consumption is undertaken in groups, or with others. Many sports, for example, require a 'team' of people to compete against another team. Attendance at professional sporting contests is always embedded in the context of large crowds, and the interactions between spectators are a large part of the sports experience. Sport sociologists are interested in determining how these group interactions shape the sports experience either through participation or as spectators. Anthropology is the study of mankind, in particular its societies and customs and the evolution of man as an animal. Sport has always been central to this form of analysis. The early origins of sport, for example, were embedded in the tribal instincts of primitive man whose skills required for survival, such as hunting, were practised and fine-tuned through sporting competitions. Viewed through the lens of anthropological analysis we can examine mankind's progress and its societies and customs

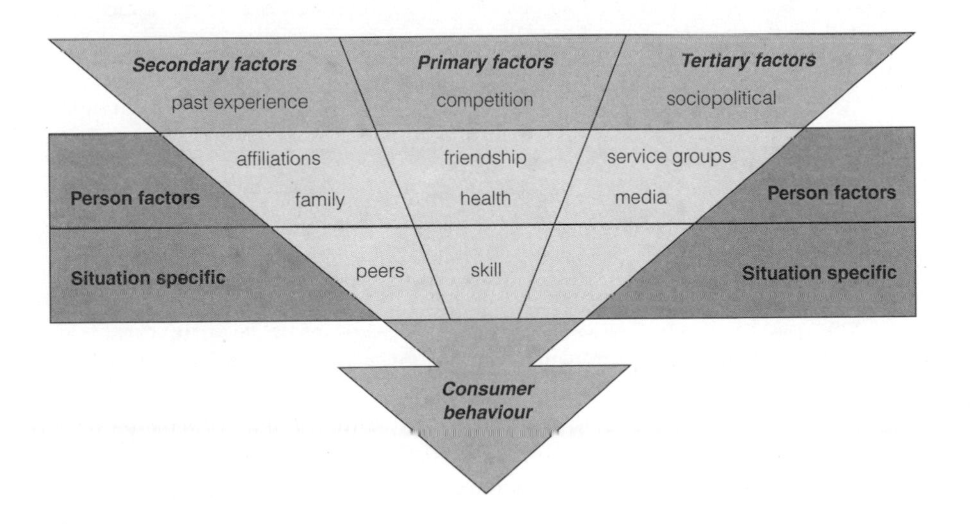

FIGURE 3.1 A model of consumer behaviour

through an institution such a sport. In other words, how does the conduct of contemporary sport explain mankind's evolution?

Funk, Haugtvedt and Howard (2000) explored the nexus between sport marketing and psychology. Delving into the social psychology literature, they determined that an understanding of attitude strength enabled the sport manager to better understand such factors as fan loyalty. In the process they suggested a framework for studying attitudes that enabled a greater understanding of fan allegiance to sport teams. Funk and James (2001) extended this analysis by establishing the Psychological Continuum Model (PCM), which was based on the four general boundaries of awareness, attraction, attachment and allegiance. The vertical model characterised 'the various psychological connections that sport spectators and fans may form with specific sports and teams' (2001: 121). Models such as the PCM are important for the sport marketer as they allow for tracking, both upward and downward, of sport fans as well as determining the threshold limit. The authors argue that the PCM model is unique to sport in that it 'focuses on the psychological relationship an individual may form with a sport object' (2001: 122). Other models explaining consumer behaviour, such as Awareness, Interest, Desire, Action (AIDA), are premised on first being aware of the product, being interested enough to focus on product benefits and having a desire to purchase. The AIDA model explaining consumer behaviour will be developed further in subsequent chapters, but it is useful to note that Funk and James (2001: 124) consider that the PCM 'concentrates on the internal psychological processes that account for different levels of psychological connection'. In other words, sport evokes interesting and varied levels of emotional attachment.

Unquestionably, certain factors are germane to all consumer decision-making processes, and the integration of such provides a framework for understanding the consumer behaviour process. Consumer behaviour is invariably the product of what may be termed primary, secondary and tertiary factors. Figure 3.1 schematically represents the interaction of these factors.

Primary factors

Primary factors are those elements that are internal to the purchaser or consumer. They are the set of beliefs that an individual holds in relation to the impact that the use of a particular product or service will have on their life. These elements are the intrinsic motivators to consume. They include issues such as the desire for health and wellbeing, and the opportunity to compete and test an individual's skills and capabilities against a variety of opposing forces, to establish new friendships or to escape 'reality'. One theoretical example of this is Brooks' (1998) sport/exercise identity. She opined that 'a sport/exercise identity appears to be formed from comparisons between an individual's sport exercise self concept (a summary assessment of physique, physical condition, athleticism, socio-economic status, age and gender) and the stereotype the individual has of participants and attributes of movement encompassed by the sport or exercise' (1998: 38). While the backdrop for this specific research was the health industry and windsurfing clubs, it would be easy to extrapolate such a theory to a wide range of sports and physical activities.

An important consideration in the pursuit of any of the preceding activities is an individual's physical characteristics. An individual weighing 65 kilograms may find contact or strength sports, especially those that do not have weight divisions, less enjoyable than sports or activities in which lightness is an attribute. Likewise, potential consumers whose centre of gravity is closer to the ground may be at an advantage where balance is a prerequisite, such as in gymnastics and skating. Conversely, physically disadvantaged individuals may find particular sports and activities a challenge to be negotiated and overcome.

The social aspect of sport has long been regarded as an important component of the consumer's decision-making process. Armstrong's (2001) study on the participation of black women in sport and fitness and its implication for sport marketing posited that, as a natural progression from the acknowledgement of women as viable sport consumers, ethnic consumers should be the focus of increased awareness. McCarthy (1998) had already examined marketing sport in the Hispanic community, but Armstrong's study was unique as she segmented it along the lines of both gender and ethnicity. Armstrong (2001: 18) concluded that 'marketing strategies designed for the mainstream market may not be effective in reaching ethnically diverse sections of the population'. Arguably, in a country as multicultural as Australia it makes sense to explore strategies for marketing to ethnically diverse groups.

Zhang et al. (2001) examined the relationship between five sociomotivational factors and attendance at sports events, in this case minor league hockey games. The five factors were: stress and entertainment, achievement-seeking, catharsis and aggression, salubrious effects, and community image. The authors suggested that three of these, stress and entertainment, achievement-seeking and salubrious effects, should be taken into account when constructing various marketing and promotional activities.

Secondary factors

Secondary factors are those elements that are immediate influences on the decision-making process. Having recognised that a need exists, the individual explores potential solutions to the problem via avenues perceived to inject quality input into the process. In this instance, each opinion held by the individual is weighted by his/her degree of respect for the source of the information.

Specifically, the most important secondary factor in the consumer behaviour model is the individual's prior exposure to the product or service. Past experience creates the evaluative mechanism on which future decisions to consume are based. Fans of the Collingwood Football Club, Arsenal, Canterbury Bulldogs or Chicago Cubs continue to watch their teams play because of their past experiences as fans of the particular club or code. If prior exposure had been less than satisfactory, spectators would have explored alternative avenues to fulfil their needs and expectations. However, in most cases fans of the above teams would be on the fourth or top tier of Funk's Psychological Continuum Model. Resistance to change characterises the fourth or 'allegiance' tier and in such cases, especially for the long-suffering generations of Cubs fans who have not seen their team win a MLB World Series since 1908, past experience creates a loyalty bond that is rarely broken.

Family is another extremely influential secondary factor. In many instances successive generations follow the same codes, clubs and practices. Interestingly, however, in some instances gender differences may determine the importance of family variables. Dietz-Uhler and Harrick (2000) determined that women were more likely to think of themselves as sport fans if they attended events with family and friends, while men more usually considered themselves fans if they played the sport. Nevertheless, there is anecdotal evidence on every sports field and at every venue of the impact of family on the decision to be a sport participant or spectator. If one family member plays golf, netball, soccer or volleyball, there is a higher possibility that children or siblings of the same gender (in gender-specific sports) will adopt that activity. In Australian V8 motor car racing, the Richards father-and-son combination is legendary. Similarly, while Tommy Smith is regarded as one of the greatest horse trainers Australia has produced, his daughter Gai Waterhouse has built a similar profile in this very competitive industry.

There is little doubt that if a parent is an avid fan of the National Rugby League (NRL) or the Australian Football League (AFL), it would be rare for a family member to support an alternative code of football. Even more significantly, a family divided by club loyalties—Carlton vs Collingwood, Manchester United vs Arsenal or Parramatta vs Canterbury—would be the source of interesting dinner conversations whenever the opposing teams met.

Peers are also an important secondary factor. The behaviour and choices of companions often stimulate an individual to act. If a particular group is heavily involved in the consumption of basketball through playing, watching and reading, the pressure to conform to the group is strong. Individuals can either conform to the behaviour of the group or seek other groups whose interests are more in keeping with their own.

Other significant secondary factors may include clubs with which an individual is affiliated, schools or universities attended, or ethnic groups one is associated with. The values and beliefs of Scouts and Guides organisations, or the local Surf Lifesaving Club, will be incorporated into the individual's set of beliefs and influence the decision-making process. Similarly, a private school that provides a variety of extracurricular sport activities, such as rowing, skiing and mountain climbing, offers very different possibilities from a state-funded, inner-urban high school that is cramped for space and perhaps lacking the level of resources to purchase large-scale capital equipment. In such instances the academic focus may be on other areas of the curriculum, such as music, drama or visual arts, an environment providing a very different set of experiences. Moreover, a sport fan who is a recent immigrant to Australia will most probably follow a sport that resonates with his/her nationality before sampling more indigenous offerings. The ethnic association of many of the National Soccer League clubs provides an opportunity for the sport fan to bridge the gap between the old and the new sport experience.

Geographical considerations are also important. The sport offerings of country or coastal schools and universities can be very different from those of their city cousins. Furthermore, climate cannot be ignored. Differences in sport consumption between Darwin and Hobart would be expected to exist, based on climatic differences.

Finally, although many Australians believe that they live in an egalitarian society, differences based on class, predominantly linked to economic considerations, do exist. While individual wealth will enable the purchase of the equipment to undertake a particular sport or activity, membership may be restricted for a variety of reasons. It may be easier to join a local golf club than the Royal Sydney or Royal Melbourne, even though the same equipment will serve at all venues. Moreover, unless you are a prime minister, the wait to join the Royal Canberra Golf Club may be very long indeed.

Tertiary factors

Tertiary factors are those elements that are beyond the immediate sphere of influence, and should be recognised for what they are. In most instances they are attempts to modify or construct individual behaviour, not just for the consumer's benefit but also for the benefit of the external group. Products, events and media provide information to the consumer in a manner that it is believed will encourage the consumer to buy. Occasionally, such groups may be at odds with each other.

An incident on a sporting field may be downplayed by the organisation concerned as it does not want adverse publicity, which could result in reduced attendance or a lessening of participation. Conversely, the media may play up the event, in the belief that graphic pictures or salacious commentary will sell additional newspapers or that television consumers will view other components of the host program or indeed other programming. In most cases, media sources suggest that they are engaging in responsible journalism by presenting the product in toto. Equally, the ongoing discussion associated with an incident may prove a boon to talkback radio and discussion-type sport shows. Two examples from 2002 were the resignation of AFL Kangaroos captain Wayne Carey for personal, non-football reasons and the loss of all premiership points by the NRL's Canterbury Bulldogs for salary cap breaches. In both instances the amount of media coverage devoted to these stories was arguably disproportionate to the nature of the events themselves. In the case of Carey, his private life was exposed in very public forums; in the case of Canterbury, it would be a brave sport fan or commentator that suggested that the Bulldogs were the only team in contravention of the salary cap. Nevertheless, various sections of the media capitalised on both incidents when there is no doubt that both the individual and club in question would have preferred a much lower profile.

Political, religious, cultural and service groups often use sport to place their organisation in a positive light or to piggyback on the popularity of a particular sport or activity. A local Rotary club's support of a community fun run is conceptually not very different from the entry of various church groups into a debate concerning the sporting use of religious holidays. In such instances, both groups are trying to establish a positive community profile. By linking themselves to sport and leisure they are endeavouring to position themselves as a similar product for consumption purposes.

Finally, an interesting trait on the part of our political leaders has been their willingness to be seen at a variety of sport events, to be photographed wearing a particular team's jersey or to stand in the winner's circle with the victors. It is an attempt on the part of politicians to be seen as just like 'the person in the street'. Here sport is being used as a fundamental link or lure to encourage the individual to consume a particular ideology. Although most senior politicians in Australia align themselves to one or other sport code or team, the connection has usually been ephemeral at best. Yet there is no doubt that Prime Minister John Howard is one of the nation's great sport fans. Whether at the 2000 Olympics, where he was a regular attendee at all sports, not just the high-profile ones, attending rugby league or union games or watching perhaps his greatest sporting passion, cricket, his unabashed zeal for viewing sporting contests is legendary. Former Australian Test captain Mark Taylor referred to the prime minister as a 'cricket tragic' and it has been suggested, perhaps apocryphally, that if he had a choice between being prime minster or batting first wicket down for Australia, he might take the latter.

The sport consumption decision-making process

As previously mentioned, all the major steps in the sport consumption decision-making process are influenced by various elements. Person-specific factors (whether situational or demographic), psychological influences and social forces all play a part in constructing the context from which the decision to purchase is made. Figure 3.2 illustrates the major steps in the decision-making process.

Given that sport consumption is not unique to any one of the above, the potential starting point for a specific decision-making process is almost indiscernible. However, the following six steps represent the major components in the way the sport consumption process unfolds. To exemplify this process, an individual's decision to ultimately attend Australia's premier tennis event, the Australian Open, is used.

Step 1: Problem recognition

Problem recognition is usually a result of the depletion of existing goods or services (*...I don't have much to do regarding entertainment late January...*), change in motivation

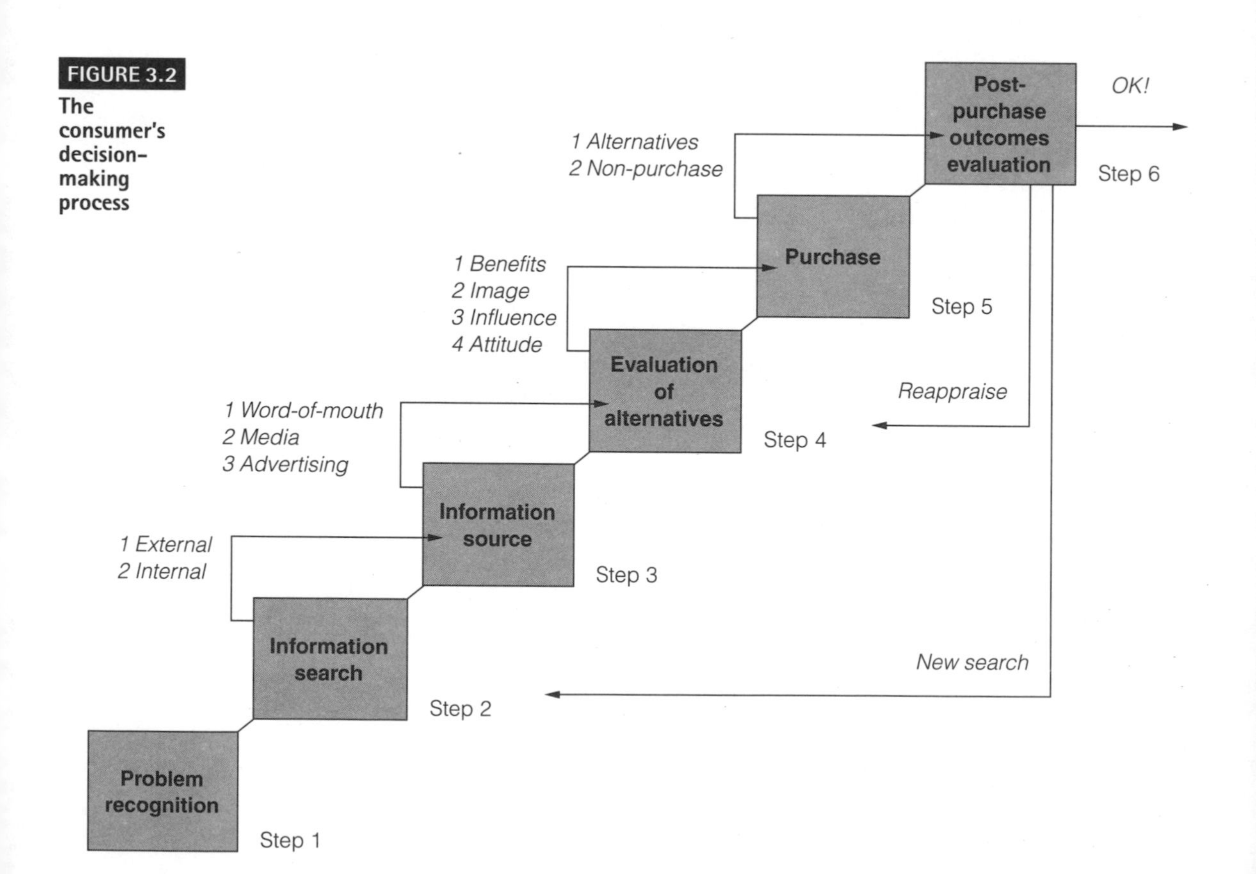

FIGURE 3.2 The consumer's decision-making process

(*...I always go to the movies but it does not allow me to have a chat with my friends...*), change in reference groups or family situation (*...I hang out a lot with my new friends from the physical education course I do at uni...*), and new information, which may be interpersonal or the result of mass communication (*...judging by the television and newspaper advertising, going to see outdoor events will be a lot of fun...*). Recognition of the problem (to find a new form of entertainment that will accommodate particular social needs) will lead to the search for information needed to make the decision.

Step 2: Information search

The information search can take either of two forms: a recall of stored knowledge in the memory, or a seeking of additional information. Some goods and services are bought solely on the basis of an internal search (recalled memory) and are usually related to habitual or routine decision making. Here, the evaluation of alternatives is limited and based on what is remembered (*...I know there is a range of entertainment options available, such as the movies, going out to dinner, to see a show at the theatre or attend a sporting event...*).

With an external search the consumer is seeking information not contained in the memory. The adoption of an external search is usually a response to two factors: recognising that there is a risk involved in making the purchase (price and negative consequences of poor choice), and believing that this type of search will greatly increase the chances of making a correct choice (*...Perhaps I should find out the cost of the tickets, catering or the packages available, and see what some of my friends feel like doing...*). This leads to the consumer sourcing the information. At this stage, general information about the range of entertainment options available, complemented by more specific information about critical product characteristics (*Can I go with my friends? Can I have a chat during the event? etc.*), is collected.

Step 3: Information source

Some sources of information are more powerful than others. For the sport marketer it is important to identify which information sources are most powerful when preaching the sales gospel. For example, a major source of information is via 'word of mouth' through family, friends and opinion leaders (*...My parents go to the theatre on regular occasions, so that might not be the coolest option for me and my friends...*). Another source of information is through general media forms, which include magazine and newspaper articles, new product reviews, and television coverage of events where the product is used. In the sport industry, the wide media coverage received by most sport organisations allows for great opportunities to present sporting events as the preferred entertainment options to customers (*...I certainly see a lot of information about tennis in the papers since Hewitt retained his number 1 position in the rankings...*). Finally, information can be obtained through promotion media, which include myriad forms of advertising (*...If my memory serves me well there was an Australian Open insert in the last edition of* Inside Sport...). It can be seen that the information that is available combined with the source of the information will allow certain providers to position themselves favourably while the potential consumers are evaluating the alternatives available to them.

Step 4: Evaluation of alternatives

An evaluation of alternatives is conducted according to a set of product selection criteria that may include the product benefits, the image of the product and/or the company, and the importance weighting of the range of product attributes according to the different groups of buyers (*... The theatre is for old people, during the movies we can't talk, going out for dinner is too expensive. Going to a sporting event offers scope on all those issues. But Melbourne can be very hot in January; it might be better to attend either indoor events or night matches at an outdoor venue...*). Here, the Australian Open tennis is very much part of the considered set of products. The evaluation of alternatives is also affected by the belief held about a certain product, the purchaser's attitude towards it and the intention to buy (*... Centre Court tickets are a bit expensive and I really don't know how much fun it will be to sit in the one place all day. Perhaps I will just buy the ground pass, where I can move around more. Then I do not have to worry about getting that ticket in advance...*). Only after evaluation does the decision to buy take place. Consumers have now decided that to attend the Australian Open will satisfy the range of needs identified during the problem recognition stage.

Step 5: Purchase

The decision to purchase a particular product or service can best be described as:

Choice = Intention + Unanticipated circumstances

Having made the decision to buy, consume or use, the individual proceeds with that intent in mind. However, at the last moment the individual may find that the store is out of stock, the stadium is full or the event has been postponed. Here a decision has to be made whether to consume an alternative offering or to wait for the selected item to become available (*... Everyone in the city must have turned up today, as all the ground passes are gone. However, it does not matter that much as I am on holidays. I will buy a ticket for tomorrow while I am here today just to be sure...*). Future product consumption is the result of post-purchase outcomes and evaluation.

Step 6: Post-purchase outcomes/evaluation

Invariably there are three major outcomes possible during this stage: (a) The consumer is entirely satisfied with the purchase and no further information is required (*...that was the most fun I have had at sporting event in quite a long time. Affordable, great action. I got to see some budding stars of the game, and I had a great time with my friends...*). (b) The consumer is not entirely satisfied with the decision and may need to reappraise the alternatives gathered through the initial information search, or may indeed seek out new information (*... The day was OK but I do not know if I would rush back. Too many people, all the good matches were on Centre Court and the price of food and drinks was a bit over the top...*). (c) The consumer is totally dissatisfied with the experience, may decide that the resolution to the initial problem may not be forthcoming from the sport/exercise experience, and may look outside this domain for satisfaction (*... That was no fun. Perhaps I should just spend my summers at the beach!!...*).

Establishment of the process by which individuals arrive at the decision to buy a particular product or service does not necessarily imply that each step in the process is always followed. Depending on the type and nature of the purchase, an individual may devote a significant amount of time and effort to the decision-making process, or may make a snap or 'spur-of-the-moment' decision. The latter usually occurs when the adverse consequence of a poor choice is minimal or the purchase has become habitual behaviour. If a person purchases a ground pass each year for the early rounds of the Australian Open, then the purchase has become habitual with the outcome of the experience essentially known in advance.

Involvement in the decision-making process

The amount of thought, and individual involvement, given to a decision to purchase can vary considerably. While the purchase of new laces for basketball shoes requires little involvement, the purchase of the initial footwear is often the result of a far more protracted process. The cost of a club membership often has to be weighed against a series of competing forces for disposable income, yet an individual may make the decision to attend a game at the last moment. The membership (or shoes) is a high involvement purchase; the single game (or laces) is a low involvement purchase.

High involvement purchases

High involvement purchases make full and extended use of the decision-making process. Expensive, complex and high-risk purchases fall into this category. In these cases the consumer will invariably undertake a thorough information search and carefully and selectively examine comparable services or products. The consumer may assess value for money, although cost may not be the major factor where special features, status or functionality are required. Finally, time will be allocated to the decision-making process and the positives and negatives of the purchase weighed. Once a tentative decision to buy has been made, affirmation may be sought from an expert in the field or from a significant other. Yachts, golf clubs, snow skis and club membership may fall into this category.

Sport-marketing strategies aimed at consumers involving a high involvement purchase process often relate to sponsor products, and include pointing out the specific or unique features of the sponsors' offering through the sport as a communication vehicle. This may include the provision of maximum technical or personal support for the service or product's use, and reinforcing the wisdom of the purchase choice. Advertising should be selective. It should target appropriate demographic-psychographic market segments as well as affirm lifestyle and connote quality and excellence. The following examples include high involvement product purchases such as cars, mobile phones and other communications services (that require long-term commitment through contracts with the communications suppliers). Using sport in their sponsorship communications mix, the threshold of purchasing high involvement products, theoretically, should be lowered by offering attractiveness, recognisability and credibility.

In 2003 Kia used the Australian Tennis Open, while in 2002 Vodafone used the Australian Rugby Union and Skyy Vodka the 2002 Motorcycle Grand Prix at Phillip Island, to link their products to fans of tennis, rugby and motorcycle racing respectively. Likewise, in a historic move in July 2002, Telstra bought the naming rights to both the former Colonial

Stadium (now Telstra Dome) in Melbourne and Stadium Australia (Telstra Stadium) in Sydney, which enabled the Telstra brand to be connected with two of the top, state-of-the-art sport and entertainment facilities in the country.

However, it is not just products that use sport to reach potential clients. Financial services, bank organisations and private health funds all use sport to promote their services, believing that purchase involvement is invariably linked to that with which the consumer has some familiarity. In the early 1990s, QBE commenced a long-term sponsorship of the AFL's Sydney Swans in an attempt to penetrate the AFL-saturated state of Victoria. Whether it is insurance, cars or telephony, purchasers have a high involvement in the decision-making process. Sport selectively targets and segments audiences for sponsors, thus the connection between the sponsor's product and the sport creates a win–win situation.

Low involvement purchases

Evans and Berman (1987) define low involvement purchases as the decision-making process undertaken when the products or services to be consumed are socially or psychologically unimportant. In these cases information is acquired passively, the decision to act is made quickly, and the product is often evaluated when the purchase is made. The choice is usually routine or habitual; the level of prior experience with the product is high, as is the frequency of purchase; the pressure or time may be significant, but the consequences of poor choice are minimal. The purchase of a weekly sports magazine can be thought of as a low involvement decision.

In establishing a strategy aimed at consumers exhibiting low involvement in the purchase process, sport marketers need to provide repetitive advertising and information, encourage familiarity, offer a variety of inducements, create attention-grabbing point-of-purchase (POP) displays and, if possible, distribute in multiple outlets. Sportview 3.1 explores high vs low involvement in the purchasing of tickets for the 2000 Sydney Olympic Games.

SPORTVIEW 3.1

The Sydney Olympic ticket policy

The Sydney Olympic Games provides an excellent vignette of the high/low involvement purchase strategy. Potential spectators at the Olympic Games in Sydney 2000 were faced with numerous choices not only as to the events they could view but also as to the amount they could pay to see such events. The Sydney Organising Committee started its ticketing campaign in early 1998, with approximately 9.6 million tickets at its disposal. The key marketing messages of the campaign were that 88% of the tickets cost under $100 and 4 million tickets were directly available to the Australian public.

According to Thamnopoulos (2000), the criteria SOCOG set for the pricing of tickets were size of venue and seating availability; sport popularity; venue location and timing; the likelihood of Australian athletes performing well; the zoning of seats; and finally comparative prices at previous Games. Moreover, the prices were divided into four segments. The first segment, which focused on the finals and the most popular events, was titled 'super premium', with prices in excess of $350. 'Premium' tickets were generally between $100 and $200 and were for early rounds of popular activities and finals of less popular sports. Sports less popular in Australia but with international appeal (judo, handball, baseball, soccer, etc.) were priced at under $100, and the fourth segment, entitled 'the experience', sold for less than $60.

As Thamnopoulos readily demonstrates, for fans who simply wanted to be part of the Olympic experience, tickets were quite inexpensive, and the choice of sport was essentially a low involvement purchase, as being there was the important thing. For individuals who wanted to attend sports in which Australians might win medals, or who wanted to see the more high-profile Olympic sports, a higher involvement in the purchase was required. Interestingly, the Opening Ceremony could be seen for around $1500 or less than $200, although the likelihood of getting tickets at the higher price was far greater than at the lower. Once again the relative importance of seeing the event brought into play the high/low involvement purchase paradigm.

Finally, fans who wanted a guaranteed seat at all events at the Olympic Stadium also had that option available. In 1996 Stadium Australia issued a prospectus offering 34400 golden memberships at $10000 each and 600 platinum memberships at $30000 each. As part of the membership package the purchaser was entitled to attend all Olympic events held in the stadium. There is no doubt that a resolution to purchase such a package was a high involvement decision.

A number of companies use sport to saturate the whole market with their message, as opposed to identifying a specific segment. Soft drinks and fast foods are examples of products that are omnipresent in the sports environment. It is hoped that the purchase of their products will become habitual. Furthermore, athletes are often used to promote basic everyday purchases. The Australian Cricket Team has promoted breakfast cereal, Kieran Perkins has promoted the virtues of milk and Grant Hackett has been seen chomping on Uncle Toby's muesli bars. Manufacturers believe that using athletes in marketing their products makes them stand out in a cluttered environment. Chapter 13 examines this concept at length.

Consumer characteristics

Demographics

Demographics provide a statistical profile of a particular segment of a marketplace. Some of the more frequently recorded demographics include gender, age, marital status, household size and income, educational level and occupation. There may also be instances when information regarding an individual's religious or political affiliation, ethnicity and even class is required. Sportview 3.2 discusses the increasing financial contribution made to sport by the gay and lesbian market, specifically connected with the Gay Games in Sydney in 2002. Through the combination of these variables, sport marketers can pinpoint both expanding and declining markets.

SPORTVIEW 3.2

The Sydney Gay Games 2002

In the June 1997 issue of *Inside Sport*, Doug Booth and Colin Tatz discussed the concept of the 'pink dollar' and its impact on the sport and leisure industry. The term 'pink dollar' in this context referred to the financial contribution made [to sport] by the gay and lesbian community. The authors provided evidence that in excess of 560 000 members of the gay and lesbian community were actively involved in sport and leisure, and argued that this segment made a sizeable contribution to the sport and leisure dollars generated by Australians each year. Major sponsor Aussie Bodies was using the event to boost the brand awareness of its range of health foods and fitness supplements to the gay community, while Southcorp believed it would provide an opportunity to consolidate the recognition of its Rosemont Estate brand in the USA. There is little doubt that the economic impact of this group is far-reaching.

However, it is in the tourism industry where the impact of the 2002 Gay Games was most felt. In 1998 the Gay Games were held in Amsterdam, for the first time outside the USA. In 2002 the Games were held for the first time in the southern hemisphere. As of September 2002, 12 700 athletes had registered to take part in a program of 97 events. According to Dennis (2002), the Gay Games had more participants than the Olympics and helped confirm Australia as a gay and lesbian tourist destination. The Australian Tourist Commission obviously agreed, and spent $400 000 in the US gay media to leverage the event. Just prior to the Games it was believed that 8000 North Americans would be in Sydney. According to Eccles (2002), the total numbers expected were in the vicinity of 35 000. As such, it was billed as a bonanza for the tourism industry, with a potential return to the NSW economy of approximately $140 million. Clearly, this is a market of considerable purchasing power.

As indicated in the headline story, the Australian Bureau of Statistics reported in 1999 that up until April that year 2.5 million people had attended an AFL match at least once in the preceding 12 months. They also reported that more than half (55%) of all men attended compared with 40% of all women; nevertheless, both these percentages were up on the 1995 survey. However, while AFL was the number 1 choice for groups, motor sport came in second for men while horseracing was the second choice of women. The research also posited that sports attendance declined with age. This trend can be seen as a positive or negative for sport marketers. While it is well documented that society in general is ageing and the baby boomers of the late 1940s and early 1950s are well and truly in the latter stages of middle age, this cohort is increasingly composed of empty nesters. Moreover, in the main they are in good health and retain a zest for life. Sport marketers would do well to determine the participation and spectator needs of this group and provide services accordingly. Finally, the survey determined that the Northern Territory had the highest rate of attendance (at 59%), while New South Wales (42%) and Queensland (43%) had the lowest. It would be interesting to undertake comparative research to determine reasons for the near 20% discrepancy.

Lifestyle

Psychographics divides the market into segments or subgroups based on certain behaviours that relate to attitudes, lifestyles or values. Psychographics can be more important than demographics in the consumer decision-making process; however, they can be more difficult to quantify. For example, Lyons and Jackson (2001) examined factors that influenced African-American gen-Xers to buy Nikes and determined that this group placed importance on the style of the shoe, especially as it related to status. They argued: 'African-Americans tend to shop, purchase and consume apparel at a greater rate than do people of other races. The impetus for this above average consumption is the desire to "fit in" or look good.' (2001: 100) There is thus little doubt that such variables are lifestyle factors. However, while the variables 'to fit in' or 'to look good' are relatively easy to articulate, they are rather subjective, making formulation of marketing strategies around such concepts difficult. Here the use of focus groups is very important.

Personality

Hawkins et al. (1992: 307) suggested that 'consumers tend to purchase products that most closely match their own [personality] or that strengthen an area they feel deficient in'. In most cases personalities are individual, constant and enduring. They can change, of course, but this is usually due to the impact of a major life event. The two most common approaches to understanding personality are individual learning theories and social learning theories, more commonly referred to as trait vs state theories of personality.

Individual learning theory argues that personality traits are usually formed in the early stages of an individual's development and remain relatively constant into and through adulthood. Reserved, quiet, shy, extroverted, relaxed or confident are examples of this type of personality. It is easy to see why certain individuals prefer the cinema to day/night cricket, bushwalking to basketball, or golf to aerobics, based on their individual personality characteristics.

Social learning theory argues that environment is an extremely important determinant of human behaviour. In such cases the personality of the individual may alter depending on the situation. An introvert in one instance can be an extrovert in the next, whereas an assertive, aggressive individual can very quickly become timid when faced with a particular fear or phobia. Bungy jumping is a good example: bravado and confidence disappear in the moments before the leap.

In marketing sport and related activities it is necessary to cater for all personality types. For every fan who wants to stand in the outer among 'like-minded supporters' and cheer him/herself hoarse for a favourite team or athlete, there is another fan who wants to watch the action unfold while seated and in a less emotionally charged environment. For every consumer who wants the latest, brightest and most expensive athletic apparel, there is another who is more than comfortable in a nondescript tracksuit and functional footwear. It is important that the product fit the consumer's personality and vice versa. An understanding of basic personality types ensures that as wide a range of consumers as possible is being catered for in the marketplace.

Environmental factors

In the latter half of the 20th century environmental issues such as pollution in its various forms, rainforest destruction, overpopulation, urban sprawl, and the general degradation of land and ocean were pushed to the forefront of public consciousness. However, while society's relationship to the physical environment is usually viewed from a negative perspective, judiciously utilised changes in technology have the potential to provide the modern sport consumer with great benefits.

Computer technologies and land management have allowed golf courses and resorts to exist side by side with rainforests and sensitive wetlands; sensible urban planning and council bylaws have allowed the establishment of new stadiums or facilities that are sympathetic to local architecture and demographics; and government legislation has been enacted to protect both the rights of individual consumers and the collective good. It is important that the views of all categories of consumers, whether long-term, new, emerging or potential, be taken into account when sport promotion takes place.

Summary

Understanding the sport consumer is not a simple task. The sport marketer needs to be aware not only of the primary, secondary and tertiary factors that influence consumer decision-making–he/she also needs to comprehend both the process and the level of involvement by which the decision to buy or consume is arrived at. Other important determinants that must be considered before establishing marketing strategies include the specific demographics and psychographics of the constituent group, along with germane environmental factors.

While comprehending the complexity of the sport consumer's decision-making process is one of the more intricate tasks facing the sport marketer, unquestionably it has become a critical part of marketing management strategy. Although it is not always possible to fully understand how this process takes place, assiduous attention to the unique characteristics of specific consumers, coupled with a broad awareness of how decisions are reached, will provide the sport marketer with a solid framework within which marketing strategies can be developed.

CASE STUDY

The impact and consumption of the Australian Tennis Open

There is no doubt that events are one of the fastest-growing sectors of today's leisure and tourism industry, and Australia has capitalised on this with the Formula 1 Grand Prix, the MotoGP, the Indy Car Series and most recently the 2000 Olympic Games in Sydney. However, one stand-out international event that annually returns to Australia is the first Tennis Grand Slam of each year, the Australian Open. Madourou (2000) compared the 1997 and 1999 Australian Tennis Opens to examine changes in economic impact and tourism flows and to determine the utility of such findings to the Greek context, where such events are currently underdeveloped.

The Australian Tennis Open dates back to 1905, when the Australasian Championships was held at what is now the Albert Ground on St Kilda Road, Melbourne. Since 1905 the event has been held every year, except during the World Wars and in 1986, when the date was shifted from December to January. In 1972 the event found a permanent home at Kooyong Courts, but when it became obvious that this venue was too small the Victorian state government began the construction of what is now known as Melbourne Park. The first event was held at the new facility in 1988 and was an instant success, with an over 80% increase in attendance over the previous staging at Kooyong. The Australian Open is a world-class competitive tennis event and is one of the four international tennis events that constitute the Grand Slam (the other three being the US Open, the French Open and Wimbledon).

In 1997, 391 500 spectators passed through the gates of Melbourne Park; two years later an all-time record was set when 473 296 patrons attended the event over fourteen days and nine night sessions. This represented an increase of 21% over 1997. Madourou (2000) contends that the gross benefit to the Victorian economy in 1999 was $97.1 million, which was up 38.5% on the 1997 figure of $70.1 million. She adds that state government tax receipts related to visitor expenditure on local goods and services were up 18.4%, from $6.2 to $7.6 million. Other interesting factors of note included the generation of an additional 65,000 visitor nights between 1997 and 1999, a generation of an additional 200 permanent employment positions and a perceived induced tourism benefit increase of approximately $31 million.

However, although there was a perception of an increased tourist benefit in 1999 there were fewer tourists from overseas attending the event while interstate and Victorian persons accounted for only an additional 10 000 of the total attendance. By far the biggest increase in attendance came from the residents of the host city, Melbourne, which provided 114 000 of the spectators in 1997 and 140 000 in 1999. The decrease in overseas visitors was a concern as it represented additional expenditure whereas local, regional and national visitors often only represent switched expenditure. Hence the perceived tourism benefit to Melbourne may have been at the expense of other events, sites or festivals. Nevertheless the point is well made that the Australian Open is an event that serves as a destination promoter and enhances the image of a host place. As such the acquisition of special events should be a policy of cities which are trying to enhance the domestic and international profile of their location.

Source: Adapted from Madourou (2002).

Questions

1 Explore a potential reason for the strong increase in urban tourism and provide a brief explanation as to why you think it is the result of primary, secondary or tertiary factors.

2 What are some of the factors that you believe may have led to the fall in international tourist numbers and how would you overcome them?
3 What additional consumer information (characteristics) would you like before you attempted to implement a similar hallmark event?
4 What are some of the potential downsides to hosting a hallmark event?

4

Market research: segmentation, target markets and positioning

Stage 1—Identification of marketing opportunities

Step 1 Analyse external environment (forces, competition, publics)

Step 2—Analyse organisation (mission, objectives, SWOT)

Step 3—Examine market research and marketing information systems

Step 4—Determine marketing mission and objectives

▼

Stage 2—Strategy determination

▼

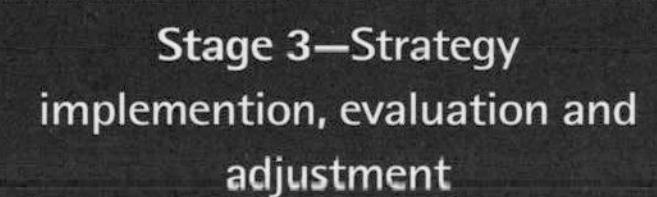

Stage 3—Strategy implemention, evaluation and adjustment

CHAPTER OBJECTIVES

Chapter 4 examines the development of marketing research and its use in segmentation, the selection of target markets and positioning. It demonstrates how marketing missions are created, objectives established and target markets selected. Furthermore it highlights how positioning is used to effectively locate a product or service within that target market.

After studying this chapter you should be able to:

1. Create a basic marketing information system.
2. Articulate the components of small-scale market research.
3. Comprehend the market segmentation process.
4. Understand the rationale for the selection of target markets.
5. Appreciate the concept of positioning.

HEADLINE STORY

'I'd rather mow the lawn!!!'

As it does regularly, the 6 March 2001 edition of *The Bulletin* reported on a piece of research conducted by the Roy Morgan Research Centre. This special study presented data relating to the leisure habits of the Australian population, and, somewhat surprisingly, determined that the leisure activity of choice for many Australians was not swimming, walking, golf or fishing—but gardening. In a three-month period the research found that 64% of those over the age of 14 had worked in the garden, and this response rate was common for the genders. While those over the age of 50 (75%) were more likely to engage in this activity than those between the ages of 14 and 24, this later group had a stronger preference for gardening (31%) than for attending professional sport contests (22%). In fact, across all age groups, attending professional sport contests (16%) was less popular than playing video games (20%), working on a car (23%), playing sport (30%), hobbies (33%) and formal exercise (39%). (Morgan Poll 2001: 20).

The significance of the above figures does not necessarily lie in the leisure time choice of activities, as interesting as these may be, but is rather indicative of the competition the sport marketer has for the discretionary resources, time and money of the consumer. Armed with such data the sport marketer can establish strategies to leverage off other leisure time pursuits. The creation of myriad football (all codes), basketball, cricket, racing and video games, often officially endorsed, is one example of how the knowledge gained from good market research can turn what at face value appears to be a negative position into a positive marketing strategy.

Market research and strategy

Mullin et al. (2000: 99) suggest that:

> the most critical factor in marketing success is the marketers' ability to collect accurate and timely information about consumers and potential consumers and to use this data to create marketing plans that are specifically targeted to meet the needs of the specific consumer groups.

There is little doubt that to make informed decisions organisations need information, and lots of it. However, the collection of this material is only a starting point for the construction of a Marketing Information System (MIS). Once compiled, this information must be integrated, analysed, and used to guide the direction of the organisation. Time spent on its assembly, maintenance and development can be the most effective marketing tool at an organisation's disposal.

Developing marketing information systems

Stanton et al. (1995: 48) suggest that an MIS is an 'ongoing, organised set of procedures and methods designed to generate, analyse, disseminate, store and later retrieve information for use in decision making'. Nevertheless, they also acknowledge that for the MIS to be successful the data should be not only of high quality but also be used in a realistic manner and adopted as a source of decision making by the organisation. Figure 4.1 provides a basic design for the construction of an effective MIS. In this instance the population is divided into consumers and non-consumers, and relevant information is obtained using appropriate data-collection methods. The information is then collated and integrated. From this resource base marketing strategies can be formulated, along with mechanisms for monitoring effectiveness.

The current need for ongoing market research and the establishment of increasingly sophisticated MISs are the result of a dynamic, constantly changing sport environment. With less time for deliberation, increased accountability, growing consumer expectations and the ever-expanding scope of marketing activities, sporting organisations need rapid access to reliable information that will result in clear, appropriate decision making. Fortunately for sport, the quantity and quality of available information are constantly expanding. Matthews (2002) reported that an additional two golf courses were being added 'to what was becoming a crammed precinct on the Mornington Peninsula in Victoria'. However, the director of the Melbourne-based golf club properties was not concerned with the oversupply, stating that 'market research shows it's viable and we have had lots of talks with Tourism Victoria. The predictions are that this will become a mecca for golfers.' (2002: 75) How such information is used is the real key to organisational success.

In order to develop an extensive MIS, sport marketers need to collect general market data, data on individual consumers, and data on competitors and their participants.

General market data include all the information which relates to the broad environment in which the sport operates. Within its area of operation, most commonly referred to as its critical trading radius, the organisation needs to establish size, demographics, the consumer habits of residents and workers, the way such individuals choose to spend their leisure time, and any specific trends that will affect the sport positively or negatively. This information

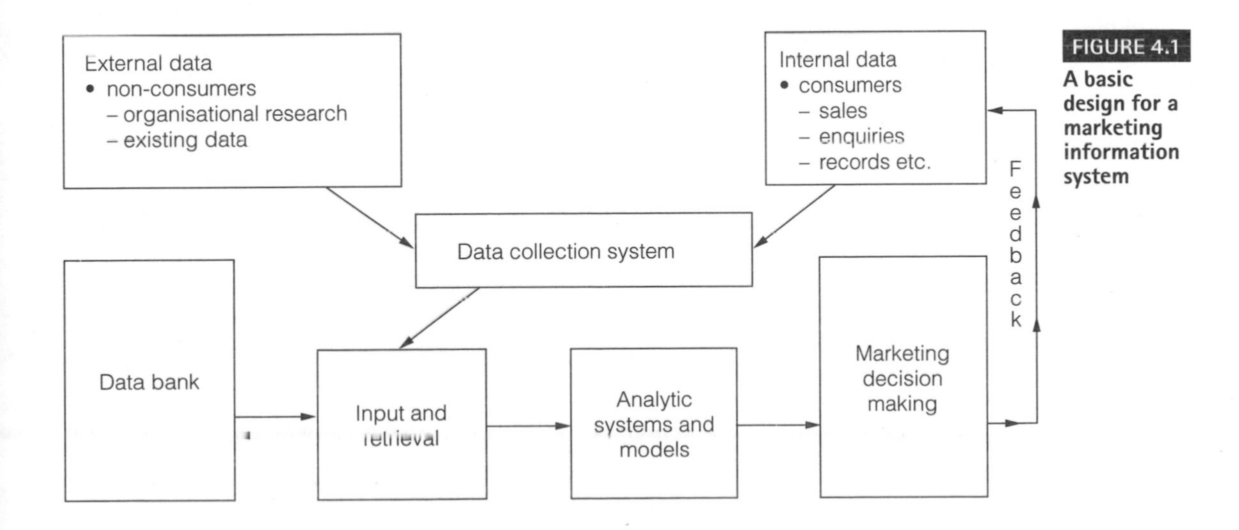

FIGURE 4.1 **A basic design for a marketing information system**

is particularly important for sports hoping to expand nationally and be successful. The profile of the specific sport fan needs to be well represented in the new market for the sport to have any hope of success. The Sydney Swans believe that there is a potential AFL base of approximately 640 000 supporters in the city, and the NBL's Sydney Kings obviously felt that the shift back to their home court of the 1990s, the Entertainment Centre in downtown Sydney, would bring back the fans they had lost, and assist in the resurrection of a club that had foundered in the new millennium at the basketball Superdome purpose-built for the Sydney Olympic Games.

Once *individual consumer* data have been collected and entered on the appropriate database, the sport marketer has a multitude of information available with which to establish marketing strategies. Name, address, phone number, gender, age, occupation or student type, purchase patterns and payment methods are a small representation of the type of information that can easily be collected by sporting organisations. Quick (1998, 1999) noted that the New South Wales Rugby Union Super 12 fan surveys in 1998 and 1999 offered inducements to fans to supply their names, addresses and phone numbers when responding.

A third source of information for sporting organisations relates to *competitors and their participants*. It is critical that sporting organisations not only be aware of who their competitors are but also know the consumers of a rival's products or services. A number of sports can sometimes successfully operate in the same area, when their fans are dissimilar. Basketball, tennis, soccer and netball appear to be quite different in their support bases. So, apart from observing general promotional strategies, these sports would be best served by focusing on information that is internal to the organisation and sport-specific. Nevertheless, if a sport is jockeying for position in the marketplace, competitor pricing, promotion, and product breadth and depth need to be noted. This is particularly important when junior competitions and leagues are involved. Juniors will invariably gravitate to those sports which provide them with opportunities at the local level.

Data sources for a marketing information system

There are two major sources of data for any MIS–external and internal. External data may be primary or secondary and have been collected by the sporting organisation or an external agency. Internal data include all the information, such as basic enquiries, that the organisation collects during the day-to-day operation of its business.

External secondary data

There are numerous sources of secondary data that sporting organisations can use to assist in the formation of a strategic marketing plan. The most obvious starting point is government agencies, such as the Australian Bureau of Statistics (ABS). *Participation in Sport and Physical Activities, Australia* (2000a) and *Australians Less Active* (2000b) are two potential information sources.

ABS statistics (2000a) showed the numbers and demographic characteristics of persons involved in sport at some time during the 12 months 1999/2000. The data suggested that men had a higher participation rate in sport than women and that the Australian-born or those living in capital cities were more likely to engage in sport than their overseas-born or rural-domiciled fellow citizens. However ABS statistics also suggested (2000b) that participation rates in sport and physical activities decreased in all states and territories except Western Australia in 1999/2000. These are just two documents that provide basic information that is potentially useful for a number of sporting bodies. (Such information is readily accessible on the ABS website: http://www.abs.gov.au/)

Libraries and chambers of commerce are other useful sources of information, especially at the local level. Data relating to trends and uses of local events and facilities should be held there, as well as the various municipal rules and regulations governing the conduct of sport events. Larger community libraries, along with those attached to institutes of higher education, often contain much of the government or commercial data that have been collected in relation to sport. Chambers of commerce will hold data relating to the income and expenditure patterns of local industry, which can assist sport marketers in establishing profiles that may match their organisation.

An increasing amount of data is being gathered in various research units in Australian universities. While much of this information is proprietary, some of the findings are being presented at conferences and appearing in academic journals. Likewise, a growing number of sport-marketing academics are being used as market research consultants and are bringing an ever-increasing repository of skills and knowledge to their task.

Advertising media are constantly engaged in the collection of secondary data. While it may not be specific to the focus of the sport marketer, information relating to demographics and psychographics may be useful for sponsorship or advertising. This is particularly the case when the characteristics of the media information match a particular sport's own data.

A final source of secondary data is private organisations such as Brian Sweeney and Associates. Their publication, *Australians and Sport*, annually looks at sports participation, attendance, and television viewing and sponsorship awareness. Hirons (2002) suggested that Uncle Toby was the best recognised sponsor, that swimming was still the most popular sport participation activity and that the Orange mobile phone carrier had 'made a spectacular entry into the sport sponsorship arena'. Similarly, Roy Morgan Research, most commonly associated with the Morgan Gallup Poll, has established a variety of services and products that can provide sporting organisations with significant data. This chapter's headline story on the Morgan Gallup Poll for *The Bulletin* (6/3/2001) is a good example of this. The Roy Morgan *Monitor* covers areas such as tourism, entertainment and leisure, and the organisation annually conducts more than 60 000 personal interviews. The collection of such data provides wide-ranging information on consumer behaviour and media usage, and as such can be an invaluable secondary source for the sport marketer. For more specific data it is even possible in some instances for organisations to contract for an industry-related question to be included in a survey.

Primary data

Primary data may be internal or external, and are a product of collection methods and purpose.

The most common type of internal data are data collected from enquiries, letters and telephone calls. These may be in the form of complaints or praise. Accounts, credit card purchases and general sales can also provide a wealth of information, indicating consumer trends in relation to a sporting organisation's product or service. Other sources of internal information can include an organisation's employees, contractors, suppliers and sponsors. All can offer the sport marketer useful advice, and any such comments should be heeded.

However, there is little doubt that the best data available to the sport marketer are those which are purpose-driven by the organisation. In this way direct answers to specific questions can be obtained about the habits and consumption patterns of sport participants and consumers. Moreover, the collection of primary data through market research is not difficult. All that is required is access to the information source, time, energy and good questions!

Marketing research in sporting organisations

Basically, market research in sporting organisations seeks to answer six questions about consumers in relation to their consumption of the product. Initially, sporting organisations need to know WHO their consumers are, but this is only the tip of the iceberg. WHY they choose the particular sport product and WHEN and WHERE that consumption takes place are equally important. WHAT that consumption entails in terms of pre- and post-event activities, and HOW the product is used, are also critical in terms of establishing a complete consumer profile.

In no particular order, the information requested generally falls into the categories of general and sport-specific.

General information

Usually, the general information requested focuses on demographics such as gender, age, occupation, household size, place of residence and methods of transport.

Similarly, information is often elicited regarding psychographic issues (which are addressed in chapter 3). Fundamentally, psychographic information conveys data on the what and how of consumer behaviour, such as how many times in a given period a person visits a particular establishment (e.g. restaurant, hotel or facility), the number and type of vehicles in the household, and the various electronic items they use. This last issue is becoming more and more important as sporting organisations endeavour to ascertain how many of their consumers not only use personal computers but also have access to the Internet. With many sporting organisations establishing interactive home pages, new opportunities for establishing enhanced databases are plentiful. The AFL's Sydney Swans is just one example of a professional sport franchise that communicates with its members on a regular basis via the Internet. Between 21 and 27 August 2002 the Swans were in touch with members via e-mail five times on matters as diverse as player retirements to 2002 final home and away game promotional activities.

An equally important general question relates to where consumers get their information. Frequency and type of newspapers read, radio stations listened to, television stations and programs viewed, and magazines read, both general and specific, are crucial factors in determining promotional strategy.

Results from a 1999 fan survey conducted for the New South Wales Rugby Union at Waratahs home matches indicated that 48% of all people listened to radio at breakfast time, Channel 9 was by far the most watched TV station, and 68% indicated that they read *The Sydney Morning Herald*. The most popular radio station for these rugby fans was the commercial-free, ABC's 2BL (Quick 1999). Research has generally indicated that television is the major source of event information, with radio rating poorly. The Waratahs scenario does little to disprove this belief. However, there are two other issues that need to be considered.

The word-of-mouth variable is a constant response, and a market research strategy needs to be developed to control this. Moreover, although general questions about magazines read almost invariably result in a sport-specific magazine response, magazines targeted at women often feature strongly. With the increasing female acceptance of and adherence to many sports and recreational activities, perhaps it is time that sport marketers allocated a portion of their advertising budget to this expanding market segment.

Sport-specific information

Sport- or activity-specific questions often relate to attendance patterns, influences to buy or consume, and levels of satisfaction with various aspects of the event.

In relation to attendance, organisations need to be aware of both the depth of product or service use and the breadth of use. Obviously, years of membership or season ticket holding is an example of depth, but the range of single-match buyback programs, offering incentives to members who do not attend a particular match to place their seat/ticket back in the pool for general sale, is an increasingly popular example of the latter.

Likewise, organisations need to know what influences the consumer's decision to buy this particular product when faced with the diverse and ever-expanding range of options in the sport or entertainment marketplace.

Finally, organisations need to be apprised of the customers' levels of satisfaction–that is, their perceptions of the range and quality of the merchandise and concessions sold, of the scope and type of services offered, and of the way in which the organisation conducts its business.

By asking such questions of sport fans and consumers, organisations can establish comprehensive profiles of their customers, which in turn allows the organisation to strategically market its products or services in a diverse marketplace. As Huggins (1992: 40) notes:

> the principal focus of the marketing function in sport is not so much to be skilful in making sport fans or participants do what suits the interest of sport as to be skilful in conceiving or doing what suits the interest of the fans or participants without changing the sport itself.

The marketing mission

Before identifying the components of the market research process, it is useful to consider the benefit of determining the marketing mission. The mission of the whole organisation, in many ways, will also assist managers in setting direction for their respective departments, one of which can be the marketing department.

Cheverton (2000) suggests that, rather than being platitudinous comments, good mission statements actually guide the organisation with some consistency through the decision making process in a way that minimises conjecture or misunderstanding. Moreover, he argues that there are five key aspects to a mission statement. These are: acknowledging the business the organisation is in; knowing the aspirational position; being aware of the core competencies that are needed to guide the organisation toward that vision; knowing which consumers or target market will best assist in reaching the position; and understanding how an organisation knows when it has arrived. In other words, what are the measurements of success? Baker (2000), however, concludes that the mission is more than just a strategic plan: it is the 'cultural glue' that enables a collective engagement in the marketing process, and it is this approach which is most appropriate to the sport-marketing environment. There is no doubting the importance of strategy in sport marketing (hence the title of this book), but given that sport organisations are eclectic organisations, the overarching mission or vision is the focal point around which such diverse units can congregate.

The Australian Sports Commission (ASC) (2002: 9) has a very simple mission, and that is 'to enrich the live of Australians through Sport'. This mission is to be achieved through the development and maintenance of an effective national sports infrastructure, increased sport participation, and enhanced sport performance. Moreover the ASC argues in its 2002–2005 Strategic Plan (2002) that it works towards this mission by developing a national policy framework, coordinating and contributing to the national delivery network, and via the development and dissemination of quality services, programs and products.

Inherent in such strategic plans, stated visions or marketing missions are the objectives by which the desired outcomes might be realised. Once again in keeping with this text, such objectives are strategic in that they carefully elucidate the manner in which the organisation reaches its stated goal. There are numerous types of organisational objectives, but in the main they fall into either of two major categories: sales or communication. Furthermore, there are a number of acronyms in existence (e.g. SMART = Smart, Measurable, Achievable, Realistic, and Timely) that guide the objectives construction process. But the fundamental underpinning in the selection and creation of strategic objectives remains their evaluative benefit. The success or otherwise of the marketing mission is determined via the ongoing monitoring and evaluation of the stated objectives. The ongoing scrutiny of results against the framework of organisational objectives is necessary because of their basically organic nature. Organisational objectives will change as intermediate goals are obtained, or with the realisation that a structured strategy is not delivering the desired results, or if an external trigger necessitates an internal change. Quality market research further enables the sport organisation to collect the information that is necessary to keep the organisation on the right strategic course.

The market research process

The days are gone when sporting organisations could rely on general sport market research to inform their decision making. It is not difficult for sporting organisations to conduct their own market research, to engage a specialist to assist in part of the research, whether it be questionnaire construction, data analysis or interpretation, or to contract a consultant to deliver product-specific information. Organisational decisions should be based on the needs and expectations of the consumer, and the only way this can be ascertained is to ask. While the phrase 'use it or lose it' is a sport cliché, when applied to market research there is not a more appropriate sentiment.

The market research process principally consists of five distinct phases. In order to guide the complete process, and to achieve maximum results with limited resources, the first step in the process is to clearly define the research problem and set a number of measurable objectives. The research problem and objectives often are a direct derivative of the marketing mission of the organisation. The second step in the process is to develop a research methodology—that is, to determine which data sources are needed (primary or secondary), and which methods of data collection (see below) are best used in the context of the research. The third step then involves the research planning and data collection, who collects the data, when and where. When all data are collected they need to be analysed. Data analysis, as the fourth step in the process, can involve the crunching of quantitative data with the help of statistical analysis software programs or the interpretation of more qualitative (e.g. interviews) research data. The final step in the research process is the presentation of the findings so that the research objectives are achieved and the research problem is best answered.

Data-collection methods

Surveys

The personal survey is still potentially the most useful of all research methods, as it allows the sport marketer to source first-hand information on the purchase and consumption patterns of sport fans. These data can be collected at the event, by going door to door in a defined geographical area, at a shopping centre (mall intercepts) or via the telephone (telemarketing). Most sport organisations that are serious about providing services to their constituency regularly engage in this type of research. Moreover, a serious sport organisation is not just a professional or semi-professional franchise. Local clubs and groups can often use the survey format to gain consumer or participant feedback. Obviously, the more professional an organisation is and the larger its stakeholder base, the more sophisticated the survey and its accompanying tools of analysis will become. Nevertheless, the underlying philosophy remains constant, and that is the collection of quality information that will assist in decision making and guide the running of a successful club.

Focus groups

The Sydney Swans is just one organisation that is using focus groups to assist in the creation and refinement of marketing strategy. A focus group is a small group of interested individuals gathered to talk about the issues that an organisation and its consumers believe are important. Usually the size of the focus group is less than ten, which provides everyone present with an opportunity to contribute. This method encourages individuals to engage freely in dialogue with each other, with the data collector in this instance prompting, guiding and recording. Trends and issues emanating from focus groups are often the catalyst for more structured, follow-up research.

Observation

Although not always undertaken in a formal manner, the observation technique should be used by the sport marketer on an ongoing basis. From Bill Veeck with baseball during the 1940s, to Kerry Packer and World Series Cricket in the 1970s, to Michael Wrubleski and the National Basketball League (NBL) in the 1990s, good sport promoters have recognised the value of getting out and both talking to the fans and watching their behaviour. This simple act can inform sport marketers about which aspects of their market strategies are having the desired result and which need some work. Ideally, the observation will lead to the focus group, which could lead to the structured survey, which should then lead to action based on rigorous data collection.

Experimentation

Experimentation can be useful to the sport marketer in specific circumstances. Here the researcher or promoter manipulates one variable while holding all others constant. Changing the venue, time or day of event, or altering uniforms, are just a few of the variables that professional sport clubs manipulate during a pre-season competition in order to gauge reaction to such changes. If the changes prove popular, they may be adopted for the regular season. If not, the previous modus operandi is utilised.

Research design

Although types of research design are as varied as the sports products and services being researched, there are a number of basic principles that should be adhered to:

- Sport marketers should ask only questions they need to know the answer to. If responses to perceived personal questions, such as income levels, are not needed, they should not be asked for, as incorrect responses can bias results.
- For ease of analysis, questions should be closed, mutually exclusive and free of ambiguity.
- While questions should be thematically linked, each response should provide a unique piece of information. This approach means that a questionnaire or survey can be reduced to sections, which can then be used and manipulated as a stand-alone instrument.
- The research design should be of sufficient scope to provide all necessary information, but short enough to encourage broad-based participation in the process.
- Mullin et al. (2000) suggest that the sport marketer needs to have a feel for the kind of answers expected. While it could be argued that this may introduce bias into the project design, most research is initiated through some type of intuitive process.

Potential uses of marketing research

Sport-marketing research generally can have numerous outcomes, although the following are the most common uses:

- It can enhance the flow of communication between the organisation and the customer.
- It may facilitate the creation of promotional strategies or the development of sponsorship proposals.
- It should assist in general decision making and programming.

Sportview 4.1 illustrates how a small-scale market research project may be devised, constructed, administered, analysed and interpreted.

SPORTVIEW 4.1

The inaugural Cathay Pacific Australian PGA Par 3 golf championship

In 1995 the organising committee of the inaugural Cathay Pacific Australian PGA Par 3 Golf Championship commissioned a small market research project from a group of sport marketing students at a Sydney university, specifically an on-course consumer behaviour survey (Moore et al. 1995). The major objective of the research was to provide the organising committee with consumer information that would enable the construction of a database. Other objectives related to the provision of a mechanism for the evaluation of the current championship and the establishment of criteria for future promotion strategies and market research.

The questionnaire was the result of the collaboration between the chairman of the organising committee and the research group, and resulted in the collection of 100 surveys over the three days of the championship (the estimated attendance for the three days was 900). Surveying was conducted over a two-hour period each day, with each member of the research team covering the entire course three times each day.

The researchers believe that the following exogenous variables may have been influential in encouraging visitors to attend the championship: the novelty factor associated with an inaugural event, the long weekend factor, and the general abundance of sport available to sport consumers at that time of year, which included the AFL Grand Final, the Bathurst 1000 motor race and the ARL Grand Final the previous week.

Consumer information gleaned from the survey included gender, postcode spread and density, occupation, golf club membership, media analysis, reasons for attending the tournament, and ratings for features such as food and beverage, staff helpfulness and availability, toilets and leader boards. Respondents were also asked about future consumption patterns related to the tournament. General comments were also asked for, and frequencies for these were established.

The research team established a number of significant points, such as that local and non-local respondents had different reasons for attending the event and that there was a low attendance rate by golf club members. The research team brought these and other issues to the attention of the organising committee and suggested topics and areas for future research. These included scheduling, merchandising, golf vs sport fans and an education process aimed at ensuring understanding of the specific nature of the competition.

Segmenting the sport market

On any given weekend, Australian sport attracts millions of spectators and participants who participate for myriad reasons. Moreover, members of the same family or household may witness or participate in a particular activity for a variety of motives. In an attempt to encourage such groups to initiate or maintain their involvement in the sport or activity, different marketing strategies must be developed that are specifically aimed or targeted at such groups or market segments.

What is market segmentation?

Stanton et al. (1995) suggest that market segmentation is the process of dividing the total, heterogeneous market for a product or service into several segments, each of which tends to be homogeneous in all similar aspects. The advantage of market segmentation is that it is a consumer-oriented philosophy and as a result endeavours to satisfy as many needs and wants in the marketplace as possible. Moreover, by segmenting the marketplace promoters can more judiciously allocate marketing resources, and this should result in greater returns on the investment, or 'more bang for the bucks'.

Mullin et al. (2000) further suggest that segmentation is central to an understanding of consumers, as it recognises differences in consumer behaviour, which directly informs marketing strategies. Consequently, the task facing sport promoters is first to determine how consumers use sport products or services to meet individual needs, and then to determine which factors are common. This allows the sport marketer to categorise or group customers according to the type of people they are, the way they use the product or service, and finally their expectations of it.

Although the segmentation possibilities are endless, there are a number of broad-based variables that provide an effective starting point for segmentation strategy. Commonly, consumers are segmented on the basis of demographics, psychographics and behaviour towards the product. This latter category is further divided into the benefits wanted from the product and product usage, or how the product is used. Figure 4.2 represents such variables schematically.

The market segmentation process

Demographic segmentation

Demographic segmentation is the most common form of segmentation, with the most important demographic determinants being gender, age, religion, income, occupation, level of education, marital status, geography, and stage in the family life cycle. Social class is another important consumer demographic but is usually an amalgam of other variables.

Although all demographic variables are potentially important, stage in the family life

FIGURE 4.2 **Market segmentation variables**

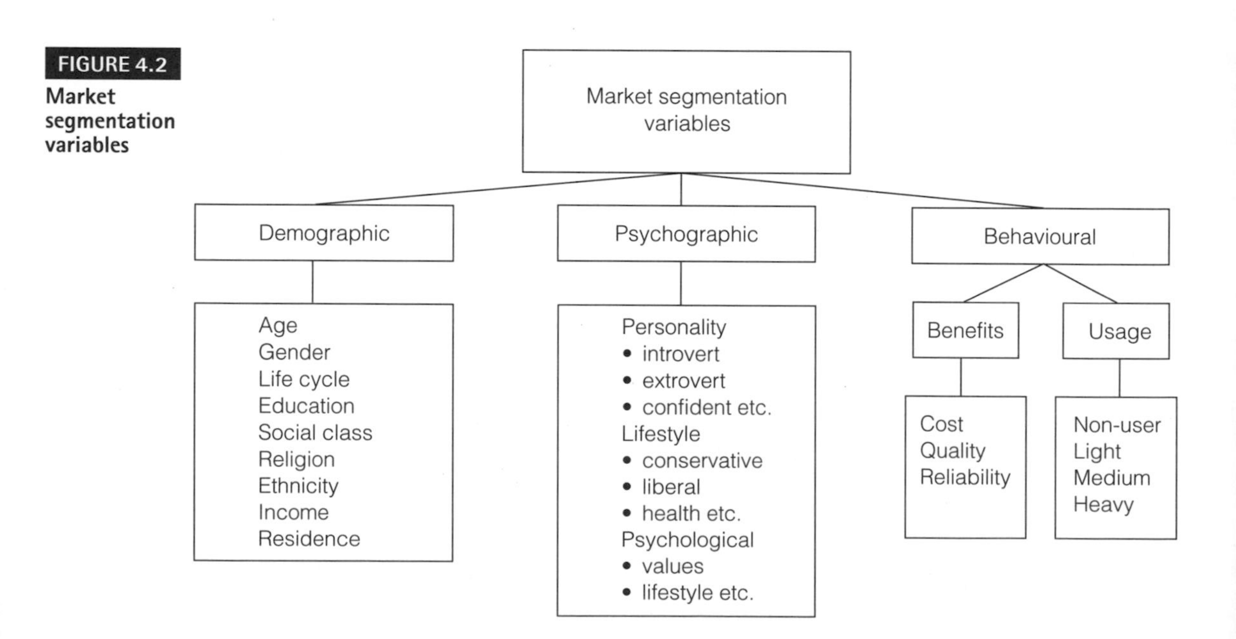

cycle has the greatest impact on sport consumption. Traditional life cycle stages include singles, married couples with and without children, 'empty nesters' and elderly singles. However, single parents, older childless couples and divorced individuals are increasingly representing alternative stages in the family life cycle. Stages in the family life cycle directly affect consumer behaviour, and it is essential for sport marketers to provide mechanisms that encourage customers to remain loyal from childhood to senior years.

Geographic issues such as regions, city size, the urban-rural dichotomy and even climate can also influence strategic sport marketing. While it may appear safe to assume that spectator expectations in country and regional areas are quite different from expectations in the city, even the cities cannot be treated as homogeneous for the sport marketer. While ease of event access, parking and travel time are often important to the suburban commuter, public transport and additional entertainment possibilities may be far more important to the inner-city dweller.

Psychographic segmentation

While demographic information can inform the sport marketer who the consumers are, this information alone does not tell why they consume. To partially answer this question, consumers need to be further categorised according to psychographics. Psychographic segmentation is based on variables that are associated with personality types or lifestyles. This approach attempts to explain consumer behaviour in terms of the reasons for purchase and the needs it meets. In the process, categories of values and lifestyles are established, such as outer-directed, inner-directed and need-driven (Mullin et al. 2000) or socially aware, visible achievement, traditional family life, young and optimistic (Stanton et al. 1995).

However, while the nomenclature may differ, basically the sport marketer must cater not only for the consumer who is confident and assertive, believes that there are advantages in being associated with the sport product and wishes to be seen to be involved with it, but also for the consumer who wishes to satisfy intrinsic as opposed to extrinsic needs. Such intrinsic needs may vary from personal development to pure escapism. Hence individuals may buy a snowboard because they can, or because they like the scene associated with snowboarding and want to fit in or belong. Likewise, they may see the purchase as an opportunity for individual growth through the development of new skills.

Irrespective of the reasons for consumption, all individuals must be catered for if possible.

Behavioural segmentation

Behavioural segmentation refers to the benefits and usages attributed to the consumption of the product. Stotlar (1993) comments that benefit segmentation is based on the unique benefits of a product or service that motivate a consumer to purchase–that is, on the different benefits that the consumer expects from the product or service. An important feature of this concept is that the consumer is purchasing the benefit, not the product. For example, athletes may buy an electrolyte-replacement drink not because they are thirsty or like the taste but because they believe that it will replace essential elements the body has lost during intensive exercise. Hence the athlete is purchasing the benefit, a more rapid recovery, rather than the product, a sport drink. However, the most obvious case of benefit segmentation in sport relates to the purchase of athletic shoes. Correct pronation or supination, arch support and cushioning or a glow in the dark are just a some of the potential benefits of athletic footwear.

Benefit segmentation is not applicable to only sport products. A person may choose to attend a basketball game not because he/she has an innate love of the sport, but because a friend is going. Here the benefit inherent in going to the game is the opportunity for social interaction. If the friend were going to the zoo, the idea of attending the basketball game would be moot. In this instance the chance for social interaction is just one benefit that the sport promoter provides. Similar benefit segmentation strategies can focus on the entertainment aspect of the event or the opportunity to escape from the rigours of the daily grind and indulge in recreative activity, to be involved in the production and presentation of an event or activity, or simply to be seen at an event. The volunteers for the Sydney 2000 Olympic Games became involved in the event for many and varied reasons. However, although the inherent benefits were numerous, many individuals chose not to continue and left the volunteer corps prior to the Games' commencement. Sportview 4.2 overviews the reasons for this attrition.

SPORTVIEW 4.2

Volunteer attrition: The case of the Sydney 2000 Olympic Games

The Sydney 2000 Olympic Games were a major triumph, with volunteers making a substantial contribution to that success. So significant was their contribution that the volunteers were rewarded in the post-Olympic euphoria with their own parade through the streets of Sydney. According to Stavros Sofios (2002: 19), the 74 000 Olympic volunteers were further immortalised in history when their names were listed on 300 poles at Sydney Olympic Park; he concludes that in the process the 'volunteers entered Australian mythology as the perfect example of the uniquely Australian character'.

However, while there is no doubt that the popular perception of the volunteer component of the Sydney Olympics being an outstanding success is accurate, there was some volunteer attrition in the pre-Games period. Gritsi (2000) used the Sydney Games as a case study for volunteer attrition. Although she concluded that the attrition rate was generally low, around 4.5% (2115 volunteers), she demonstrated that attrition was far higher in spectator services (12%) than in other functional areas. On examination, the higher rate of attrition in spectator services was the result of a number of interesting conditions.

The key reasons why potential volunteers chose not to continue included poor communication, inadequate training sessions, a failure to be appointed to the venue of preference, reporting to multiple supervisors, and the apparent perception that the environment was less than caring and supportive. Other reasons included a less than demanding position, the inability to actually see events, an inability to interact with athletes, an apparent lack of a comfortable uniform, a perception that the food was lacking in variety and quality, an inability to make new friends and, finally, plain boredom. This is an expansive and wide-ranging list of apparent grievances.

In all the above-mentioned cases the benefits that such individuals expected from their association with the Olympic Games were not forthcoming. Fortunately, the number was not large and attrition was not a problem. However, Gritsi's (2000) study demonstrates the variety of seemingly inconsequential reasons that influence the consumer decision-making process as it relates to expected benefits.

Usage segmentation focuses on the amount of the product or service consumed by the customer. The usage pattern for a product or service is especially applicable to spectator sport. In attempting to define the consumer in respect to usage patterns, broad categories including non-user, light user, medium user and heavy user are established. Chapter 9, which examines the sport promotion mix, discusses usage patterns in light of the escalator principle, so only passing reference will be made to it at this stage.

While it is often desirable to encourage consumers to elevate their level of consumption, this is not always possible or even desirable. For example, Spolestra (1991) believes that in terms of the consumption of professional sport, the season ticket or membership is not for everyone. Whether it is due to lack of finance, time or even interest, consumers often find that attending every game is not possible. Hence he argues that the concept of seat sharing, whether corporate or with friends, results in maximum use of a particular seat. By adopting an approach called full-menu marketing, the organisation provides numerous packages that allow fans to consume at a level with which they are comfortable. Here the market has been segmented based on usage.

Multiple segmentation

The establishment of a segmentation strategy depends on a number of features such as size, reachability and receptiveness of the target market. As such, multiple segment strategies are often developed, which enable the sport marketer to construct different yet coordinated strategies for delivering a product or service. The establishment, maintenance and ongoing addition to an organisation's MIS will assist sporting organisations to become increasingly discerning and creative in their target market segmentation strategies.

Examples of sport spectator segments

In 1995 Graham Halbish, former chief executive officer of the Australian Cricket Board (ACB), identified four target audiences that had developed since the World Series Cricket era:

- the purist, who understood the nuances of the game and often had a history of active participation in the sport;
- the sport enthusiast, who followed a wider range of activities;
- the follower, who, while unlikely to attend matches, avidly followed the game via the media; and
- the entertainment seeker, who sought action and excitement.

Each segment was important for distinct reasons. While purists were perceived as essential for Test match cricket longevity, enthusiasts were important for their current level of interest. Similarly, while followers were important because of their desire for cricket information, entertainment-seekers provided for an important segue into the female and youth market.

Smith and Stewart (1999: 174) devised a classification of team-sports spectator behaviour and developed five spectator categories and motivations for adoption of such categories:

- the passionate partisan, who displays undiminished loyalty to a team over time and identifies closely with winning and losing;
- the champ follower, whose loyalty is essentially a function of team success;
- the reclusive partisan, who displays strong identification, which does not necessarily translate into actual support;
- the theatregoer, who seeks a close encounter and wishes to be entertained; and
- the aficionado, whose loyalty is to the game rather than the team.

In many instances, especially related to sport consumer behaviour in the context of seasonal sport competitions, the passionate partisan is an important target market. Each of the other target markets requires different marketing strategies aimed at the specific orientation of potential consumers held by the market. As we saw with the product market grid, discussed in chapter 2, each distinct market segment may require a separate product offering or variation. When we decide that a particular market segment is going to be the focus of a sport organisation, we have selected a target market.

Target market selection

The selection of the appropriate target market follows the process of segmentation. Having identified the segmentation variables and developed profiles of the different segments, the next step is to identify the attractiveness of each of the segments. To enable the sport marketer to identify attractiveness, market segments must be substantial enough to justify consideration, their size and attractiveness must be measurable, the sport organisation must have access to the segment, and must have the resources enabling the organisation to approach the segment, and the segments must enable differentiation from other segments. When these criteria are fulfilled, the sport marketer can assess the segment's size and growth potential, the segment's structural attractiveness (this can be identified by applying Porter's five forces analysis), and whether the segment offers scope to achieve the organisation's strategic objectives and generate vital resources. Based on this information the sport marketer is in a position to select a (number of) target market(s). Target market selection strategies include the selection of a single segment, a number of unrelated segments, a number of segments that are selected on the ability of the sport organisation to deliver a particular product (e.g. football spectator services), a number of segments that are based on the ability of the sport organisation to serve a particular market (e.g. the Melbourne metropolitan football market) very well, or a full market coverage strategy, targeting the market as a whole.

The growth of snowboarding since the 1980s may serve as an interesting example. Capitalising on the popularity of skateboarding and surfing and the growth in extreme sports, snowboard promoters identified a target market that was young, had discretionary income, eschewed the normal alpine skiing activities of their parents, and wanted to be seen at the leading edge of a new recreational activity. While initially the alpine industry examined ways to ban the sport from many resort areas, snowboarding quickly gained a foothold and debuted as an Olympic sport in 1998. A sport once considered fringe is now at the forefront of winter activity. Moreover, resorts that had previously turned their back on this particular segment now aggressively market to this cohort and establish areas on the slopes where they can pursue their sport to the full. Some resorts even try to position their location as the place for snowboarding.

Positioning

Before we move into marketing 'action'—that is, the application of the marketing mix—the final piece in the puzzle of preparing for action is the identification of positioning strategies for each of the segments that we have chosen to target. In this process it is important to remember that the key to successful positioning lies in the sport marketer's ability to differentiate the product offering from segment competitors. Whatever is different in the offering of the sport organisation needs to be important and distinctive for the consumers to consider the (alternative) offering. For example, positioning can focus on the benefits that consumers seek in consuming the product; quality or price can be used to set the offering apart from others; or the image of the product or organisation can sway consumers to purchase a trendy 'brand' rather than a non-branded product.

In their far-reaching text, Ries and Trout (1986: 5) suggest: 'the basic approach of positioning is not to create something new and different, but to manipulate what's already in the mind'. In other words, positioning is really about what the marketer does in the mind of the consumer. In reality, there are probably two ways in which sport can be positioned in the mind of the consumer. As Ries and Trout indicate, the best option is to be first; but if you can't be first, be different. When it comes to sport, marketers and promoters constantly try to effectively position their product or service in the mind of an increasingly discerning consumer. Furthermore, given that consumer preferences are in a constant state of flux, the positioning process demands creativity, responsiveness and perspicacity.

For example, Teutsch (2002) refers to the September release by the president of the Australian Medical Association of the results of a national health survey. This survey quizzed more than 1000 people about their sport and exercise habits. While former trendy sports such as rollerblading and aerobics were considered passé, activities such as yoga, Pilates, 'boxing-type' classes, personal training, and adventure activities such as snowboarding, climbing and sailing were considered to be growth areas. While it is hard to argue against snowboarding being a sport of the future given its current Olympic standing, there is little doubt that it is rapidly moving from cult to mainstream status. Darby (2002), writing in the travel section of the *Herald Sun* (Melbourne), discussed skiing in the Rocky Mountains and suggested Canada as a valuable destination for skiers and snowboarders. Of the ski area Fernie, he noted that cult skiers were drawn there 'by the five big bowls, the stunning features, the great skiing and the naturally good snowboarding terrain' (2002: T06). However, he also indicated that the area was fast making the transition from cult to consumer destination. Hence, it can be reasonably concluded that snowboarding, initially positioned as a cult activity with a clearly defined non-mainstream target market, rapidly progressed through stages of development (which included alpine resorts endeavouring to position themselves as snowboard-friendly) to a point where it is positioned as a mainstream sport of the future.

Given that the sport marketplace is so dynamic and constantly in a state of change, sport marketers must not only recognise change but be strategically ready to respond to it quickly. Moreover, the speed at which change occurs will only increase in the future, and sporting organisations, already sensitive to market share (if mergers and franchise relocations are any indication) will need to be increasingly creative in their segmentation strategy. Defining product position and its application is considered in more detail in chapter 5.

Summary

In the 21st century, ongoing data collection is essential for the adaptation of an organisation to a volatile and changing marketplace. Moreover, such data need to be collected in a systematic ongoing manner and stored in a marketing information system (MIS). The MIS should not only allow for ready accessibility but also enable ongoing decision making and strategy selection.

The major sources of information for an MIS include both external and internal data. External data may be classified as primary or secondary, and includes data that have been collected by the sporting organisation or an external agency. It should be understood, however, that while some general market and sport market research may have universal applicability, the sporting organisation cannot do better than collect its own data.

Market research in sporting organisations seeks to answer the questions of who, when, where, what, how and why. While the survey is the most popular mechanism for gathering sport-related data, mall or shopping centre intercepts, focus groups, observation and even experimentation are becoming increasingly popular. Collected data should explore general market conditions, individual consumers and competitors. Internal data consist of information that the organisation collects during the conduct of its business.

A major advantage of solid market research is that it allows the sport marketer to divide the total market into several segments. Commonly, consumers are segmented on the basis of demographics, psychographics and behaviour. This latter category is further divided into the benefits wanted from the product and product usage. Finally, it should be remembered that the sport marketplace is in a constant state of change. Sport marketers must place themselves in a position to not just respond to change but even anticipate it.

CASE STUDY

Tai Chi—The gentle art of relaxation

This case study was originally prepared by Ken Slinger, University of Western Sydney, Nepean.

Tai Chi, the oriental form of relaxation and exercise, has gained enormous popularity in Australia since its introduction in 1970. Currently the largest group offering Tai Chi classes to the community is the Australia Academy of Tai Chi. This institution is controlled and run by the Khor family. The founder, Gary Khor, was a Malaysian student attending university in the mid 1970s, who began conducting classes for his fellow students. As word-of-mouth publicity caused his classes to expand beyond the university campus, a second brother, Eng Khor, was brought from the United Kingdom to assist with this fledgling operation. From its early beginnings the academy has grown to 6000 members with 100 instructors spread across Australia's major cities. Increased awareness by the Australian community of health and relaxation has led to a rapid expansion of this form of exercise and relaxation.

In establishing the early market for Tai Chi, the founders were faced with the task of identifying their market. In addition, suitable locations or sites had to be acquired so that students could assemble in areas that provided firm footing, good lighting and easy access. Early sites were developed in Paddington and the upper north shore of Sydney. Community awareness was considered to be of prime importance; so demonstrations in shopping centres were conducted to make the community aware of what Tai Chi represents.

A profile of Tai Chi consumers identified an age range of 20–80 years, from all walks of life and most suburbs of Sydney. In addition to shopping centre demonstrations, external lessons and demonstrations in public parks and on beaches were also conducted. Brochures outlining the history of Tai Chi and its development in Australia were produced and distributed to interested members of the community. Testimonials were secured from doctors, physiotherapists and others testifying to the physical benefits of Tai Chi, while other testimonials were secured that acknowledged the benefits in the area of relaxation and stress reduction.

Tai Chi was conducted according to levels of competence. Most students would progress to Level 6, with a lesser number of competent students moving on to more advance classes. To further supplement the promotional strategies, advertisements were taken out in regional newspapers, but ultimately word-of-mouth or a referral system was the best method of acquiring new students. To date, 65% of the students are female and 35% are male, with age or physical handicaps being only a minor barrier.

Source: Adjusted from Stanton (1995).

Questions

1 Develop a target market for Tai Chi in the following areas:
  (a) your city;
  (b) Australia.

  Consider the above in the light of demographic, psychographic and behavioural segmentation.

2 Develop a strategy for improving consumer perceptions of Tai Chi or changing any incorrect preconceptions.

3 Discuss expansion strategies for this form of exercise and relaxation.

PART II

Strategy determination

5

The sport product

Stage 1—Identification of marketing opportunities

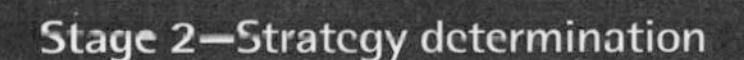

Step 5—Determine core marketing strategy

Marketing and service mix—sport product

Stage 3—Strategy implemention, evaluation and adjustment

CHAPTER OBJECTIVES

Chapter 5 introduces the first variable in the marketing mix: the sport product. This chapter also moves to Stage 2 of the strategic sport-marketing planning process (SSMPP): strategy determination. During this stage, marketing mix variables are reviewed and combined in such a way as to determine the core marketing strategy. It is first important to identify and understand the product and its attributes. Key tools to assist in determining the core marketing strategy are introduced, including perceptual mapping and product life cycle.

After studying this chapter you should be able to:

1 Identify the difference between core and product extensions in sport.
2 Describe the characteristics of a service.
3 Understand why sport is classified as a service product.
4 Identify the dimensions of quality service.
5 Understand the strategic importance of product positioning.
6 Understand the strategic significance of the product life cycle.

HEADLINE STORY

Adelaide's wheels of fortune

Another sort of road race—international-level cycling, replacing the sadly departed F1 Grand Prix—looks set to deliver big rewards. When Melbourne ripped away Adelaide's Formula One Grand Prix in 1994–95, the South Australian capital was quickly sidelined as the home of beautiful churches and pubs and not much else. Desperate to sharpen the capital's sporting edge, the State Government poured money into attracting new events and played host to Wagner's Ring Cycle, horse trial events including the Adelaide International Three-Day Event and cycling's Tour Down Under, the V8 touring car race, Clipsal Adelaide 500, and the Le Mans sportscar endurance event. It seems to have worked. Adelaide is back in the international sporting spotlight. The Tour Down Under is an annual race billed as the most important cycling event in the Southern Hemisphere. Cynics point out that the Southern Hemisphere isn't known for its cycling talent and doesn't offer many other international races. But the 757 km race—gearing up for its third year—has been approved by the international governing body, Union Cycliste Internationale, attracts big-name cyclists and has high-profile corporate sponsors.

It's not yet on the same level as the 1994 Adelaide Formula One Grand Prix, which garnered $13 million in corporate sponsorships, merchandising and licensing on the expectation that more than 127000 people would turn up to watch Nigel Mansell win. But last year, the cycling event was estimated to generate $20 million, including $11.5 million from international and national media, and was viewed by about 200 million people. This year, organisers expect more than 500000 people will line the streets during the six-day competition as eight international teams whiz past. Lending further weight to the sponsorship clout of the event is the growing recognition of the Tour Down Under in sporting circles...Wine producer Orlando Wyndham has snared the most high-profile sponsorship prize—the naming rights—for its Jacob's Creek label, and will have its logo stamped on the yellow leader's jersey. The other big corporate sponsors for the race are Malaysia Airlines, Mitsubishi Motors and Hilton Adelaide. Other jersey sponsors include Clipsal (leading team jersey), Share the Road (young rider's jersey), Century 21 (most aggressive rider's jersey), optical retailer Laubman and Pank (king of the mountain jersey) and the omnipresent TAB. (Whyte 2001: 9)

Adelaide, and Australia generally, have not typically been regarded as the home of world-class cycling events. Although Australia's record in Olympic and World Championship cycling has been excellent, it is not a high-profile Australian sport. Modelled on the world-renowned Tour de France, the Tour Down Under has been conceived to promote Adelaide to a world television audience as well as promote cycling as an international sport of prominence. Increasingly, state governments are using major sporting events as a means of promoting the capital city and state generally as a tourist destination. Major sporting events have the capacity to draw attention to a city and state. However, for broader tourism objectives to be met, a quality sports event must be staged—one that will entice world-class athletes to attend, and one that the athletes themselves believe to be a quality event. Equally, spectators must view the event as exciting and one worth attending, as must sponsors. The Tour Down Under is a unique event in that it cannot be watched from the comfort of a stadium, as it is spread across 757 kilometres. This presents some obvious problems for organisers to ensure a quality product matched by service standards commensurate with a world-class event. Sponsors, however, are more easily appeased if their products appear on television screens throughout Australia and beyond. The purpose of this chapter is to examine the place of the sport product in the marketing mix and illustrate the importance of service provision of the sport product. As can be seen from the headline story, the sport product comes in many sizes, shapes and configurations, complicating the capacity to apply standard service solutions.

The sport product

Boyd and Walker (1990: 385) describe a product as being 'anything that satisfies a want or need in terms of use, consumption or acquisition'. Moreover, the authors note that a product is a problem solver in that it is purchased because of the benefits provided. Essentially, consumers buy benefits, not the product.

Quality is another feature of perceived product benefits. McCarthy and Perreault (1990: 219) define quality, from a marketing perspective, as 'the ability of a product to satisfy a consumer's needs or requirements'. As the authors point out, this definition focuses on the consumer's view of what quality may mean, or of a product's suitability for some specific purpose. In sport, the product is easily discernible; however, the quality of the core product is something over which the sport marketer has no control. This is a distinctly unique aspect of sport and sport marketing. For this reason, it is important to recognise a broader definition of the product than simply the game.

Mullin (1985) identifies the playing of the game as the core product and all the related activities, such as food and beverage, merchandise, half-time entertainment, video screens and the facility itself, as product extensions. For example, the Australian Tennis Open and the Melbourne Park facility and all the services provided within and during the tournament are crucial in measuring the overall success of the event. Ultimately, once players have agreed to play in the Australian Open there is little organisers can do to ensure quality matches. Even matches receiving 'top billing' such as Hewitt vs Agassi or Williams vs Hingis do not always guarantee quality contests. The quality of the supporting product extensions, however, can be guaranteed. It is at this point that similarities are observed between the importance of quality service provision and quality product extensions. Often, most product extensions possess an element of service provision, and hence quality is important. As a consequence, product extensions have the capacity of ensuring that spectators at the tennis have an enjoyable day despite on-court results.

Branch (1992: 25) supports the need to broaden sport product position and program concept, observing that:

> Forward-thinking professional sport marketers realise that the game, sport's 'core' or primary product, is not the organisation's only or most important product... diversifying sport's

program concept in this manner, the core product accrues substantial 'value added' qualities. In other words, the event becomes a more consistent buy for sport consumers. The challenge is to focus less on the game's outcome and more on a positive customer experience.

Sportview 5.1 demonstrates the relevance of this argument by emphasising the success of the National Basketball Association's (NBA) Charlotte Hornets basketball franchise. The Hornets entered the NBA as a new franchise in 1988, primarily comprising cast-offs from other teams. On-court success was not realistic, so attention to detail and customer satisfaction with the experience of the event became benchmarks for the Hornets' marketing efforts (Macnow 1990).

SPORTVIEW 5.1

A winning game plan

The Charlotte Hornets' 43rd consecutive sold-out home game belied the team's on-court record. Having won less than a quarter of their games since joining the NBA, they seem to have proven the sport traditionalists wrong. Conventional theory has it that teams must win games to consistently play in front of sell-out crowds. Not so in Charlotte, with the 23388 fans filling the stadium.

The Hornets may be the most thoroughly packaged franchise in sport, with everything from half-time shows to players' uniforms designed down to the most minute detail. How well does it work? Consider these figures:

- In their inaugural season, the Hornets led the NBA in attendance, drawing more than 950000 fans despite losing 62 of 82 games.
- The franchise turned a larger profit than any other NBA team.
- The club's fans spend money not just on tickets but also on ancillary products. In 1989, fans spent an average of 39 cents per person at every game on shirts, mugs, key rings and other licensed souvenirs.

Attention to detail and total customer satisfaction with the experience of the event are benchmarks for the Hornets' marketing efforts. 'We've borrowed the philosophy from Disney that the small things count,' says general manager Scheer: 'To us, taking the fans for granted is the ultimate sin.' What plays in Charlotte now is the Hornets. And though they've lost more than they've won so far, they are playing to great reviews.

Source: Adjusted from Macnow (1990: 82–4).

The Charlotte Hornets illustrate another important concept in product planning–branding: 'Branding means the use of a name, term, symbol, or design–or a combination of these–to identify a product.' (McCarthy & Perreault 1990: 235) The Hornets represent a brand within the NBA competition. Brands are important to their owners, as they help consumers to recognise a company's products; and if brand recognition and acceptance are high, there exists the potential for high brand loyalty. In sport, teams and clubs such as the Hornets are examples of a brand, and it is through team and club loyalty that prominent brand recognition is achieved. (The issue of branding is considered in more detail in chapter 16 when the role and purpose of promotional licensing are reviewed.) Developing highly recognisable brands as trademarks and logos is an important source of revenue and promotion for sporting organisations and athletes. These trademarks form the basis of merchandise and licensing programs, an important form of product extensions.

This section has stressed the importance of quality service provision in the product extensions, so it is appropriate now to consider in more detail how and why sport is a service product.

Sport as a service

Services marketing has grown in importance across a wide range of industries during the past decade. In Australia, the Department of Industry, Science and Resources in collaboration with the Australian Services Network (2000: 2–3) has noted that:

> The Australian service sector makes up the largest proportion of the Australian economy in output terms. In fact, for the 12 months to June 1998, output of the sector contributed to over 76 per cent of total output of the Australian economy (excludes ownership of dwellings). Similarly, the sector also dominates employment, employing over four of every five Australian workers (just under 82 per cent)... Between February 1990 and May 1999, a net total of 913,700 jobs were added to the Australian economy, of which the service sector contributed 1,057,800. The difference arose due to a decline in the number of non-service sector jobs of the period of 144,100... the service sector was the main driver of economic growth, averaging annual real output growth of 3.2 per cent per annum compared with 2 per cent per annum for the non-service sector, and 3 per cent for the economy as a whole.

Sport is an important contributor to the service economy. Unfortunately, sport's contribution is contained within the broader classification of 'Cultural and Recreational Services', which consists of motion pictures, radio and television services, libraries, museums and the arts, sport and recreation, and gambling services. It is not possible to be specific about sport's contribution, but the 'real output of the Cultural and Recreational Services group grew by an average 3.3 per cent in the eight years leading up to 1997-98' (DISR 2000: 48). The industry's share of service sector output grew from 2.5% to 2.9% and employment rose from a low of 145 000 in 1990 to 217 000 in May 1999 (DISR 2000). Major sporting events such as the Ford Australian Open and Formula 1 Grand Prix have the capacity to add to the strong performances indicated in the tourism-related, cultural and recreational service activities. The number and magnitude of sporting events in Australia have seen the evolution of sports tourism as a niche classification within tourism, which ultimately contributes to service sector output across a number of areas, including accommodation, cafes, restaurants and transport.

Service defined

Why is sport considered a service? This section will answer this question by discussing the characteristics that distinguish a good from a service. A common theme of authors writing on sport marketing (Mullin 1980, 1985; Mullin et al. 2000; Shilbury 1989, 1991; Sutton

& Parrett 1992) has been their agreement on how the unique characteristics of sport as a product require marketing personnel to adopt different strategies from those traditionally espoused. Although many of these writings are devoid of specific references to services marketing, the discussions pertaining to these unique characteristics align sport to the attributes of a service.

Zeithaml et al. (1985) summarise the characteristics distinguishing a good from a service. This summary helps in describing sport as a service:

- *Intangibility.* Services cannot be seen, tasted, felt or smelled before they are bought. Services are performances rather than objects. For example, is it possible to describe what product benefits people take home with them after playing sport? Or the benefits derived from watching a game of basketball? There is no tangible take-home product in this example.
- *Inseparability of production and consumption.* Services are simultaneously produced and consumed. The product cannot be put on the shelf and bought by the consumer. The consumer must be present during production. For example, consider getting a haircut, attending a sporting contest or visiting a physiotherapist. You need to attend during the process.
- *Heterogeneity.* Services are potentially variable in their performance. Services can vary greatly depending on who performs them. Many different employees can come into contact with the consumer; therefore, consistency becomes an issue. Few sporting contests are the same from one week to the next, and the consistency of service delivery by people working at such an event can also vary.
- *Perishability.* Services cannot be stored. Hotel rooms not occupied, airline seats not purchased or tickets to a sporting contest not sold cannot be reclaimed. Simply, it is lost revenue and indicates the importance of understanding that services are time dependent.

Perhaps the most significant difference between a good and a service is the simultaneous production and consumption of a product. The implications of this for marketing are examined specifically in chapter 7, when the convergence of the marketing and operations functions are considered in relation to the 'place' of the facility in the marketing mix, and expanded in chapter 8 in relation to service quality and customer satisfaction.

> A *service*, then, is predominantly any activity or benefit that is intangible and does not result in ownership.

Both spectators and participants take from the game a series of experiences, none of which is physically tangible. Students of sport marketing should be careful not to confuse some of the tangible products that can be bought as a consequence of the game or sport (product extensions) with the game or sport itself (core product). Without the sport, the merchandise would not exist.

Classification of services

When classifying services we need to determine the extent to which the customer must be present. To assist in making this determination, Lovelock (1991) uses a four-way classification scheme, involving:

TABLE 5.1 Understanding the nature of the service act

What is the nature of the service act?	Who or what is the direct recipient of the service?	
	People	**Possessions**
Tangible actions	*Services directed at people's bodies* Health care Passenger transportation Beauty salons Exercise clinics Restaurants Haircutting	*Services directed at goods and other physical possessions* Freight transportation Industrial equipment repair Janitorial services Laundry and dry cleaning Landscaping/lawncare Veterinary care
Intangible actions	*Services directed at people's minds* Education Broadcasting Information services Theatres Museums	*Services directed at intangible assets* Banking Legal services Accounting Securities Insurance

Source: Lovelock (1991: 26). Reprinted with the permission of Prentice Hall, Inc. Upper Saddle River, NJ.

- tangible actions to people's bodies;
- tangible actions to goods and other physical possessions;
- intangible actions directed at people's minds; and
- intangible actions directed at intangible assets.

Table 5.1 illustrates Lovelock's schematic with examples.

Considering the classification used in Table 5.1, where would sport be placed? This is an interesting question, as the answer might depend on whether we were being specific about physical participation or attendance. Physical participation could be classified as a people-based service directed at people's bodies. Attendance at sporting events could more accurately be classified as a people-based service directed at people's minds. The context of participation in sport is important in framing marketing strategies. The most obvious example is the formation of marketing strategies aimed at attracting players to participate in a competition or sport and the marketing strategies required to attract people to attend a sporting event. In either case, it is necessary to ask why such a classification scheme is important.

Lovelock (1991: 27) notes the following, which helps to answer this question:

1. Does the customer need to be physically present:
   (a) throughout the service?
   (b) only to initiate or terminate the service transaction?
   (c) not at all?
2. Does the customer need to be mentally present during service delivery? Can mental presence be maintained across physical distances through mail or electronic communications?
3 In what way is the target of the service act 'modified' by receipt of the service? And how does the customer benefit from these 'modifications'?

If, as is the case in sport, customers need to be present to play or watch a live event, they must enter the service factory, returning us to the importance of simultaneous production and consumption. When spectators or participants enter the sport factory, this has an obvious implication for the sport marketer. The sport factory is best known as the facility, and the implications for managing the customer in the sport factory or facility will be specifically investigated in chapter 7. However, the major implication of the consumer entering the sport factory or facility is that sport spectatorship, in particular, is a service experience.

In sport, it is hard to overcome the winning (I had a good day/night) or losing (I had a bad day/night) syndrome. Although this special range of emotions will never be removed from the sport product, their importance can be diminished by ensuring that the quality of service is very good. Again, the importance of the product extensions through quality service provision is highlighted. Slowly, sporting organisations are beginning to recognise the need to plan for service quality.

Service quality

Service quality research has become prominent in the marketing literature during the past decade. Much work has been conducted to identify the key attributes of quality service. These attributes have been developed from the perspective of the consumer. Extensive research using focus group interviews, conducted by Parasuraman, Zeithaml and Berry during the 1980s, identified the ten dimensions of service quality shown in Table 5.2. Parasuraman et al. (1985: 46) note that, 'regardless of the type of service, consumers used basically similar criteria in evaluating service quality'.

TABLE 5.2 Dimensions of service quality

Dimension	Description
Tangibles	Appearance of physical facilities, equipment, personnel and communication materials
Reliability	Ability to perform the promised service dependably and accurately
Responsiveness	Willingness to help customers and provide prompt service
Competence	Possession of the required skills and knowledge to perform the service
Courtesy	Politeness, respect, consideration and friendliness of contact personnel
Credibility	Trustworthiness, believability, honesty of service provider
Security	Freedom from danger, risk or doubt
Access	Approachability and ease of contact
Communication	Keeping customers informed in language they can understand and listening to them
Understanding the customer	Making the effort to know customers and their needs

Source: Lovelock et al. (1990: 22).

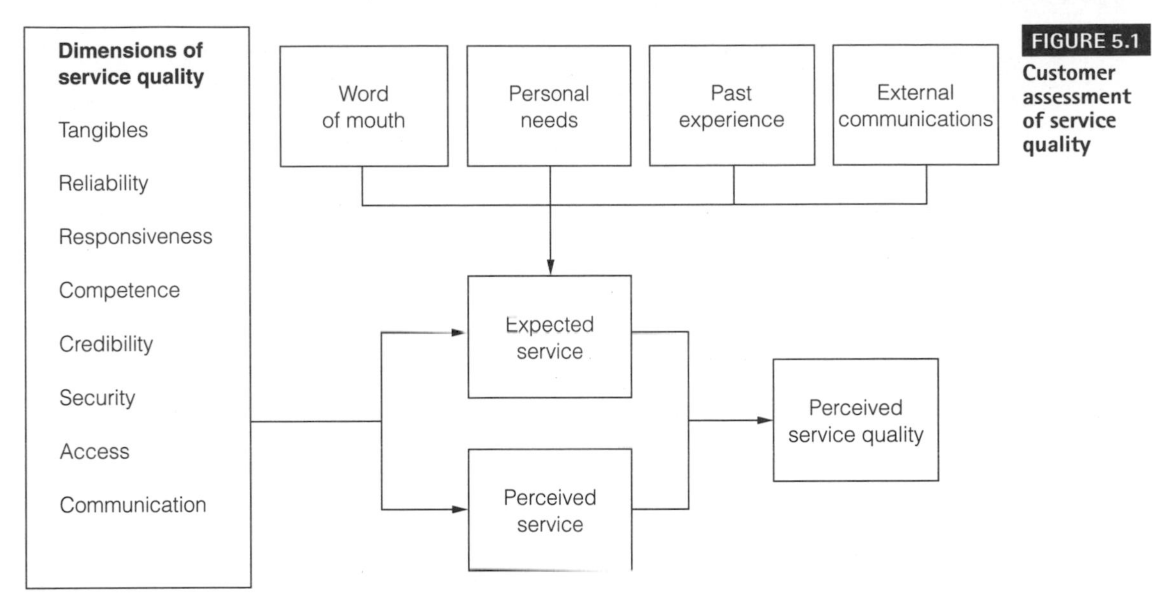

FIGURE 5.1 **Customer assessment of service quality**

Source: Reprinted with the permission of The Free Press, an imprint of Simon & Schuster Adult Publishing Group, Copyright 1990, by The Free Press.

Figure 5.1 illustrates the application of the ten dimensions in relation to the way the consumer views quality: 'Perceived service quality is the result of the consumer's comparison of expected service with perceived service' (Parasuraman et al. 1985: 47). Figure 5.1 illustrates how word-of-mouth, personal needs, past experience and external communications build up a level of expected service quality. Word-of-mouth is a particularly strong source of pre-consumption information that determines the likelihood of purchase.

The lack of tangible clues creates difficulties for consumers in making decisions about service product purchase. In relation to purchasing a good, it is often possible to try out the product before purchase, or at least to see it in action. This would be the case with the purchase of a car or computer. As services are time-dependent, it is often not possible to try out the product before purchase. Consumer recommendation about a service is a powerful influence in pre-purchase decisions. Similarly, past experience with a service provides the same opportunity to develop perceptions about the quality of the service being considered. Finally, external communications, via advertising, create levels of expectations about service quality.

The gap that ultimately exists between 'expected' service and 'perceived' service is a result of the four factors consumers bring to product consumption. Companies should ensure that they do not promise more than they can actually deliver, as unrealistic expectations created by a company can negatively affect the level of perceived quality, when in reality the level of service quality was good. By implication, a firm needs to understand customer expectations as well as to have an intimate knowledge of the product attributes, which are the genesis of the expected service levels and product positioning. (The importance of service quality, its application to customer satisfaction and how to measure service quality are considered in more detail in chapter 8.)

Positioning the sport product

Positioning the sport product in the marketplace is strategically important, as it plays a pivotal role in marketing strategy. Product positioning links the market research and market segmentation phases described in chapter 4. In essence, positioning is the perceived fit between a particular product and the target market. To a large extent, the success of a product within a chosen market depends on how effectively it has been positioned. The sport product, like any other product, is subject to the same range of preferences and perceptions by consumers.

Defining position

Use of a perceptual map to define positioning is helpful. The perceptual map is formed by asking consumers to rank certain product attributes. In much the same way as attitude is measured, key attributes of the sport product are identified. In a hypothetical example, two simple bipolar scales measure level of excitement of the sport and expense, or cost to attend. The two attributes are put together to form a two-dimensional diagram, as is illustrated in Figure 5.2.

Location of the product in a product space is called a position, and is a crucial step in defining the market that a product is targeting. In the example shown in Figure 5.2, only sport products are considered. This is important, as the sports chosen here include the major professional sports played in Australia. An astute marketer would realise that the sport product should be positioned within a larger competitive frame than just sport, as professional sport is part of the much larger entertainment industry. However, to ensure that this example does not become too complex, it has been restricted to just sport entertainment. Costs for entry to the sports shown in Figure 5.2 are based on 2001/02 ticket prices. It is also important to note that under normal circumstances the market researcher would ask the sport consumer about the attributes used in this perceptual map. Spectators would be asked, for example, to rate the excitement level of rugby league, or cricket or basketball.

Figure 5.2 highlights the intense competition that exists for the consumer's disposable income during the winter season. The Australian Football League (AFL), for example, is seeking a segment of spectators looking for high levels of excitement at moderate to low cost. Rugby league, through the National Rugby League (NRL) competition, is a direct competitor and thus a substitute for the AFL, given that both games are played during the winter. The genuine likelihood of substitution, of course, assumes that both codes are played in the same market. In Sydney, Melbourne and Brisbane this is the case. In Melbourne, the National Basketball League (NBL) also appears to be a major competitor to the AFL. Figure 5.2 shows that the product attributes of the AFL and NBL are similar, as is demonstrated by the product space both occupy, although the NBL in trying to distance itself from the AFL moved from a winter to a summer season in 1998. Now, in an endeavour to identify the right product position, the NBL is considering the prospect of a season commencing in July and concluding around the end of the year. This would mean the NBL season, in part, returns to the winter product space, competing with the AFL and NRL. Some of this

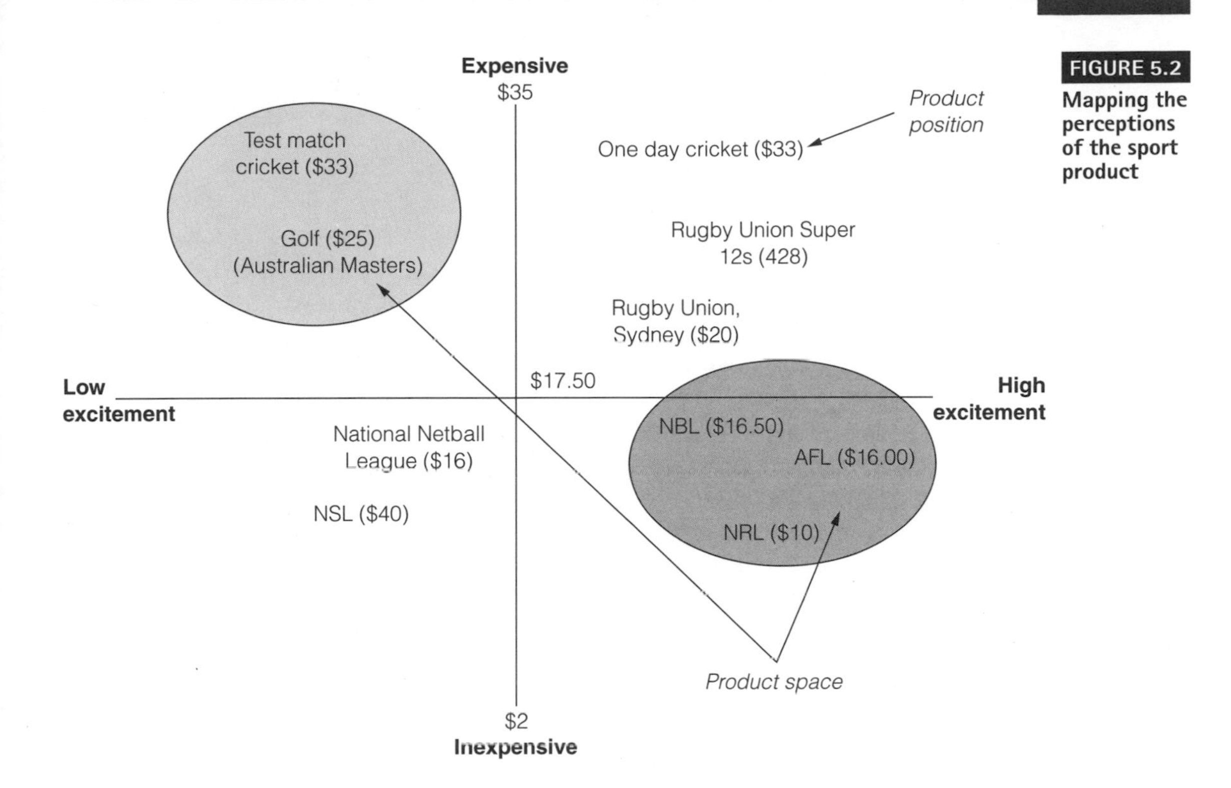

FIGURE 5.2 Mapping the perceptions of the sport product

competition would be offset by at least half the season, including finals, being played in the summer and in a product position considered less competitive.

Establishing position

Establishment of a desired position in the marketplace is a priority for the sport marketer. This can be achieved in two ways: by physical design, and through advertising.

Physical design refers to the rule changes and modifications that can be made to render a sport more attractive to certain segments of the market. Cricket is the best example of this. The two forms of the game shown in Figure 5.2 exemplify the way in which a sport has been modified to capture different segments of the market.

Establishing a product position through advertising is being used more and more by sport marketers. The most notable campaign aimed at repositioning a sport was the former NSW Rugby League's (NSWRL) advertisements featuring Tina Turner. In 1989 the NSWRL embarked on an advertising campaign aimed at presenting rugby league as a glamorous, racy and exciting game. This was necessary, as the league was emerging from a period where the game was beset by image problems such as excessive on-field violence and a struggling image at both club and league level. The 'What you get is what you see' and 'Simply the best' campaigns were extremely effective in creating a new and different image for the game. In effect, the game was being repositioned to broaden its appeal, which had been predominantly to the blue-collar male market. Between 1983 and 1990, when the league embarked on its turnaround strategy, attendances doubled and television ratings rose by

70%, indicating some success in broadening the appeal of the game. This is also indicative of the phases through which products pass in varying stages of their life cycle.

Product development

Kotler et al. (1989: 354) note that 'a company has to be good at developing new products. It also has to be good at managing them in the face of changing tastes, technologies and competition'. Every product, including sport products, seems to pass through a life cycle. Typically, this follows a consistent pattern: the product is conceived or born, and develops through several phases of maturity before dying as new and improved products emerge. In sport, it is also true that various sports oscillate within this described life cycle.

There are some differences, however. In general, it is unusual for a sport to die. It is possible to trace the history of many sports worldwide and to note how the majority have stood the test of time. Not all sports have always been successful, but they have continued to exist and experience varying levels of success. Rather than the actual sport dying, sporting competitions, events, tournaments and clubs or teams tend to disappear or require marketing strategies designed to extend their life cycle. Relocation of teams, rule changes, mergers and the provision of new facilities all constitute ways in which various forms of the sport product endeavour to avoid decline. The other major difference is that sporting organisations do not often release new products in the way that the car and computer industries do. The sport product is again seen to be reasonably stable.

The NRL, like the AFL, is an example of a sport that has had to rejuvenate its products. Expanding to form national competitions was one way in which this was achieved. In rugby league, the previously described Tina Turner advertising campaign was an integral part of relaunching a sport that was losing market share or, in product life cycle terms, was in decline. Other strategies included expanding the competition to Queensland, the ACT, Victoria and, for a brief period, Western Australia. Within Sydney itself, some clubs were closed or relocated to overcome changing or declining inner-city populations. For example, the Balmain Tigers survived 87 years on the dedication of its fans and working-class traditions. As the demographic profile of the Balmain region changed, the club was forced to look elsewhere to maintain the necessary financial infrastructure to continue participating in the league. The club's name was changed to the Sydney Tigers, broadening its appeal, and it relocated to a new facility in Parramatta.

The product life cycle curve

Figure 5.3 illustrates the product life cycle (PLC). The typical PLC curve is S-shaped and characterised by four different phases:

1. Introduction is a period of slow sales growth. Profits are non-existent at this stage because of the heavy expenses of introducing the product to the market.
2. Growth is a period of rapid market acceptance and increasing profits.
3. Maturity is a slow period of sales growth because the product has been accepted by most potential buyers. Profits stabilise or decline because of increased marketing designed to defend the product against competition.
4. Decline is the period when sales show a strong downward drift and profits erode.

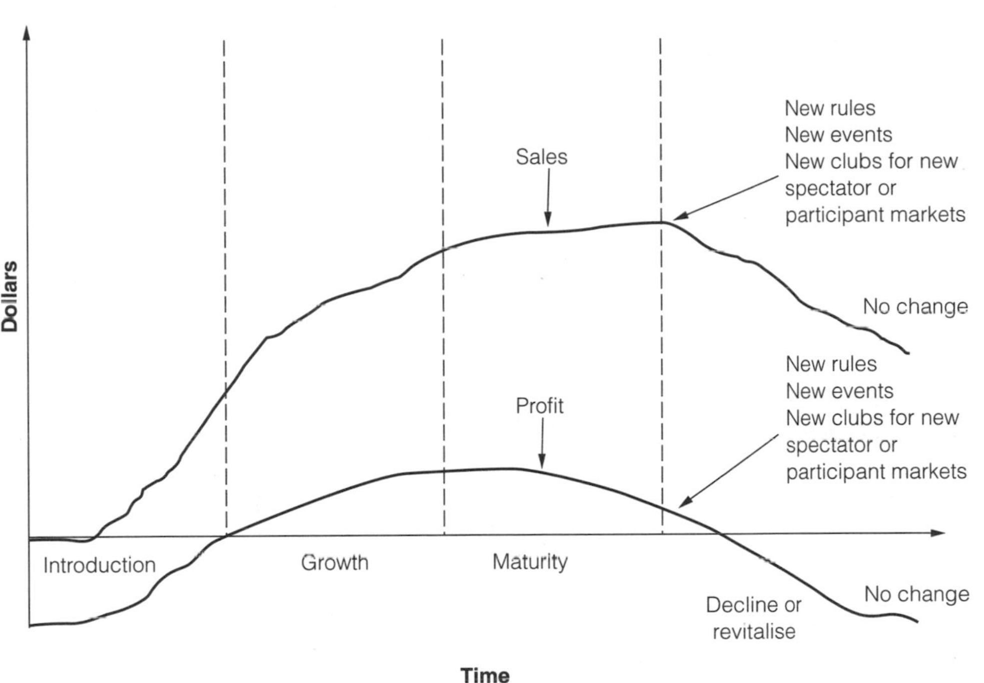

FIGURE 5.3 **Product life cycle**

In the late 1970s and early 1980s a number of traditional Australian sports entered the decline phase of the PLC. Cricket, the Victorian Football League (VFL) and NSWRL all struggled as Australians' appetite for sport and leisure options began to diversify. A subsequent surge in interest for individual sport and recreational activities such as jogging, triathlon, aerobics and cycling saw the profits and previous market dominance of these sports begin to erode. Also in 1979, the NBL was formed, capitalising on the trend towards the professionalisation of sporting competitions. The NBL entry was indicative of the heightened intensity of competition that has emerged in the professional sport sector.

The NBL presents an interesting example of the way in which the PLC can be used to assess the phases of development of a product. Sportview 5.2 explains in more detail the progress made by the NBL since its inception in 1979. What can be understood from this information is that by 1995 the NBL had reached the maturity stage. Attendances and level of support seemed to have plateaued. This was not a special feature of season 1995, but a trend that had become apparent during the 1993 and 1994 seasons. Attendances had peaked at about 80% of stadium capacity, sponsor interest had levelled, and the NBL was still experiencing problems in attracting good television ratings.

The challenge for the NBL was what to do to arrest the decline. One solution examined during 1996 was to change the playing season, moving it to the summer. Not only would this provide the impetus to relaunch the NBL as a summer game–it would, as shown in the perceptual map, have the capacity to alter its direct competitors, including the capacity to obtain more television time. Moving to summer would see the intense competition provided by the AFL, NRL and Super 12s reduced, at the risk of moving into cricket's competitive space.

The National Soccer League (NSL) would become relevant competitors, but the NSL does not have the same product intensity as the AFL, NRL or Super 12s. Cricket, in particular one-day cricket, does have the competitive intensity to create difficulties for the NBL. Programming of cricket is not as intense or as weekend-oriented as that of the AFL and NRL. In winter, the AFL often schedules matches on Friday night, Saturday afternoon, Saturday night and Sunday afternoon. This creates difficulties for basketball in terms of both television and live attendance. Cricket has fewer matches, and these tend to be concentrated in one major city on any given weekend. The opportunity to rejuvenate the NBL was therefore presented through the season change that ultimately took effect in the summer of 1998.

SPORTVIEW 5.2

The NBL—product development

A substantial drop in attendance figures forced the NBL to review its marketing strategies, in a bid to generate more excitement and momentum in the early part of the 1993 season. After ten rounds, the NBL—which trumpeted a sensational growth in attendances throughout the 1980s and early 1990s—was down by almost 270,000 fans. (Brown 1993:6)

The ten-team NBL competition commenced in 1979 as an outlet to provide a regular opportunity for its elite players to play top-line basketball. It also quickly became the promotional vehicle for basketball in Australia. The gate for the first season was 196 000 for all home and away games. By 1995, as is shown in the table, attendances had risen to 1 097 678 from 201 games played across the country. An average of 5461 fans attended games in 1995. From 1979 to 1984 attendances grew 82%, to 355 828 spectators; but in the five years to 1988 they jumped 130%, clearly demonstrating the sport's appeal, and in the five years to 1993 they rose to just over 1 million. Seasons 1993–95 show that growth then slowed and that the NBL in terms of attendances had plateaued.

NBL attendance 1984–98

Year	Attendance	No. of games	Annual increase/ decrease (%)
1984	242 022	209	–
1985	317 372	187	31
1986	394 685	189	24
1987	483 467	192	22.5
1988	563 493	166	11
1989	662 493	170	23.5
1990	887 443	195	34
1991	825 645	194	(7)
1992	945 117	173	14.5
1993	1 083 490	199	14.6
1994	1 127 033	198	4
1995	1 097 678	201	(2.6)
1996	1 019 988	201	
1997	896 449	177	
1998	755 000	–	

Source: NBL

The success of the NBL in capturing the public's imagination in the 1980s can be traced to several reasons. It was a highly entertaining game, played in a comfortable, warm stadium, enjoyed by men and women, and revered by children. Hype generated by the NBL was also fostered by enormous goodwill from the print media and radio media. There was no question that this most American of sports had taken off in Australia, but to continue to grow it needed television to play a more significant role (Brown 1992). The Seven network, which held the rights to televise basketball in Sydney and Melbourne prior to 1992, was reluctant to give basketball a greater profile. Channel Ten took up the rights to televise the NBL in 1992 on the promise that the NBL would be shown in prime time. As season 1992 unfolded the Ten network realised that NBL programming was suffering from low ratings. The only exception to this was Perth. Following the break for the 1992 Olympic Games, the Ten network removed the NBL from prime time television.

Television remains a source of frustration for the NBL. In 1995, the NBL made the following observations in relation to television and its impact on product development:

> With television we found ourselves in a difficult situation. In order to make television work, the NBL will have to become much more flexible in its scheduling (playing in non-competitive days and times), consider changing the time of year we play, clean up the court clutter (to increase NBL branding and strengthen television advertising). All of these strategies may have a cost to the clubs. This cost will not be initially met by television rights revenue. But without making some or all of these changes, television rights revenue may never reach the level to be able to finance the changes. Almost every aspect of the NBL/Club business now comes back to creating success on television. Marketing, merchandising, attendance, rights money and sponsorship levels all point to television needing improving. The television ratings are a mystery. Our worst rating performance in recent history comes at a time when a new ARM Quantum survey shows that basketball has increased its stranglehold on the youth in this country. Basketball ranks as the top sport played by boys (10–17) at 59%, 12 points above the next team sport, cricket (47%). For girls, basketball ranks third at 31%, behind swimming (52%) and netball (36%). There are more mysteries in the result of the survey that indicates what the youth market are watching on television. Basketball is way out in front at 50%, ahead of cricket at 38%—significantly improving its position since the last youth monitor three years ago. Finally, in the 10–17-year group, basketball is the best attended sport at 22%, ahead of rugby league at 17%. (NBL 1995)

In 1996 the NBL made the decision to move the NBL season from its traditional winter season to a summer season. This necessitated a transition, or interim season, from January to July 1998. The new summer season commenced in October 1998. The rationale for the change according to the NBL (2000) was (a) to improve television arrangements, (b) increase media coverage through reduced clutter (i.e. less AFL media), (c) maintenance of sponsorship, although it was recognised that reduced attendance might result from the change. Although the interim season had a negative impact in terms of club mergers and further erosion of the fan supporter base, television coverage improved, albeit mainly through pay-TV Fox Sports supported by ABC coverage. Attendances grew 8% in the first full summer season, compared to a 5% decline in the interim season. The second summer season allowed the NBL to experiment with innovative fixturing, such as the pre-season blitz, double-headers, an open-air game at Rod Laver Arena, Melbourne Park, as well as promoting local derbies. Attendances also rose by approximately 14%, with average weekly television audiences of about 580000.

By season 2002, however, the NBL and its teams were experiencing difficulties. Dampney (2002: 101) noted that 'two clubs appointing administrators, no naming rights sponsor, no free to air television rights—no national basketball League?' Both the Victorian Titans and Sydney Kings appointed administrators in 2002, although a consortium—including former Australian boomer Shane Heal and Bob Turner, a founding member of the NBL in Australia—eventually bought the Sydney Kings. The Victorian Titans' future was less certain mid-2002. Leading into season 2002/03, the 11 teams in the NBL competition were facing a series of collective challenges. As Dampney (2002) asks: 'Is all hope lost for a game once labeled the world's fastest growing participation sport?' Product development is again a major issue confronting the NBL.

Stages of the product life cycle

It is worth returning to the stages of the PLC shown in Figure 5.3 for further examination.

Introduction

The introductory stage is characterised by the need to communicate the existence of the product to potential consumers. This can be very expensive, and accounts for the high start-up costs for a new product. The principal objective in this stage is to build awareness. Returning to the NBL example, building awareness of the new competition in 1979 was the primary objective for competition organisers. Successfully achieving this goal was inhibited, as basketball was not a traditional sport in Australia. Typically during the introductory stage, profitability is low or negative and sales near zero. Attracting 190000 spectators in the first year of the NBL competition compared to just over 1 million in 1995 illustrates the initial difficulties of developing a market segment for basketball. The other important consideration in this introductory stage is identifying the channels through which the NBL is distributed. Each club in the league was based in a major capital city or regional centre, with the intention of developing product awareness in that city or region. The most difficult phase of developing product awareness was trying to build team loyalty and team rivalry.

Growth

As product awareness began to build for basketball it moved into the next stage of the PLC: the growth stage. The NBL attendances grew to 242022 by 1984 and to just over 800000 by 1990. In this period considerable growth was achieved as many clubs moved to larger playing facilities. During the growth stage, the range of product offerings tends to widen, and refinements are made to the way in which the product is offered. The NBL found it necessary to provide large comfortable facilities as well as quality product extensions. It was through product extensions that the NBL made its greatest change to product offerings. Merchandise and licensing programs emerged, associated television programming appeared, and basketball began to identify and open up new market segments. To overcome the high cost of enticing new consumers to NBL games, the clubs began to recognise the importance of retaining their members and loyal supporters. This marked the transition from the growth to the maturity stage. The clubs themselves became the most important marketing vehicles for basketball. Brand loyalty via individual clubs became important, and club memberships began to stabilise post-1990.

Maturity and revitalisation

The mature stage is characterised by a plateau in sales–in the NBL's case, sales in the form of attendance, memberships, sponsorships and merchandise. As has already been discussed in this section, action needs to be taken to extend the PLC. This returns us to the reasons why the NBL is considering a change of season, to recycle or extend the capacity of the NBL to capture market share. Given that the NBL is a relatively new sport product in Australia, it will be worth seeing what other action the NBL takes to extend the PLC of basketball.

Variations from the PLC curve

The PLC is a useful tool for the sport marketer to assist in strategy development for sports and sporting league and associations. The S-curve indicated in Figure 5.3, however, can be misleading. Not all products progress incrementally through the stages of the life cycle described, making it harder to discern at what stage of the PLC a product can be classified. Another complication is the time taken to progress through the stages of the PLC. It is very hard to predict how long it will take a product to move from an introductory stage to maturity. Indeed, the NBL has been caught in this situation of taking at least two years to identify maturity, and a subsequent levelling off of interest.

Variations from the PLC S-curve **FIGURE 5.4**

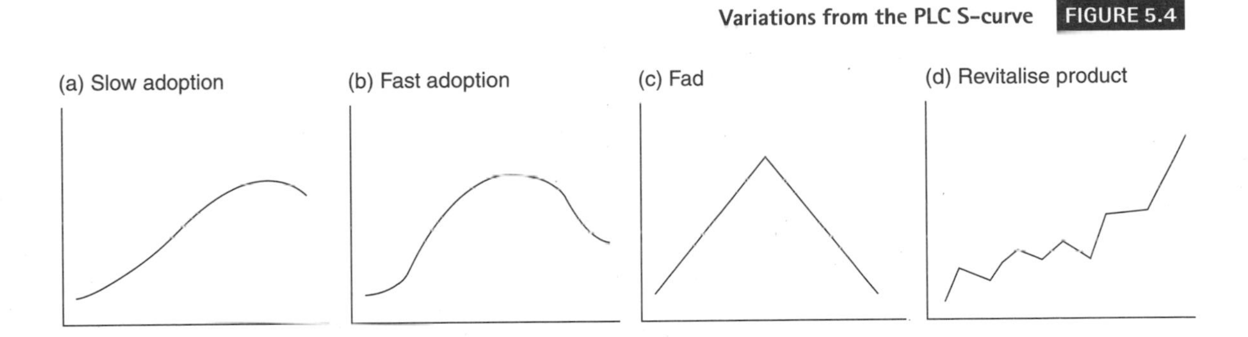

Figure 5.4 illustrates some of the more common variations from the normal S-curve shown in Figure 5.3. The first curve (a) shows a product that has a long introduction stage because it is adopted slowly by consumers. The second curve (b) illustrates products such as one-day cricket, which are rapidly accepted and have a shorter introductory stage. The third curve (c) represents 'fad' products that typically have a rapid rise and rapid fall. The fourth curve (d) shows a product that has been frequently revitalised, going through stages of decline followed by growth. The Olympic Games provide a good example of the fourth curve, as it has ebbed and flowed in terms of growth and popularity during the past 100 years. At present, the Olympic movement could be described as being in a growth phase,

although as recently as 1980, leading up to the 1984 Los Angeles Games, it was in a state of decline. Los Angeles proved the catalyst that provided the necessary revitalisation for the Olympic movement.

Like all the models presented in this book, the PLC provides the sport marketer with a framework on which to base decision making. There will always be variations on the models and theories discussed. However, it is incumbent on the sport manager to temper theory with the peculiar nature and development of each product.

Sport and television

Earlier in this chapter we discussed the benefits provided by a product as being vital to the consumer's decision to purchase. In sport, television has emerged as an important substitute for attendance at the live event. Another question is whether sport on television is the same product as the live event.

Sportview 5.2 has highlighted the importance of television to the NBL in developing its product to its full potential. The exposure and promotional benefits to be gained by a sport from televising its games or events have been central to most sport-marketing strategies in the professional sport sector.

At issue also has been the revenue aspect of televising sporting contests versus the live game. That is, consumers have the choice either to attend the event or stay at home and watch it on television. For sports where consumers may decide to stay home and watch the event on television, this choice represents direct lost revenue. It is, however, also revenue that may find its way back to the sport indirectly in the form of television rights as a consequence of high program ratings. Alternatively, the short-term lost revenue may result in a long-term revenue gain as the consumer is enticed to attend future games because the televised game was entertaining and enjoyable. The relationship between television and sport has always been prickly, as the balance between live coverage, delayed coverage and 'blacking out' home markets has created tension between respective sports and the television networks. Other tensions are observed in the form of scheduling, as television looks to the most favourable programming options to maximise its investment via television rights.

In this book we consider the televised form of sport to be different from attendance at the live event. In other words, the benefits offered by watching the game on television are different from those gained by attending. Television offers different features, including commentary, slow-motion replays, live interviews and, depending on the sport, close-up action, which can sometimes detract from observing the build-up to the central action.

The television–sport relationship is considered in greater detail in chapter 11. Specifically, chapter 11 will examine why television has become such an important component of the economics and marketing of professional sport. Television is also discussed in chapter 7 in relation to its role in distributing the sport product.

Summary

This chapter defined and described sport as a product. A product is anything that satisfies a need or want and is acquired to do so. In relation to sport, two important concepts have implications for sport marketing. The first is the core product, defined as the actual game, over which the sport marketer has no control. The sport marketer must be very careful not to overpromise in terms of how good the game will be or how well specific athletes may perform. The second concept is the importance of product extensions to the overall marketing effort. It is here that the marketer can ensure that acceptable levels of quality are achieved. Discussion in this chapter also focused on the importance of delivering quality service. The dimensions of quality service were discussed and the areas requiring attention in the delivery of product extensions indicated. These include anything that affects spectators' attendance and enjoyment of an event.

Issues of strategy were also considered when discussing product positioning and the product life cycle. In both cases these techniques allow the marketer to assess the relative standing of a product in relation to competitors and the phases of product growth. The perceptual map was used to illustrate the concept of product space and the way in which this defines direct and indirect competitors. Perceptual mapping also highlights the importance of key product attributes and their ability to entice consumers to purchase or attend games. Level of excitement was used as an example of a key product attribute. In this example, it was possible to determine the direct competitors of the NBL and other sports. The NBL was also used to illustrate the application of product life cycle analysis, which revealed some interesting challenges confronting the NBL in its quest to arrest the plateau in the fortunes of its competition.

Finally, the importance of television to sport was noted. A distinction was made between the television product and the live product. It was posited that televised sport is a different product from the one viewed live. Different benefits are offered, so a different range of options is considered in the pre-purchase process.

CASE STUDY

The tradition continues—Masters of anti-sports marketing

For golf fans, nothing signals the start of another season quite like 'The Masters'. The tradition-rich tournament that runs from 6–9 April is a soothing wake-up call for duffers, beckoning them back for another year of lofty ambitions and erratic shot-making. Yet an accident of the calendar doesn't quite explain the grip this tournament has on golf. The mystique of The Masters is probably best summed up by a simple principle: less is more. The buttoned-down, tight-lipped members of the Augusta National Golf Club who run The Masters have proven themselves masters of managing supply. If you have week-long passes, you probably inherited them from your great-grandfather. The estimated 40000 badges are the most sought-after in sports, and the waiting list closed two decades ago. Masters golf paraphernalia isn't much easier to come by. Shirts, visors, towels and other items carrying the distinctive flagstick logo are sold only at souvenir pavilions and the pro shop—and only during tournament week.

Unique

If The Masters peddled its wares on the Web or loosened curbs on corporate hospitality tents (only a few longtime sponsors have them) it might be one of the great cash cows in sports, alongside the Super Bowl and NCAA Final Four. As it is, The Masters is no pauper. Although the club zealously guards its numbers, revenue estimates run from $20 million to $25 million. Rest assured, however, that The Masters will continue leaving money on the table. Its almost cavalier attitude towards cash allows the all-male, overwhelmingly white membership of Augusta National to retain steely control. The less these anti-sports-marketers trumpet their tournament, the larger its legend seems to grow. 'The Masters is absolutely unique in all of sports. There's a real feeling that they want you to worship from afar. See it, experience it, but don't get too close', says sports-marketing consultant William A. Sutton.

That aura is as old as the tourney itself. Conceived by golfing legend Bobby Jones in 1934, The Masters began as an intimate get-together of Jones's friends on the picture-postcard course that weaves through groves of Georgia pines. And to this day, 'The National' retains its exclusivity. Citigroup's Sandy Weill, GE's Jack Welch, Bank of America's Hugh McColl and former Secretary of State George P. Shultz are or have been members. Microsoft Corp's Bill Gates would like to be one but hasn't gotten in.

'If you're launching a sporting event now, you're fighting every day for people's attention. First thing, you throw up a Web site. Then you try to get writers buzzing about it', says Sutton: 'The Masters is just the opposite. It doesn't need to do any of that. It's positioned itself as this regal event'. Television helps with the tease. CBS has been the only network to televise The Masters since its TV debut 45 years ago. It has held on to this plum largely because it abides by a list of unusual terms dictated by the club: a limit of four minutes of commercial breaks per hour, a ban on annoying promos for regular network shows, and a sharp limit on air time.

Unlike NBC's coverage of the US Open, which follows the leaders from the first tee, The Masters decrees that coverage begin mid-round, focusing the drama on the famous Amen Corner holes of the back nine. Given a chance, CBS undoubtedly would expand coverage to both nines and maybe the lot where the golfers park their courtesy cars. But Masters Chairman Hootie Johnson isn't budging. 'We've talked about this very subject', says CBS Sports President Sean McManus: 'If the club felt strongly we should do something to improve our coverage, we'd obviously have an open dialog'.

In only one area has The Masters eased up on its less-is-more philosophy—prize money. Last year's champion, Spaniard Jose Maria Olazabal, banked $800 000, a hefty raise over the 1998 winner's check of $576 000. And let's not forget that the pros do get to spend a week playing 'The National'. The men in the green jackets no doubt think that's reward enough.

Source: Adapted from Hyman (2000: 7)

Questions

1. Identify the product attributes of The Masters. What product benefits can you identify from the professional golfer's, spectators' and television perspectives?
2. Describe product quality as it might apply to The Masters.
3. Identify the positioning strategy used by Masters organisers.
4. In product life cycle terms, at what stage would you place The Masters? Is this stage sustainable given the sport marketing strategy described?
5. Describe the product positioning of The Masters. Using your research skills, identify potential sports and allied products that might occupy a product space on a perceptual map.

6

Pricing strategies

Stage 1—Identification of marketing opportunities

▼

Stage 2—Strategy determination

Step 5—Determine core marketing strategy

Marketing and service mix—sport product, pricing

▼

Stage 3—Strategy implemention, evaluation and adjustment

CHAPTER OBJECTIVES

Chapter 6 introduces price as one of the marketing mix variables. Pricing strategies are discussed in this chapter in relation to overall organisational and marketing goals. Pricing as a process is defined as setting or adjusting a price charged to a customer in exchange for a good or a service. The techniques used to determine price and the role of price in the marketing mix form the basis of this chapter. However, through the headline story, and one of the sportviews, the macro-perspective of achieving positive overall outcomes is discussed as well. As will be shown, the 'big picture' cost–benefit analysis should always be the overriding measure of pricing effectiveness.

After studying this chapter you should be able to:

1. Distinguish between factors that influence the pricing process.
2. See pricing in the context of organisational strategy.
3. Determine demand and supply relations and the price sensitivity of markets.
4. Apply a strategic pricing approach in setting or adjusting the price of sport products.

HEADLINE STORY

The relative 'price' of hosting major sporting events

If you believe the protestations of the 'Save Albert Park' group, the committee which has vehemently campaigned against the location of the Australian Formula 1 Grand Prix at the Albert Park circuit in Melbourne, a city would be unwise and irresponsible to consider attracting and hosting an international sport event. Noise and air pollution, the destruction of inner-city parklands, restricted access to public property, significant expenditure of public monies, grossly overstated economic benefits for the local community and political opposition all await the city that hosts hallmark events. On the other hand, the socio-economic conservationists are continually overwhelmed by the mass public and political appeal that hallmark events forge. In addition to the economic stimulus, research on hallmark events tends to reveal that their social impact is positive, providing a normative glue fastening parochial sport fans and even the less frequently interested sport theatregoers with a vast bonding of collective identity and vicarious experience. Indeed, studies suggest that the outcomes of most cost–benefit analysis are positive; that is, the benefits (such as in Melbourne's case, the exposure of the city and revenues from tourism) outweigh the costs (such as air and noise pollution and the re-development of parklands). The Grand Prix will remain in Melbourne for a minimum of another five years. With record attendances in 2001 of half a million people over the four days of the event and 120,000 for the big race, this time period seems modest. For the moment, at least once a year, Albert Park belongs to the petrol-heads and speed-freaks. The 1 million dollar question, however, remains: who pays the final price? (Westerbeek & Smith 2001: 24)

Pricing, as a process, can simply be defined as setting or adjusting a price charged to a customer in exchange for a good or service. Pricing a product or a range of products properly is of utmost importance to an organisation. The level of pricing determines how many customers are inclined to buy the organisation's products. At the end of the day, the price multiplied by the number of products sold must at least cover the costs of production. This is, however, a simplified version of reality, which will be elaborated on during this chapter.

In chapter 5 it was shown that the sport product is made up of different components: the core product and product extensions. Although the core product may be the main attraction for customers, product extensions, in terms of potential income, make up a considerable part of overall revenue for sporting organisations. This is one reason why, for example, the Australian Football League does not price its core product (tickets to attend a football match) at a higher level. The core spectator product is priced relative to the product extensions (such as sponsorship services and television rights) or, in other words, the total product mix. Throughout this chapter, examples of this 'big picture perspective' will be given in relation to hosting major sporting events and city marketing.

In this chapter, the pricing process will be examined from a strategic perspective. After presenting a strategic pricing model, the different steps of this model will then be discussed.

The strategic pricing process in sport

The importance of recovering the costs of production through setting the right price is highlighted in the headline above. Cost of production, however, is only one of the variables to take into consideration when setting or adjusting price. The strategic pricing process incorporates both internal characteristics of the organisation and its products (e.g. goals and objectives) and external characteristics (e.g. competitors' pricing behaviour). This will enable the marketer to create a pricing strategy beyond the short-term future of the organisation. Figure 6.1 describes the strategic pricing process for sporting organisations.

Step 1: Determine pricing goal(s)

Although there exists a subtle difference between introducing a product then setting a price and adjusting the price of an existing product, the pricing goal must be determined for both. It is vital to recognise the influence that price has on customers' perceptions of the product. A relatively high-priced product will often be perceived as a high-quality product. Pricing, in other words, has a strong impact on the positioning of the product.

Determining the pricing goals should be a direct derivative of the organisation's reason for being (i.e. its mission) and the resulting marketing goals. Marketing goals of different organisations and derived pricing goals are shown in Table 6.1.

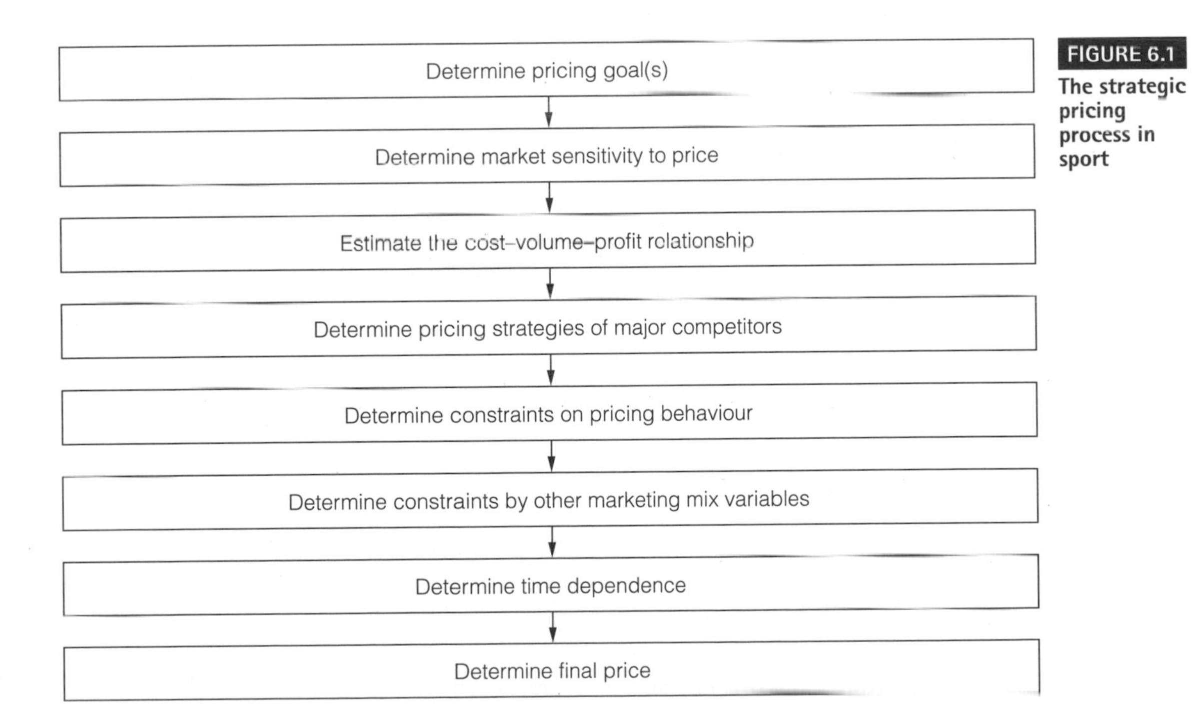

FIGURE 6.1 The strategic pricing process in sport

TABLE 6.1 Marketing goals and derived pricing goals

Marketing goals	Derived pricing goals
Maximise shareholder value	Maximising profit Maximising sales growth Maximising revenue
Be the most innovative in the business	Market skimming
Deliver the highest quality products	Premium price
Be accessible to all members of the community	Full cost recovery Partial cost recovery

Maximum shareholder value

Private enterprises and privately owned sport franchises often pursue goals designed to maximise shareholder value. In order to achieve maximum shareholder value, pricing goals would include maximising profit, maximising sales growth or maximising revenue.

Maximising profit is often seen as a short-term goal concentrating on current financial performance, assuming little influence from competitors (i.e. to undercut the set price).

Maximising sales growth is a long-term pricing goal. Although profits could be higher, the organisation aims to sell its products at a lower price to as many customers as possible. The goal is to obtain a large share of the market and reap the subsequent long-term benefits.

Maximising revenue can be the pricing goal of, for example, the organisers of Wimbledon. With an infrastructure (buildings, equipment and personnel) in place, every extra customer adds to the revenue of the organisation. The organisation itself is incurring little extra cost by providing services to that one extra visitor, and this makes selling the extra tickets, such as ground passes, extremely attractive.

Most innovation

If an organisation aims to be an innovative company, the pricing goal may be to skim the market. Nike, as an athletic footwear manufacturer, establishes a price high enough for a small segment of the market to buy its products. As soon as competitors introduce similar products, Nike lowers the price to sell to the segment below the 'early adopters'. Nike skims the market by receiving the maximum price from the different segments in the market. Nike can adopt this strategy because it ensures that it is the first to introduce a new, trendy, high-quality product.

Highest-quality products

If an organisation aims to deliver the highest-quality products, a premium pricing strategy may be an alternative pricing goal. In order to communicate the high quality of the product (e.g. a world title boxing contest), a correspondingly high price is set. Customers, valuing the high-quality features of the product, will pay the premium price, and the organisation will achieve an above-average return.

Community accessibility

Not-for-profit organisations, government organisations and many sporting organisations often set pricing goals such as partial cost recovery or full cost recovery. Public hospitals, for example, may set prices in order to recover their costs because they do not need to make a profit, their main goal being to serve the community. National sport-governing bodies can price their products in order to break even, incorporating funding from the federal government (partial cost recovery). Setting or adjusting the price depends not only on the goals of the organisation but also on the other elements of the pricing process. This will become clear in the following sections.

Step 2: Determine market sensitivity to price

How sensitive customers are to a change in price is important in determining a range in which the final price may be set. It is also vital to know the estimated size of the market and how the market is segmented. In this section it is assumed that this information is available. The concepts of demand and supply, price elasticity and non-price factors are important in determining market sensitivity to price. Given the marketing focus of this book, we start by discussing the concept of demand.

Demand

The quantity demanded of the product by potential customers depends on the price assigned to the product. In general terms, the higher the price of a product, the lower the quantity demanded. Figure 6.2(a) shows that for a certain product a demand curve can be drawn demonstrating the linear relationship with the price. The quantity demanded also depends on the prices of other factors, such as product (substitutes and complements), income of customers, expectations of future prices and the size of the population.

Substitutes are products that can be used in place of another product (e.g. spectator tickets to a football match and to a basketball match). If the price of a product (football tickets) rises, the quantity demanded of the substitute (basketball tickets) is likely to rise as well because consumers will elect to purchase the cheaper substitute.

Complements are products used in conjunction with another product (e.g. golf clubs and a golf course membership). If the price of a product (golf course membership) falls, the quantity demanded of this product and its complement (golf clubs) will rise.

Generally, when the income of customers rises, demand for most goods will also rise. Expectations of higher prices in the future may prompt customers to buy now, and hence demand will rise. In general, the larger the population, the greater the demand will be for products.

Supply

When a product is providing attractive returns to producers, more organisations will be inclined to supply the product to the market than when the price is relatively low. In general terms, the higher the price of a product, the greater the quantity supplied. Figure 6.2(a) shows that for a certain product a supply curve can be drawn demonstrating the linear relationship with the price. The quantity supplied also depends on resource prices, technology, the number of sellers and the expectations about future prices.

In general, when resource prices rise, the quantity supplied will fall. Similarly, technological improvements and increasing efficiency will result in a rise in the quantity supplied because a greater quantity can be produced at the same cost. The more sellers there are, the greater the quantity supplied. Expectations about future prices are a more complicated issue. When a sporting goods firm expects prices of tennis racquets to rise after the final

FIGURE 6.2 **Demand, supply and market equilibrium**

(a) Demand and supply in equilibrium at unit price $100

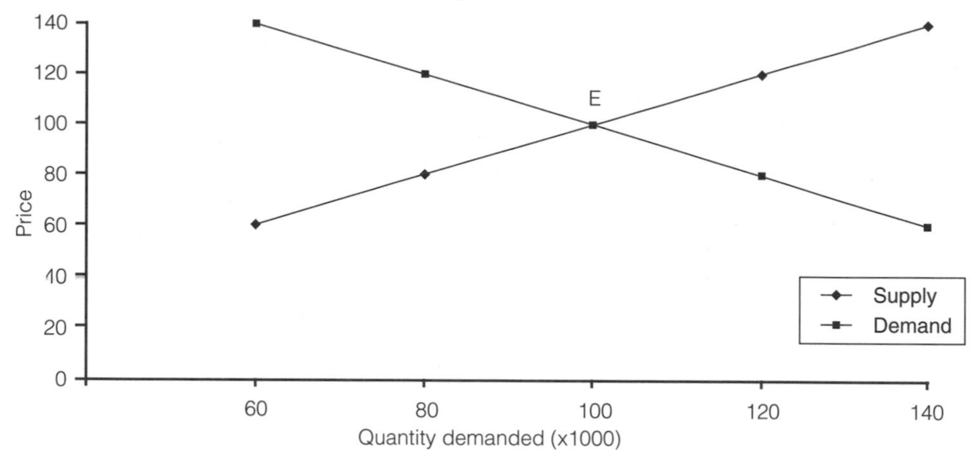

(b) Excess supply at unit price $120

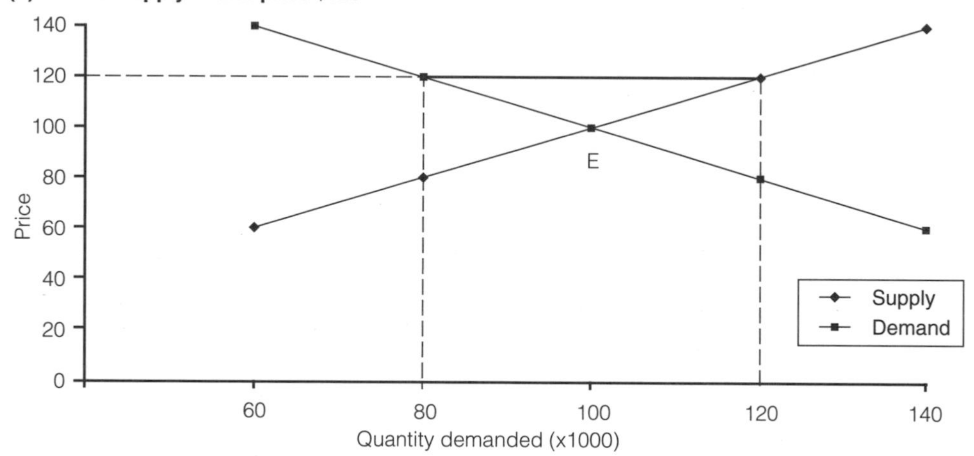

(c) Excess demend at unit price $80

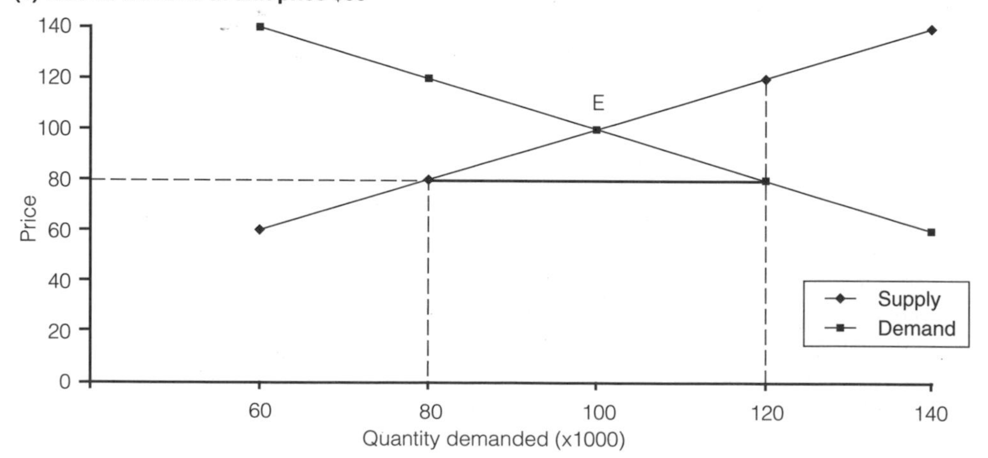

at Wimbledon, it may choose to hold back the racquets in stock in order to sell them at a higher price. Racquet manufacturers, however, may decide to increase production and supply more racquets to the market.

Market equilibrium

Figure 6.2(a) shows that, at the point where demand equals supply, the market is in equilibrium (E). This point represents the price that the market is prepared to pay, given the quantity supplied. Figure 6.2(b) shows that at a price of $120 there will be a supply of 120 000 racquets but a demand for only 80 000. There will be excess supply of 40 000 racquets. Figure 6.2(c) shows that the reverse will occur at a price lower than the equilibrium price (e.g. $80). Therefore in that situation, there will be excess demand of 40 000 racquets.

If the demand for tennis racquets after the Wimbledon final rises, the demand curve will move to the right. This will result in a rise in the quantity supplied (i.e. a movement along the supply curve) because the price will go up to establish a new equilibrium. Let us assume that people keep demanding the new quantity. With this increase in demand, new producers will be lured to the market because of the higher price, supply will go up, and the supply curve will move to the right. This again will result in a fall in price. Equilibrium will return to the point where it is not attractive enough for new suppliers to enter the market. At the end of this process the only change will be that the total quantity supplied has risen. It goes beyond the scope of this book to further elaborate on demand and supply issues.

Price elasticity of demand

We have now explored the influence that price can have on the quantity of products supplied and demanded. What we do not know is how sensitive a customer is to a change in price. Will a rise or fall in the price of a product result in a great or small change in the quantity traded? Price elasticity of demand is a measure projecting this relationship. It is calculated as the absolute value of the change (%) in the quantity demanded, divided by the change (%) in price. The absolute value can range between 0 and infinity. A value between 0 and 1 represents inelastic demand; a value greater than 1 represents elastic demand; a value of exactly 1 is called unit elastic demand.

Figure 6.3(a) shows that inelastic demand occurs where the fall (%) in the quantity demanded is less than the rise (%) in price. In other words, the organisation will benefit from raising price because the number of customers lost will be less than the gain in revenue. For example, the number of customers will not vary greatly when the price of tickets for the World Championship Soccer Final is raised.

Figure 6.3(b) shows that if the fall (%) in the quantity demanded equals the rise (%) in price, the elasticity of demand is 1 (unit elastic demand). This means that total revenue will not change.

In Figure 6.3(c) it is shown that if the fall (%) in the quantity demanded exceeds the rise (%) in price, demand is considered to be elastic. In this case, the organisation will benefit from reducing price because the gain in number of customers will be greater than the loss in revenue. For example, the number of customers will vary greatly (i.e. rise) when the price of a golf course membership is lowered.

FIGURE 6.3 Price elasticity of demand

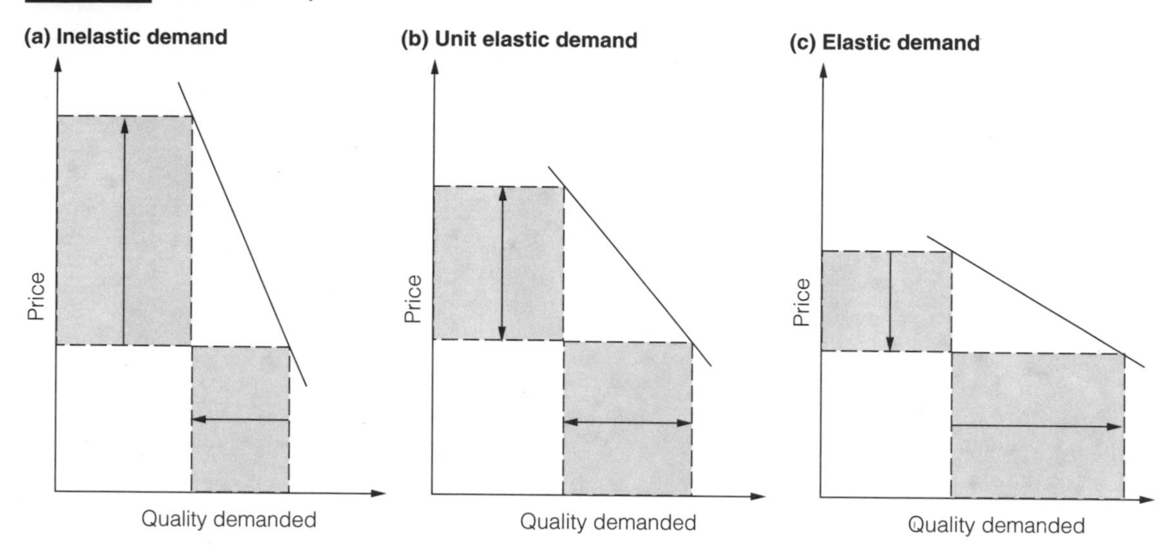

Factors determining elasticity

The size of the elasticity of demand is mainly determined by three variables:

- the substitutability of the product;
- the amount of time since the price change; and
- the proportion of customer income spent on the product.

The more substitutes there are available for a product, the easier it is for a customer to replace one product with another when price rises, hence the higher the price elasticity. A range of professional sports are playing in the metropolitan area of Melbourne less than 1 kilometre apart. A rise in the admission price for one sport will force customers to search for cheaper alternatives. A substantial price rise will result in an even more substantial loss of customers. However, existing customers of a basketball club, for example, will not immediately be able to go to a football club because they may have purchased long-term memberships.

The longer the time since the price change, the more opportunities customers will have had to find alternatives, and hence the greater the elasticity of demand.

The higher the proportion of customer income spent on club membership, the higher the elasticity of demand. If expenditure represents a large part of an individual's income, every extra dollar on top of that expenditure will be scrutinised and can make him/her decide not to purchase. If, however, a very rich person has to make the same decision, money spent on membership represents only a small portion of total income, and a price rise will not greatly affect the decision to buy. This last example shows that price elasticity of demand can differ not only between products but also between consumer groups, and provides the marketer with the opportunity to differentiate between customer segments. Different issues related to price elasticity of demand are explored in Sportview 6.1.

SPORTVIEW 6.1

AFL kicks a goal on marketing strategy

'The AFL's marketing strategy since the early 1980s has boosted football and helped to reverse the game's long-run decline in attendance, say two Melbourne economists. Research conducted by Mr Peter Fuller and Mr Mark Stewart at RMIT has rejected the belief widely held among football fans "that the AFL is conspiring against the best interests of the game. To the extent that increased attendance at football matches is deemed the yardstick by which football administrators are judged, we can only endorse their recent actions," Mr Fuller and Mr Stewart have concluded.

'The AFL's decision to hold down ticket price rises in the late 1980s, the construction of the new Great Southern Stand at the Melbourne Cricket Ground, the closer competition, the player draft from 1986, and the continued program of ground rationalisation were major factors in boosting game attendances. But Fuller and Stewart have found that the AFL could now push prices up further without suffering any loss in gate takings. In both Victoria and South Australia, attendance was in decline from 1948, "indicating football was becoming proportionately a less popular from of entertainment," the economists have found, using an analysis based on attendances as a proportion of each State's population.

'Crowds hit rock bottom in Victoria in 1987 and in South Australia in 1989. However, some of the game's popularity has been restored since those low points. According to Fuller and Stewart, this is partly because the real cost of admission has been held down in the minor round games, and partly because of improvements in administration. "Increased competitiveness allowing people the opportunity to attend games at different times, ground rationalisation and the move to the National competition (especially in South Australia) seem to have played a part in this," they said. The research has suggested that the player draft and the salary cap have helped by making games more even.

'Analysis of the impact of price changes on crowd size shows that a 10% increase in ticket prices (adjusted for inflation) eventually reduces attendances by around 6%. This means "the AFL could increase gate receipts by charging higher prices. The implication is that in terms of revenue derived from attendance, both the AFL and the SANFL are under-charging," according to Fuller and Stewart.'

Source: Excerpts from Henderson (1996: 5). Copyright © *The Australian*. Ian Henderson is Economics Correspondent at *The Australian*. Reprinted with the permission of *The Australian* and the author.

Non-price factors

Non-price factors influence buying situations and reduce the importance of price in the buying process. Non-price factors include an intangible perception of a product, resulting in a perceived value. In other words, some customers may be willing to pay a higher-than-average market price (premium price) to receive product benefits. Other customers may be willing to forgo these benefits in return for a lower-than-average market price. For marketers, it is therefore important to understand key product attributes in order to enhance the perceived value and hence charge a premium price.

In the sport industry, non-price factors are very important. The rules of demand and supply and price elasticity can be applied to sport's core product and extensions. In addition, different combinations of core and extensions can enhance the perceived value of the total product, justifying extra expenditure for customers. The core product cannot be remixed, but in combination with different product extensions the perceived value of the total package can be increased.

Also, the more important the product is to the consumer, the less important price will become. For example, a $100 repair on a bicycle of $2000 will enable the owner to ride the bicycle again. The perceived value of the $100 expenditure is likely to be higher than that of another $100 expenditure on something less important (e.g. a television repair) to the bike-rider.

If the marketer is able to enhance the perceived value of the product, customers will become less sensitive to price (i.e. elasticity will decrease), and the organisation will benefit from raising price. This applies also to the reverse situation. If the marketer is able to filter out the product attributes less valued by customers (e.g. cushioned seats or undercover seats in a sport stadium), customers will become more sensitive to price (i.e. elasticity will increase), and the organisation will benefit from lowering price.

It is clear from these examples that different segments of customers are targeted as part of the pricing strategy. The next section shows the impact of the cost-volume-profit relationship.

Step 3: Estimate the cost–volume–profit relationship

Cost-volume-profit analysis, also called break-even analysis, examines the interaction of factors influencing the level of profits. These factors, as identified by Anderson and Sollenberger (1992), are:

- selling prices;
- volume of sales;
- unit variable cost;
- total fixed cost; and
- sales mix.

The first four factors are discussed in this section, with sales mix left to the section on constraints by other marketing mix variables (product mix).

In general terms, the total costs of production represent the minimum financial figure (i.e. break-even point) that needs to be recovered from sales in order to at least break even (total costs = total revenue). Total costs are made up of a fixed cost and a variable cost component. Fixed costs are the costs that an organisation has to incur in order to operate (e.g. costs of plant and equipment, taxes, insurance) regardless of the level of production. Variable costs fluctuate in direct proportion to changes in the activity of the organisation. The cost of direct materials like leather for shoes is a good example. Pertaining to the goals of the organisation, the break-even point may vary. For an organisation with a partial cost recovery goal, this point is relatively lower than for a full cost recovery organisation. Both organisations, however, need to be able to ascertain their cost of production, enabling the organisation to arrive at a minimum price for its products by dividing the cost of production by the (estimated) number of products sold.

For a large athletic footwear manufacturer, total costs are made up of a fixed and variable component. In order to produce 10 000 pairs a day, for example, a certain infrastructure needs to be evident. Plant, equipment and labour are needed in order to start operations and represent the fixed costs of operations, which are independent of the output level. Raw material to manufacture the shoes is the major component of the variable costs, which vary with the output of the plant. Although certain levels of production will be more efficient, in this example it is assumed that the variable cost per unit of production is the same. In Figure 6.4 a break-even chart is shown.

It can be derived from Figure 6.4 that the higher the total costs, the smaller the average fixed cost in each unit of production (e.g. pairs of shoes). In other words, the fixed cost component will decrease with volume of production. If a factory with building costs of $10 million produces 100 million pairs of shoes over its productive lifetime (e.g. ten years), the fixed cost component in every pair of shoes is $0.10. The relationship between total fixed costs, price and unit variable cost can be shown in the break-even formula:

$$\text{Break-even point (pairs of shoes)} = \frac{\text{Total fixed costs}}{\text{Unit price} - \text{Unit variable cost}}$$

The formula shows that, with a variation in the unit price, the amount of shoes sold to break even varies. This relationship is shown in Table 6.2. When we turn our attention to service products, and many sport products are service products, the unit variable costs in the break-even formula are much harder to determine. Many costs are both fixed and shared across different services. In a large stadium, the building, its equipment (e.g. indoor courts, tennis nets, computers) and labour (a majority is often multiskilled in order to deliver different services) are all needed to provide the total mix of services offered by the facility. The variable costs per unit are hard to determine. What, for example, are the variable costs of providing basketball spectator services when one extra ticket is sold? Most costs have to be incurred, irrespective of the number of customers on the day or over a longer period.

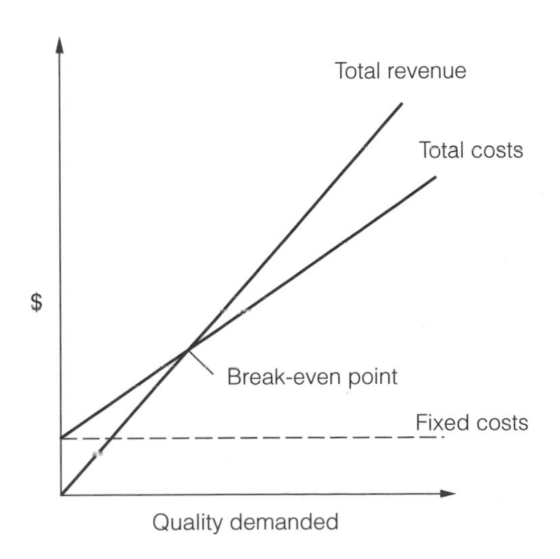

FIGURE 6.4
The break-even chart

TABLE 6.2 **The relationship between unit price and the break-even point**

Unit price	Break-even point (pairs of shoes)	Unit variable cost	Total fixed costs (per year)
10	2 000 000	5	10 million
100	105 264	5	10 million
200	51 282	5	10 million

We can state that most costs are fixed. This is why it is very attractive to entice that one extra customer: with little to no extra (variable) cost, the revenue from one extra customer is almost pure profit. This explains why, in the health and fitness industry, competition is based primarily on price. An organisation has to incur little extra cost in order to gain a substantial increase in revenues.

This also indicates the importance of managing the non-price factors in the sport industry. Because we know that most costs are fixed, it becomes a matter of sophisticated marketing in order to enhance the perceived value of the sport product. This should lead to sufficient and sustainable market share to at least cover the costs of operation.

Step 4: Determine pricing strategies of major competitors

As in any strategic-planning effort of an organisation, it is important to monitor competitor behaviour and adjust actions accordingly. The first questions that need to be answered are: Who are the major (potential) competitors? Do they operate in the same market (e.g. an amateur soccer team and a professional basketball team) or even in the same segment of the market (e.g. a central-business-district golf course and a working-class-suburb golf course)? Organisations can then determine when to respond to price changes by competitors.

The next step is to determine how competitors are positioned in terms of their relative prices, providing an organisation with an indication of the competitive price range for which the product is on offer. It would also be very useful to know which strategies of competing firms are successful.

Finally, if an organisation is able to find out what the probable responses of competitors would be to a price change, different pricing scenarios can be developed in order to make the appropriate choice.

Step 5: Determine constraints on pricing behaviour

Laws and regulations are the most obvious constraints on pricing behaviour. Most of these are a direct result of government intervention in regulating the market behaviour of organisations. Some cases of price fixing (i.e. agreement between organisations about price) can be regarded as disadvantageous for the public and are therefore forbidden by law. In order to keep government-owned facilities accessible to all members of the community, local government can set a maximum price level (ceiling). Even when a management company is hired to manage the local pool, local government can constrain it in its pricing strategies. Regulatory organisations, like national sport organisations, can set membership fees for members, clubs and associations in order to optimise participation levels.

Social responsibility constraints can also affect the pricing behaviour of organisations. If, for example, the local professional soccer club feels that disabled members of the local community should be able to enjoy a game of soccer, it will have to adjust its facility in terms of access and seating arrangements. This will have a direct impact on the fixed cost component of the total costs of the club, and it may decide to set different unit (i.e. admission) prices to recover those costs. The pricing strategy of this club will be different from that of a club focusing solely on profit maximisation. Legal and social responsibility constraints therefore limit the pricing range for the product.

Step 6: Determine constraints by other marketing mix variables

The variables of the marketing mix–product (mix), place (dependence) and promotion (mix)–all affect each other.

Product mix

Prices in supermarkets are based on the overall mix of products rather than the individual products. Some products are priced at an attractive level (e.g. soft drinks during summer) in order to entice customers to do the rest of their shopping in the same supermarket. The AFL example presented in Sportview 6.1 also exemplifies the importance of looking at the overall product mix before pricing individual products. The AFL's admission prices are low compared to other sporting codes. These prices attract larger crowds, enhancing the atmosphere for attractive television coverage and as a consequence the attractiveness of the total product for television sponsors. The AFL can offset the loss of income from gate receipts against the increase in income from television, sponsor contracts and other in-stadium purchases.

Place dependence

A majority of sport products are produced and consumed in a facility specifically designed to produce those sport products. The capacity of the facility limits the number of customers that can be serviced at a certain point in time and consequently the maximum total income. The location of the facility determines the catchment area of potential customers and hence partly determines the profile of the customer. In general terms, dependence on the place of distribution further limits the possible pricing range of the products of the organisation. Place dependence is discussed in more detail in chapter 7. Sportview 6.2 also includes some elements of place dependence–that is, dependence on a number of geographic regions (cities) of distribution.

SPORTVIEW 6.2

Hallmark sporting events can make money!

The commercial turning point for hallmark sporting events occurred over a decade and a half ago. It has been widely recognised that the 1984 Los Angeles Olympic Games created a turnaround in attitudes towards embarking on the colossal task of organising mega-events such as the Olympics and soccer's World Cup and Euro Championships. The LA Games demonstrated that when astute business ideas are applied to selling spectator sport products, money can be made. Over the past two decades, it has been the vast injections of money that have made the world of big events go round. It is the positive economic impact of events on the hosting communities that has been the critical (political) justification for investing heavily in bidding and building for the event. Hallmark events have the propensity to deliver immense economic development to a region as an outcome of the combined encouragement of government, business and visitor spending.

The economic benefits of hallmark events are typically expected to outweigh their costs. In economic terms, this is because large-scale events have a high cost–benefit ratio. In other words, their capacity to generate exports, stimulate domestic spending, improve capital utilisation, develop and regenerate infrastructure, mobilise government involvement, marshal commercial sponsorship, assemble community supporters and drive consumable manufacturing are irreplaceable, and seldom achieved via any other program or activity.

Nevertheless, despite the anticipated benefits of hosting hallmark sport events, the exponential increase in their funding, and often the need for underwriting by the local government, has driven the need for more rigorous justification of investments. As government authorities provide the lynchpin infrastructure for the events, they also assume the burden for justifying the community rewards in expending public monies. Thus, to invest in hallmark events for communal benefits, there has been a greater need to validate spending by measuring the event's contribution to the economy. For example, research (Diopter/Meerwaarde 2000) commissioned by the Dutch government identified that the Euro 2000 tournament contributed 248.2 million guilders (US$110 million) to the Dutch economy. Of this sum, 238.2 million came from foreign visitors while the Dutch spent an additional 10 million, on top of their 'normal' expenditure. This 'extra' money flowed to the four Dutch host cities of the event: Amsterdam (112.1 million), Rotterdam (71.8 million), Eindhoven (41.1 million) and Arnhem (27.6 million), ironically leading to a 'net loss' for the rest of the country of 4.4 million. On top of visitor expenditure, the Stichting Euro 2000 spent an additional 72 million (sponsor and UEFA contribution) on the organisation of the tournament, resulting in a total positive economic impact of 320 million guilders.

Source: Adapted from Westerbeek & Smith (2001: 24).

Promotion mix

The promotion mix (i.e. the means through which communication with the target markets will take place) can be constructed after product, price and place information is available. A low price strategy often needs an intensive promotional effort in order to sell as many units as possible. If the tools for intensive promotion are not available due to limited funds, the organisation will be limited in pursuing a low price strategy. The promotion mix is constraining the pricing strategy. A pricing strategy never stands on its own, as it needs to be backed by adequate promotional efforts.

One of the characteristics of services is that they cannot be stored, as services are time-dependent.

Step 7: Determine time dependence

The visitor at the Olympic Games witnesses production and at the same time consumes the product. The customer is therefore part of the production process. When the Games are over, nobody will ever be able to consume this (past) product again. Dependence on the time of consumption makes it imperative for the Games organising committee to sell as many tickets as possible, because the tickets for today's event cannot be sold the next day.

Time dependence makes sport suitable for price discrimination. Price discrimination implies that different groups of customers pay different prices for basically the same product. In the case of a health and fitness club, part of the peak demand (i.e. full utilisation of capacity) between 5 pm and 7 pm can be moved to a low-demand time slot by offering the same product at a lower price during an off-peak time. Senior citizens and parents with home duties, for example, may be able to take advantage of this offer. Pre-selling tickets to the Olympic Games is another example of price discrimination. By offering the same tickets at a lower price, the organising committee fills up seating capacity with customers who are able to plan and purchase in advance.

Step 8: Determine final price

Throughout this chapter it has been shown that many factors affect the pricing process of a certain product. Figure 6.5 summarises these factors and shows how the possible pricing range of the product narrows down after taking the influence of these various factors into consideration.

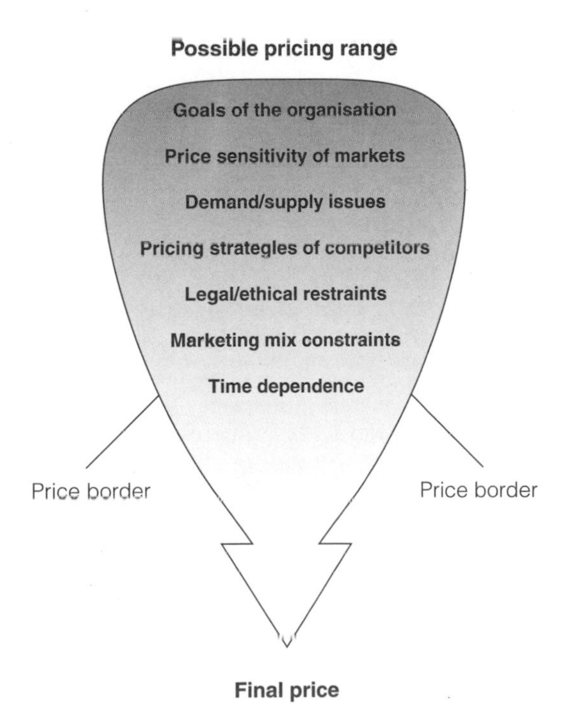

FIGURE 6.5 The possible pricing range

Final price determination is based on cost, competition, demand or a combination of the three. Most of the time, one method provides the basis for decision making, although the others often contribute. As is shown in this chapter, cost-based price determination proves to be more difficult for service-based sport products. The break-even analysis has been presented as a cost-based approach. Many providers in the health and fitness industry will base their pricing on competition. In this industry it is important to fill the capacity of the facility and thus to attract those few extra customers from the direct competitors. It is likely that the larger spectator sport organisations base their pricing on demand. In this method, the value of the product to the buyer is estimated. Westerbeek and Turner (1996: 394) found that:

> together with an increase in televisual appeal and hence income, the AFL was able to devise strategies in which demand characteristics of their markets (like elasticity of demand) could be used to optimise net income. Mass attendance at games was deemed more important than maximum profit from gate receipts. By undercharging at the gate [it was found that demand was inelastic at the current pricing level], income from TV and sponsorship could be raised, leading to greater total income rather than maximising gate receipts.

In this chapter's opening example, the state government of Victoria and the bidding organisation (Melbourne Major Events Company) will have estimated the value of the television product to the broadcast network, the sponsor product to the sponsors, and the economic, social and cultural value of the Grand Prix event to the host community. It can be concluded that, ultimately, the AFL based its pricing strategy on the perceived value of its total product mix and, along similar lines, the price charged by the Grand Prix organisers for tickets makes up only a small component of the overall pricing equation. The final price charged by Grand Prix organisers includes a significant tax contribution by the local residents of Melbourne and Victoria, not to mention a range of environmental costs. Overall, the 'final price' paid for the right to host the event is a function of the range of benefits, both tangible (economic) and intangible (social and cultural), that the event is able to generate.

Summary

In this chapter, price as one of the variables of the marketing mix was discussed in the context of setting or adjusting the price of a sport product. In order to arrive at a final price, a strategic pricing model was introduced. To enable the sport marketer to set appropriate prices, it is important to set pricing goals in concert with the overall organisational and marketing goals. Then the sensitivity of markets to changes in price can be determined and, as a consequence, the elasticity of demand. This information, combined with marketing data such as the size of the market and the number of competitors, is used to estimate cost-volume-profit relationships, leading to the creation of a break-even chart with an emphasis on a cost-based pricing strategy. When the organisation is able to base its pricing on the demand in the market—in other words, powerful enough to lead the way in setting price—the emphasis will be on demand-based pricing. It may, however, be more important to find out about the pricing strategies of competitors and to determine constraints (legal, social, other marketing mix variables) on pricing behaviour in the industry. This can lead to a competitor-based pricing strategy. When taking into consideration the time dependence of many sport products, a combination of cost-based, demand-based and competitor-based pricing will often be exercised in setting the final price or adjusting the current price.

CASE STUDY

The high price of being there

Deloitte & Touche are the accountants of England's Premier League. They produce what is probably the most comprehensive picture possible of a professional sporting league's financial business side. It is made available to the general public in their 'annual review of football finance'. In a report on television rights as an increasingly importance source of league revenues, Boon (1999: 62) observed:

> Whether they are far-sighted visionaries or not, the school of thought that downplays the importance of income from the live event (and tends to disregard the fan—'customer'—loyalty it creates) in favour of a greater impact from the (indirect) income for TV rights, is—in our view—putting the wrong emphasis on football's financial structure. It is the balance of the revenues from these different markets that is important.

Boon's 1999 observation turned out to be visionary in its own right. Individual clubs and leagues have indeed continued their efforts to achieve full capacity for revenue maximisation purposes. With even the most successful football league in the world suffering from a drop in attendance in the 2001/02 Premier League, the emphasis is back on expanding (or retaining) the fan base. In order to boost regular attendance and to turn young spectators into football devotees, half of all clubs have reduced prices. Sunderland, for example, discounted season tickets by 10% and designed a special discount scheme for children under 12 and those aged under 22. The latter youngsters are in their first jobs, and having moved out of their parental homes, are likely to be short of money. To that end clubs still aim to maximise gate takings, while leagues aim to maximise total revenue from the product mix consisting of gate, sponsorship, merchandise and TV revenues (Campbell 2001).

If sport fans in the UK feel the heat of overpriced tickets, then we should really pity the American sports nut. Team Marketing Report (2001) published the 2000/01 Fan Cost Index (FCI) for all NBA franchises. The FCI represents the total dollar value of a 'family of four' attending an NBA game. The total cost includes food and beverage (four sodas, four hot dogs, parking, two programs, two caps, two small beers) and four game tickets. For a family of four to see a New York Knicks game, the most expensive ticket in the NBA, they had to cough up US$469.59, up 3.1% from the previous year. At Charlotte Hornets, the cheapest ticket, the family was still US$183.19 out of pocket. No wonder that, according to Howard (1999: 89):

> minor leagues across a number of sports are thriving. Minor league baseball has enjoyed sustained growth in the 1990s. In 1992, 168 minor league ball clubs drew 27 million fans. By 1997, attendance had reached 34.7 million... perhaps the most surprising development of the decade has been the explosive growth of minor league [ice] hockey... The East Coast Hockey League (ECHL), for example, has grown from 5 to 29 teams in just 9 years.

Over the past four seasons, ECHL attendance has more than doubled, topping 4.7 million in 1997–1998.

Questions

1. In your opinion, how important will the income from gate receipts be, relative to the income from indirect sources such as television rights, in the near future of professional sport? Justify your answer.
2. Are there reasons, other than revenue maximisation, that underpin the importance of having a full stadium?
3. How is it possible that within the one professional league (NBA), the FCI can vary so much?
4. Why are minor leagues thriving in the USA? Consider the cost–volume–profit relationship in your answer to the question.

7

The place of the sport facility

Stage 1—Identification of marketing opportunities

▼

Stage 2—Strategy determination

Step 5—Determine core marketing strategy

Marketing and service mix—sport product, pricing, **place (physical evidence, people, process)**

▼

Stage 3—Strategy implemention, evaluation and adjustment

CHAPTER OBJECTIVES

Chapter 7 introduces the facility as the most important means by which sport services are distributed. Place as an element of the marketing mix is discussed in terms of preparing for and delivering quality service to visitors to the facility. Where to focus attention in relation to preparation for the sporting contest (planning and physical evidence) and actual delivery (people and process) are the central concepts discussed in this chapter. The practice of blueprinting is introduced to assist in this analysis. The chapter also examines different channels of distribution in sport.

After studying this chapter you should be able to:

1. Identify the critical elements of the sportscape model.
2. Identify and apply the four variable components of place.
3. Create a blueprint of how a sport product is delivered.
4. Identify the marketing channels through which sport products can be delivered.

HEADLINE STORY

Venues for now and the future

> Sydney's Olympic Plan involved the development of world class sporting facilities in two primary Olympic locations—Sydney Olympic Park and the Sydney Harbour Zone. Sydney Olympic Park is now a major new sports centre, forming part of the redevelopment of a 760 hectare site in the demographic centre of Sydney, 14 kilometres west of the central business district. The Sydney Harbour Zone incorporates existing venues on the immediate edge of the central business district. (Churches 1994: p. 10)

More than ten years before the actual Olympic Games, which were successfully hosted by Sydney in 2000, the NSW government started the physical planning of venues, villages, media facilities, training facilities, transport services and security provisions, forming the technical infrastructure for the conduct of the Games. When in 1993 Sydney won the right to host the Games, the broad structure of what to develop, and where to develop it (in terms of physical facilities), was already in place. Issues such as which sports to cater for, how many spectators to cater for, travel times to venues, maximised use of existing facilities, economically viable uses of all facilities after the Games, and the design of facilities to fit the environment and suit their use all needed to be considered. It comes as no surprise that, for example, the Olympic athletes' village is now a Sydney suburb, where real estate prices continue to move upward. However, as will be shown in the concluding case study, not all is well in regard to the future of Homebush Bay, the location of Sydney Olympic Park. Even the most stringent and well-planned developments need to consider all issues relating to the sport distribution system.

In chapter 1, place as an element of the marketing mix is described as distributing the product to the right place at the right time to allow ease of purchase. A unique characteristic of the sport distribution system is described, in that sports generally do not physically distribute their product. Most sport products are simultaneously produced, delivered and consumed at the one location, at the one point in time. The exceptions are sporting goods and broadcast sport. Given this characteristic of the sport distribution system, the sport venue or facility becomes the most important element in the distribution strategy of the sporting organisation. In other words, the place variable in the marketing mix is the sport facility.

By manipulating the elements of the marketing mix into varying combinations, different marketing strategies can be created. For one group of customers, the sport marketer will use the place variable differently from another group of customers. To be able to do this, it is necessary to identify the variable components of the marketing mix element of place. It is no coincidence that the latter three of these variable elements of place are also elements of the services marketing mix. The variable components of place are:

- facility planning;
- physical evidence;
- process;
- people.

The variable components are presented in Figure 7.1 and are discussed in more detail in following sections of this chapter. The variables are presented in the sequence shown in

Figure 7.1 because decisions made at a higher level (e.g. facility planning) dictate decisions at lower levels.

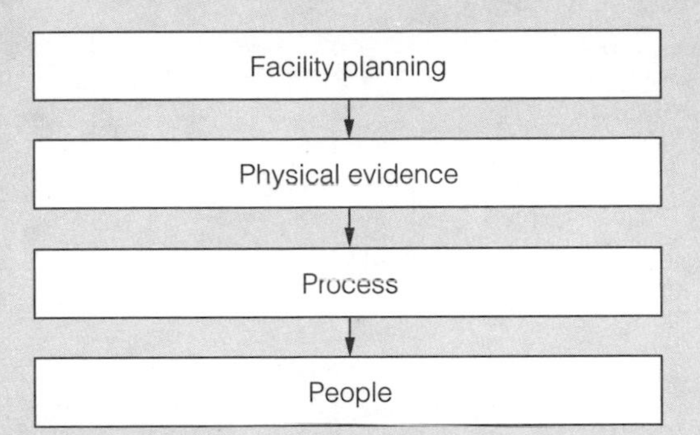

FIGURE 7.1
Variable components of place

After identifying the different variable components of place, bringing them together in an integrated fashion becomes the primary task of the sport marketer, which will be the topic of the next section. Where and when to interfere and influence can be mapped out in a blueprint, or overview, of the sport service delivery system. The chapter finishes with a discussion of more traditional distribution systems, mainly used to distribute sporting goods but, as a conceptual model, also applicable to sport service products.

Sport as a service product is briefly discussed in chapter 5 and is covered more extensively in chapter 8. But in order fully to appreciate the variable components of the (sport)place, a closer look at what makes up the sport facility or 'sportscape' is justified. We can indeed define the service environment in and around the stadium as the 'sportscape'. A considerable amount of research has been conducted into the influence of the fixed elements of the servicescape–that is, those elements that remain the same from game to game (Wakefield & Sloan 1995; Wakefield & Blodgett 1994, 1996; Wakefield, Blodgett & Sloan 1996). These elements include layout accessibility, facility aesthetics, seating comfort, electronic equipment and displays, and facility cleanliness.

The Wakefield and Blodgett (1996) study found that layout accessibility, facility aesthetics, seating comfort, electronic equipment and displays, and facility cleanliness all have a significant influence on how sport fans perceive the quality of the stadium. In turn, the higher this perceived quality of the sportscape, the higher the sport fan's satisfaction with the sportscape. If sport fans are more satisfied, they are likely to stay in the stadium for a longer period (and spend more money!); also, they are likely to return more often. These relationships between the sport fan's behavioural intentions and the sportscape are presented in Figure 7.2.

Now that we have established the importance of the inanimate and permanent structure that is the sport facility, and its impact on sport fans' response to the distribution of sport products, it is time to introduce the first variable element of place. The example of the Sydney Olympic Games at the start of this chapter further serves as an example of the first important consideration pertaining to planning the sports distribution system: facility planning.

FIGURE 7.2 Sportscape model

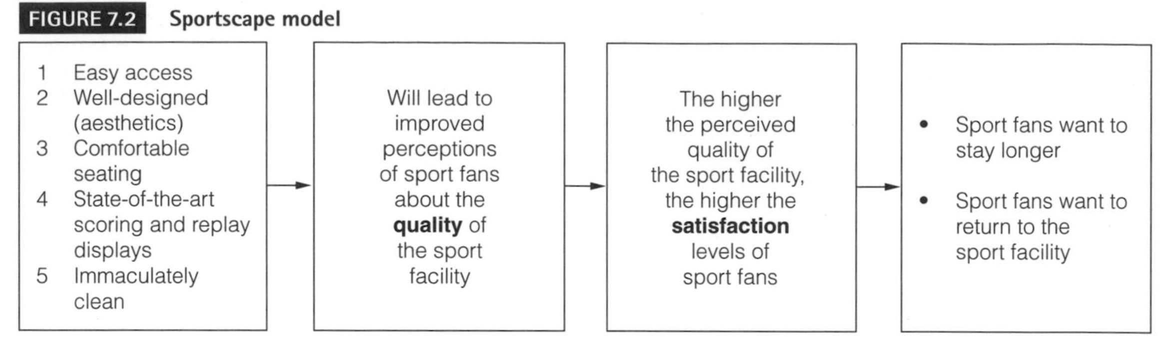

Source: Adaped from Wakefield & Blodgett (1996: 46).

Facility planning

Planning of facilities for mega-events like the Olympic Games, or facilities for a professional basketball club, or facilities for the local sport clubs, all should involve a long-term perspective in terms of the prospective usage of the facility. With production and consumption of the sport products taking place in the facility, both current and future provision need to be taken into consideration. It is extremely costly to redevelop and redesign existing facilities. It is also shown in Figure 7.2 that those elements that directly derive from how we plan for the development of the facility affect the purchase behaviour of sport fans. In that regard, does the sport facility as it is significantly determine opportunities and limitations for sport product provision? The Olympic Park soccer stadium in Melbourne, for example, due to its size and design, is not able to host a cricket or Australian Rules football match. Soccer matches cannot be played at Olympic Park during excessive rainfall, which, due to poor drainage, floods the field. The Amsterdam Arena in the Netherlands, on the other hand, can host soccer matches at any time of the year. Opened in 1996, it is the world's first 'real grass' soccer stadium with a retractable roof. Excessive rainfall, in this case, is not a potential limitation. Since the opening of the Arena, other sport providers have followed suit. For example, the Telstra Dome in Melbourne has a retractable roof, allowing for soccer, 'indoor' cricket and Australian Rules football matches through its unique Australian design. It must be noted that the Amsterdam Arena in particular has had problems ensuring that the 'real grass' playing surface is of sufficient quality (due to limited daylight exposure) to play premier league soccer matches. This just shows that when you plan to solve one problem, another may arise.

Many sporting arenas around the world were originally developed and built to host sporting events and enable a certain number of spectators to watch the game. Few of the older arenas, however, were built to host guests in corporate boxes. With many sporting organisations dependent on corporate dollars, an old stadium can become a severe competitive disadvantage. In other words, the ability to cater for a range of sport products is highly dependent on the planning and design of the sport facility. Sportview 7.1 further discusses the importance of the sport facility and its physical environment.

SPORTVIEW 7.1

The importance of the servicescape for sport consumers

In the case of leisure services, it is more than just the perceived quality of the service rendered (e.g. whether a meal was delivered in a timely fashion) that influences whether consumers are satisfied with the service experience. For example, the purpose of going to an amusement park, a theatre, or a sporting event would seem to be for the excitement and stimulation of the experience. This kind of situation differs from a trip to the dry-cleaner, in which the customer is not likely to have any expectation of emotional arousal.

Because the sport product is generally purchased and consumed simultaneously, and typically requires direct human contact, customers and employees interact with each other within the organisation's physical facility. Idally, therefore, the organisation's environment should support the needs and preferences of both service employees and customers simultaneously. Even before purchase, consumers commonly look for cues about the organisation's capabilities and quality. The physical environment is rich in such cues and may be very influential in communication the organisation's image and purpose to its customers.

Bitner (1992) found that the facility itself, or the *servicescape*, may have a substantial effect on the customer's satisfaction with the service experience, and hence will play an important role in determining whether the customer will repatronise the service-providing sporting organisation. The important aspects of the servicescape are the spatial layout and functionality of the facility and the elements related to aesthetic appeal.

Wakefield and Blodgett (1994) tested the importance of the servicescape on Major League Baseball (MLB) consumers.

The effect of the servicescape has been gaining increased attention by owners of MLB teams, as rising attendance and increased fan satisfaction have accompanied new stadiums in Baltimore, Cleveland, Texas, Toronto and Chicago. MLB stadiums provide a good setting in which to explore both the layout and functionality aspects of the servicescape, as well as the aesthetic appeal. The ways in which seats, aisles, hallways and walkways, food service lines, restrooms, and entrances and exits are designed and arranged influence fan comfort, while the external environment, the architectural design, facility upkeep and cleanliness, use of decorative banners and signs, and personnel appearance all influence the ambience of the place.

Wakefield and Blodgett (1994) exposed potential customers to two different servicescapes: one old, low quality servicescape stadium and one new, high quality servicescape stadium. They found that the old stadium was being perceived as a significantly lower quality servicescape compared to the new one.

Respondents who perceived the servicescape to be of high quality reported higher levels of satisfaction with the servicescape, and hence were more willing to attend future games. Respondents who perceived the servicescape to be of high quality also experienced greater levels of excitement, and hence satisfaction with the servicescape. It was also found that respondents who felt crowded were less excited about the servicescape and perceived the servicescape to be of lower quality.

The results of the study may have direct implications for those who have investments in stadium projects. A return in increased gate receipts might be expected owing to new stadiums or renovations. Spectators are likely to be more excited and more satisfied when in a high quality stadium and therefore more likely to come back. Consistently fielding a winning team is increasingly expensive and difficult owing to uncontrollables such as player injuries and changes in competitors' performances. Thus another basic recommendation coming from this study is that owners/managers should be sure that the controllable aspects of the servicescape are properly managed to maximise stadium capacity.

Source: Adjusted from Bitner (1992: 57–71 and Wakefield and Blodgett (1994: 66–76).

Based on extensive market research, economic trend analysis and environmental scanning, the sport marketer can determine current demand and predict future customer needs. This should lead to market information on which specialists such as the architect and the engineer can base their sport facility planning and construction. If the sport marketer can influence facility location, design and construction decisions, the place variable will be optimised in terms of facility opportunities. It should be noted though that many sport marketers have to work with existing sport facilities. Nevertheless, identification of the service provision opportunities and limitations of the facility remains a task to be performed by the sport marketer in order to move on to the next step: supplying physical evidence.

Physical evidence

As described in chapter 1, the sport product itself is intangible and subjective, making it harder for the sport marketer to sell the sport product as a commodity, standardised in quality and physical shape. Legg and Baker (1987) identify three major areas of concern that customers face when purchasing services:

- understanding the service offering;
- identifying the evoked set of potential service providers; and
- evaluating the service before, during and after purchase.

Stated differently, it is hard for the customer to judge the quality of the product, and compare it with other products (providers) to arrive at a final purchase decision. If the sport marketer is able to make the sport product more tangible for the customer prior to purchase, the customer is more likely to buy it. The sport marketer has to lend the sport product physical evidence.

Physical evidence should support the quality characteristics of the product, because the majority of customers will judge the product on its quality. Physical evidence can be enhanced by optimising:

- sport facility design;
- promotion material and advertising; and
- service provision.

The third factor, service provision, is discussed below.

The sport facility

The sport facility is the most tangible and visible physical evidence sport marketers can have for their products. The name of the facility can be displayed and marketed as the place where exciting events occur. The FA Cup at Wembley, the Australian Football League (AFL) Grand Final at the Melbourne Cricket Ground and the National Basketball Association (NBA) playoffs at Madison Square Garden are all examples of events growing in their perceived quality in combination with the respective venues. Who would get excited about the FA Cup at Queenstown football ground, the AFL Grand Final at Bendigo football oval or the NBA playoffs at Pinola basketball stadium?

High-tech scoreboards showing instant replays and the provision of sports trivia enhance the tangibility of the event (and hence the perceived quality of the sportscape, as shown in Figure 7.2). In addition, banners, photographs or statues of sporting heroes can decorate the outside and inner walkways of the facility. All past Australian Open tennis champions decorate the inside walkways of Melbourne Park. Video or television screens and trophy exhibitions can show the famous moments of success of the teams playing in the facility. The museum at Barcelona Football Club's Nou Camp stadium in Spain has a continuous video display of Ronald Koeman's winning goal in the final of the 1992 European Club championships at Wembley football stadium. To add impact, the European Cup stands next to the video display.

Promotion

Because of the intangibility of the sport product, promotion is another way to add to the physical evidence. Adding this physical evidence is not specific to distribution through the facility, and examples are therefore not necessarily facility-linked. Through either advertising or promotions, distributed among potential customers or distributed by direct mail to selected markets, the quality image and brand name of a sporting organisation can be enhanced. Legg and Baker (1987) suggest that advertisements should be vivid, using relevant tangible objects, concrete language and/or dramatisations. Photographs of past events, listings of services and explanations of different product offerings will materialise intangible services offered by the organisation. Media channels are another important consideration. Satisfied customers prepared to participate in these promotions can be used to endorse the different products, communicating their satisfaction. Celebrities, or even athlete celebrities, can also be used in this process as an influential and forceful communication channel. This type of promotion is explored in chapter 13.

Irrespective of the media channel used, the sporting organisation should try to link pictorial (posters, merchandise, advertisements) and written (brochures, flyers, advertisements) physical evidence to the name of the organisation. Licensing strategies (team merchandise) used by the LA Lakers, the Australian Cricket Board (ACB) and Manchester United Football Club are excellent examples of sporting organisations adding to their physical evidence and making money with their marketing promotions. These organisations also show that the fit between the name of the organisation and physical evidence is very important when considering a licensing and merchandising strategy. This topic is discussed in chapter 16.

Process

So far only the variables that can be manipulated when preparing for the customer to come to the facility to buy and consume the product have been discussed. Purchase and consumption involve the process by which the sporting organisation actually distributes the product to the customer. Sport marketers heavily involved in this sport service delivery process can influence and optimise the contacts between the customer and the sporting organisation. Shilbury (1994: 31) notes that 'the facility is of paramount importance because it represents the convergence of the marketing and operations functions'.

The marketing function

Grönroos (1990) distinguishes between the marketing department and the marketing function of an organisation. In traditional consumer goods marketing, the marketing department is the unit responsible for planning and implementing marketing activities. How to market a can of beans is almost the sole responsibility of the marketing department of the manufacturer; the retailer has only to put it on the shelf and sell it.

In an emerging service economy, however, marketing activities (delivering the service as opposed to selling the beans) cannot be taken care of solely by the marketing department. Contacts between the service provider (e.g. the basketball club) and the customer are so important in overall customer satisfaction that marketing activities have to be carried out by the whole organisation, not only the marketing department. Ushers and food and beverage sellers are producing and delivering parts of the overall service package and can be identified as 'part-time marketers'. They belong to what Grönroos (1990: 177) defines as the marketing function, 'including all resources and activities that have a direct or even indirect impact on the establishment, maintenance, and strengthening of customer relationships, irrespective of where in the organisation they are'.

Sport servuction model

The process of how the overall package of services is planned, produced and delivered to the customer can best be explained with the help of the sport servuction model shown in Figure 7.3. This model will be further explained by using service delivery at a basketball match as an example. The term 'servuction' refers to the visible production and delivery of the service experience.

The sport servuction system model portrays the invisible and visible parts of the organisation. In the invisible part, facility management and the two basketball clubs' managements combine to organise and plan for game night. This can be classified as the traditional marketing department role. The visible part of the organisation consists of the facility itself, the inanimate environment (physical evidence) and the service providers (contact people). The importance of the inanimate environment was described earlier in this chapter. Contact people, like ticket sellers, ushers and food and beverage sellers, but also the basketball players, provide the different services to the customers. This accumulation of services represents the customer's overall perception of their interaction with other customers, facility staff and players.

It is in the invisible part of the organisation that managers put together the service delivery process. Questions like where do we locate merchandising stands, how many

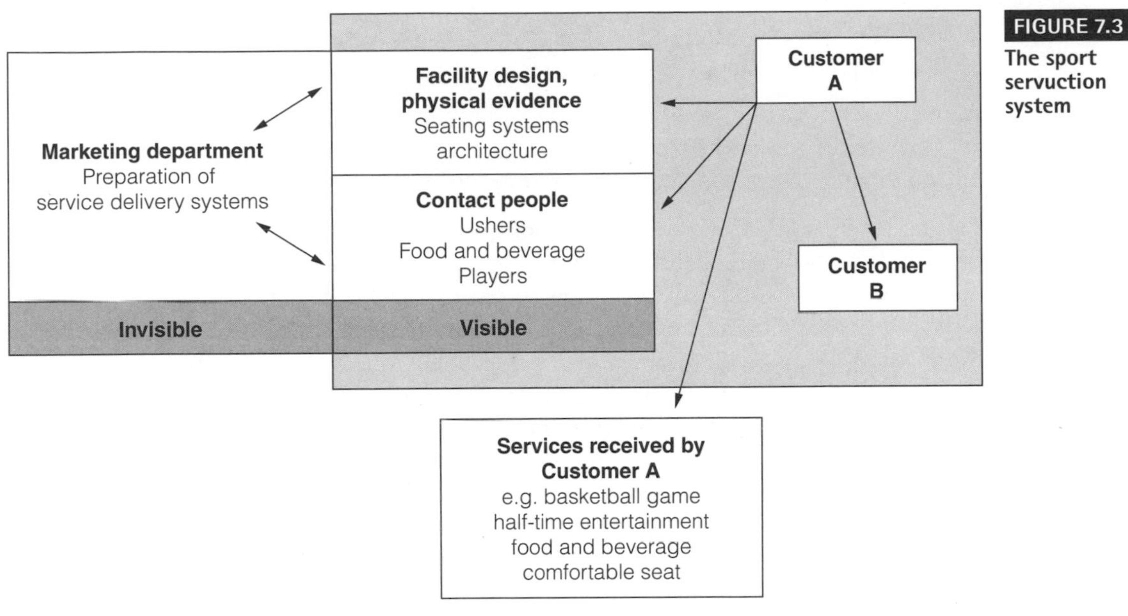

FIGURE 7.3
The sport servuction system

Source: Adjusted from Langeard et al. (1981). Reprinted with the permission of the publisher.

ticket sellers and ushers do we need, how do we want ticket sellers and ushers to approach customers, and how many food and beverage stands will we operate are asked in the cause of optimising the service delivery process. Later in this chapter, the sport service delivery system is blueprinted, based on the sport servuction system model. First, however, it is necessary to include people as the final variable component of place.

People

Staff are responsible for the delivery of the product, and as a consequence are the main distinguishing quality factor in the consumption process. The outcome of the basketball game cannot be guaranteed; therefore, consistency in service delivery is of the utmost importance in determining the customer's overall perception of the quality of the sport product. In chapter 8, five criteria that customers use to evaluate service quality are further introduced. These are:

- tangibles;
- reliability;
- responsiveness;
- assurance; and
- empathy.

These five criteria show the importance of marketing function personnel in the delivery of quality service. Apart from tangibles (partly personnel) and security, all the criteria are fully dependent on the training, skills and abilities of people in delivering high levels of service quality. The selection and training of human resources for service delivery in sport are tasks in which the sport marketer should have strong involvement. The level of training, skills and abilities of potential employees of the sporting organisation become 'people variables' that will make the difference between mediocre and excellent service provision.

Blueprinting the sport service delivery system

Having identified the four variable components of the marketing mix element place, and knowing how one component can be varied independently from the other components, the sport marketer can start looking at how to combine the different components in an integrated fashion. By identifying operations (service preparation and service delivery) within the physical design of the sport facility, it is possible to make an overview or blueprint of the sport service delivery system. The blueprinted sport service delivery system will incorporate the four variable components of place. It now is up to the sport marketer to create the right mix of what is to be produced and consumed in the system.

Figure 7.4 displays a blueprint of the sport service delivery system for a basketball match. It follows the flow of customers through the facility and identifies different parts of the sport facility where interactions between the customer and facility personnel take place. The accumulation of these interactions contributes to the overall service experience of the customer.

Facility planning and physical evidence directly affect all visible operations. The design of the facility determines how easy it is for customers to move between their seats, restrooms, and food and beverage stands. Physical evidence such as signage not only tells customers where to go and what is going on in the facility during their visit, but can also be used to advertise or communicate upcoming events. Poster and video displays of past events can increase the customers' perception of being in a place where the product is basketball entertainment.

Facility planning has an equally important influence on invisible operations. How monitoring, maintenance and television operations take place is highly dependent on provisions made in the design and construction of the facility.

Figure 7.3 showed that the planning and preparation of the service delivery system took place in the marketing department (invisible part of the organisation). This involved process and people issues such as how to approach customers, how to supply them with information or food, how many employees will be needed on game night and in which functions (ushers, food and beverage sellers, ticket sellers), and how often and when to clean restrooms. With larger crowds, parking issues and crowd flow to and from the facility become important.

The blueprint tracks the customer from entering the facility to exiting the facility and maps all possible interactions with the sporting organisation and its personnel. The blueprint identifies where the sport marketer can influence and vary the different components of place. A blueprint therefore is a vital instrument for the sport marketer in optimising the service experience. It is, however, only a start. As described at the beginning of this chapter, the actual delivery of service is the key to success.

In the final section of this chapter, traditional marketing channels are discussed, using the basketball example again to relate these channels to the distribution of sport products.

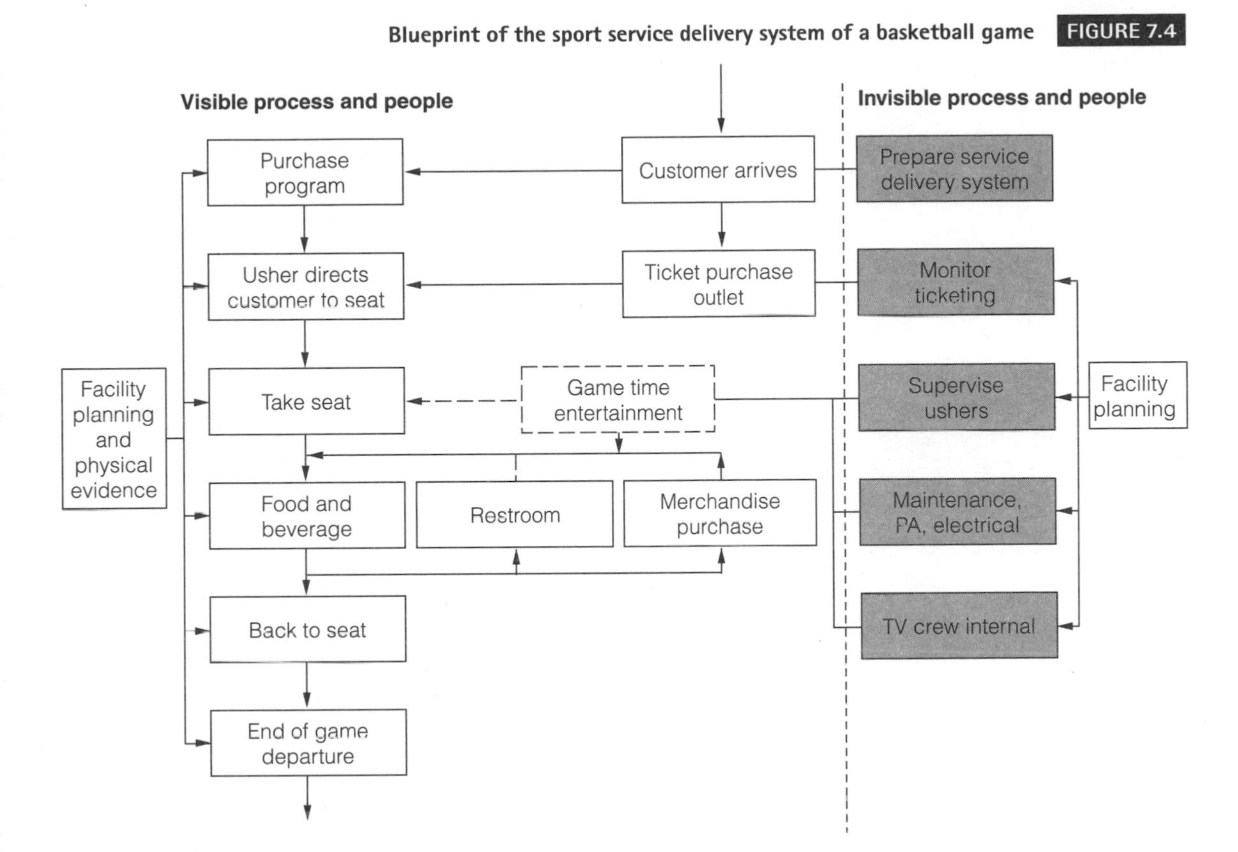

Blueprint of the sport service delivery system of a basketball game FIGURE 7.4

Marketing channels for sporting goods and services

It was noted earlier that most sport service providers deliver the sport product to the customer directly. The organisations involved in the process of making the product available for consumption or use are jointly called a marketing channel. The marketing channel performs different functions in order to enable producer and customer to exchange goods or services. Boyd et al. (1995) identify the following functions of marketing channels:

- transportation and storage;
- communication of information via advertising;
- personal selling;
- sales promotion;
- feedback (marketing research);
- financing; and
- services such as installation and repair.

A trade-off between costs and benefits will decide whether channel intermediaries are necessary to perform some of these channel functions. Figure 7.5 shows different marketing channels for sport products.

FIGURE 7.5
Marketing channels for sport products

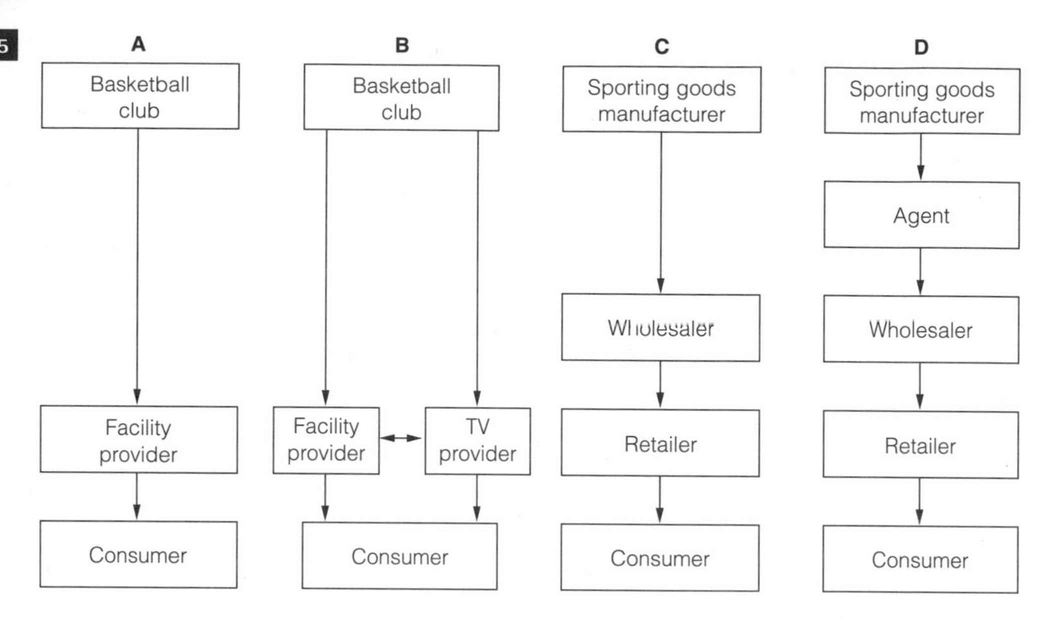

Channels A and B are the most important marketing channels for sport products. The majority of sport service products will be delivered through those channels, as discussed earlier in this chapter. Channel A shows the delivery of the sport product through the sport facility. Because the facility usually is owned and operated by a third party, the facility provider is the channel intermediary. Channel B shows the distribution of televised sport and distribution through a facility provider. Both the television station and the facility owner are channel intermediaries at the same level in the channel. They depend on each other to get the product to the consumer.

Channels C and D are more applicable to sporting goods. Manufacturers of sporting goods will often use wholesale organisations or even agents (persons selling to wholesale organisations) to channel their product from the manufacturing plant to the retailer and ultimately to the final consumer. Manufacturing organisations use other organisations in the marketing channel to concentrate on what they do best–namely, manufacturing. Overall costs will become too big for the manufacturing organisation if it has to fulfill all marketing channel functions (e.g. marketing and sales to the final consumers of the product). The manufacturing organisation therefore hires other organisations to perform those functions.

The longer a marketing channel, the less control an organisation has over delivery of the product to the final consumer. Because actual service delivery is critical to consumer satisfaction, sport service organisations should aim to keep their marketing channels as short as possible, as shown in channels A and B.

In the headline story, the organising committee of the Sydney Olympic Games has used all described marketing channels to distribute the variety of sport products. Olympic sport events were distributed through newly built facilities or existing/renovated government-owned facilities. Some events were not shown on television (channel A). The majority of events, however, were broadcast throughout the world on television (channel B). Huge amounts of Sydney 2000 Olympics licensed merchandise were produced by many different manufacturers around the world, using channel C or D as their means of distribution. After the Games, ownership of the facilities and actual users was largely separated, and the distribution of sport products now predominantly takes place through channels A and B. Both before and during the distribution process, facility planning, physical evidence, process and people are all place variables to consider in the short and long term. Quality service delivery both during and after the Games was and will be of the utmost importance to ensure that the Sydney Games are remembered as the best of the 21st century.

Summary

This chapter described and explained the unique characteristics of the sport distribution system. Identifying sport products primarily as service products, it was explained how layout accessibility, facility aesthetics, seating comfort, electronic equipment and displays and facility cleanliness all have a significant influence on how sport fans perceive the quality of the stadium. In turn, the perceived quality of the sportscape affects the sport fan's satisfaction with the sportscape. And if sport fans are more satisfied, they are likely to stay in the stadium for a longer period, spend more money, and return to the stadium more often.

Following the importance of the inanimate stadium, the chapter continued by discussing the four variables of place: facility planning, physical evidence, process and people. Sport product delivery can be enhanced by planning and designing the facility to suit customer and management needs. Providing physical evidence to the intangible sport service product can enhance distribution of the sport product and the actual service delivery process, and the people involved in this process are crucial for the success of the sporting organisation. Where and when to intervene, and how to influence the service delivery process, were highlighted by introducing the blueprint, or an overview of the sport service delivery system. The chapter finished with a discussion of distribution systems or marketing channels used to distribute sport products.

CASE STUDY

The future of the sportplace: build it and they will come...?

As observed by Westerbeek and Smith (2003): 'the issue of stadium capacity is a double-edged sword. On the one hand stadia with limited capacity will lead to occupants not profiting from maximising their gate receipts. On the other hand, too large stadia contribute to increased operational costs, lack of atmosphere and consequently, lack of support from the fans, impacting on other business areas of the club like sponsorship, corporate hospitality and TV revenue'. Although the trend in international sport business is for the importance of gate receipts as a component of the overall revenue picture to decline, a comparison of six European football leagues shows how important this income stream still is.

FIGURE 7.6

Income (% of total) from ticket sales in six major football leagues in Europe

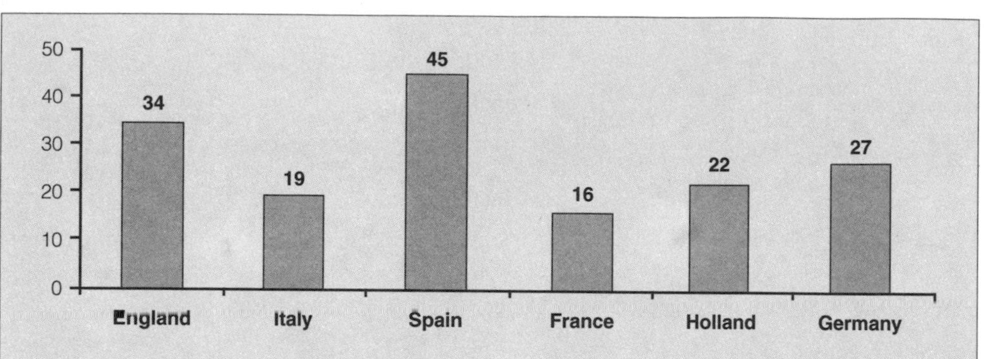

Sources: Boon (1999, 2001).

The multipurpose requirement

Most modern-day stadia cannot afford to be built for single-sport usage. According to Rod Sheard, senior principal at sport architects HOK, 'stadia need to be future proofed by building a critical mass of other facilities that will ensure the project's economic survival in another 20 years' time' (Menary 2001: 46). As a result of the changing functionality of sporting arenas, the current (fourth) generation of stadia incorporate facilities such as office space, hotels, restaurants, retail arcades, exhibition pavilions, television studios, business centres health and fitness areas, and late-night activity options such as bars and night clubs.

The corporate push

The cost structure of building new stadia has traditionally been based on the standard 'cost per seat'. Dependent on the standard of quality required—and this largely relates to the type of league the club is playing in, and the type of customers it wants to target—stadium construction costs start as low as US$700 per seat. According to Colin Fearns, director of Birse, the contractor building Leicester City's new stadium, you can get a nice stadium, including executive suites, for about US$1120 per seat (Menary 2001), which is very reasonable compared to the US$1750 per seat costs of the Bolton Wanderers Reebok stadium. The fact is that average income from corporate seats can amount to US$4200 per season, whereas the average income from a regular attendee will probably not exceed US$1000 per seat (per season). This explains why so many sport organisations devote more space to developing their corporate facilities. With this increased preoccupation with building, and hence catering for corporate hospitality, comes the impact on attendance (patterns) at matches. Not only is the corporate dollar an increasingly important source of revenue for facility operators, the space in the stadium devoted to corporate facilities, the architectural building style and multiple relationships with other stadium stakeholders also requires a reassessment of the facility's positioning strategies. In other words, the facility operators need to reassess their target markets.

The Sydney 2000 hangover

In the aftermath of the enormous success of the Sydney 2000 Olympic Games, it cannot be ignored that Sydney is slowly coming to terms with the Olympic Park facility hangover. Irrespective of the thought that went into planning Olympic facilities beyond their usage during the Games, the first and foremost planning objective was that 'the Games had to go on'. Montreal and Barcelona taxpayers, in particular, will wholeheartedly concur. As observed by Gaudron (2002: 37), Sydney Olympic Park 'encompasses a sprawling space incorporating nine world-class sporting and entertainment facilities, five star hotels, cafes and eateries, the Sydney Showground and huge parklands. But it has one missing element: regular crowds... In a space designed to accommodate the daily arrival of hundreds of thousands of Olympic spectators, the New South Wales government's key priority is to lure people back to the historic site'. The Sydney Olympic Park Authority aims to increase the number of people visiting the site from 2000 to 10000 per day, largely by developing Olympic Park into a vibrant and 'happening' residential and commercial precinct. Residential development is well underway through the transformation of the Olympic athletes' village into a suburb, but the site surrounding the biggest 'white elephant', Stadium Australia, needs a complete overhaul so that people don't feel lost in the vast spaces around the stadium. A few more sell-out events would also help the stadium approach a break-even financial scenario. Not all is bad: the Sydney International Aquatic Centre has performed well, attracting an average of 1.3 million visitors per annum; and the Sydney International Tennis Centre, as new host of the Adidas International, has attracted good crowds. However, Sydney's Olympic planning cycle may turn out to span a period of 20 years or more.

Back to the future?

Ironically, in the USA recent stadium development projects have turned back the clock in different ways. At least on the field there seems to be a push towards re-establising single-purpose stadia, in particular in soccer and baseball. Off-the-field multipurpose space allocation (office space, restaurants, retail etc.) does, however, remain the norm. Baseball teams in particular have recognised the value of the past, and have embarked on redeveloping existing ballparks, or building new ones, that reflect the history and tradition of the game, ensuring that the architecture blends in with the early 1900s inner-city buildings, yet incorporating the latest technology that the modern-day fan requires to enjoy the game to the fullest—better views, in-seat interactive video screens, multiple replay screens in the stadium, comfortable seats, automated payment systems at concession stands, and interactive games for the kids prior to, during and after the match. You may even want fries with that.

Sources: Boon (1999, 2001); Gaudron (2002); Mcnary (2001); Westerbeek & Smith (2003).

Questions

1 Comment on how the variables 'facility planning' and 'physical evidence' apply to the different sections of this case study.
2 Comment on how the variables 'people' and 'process' apply to the different sections of this case study.

3. Can you think of other standards that may replace 'cost per seat' as a better means to account for facility construction costs? Justify your answer.
4. Given the different distribution channels presented in Figure 7.5, can you argue the most likely (future) distribution channel for spectator sport? You may want to consider the strategic distribution principle of 'vertical integration'.

8

Customer satisfaction and service quality

Linda van Leeuwen

Stage 1—Identification of marketing opportunities

▼

Stage 2—Strategy determination

Step 5—Determine core marketing strategy

Marketing and service mix—sport product, pricing, place (physical evidence, people, process), **customer satisfaction**

▼

Stage 3—Strategy implemention, evaluation and adjustment

CHAPTER OBJECTIVES

Chapter 8 introduces customer satisfaction and service quality, two constructs central to customer retention and therefore organisational success. The chapter details why it is important for sport organisations to provide high-quality service and to satisfy customers (i.e. spectators and participants). It describes the various aspects of sport products that spectators and participants evaluate and provides information on how to measure and model both customer satisfaction and service quality. The chapter concludes by emphasising the centrality of customer expectations to service quality and customer satisfaction and the subsequent importance of sport marketers understanding and managing these expectations.

After studying this chapter you should be able to:

1. Comprehend the importance of customer retention.
2. Recognise customer satisfaction and service quality as two key influences on spectator and participant retention.
3. Articulate the importance of customer satisfaction and service quality.
4. Recognise the many and varied aspects of the sport service that customers evaluate.
5. Measure customer satisfaction and service quality.
6. Understand the processes by which customer satisfaction and service quality are derived.
7. Articulate the centrality of customer expectations to customer satisfaction and service quality.

HEADLINE STORY

Winning the membership race

> Adelaide continues to smash membership records, with a staggering 47 500 fans signing up for the Crows this season. Total revenue from the club's membership packages is pushing towards $6 million, more than enough to cover player salaries... Essendon still leads the race among Victorian clubs, but has 860 fewer members than this time last year and could fail to match the 2001 total of 362 227... The Western Bulldogs and the Kangaroos remain at the bottom of the membership table with both clubs struggling to break the 16 000 barrier. (*Herald Sun*, 19 April 2002: 108)

Inherent in this paragraph is the importance of a sport organisation's customers. Not only do sport organisations such as AFL clubs need to attract new customers, they also need to retain their existing customers. Indeed, the retention of customers, particularly season ticket holders in the case of AFL clubs, is absolutely essential.

The critical nature of customer retention is often demonstrated in terms of customer lifetime value, whereby an organisation calculates the value of retaining a customer over a certain period of time. Customer lifetime value is a function of the costs of serving a customer and the revenue received from the customer over the particular time period:

Time period × (Revenue – Costs) = Customer lifetime value

For example, the lifetime value of a golf club member over a 10-year period might be $6500 10 × ($900 - $250) = $6500 whereby:

- Time period = 10 years
- Annual revenue = $900
- Annual costs = $250.

Of additional relevance to sport organisations are the many product extensions that a customer might also purchase. For the golf club example, it is reasonable to assume that a member would buy food and drink from the club, as well as lessons, balls, and even clothing.

On calculating the lifetime value of customers it becomes readily apparent why customer retention is so important. Lost customers equate to lost revenue! In addition to the cost of losing customers is the expense of attracting new ones. Farber and Wycoff (1991) reported that it is three to five times more expensive to attract new customers than to retain existing customers. In brief, it makes sound financial sense for sport organisations to hold on to their customers. Despite this, some sport organisations continue to operate on the 'leaky bucket' premise.

Imagine the sport organisation as a large bucket. Organisations that succumb to leaky bucket marketing expend considerable resources on attracting new spectators and participants into their 'bucket' while simultaneously neglecting the needs of existing customers. The neglected needs of existing customers represent 'holes' in the bucket through which customers leave. That is, the sport organisation's customers simply 'leak away'—in other words, they stop purchasing. On leaving, these very same customers may take their unmet needs and therefore their money to a competitor. This is particularly so for sporting participants (e.g. golf club members and customers of tennis coaching clinics). It is also true for those sport spectators who are not avid or die-hard fans of a particular club. However, the uniqueness of the sport product, as described in chapter 1, dictates that not all dissatisfied sport customers will take their needs and therefore money to a competitor. Consider the devoted basketball fan who strongly identifies with, and has intense emotional attachment to, a particular NBL club but who was extremely dissatisfied with the season ticket experience. It is unlikely that on ceasing his or her membership he or she will take out a new membership with another NBL club, or a club from another sport league. Although the sport fan may elect not to financially support his or her once-favourite club, he or she cannot immediately transfer the strong brand loyalty and emotional attachment so often inherent in the sport product over to another club.

Even when spectators and participants do not take their dollars to competing sport organisations, however, their lost custom still represents lost revenue. Unless the sport organisation finds the balance between courting new customers and attending to the needs of its current customer base (i.e. plugs the holes in its bucket) it will be caught up in the expensive leaky bucket cycle, whereby excessive resources are expended on continually seeking new customers to replace those who have defected. In accord with the sportscape model and the work of Wakefield and Blodgett (1994) described in chapter 7, a sport organisation can plug its bucket by concentrating on providing its customers with quality service and therefore satisfying experiences. Service quality and customer satisfaction have long been known to be key to retaining customers.

Customer satisfaction and service quality are important

In addition to spectator and participant retention, there are many positive consequences associated with service quality and customer satisfaction, including fewer complaints, more positive word-of-mouth, the buying of additional products, less attention paid to competitors, reduced transaction costs, and reduced marketing expenses. Together, these positive outcomes contribute to profitability, or, in the case of not-for-profit organisations such as community sport centres and clubs, longevity.

Despite the many positive outcomes for sport organisations that provide high-quality and subsequently satisfying products, sport marketers and scholars have only recently turned their attention to service quality and customer satisfaction. This lag in sport marketing knowledge is surprising given the growing sport-business nexus and the failure of many sport organisations, whether for-profit or not, to operate at optimal capacity. Consider for just a moment the number of empty seats at many professional sport events, or the numerous community clubs confronting financial stress due to declining membership.

Sport, perhaps more than many other industries, should demonstrate additional concern for its customers' evaluations of satisfaction and service quality. This is because the sport product is discretionary and substitutable (Martin 1990). The sport product is discretionary in that it is not essential in the same way that products such as food, petrol and medical services are. That is, no one *has* to play netball or attend a basketball game. The sport product is substitutable in that there are many other organisations outside the sporting arena that can cater to the leisure and recreation needs of the would-be sports consumer. That is, the competitive market in which the sport organisation is but one player contains also the arts, cinemas and cultural organisations. Many of the needs satisfied by the sport product (e.g. excitement, escape, social facilitation) can be satisfied by products from other industries. Today, most sport marketers recognise the importance of satisfying spectators and participants and providing them with service experiences of high quality. Moreover, there is a growing acknowledgement in the sport industry that service quality and customer satisfaction can provide a competitive advantage in the quest for the sport customer's dollar.

Definitions

So what are service quality and customer satisfaction? To begin with, service quality and customer satisfaction are both a type of evaluation, and they can both mean different things to different people and in different contexts.

For the purposes of this book, service quality is defined in terms of excellence in accord with Parasuraman, Zeithaml and Berry (1988) and, more recently, Lovelock, Patterson and Walker (2001). That is, service quality is the spectator's or participant's judgement about how excellent a sport service or service component is. The more closely the spectator's or participant's perception approximates excellence, the higher his or her evaluation of service quality will be.

Customer satisfaction, on the other hand, is defined in terms of pleasurable fulfilment in accordance with Oliver (1997). That is, customer satisfaction is a judgement that a sport service, or service component, has provided a pleasurable level of consumption-related fulfilment. Like service quality, customer satisfaction is a matter of degree: that is, the greater the degree of pleasurable fulfilment, the greater the spectator's or participant's satisfaction.

Service quality and customer satisfaction are sometimes referred to interchangeably, but they are distinct, albeit-related constructs. The most readily agreed on and perhaps key point of differentiation between the two types of evaluation is that whereas satisfaction is experience-dependent, service quality is not. That is, a person must experience a sport product to be either satisfied or dissatisfied with it, but no experience is necessary to form perceptions of quality. For example, a general admission ticket holder of a sport stadium may never have experienced the spectator experience from a corporate suite but still have perceptions of the quality of that service.

Evaluations of what?

Thus far, service quality and customer satisfaction have both been referred to as evaluations. But exactly *what* do spectators and participants evaluate? In addition to the overall sport service, research demonstrates that sport customers evaluate a virtual plethora of service components, with the customers' summary satisfaction and perception of quality being a function of many different, 'smaller' evaluations.

The sheer breadth of the sport service, and thus the likelihood of multiple evaluations for the one sport product, is evident in the sport servuction model presented in chapter 7. The model illustrates the factors that influence the sport service experience. The visible part of the model has three components: the inanimate environment, or the facility itself; the contact personnel, such as ushers; and the customers. The model's invisible part consists of the invisible organisation and systems such as the marketing department. An astute sport marketer recognises that customers can and do form evaluations of the sport product pertaining to each of these components. For example, a spectator at a professional sport event might evaluate the cleanliness of the stadium's restrooms (inanimate environment), the courtesy and helpfulness of service staff (contact personnel), the management of unruly and annoying co-spectators (customers), and the ticketing (invisible organisation).

An understanding of the sport servuction model helps the marketer comprehend the sheer scope of the sport service and many aspects of the sport service, which contributes to a customer receiving a high-quality and satisfying experience. Furthermore, the model reminds us that things other than those which spectators and participants can see for themselves (i.e. the invisible component) have considerable propensity to influence customer satisfaction and service quality.

The core product and product extensions

Chapter 5 introduces two broad dimensions of the sport service (i.e. the core product and the product extensions) into which individual components of the service can be grouped. In mainstream marketing it has long been realised that customer satisfaction and service quality arise from both dimensions, with many arguing that, in the context of services, these evaluations are most strongly influenced by the non-core components. While sport marketers acknowledge the importance of both dimensions, until recently it was not known which dimension most strongly influenced customer evaluations. Australian research using season ticket holders indicates that, at least for the spectator service of professional sport organisations, the product extensions contribute most to customer satisfaction (van Leeuwen 2001). A sport specific service quality study that simultaneously addresses the differential effects of the core product and the product extensions has yet to be conducted.

The dominant role played by the product extensions in a spectator's satisfaction is good news for sport organisations because, as emphasised in chapter 5, it is the product extensions and not the game that fall under the control of sport marketers. That is, the sport marketer can more readily ensure the quality and hence manipulate customer satisfaction arising from such service aspects as merchandise and half-time entertainment than from the game itself.

Up to this point service quality and satisfaction have been discussed together. The next section will focus specifically on customer satisfaction, addressing the measurement of satisfaction, as well as its determinants and the process by which it arises. The latter half of the chapter will focus on service quality.

Measuring customer satisfaction

Given that customer satisfaction is so important, it is critical that the sport organisation is able to identify exactly how satisfied spectators and participants are with the overall service as well as with its individual components. Sport organisations can assess customer satisfaction levels both directly and indirectly, as described by Hoffman and Bateson (1997).

Indirect methods of customer satisfaction measurement include tracking and monitoring customer complaints, sales records, profits and customer retention. Although these indirect measures are useful, they should not be used in isolation. There are many other factors, external to customer satisfaction, that affect the number of complaints an organisation receives, its sales, profits and number of customers retained. Therefore, indirect measures should be combined with direct measures.

Direct measures of customer satisfaction vary. One of the most popular is the 'very satisfied–very dissatisfied' approach typically conducted via personal interviews or self-administered questionnaires. Customers are asked to indicate the extent to which they are satisfied or dissatisfied on typically a five- or seven-point scale, where 1 = very dissatisfied and 5 or 7 = very satisfied. This approach can be used for: (a) specific service aspects such as ticketing, staff courtesy and skilfulness of players; (b) broader service dimensions, such as the core product and product extensions; and (c) the entire sport experience, such as the season ticket or club membership.

For additional insight, the 'very satisfied–very dissatisfied' rating scale approach should be accompanied by a mechanism to identify why customers are either satisfied or dissatisfied. This can be achieved by simply requesting spectators and participants to identify exactly what was particularly satisfying or dissatisfying about their sport experience. This method has great diagnostic potential, as it enables the organisation both to pinpoint problems and seek ways to remedy them and to identify where the organisation is performing exceptionally well so as to ensure continued good performance. Spectators and participants can also be asked for their opinion on how improvements could be made to the organisation and its services. Sport customers are often highly identified and emotionally involved with the products they consume and are thus likely to be more forthcoming than most in providing customer satisfaction researchers with this sort of valuable information.

How satisfied should customers be?

Having conducted a satisfaction study, a sport organisation might identify that 83% of customers surveyed reported being satisfied or very satisfied. The sport organisation will probably give itself a pat on the back for having only 17% of customers less than satisfied. Another sport organisation may be equally self-congratulatory on identifying the average satisfaction rating for its customers as 5.5 out of a possible maximum of 7. However, according to Jones and Sasser (1995), the results for both of these organisations are not as good as you might initially think.

First, given suitable alternatives, less-than-satisfied customers, particularly participants and spectators who are not avid fans (as noted earlier in this chapter), are highly likely to defect to competing organisations. How many sport organisations can afford to lose 17% of their customer base (remembering the concept of customer lifetime value)? Also, customer satisfaction is a matter of degree, with customers ranging from being just satisfied through to very satisfied (perhaps even delighted). Jones and Sasser (1995) report that, in most circumstances, favourable outcomes such as loyalty and improved financial performance result only from the very highest levels of customer satisfaction. Finally, most customer satisfaction research, at least for studies involving a self-reporting methodology, reveals that the majority of respondents are satisfied (Peterson & Wilson 1992). That is, there appears to be a propensity among respondents to indicate higher than actual satisfaction levels. In other words, a sport organisation's spectators or participants may not really be as satisfied as its research indicates they are.

Sport organisations need to identify spectators and participants who are not completely satisfied in order to identify the cause of the less-than-optimal satisfaction and remedy it. Apart from asking survey respondents to identify these reasons via a customer satisfaction study, management can do this through complaint inducement mechanisms. Two strategies to encourage customer complaints described by Oliver (1997) and suitable for most sport organisations are: (a) free-to-the-customer communication channels such as toll-free numbers and postage-paid feedback cards; and (b) contacts instigated by the organisation, generally by telephone, asking customers if their sport service has been satisfactory.

The identification and successful handling of complaints has positive implications for sport organisations and the satisfaction of their customers. The work of Bitner, Booms and Tetrault (1990), for example, indicates that a well-handled complaint can alter the sport customer's evaluation of the product in a positive way. In other words, successful complaint resolution can result in what Lapidus and Pinkerton (1995) refer to as second-order satisfaction. The spectator or participant who was initially dissatisfied with some aspect of the sport service can experience satisfaction with the remainder of the service. Essentially, sport organisations should recognise the value of customer complaints. Complaints provide the organisation with an opportunity to identify and fix problems and consequently satisfy and retain their customers.

Customer satisfaction determinants

As noted earlier, it is not important merely to understand *how* satisfied a sport organisation's customers are, it is important also to understand *why* they are satisfied. Therefore a valuable body of research addresses the factors that contribute to, or determine, the satisfaction of customers. The three determinants that appear most regularly in the literature are expectations, perceived performance and disconfirmation. Together with customer satisfaction, these three determinants form the 'disconfirmation of expectations model' (DEM) as depicted in Figure 8.1. The DEM is based on the premise that customers form certain expectations of product performance, observe or experience the performance and form perceptions of the performance. It is proposed that these perceptions of performance will be compared to the customers' originally held expectations (Churchill & Surprenant 1982; Oliver 1997). This comparison can result in one of three outcomes–negative disconfirmation, zero disconfirmation (i.e. confirmation), or positive disconfirmation–which in turn influence the extent to which the customer is satisfied.

Negative disconfirmation results when performance falls short of expectations. Consider the fan attending the men's finals of the Australian Open who expects to experience a highly exciting and very close tennis match but who instead views a one-sided event that is over in three quick sets. *Zero disconfirmation*, or simply confirmation, occurs when performance equals expectations. Here our tennis fan experiences nothing more and nothing less than the quality of match she initially expected. *Positive disconfirmation* results when performance exceeds expectations. Our tennis fan not only experiences an exciting and close match but a complete 'nail biter'; to top it off she views the event from a fantastic seat and manages to secure her favourite player's autograph!

The original and simplest interpretation of the outcomes of the three different types of disconfirmation described previously is that satisfaction results from expectations being met or exceeded (with some arguing that delight, as opposed to mere satisfaction, arises when

FIGURE 8.1 **Disconfirmation of expectations model (DEM) of customer satisfaction**

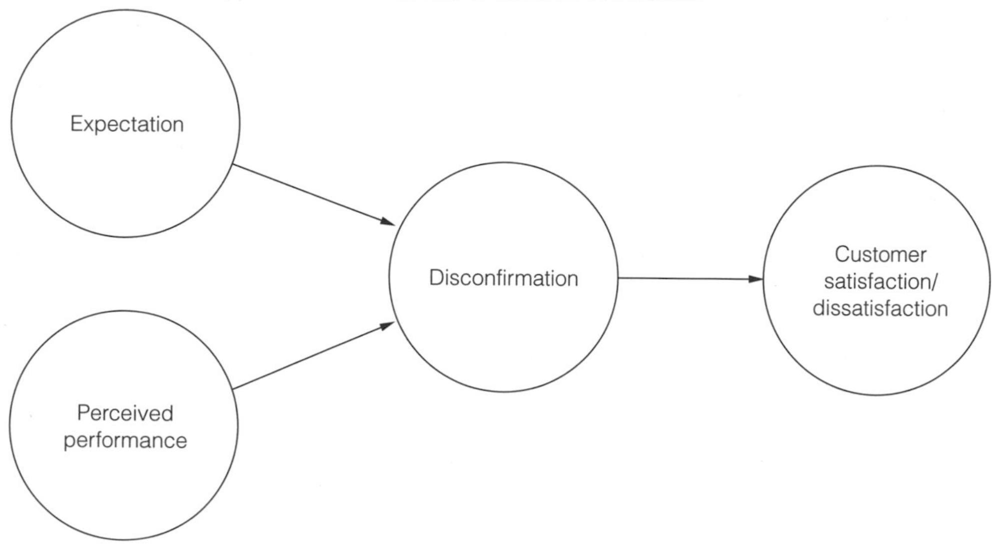

positive disconfirmation is extreme) and dissatisfaction results from expectations not being met. However, as will be outlined later, the outcomes of disconfirmation can vary with the expectation type used (Miller 1977; Swan & Trawick 1980).

Although the DEM and various extended versions of it appear regularly in the marketing literature, the model has not made inroads into the sport marketing literature. Nonetheless, some models of sport customer satisfaction have been developed. In the context of spectator sport, Madrigal (1995) found that the affective components of basking in reflected glory (BIRGing), or an individual's inclination to 'share the glory of a successful other with whom they are in some way associated' (Cialdini et al. 1976: 366), together with enjoyment, disconfirmation of expectations, team identification and quality of opponent, contributed to customer satisfaction with university women's basketball games. Also in the context of spectator sport, Wakefield and Blodgett (1994) identified that the quality of the sportscape (i.e. sport facility) as well as crowding, excitement and involvement influenced spectator satisfaction with the facility.

Perhaps the most comprehensive study of spectator satisfaction thus far is Van Leeuwen's (2001) research using a sample of season ticket holders from an Australian professional sport league. She accounted for the uniqueness of the spectator product when testing a model of customer satisfaction based on the DEM. Her model accounted for both the core product and product extensions of the spectator sport service, as well as the win–lose phenomenon of sport and the extent to which season ticket holders personally identify with a sport club (i.e. club identification). The results revealed the importance of considering the uniqueness of the sport service in sport-specific customer satisfaction research. That is, the spectator's club identification, as well as the win–lose phenomenon, was shown to greatly influence the amount of satisfaction season ticket holders experienced. The more highly identified the spectator and the more games won, the greater the season ticket holder's satisfaction. It is worth noting that the season ticket holders' identification with their club actually had the greatest influence on determining their satisfaction.

Service quality

Preceding sections of this chapter have been dedicated to customer satisfaction. This section focuses exclusively on quality. Quality in this book pertains to the perceived excellence of the sport product. The concept of quality in services such as sport is somewhat different from quality in the manufacturing sector. However, it was in the manufacturing sector that the concern for quality was born, and a basic understanding of quality as it pertains to manufactured goods provides a starting point for understanding service quality.

Goods quality versus service quality

The 1980s were marked by a quality revolution in terms of manufactured goods. Traditionally, quality had been determined by an end-of-production checking process whereby inspectors checked final products for defects. Inspectors sorted out the good from the bad, placing the defective products on the organisation's 'scrap heap'. The quality revolution of the 1980s involved a shift in focus from checking the end product to maximising the effectiveness and efficiency of the process resulting in the end product. Thus the first principle of the new quality era was doing it right the first time (Chase & Stewart 1994), with the ultimate aim being the production of zero defects.

The new way of ensuring quality was attributed to W. Edwards Deming, and is now commonly known as Total Quality Management (TQM). Deming introduced manufacturers to methods of statistical analysis that helped them to identify and reduce the variability in their production processes, thus enabling them to produce goods of consistent quality.

Although consistent quality is central to TQM, the zero-defects quality model of the manufacturing sector does not work well for service organisations. This is largely due to the unique nature of the service product, as noted in chapter 5—especially its characteristic of inseparable production and consumption, whereby the customer becomes part of the production process. For example, the NRL spectator experiences the game as it is produced, as does the netballer or golfer. The involvement of the customer in the production process inevitably results in some degree of variation in the production of the service, and where there is variation there is room for error or, in TQM terminology, a 'defective' service experience. Moreover, even if the quality of the service is without variation, service quality is a matter of perception (i.e. the customer's perception), and two people who experience the same service may thus have very different perceptions of its quality. This is particularly so in the context of sport, where two customers, whether players or spectators, are barracking or playing for opposing teams. Further, an individual's perception of service quality may vary from one experience to the next due to myriad factors often beyond the organisation's control, such as his or her mood.

All in all, service quality is more complex and more difficult to achieve than quality in manufacturing. However, sport organisations find it even more challenging to ensure the quality of their products than do other organisations. This is due to the sport organisation's inability to control the core sport product–that is, the game itself. As mentioned in chapter 5, the uncontrollability of the core sport product has resulted in marketers focusing on the product extensions. Whereas the game itself is beyond the marketer's sphere of influence, he or she can do much to influence the quality of the product extensions of the service, including the half-time entertainment, ticketing processes, merchandise, and design and cleanliness of the facility.

Modelling service quality

Sport marketers can improve the quality of their services by first understanding how service quality is determined. The service quality process can be understood in terms of a number of gaps, as described by Parasuraman, Zeithaml and Berry (1985) and depicted in Figure 8.2. These are gaps between the expectations and perceptions of three different groups: customers, management, and employees. The most important gap, the service gap, is the difference between what customers expect from the service and what they perceive they have actually got. The service gap is a function of four other gaps, including the knowledge gap, standards gap, delivery gap and communications gap. Each of these four gaps is described below.

FIGURE 8.2 **Conceptual model of service quality**

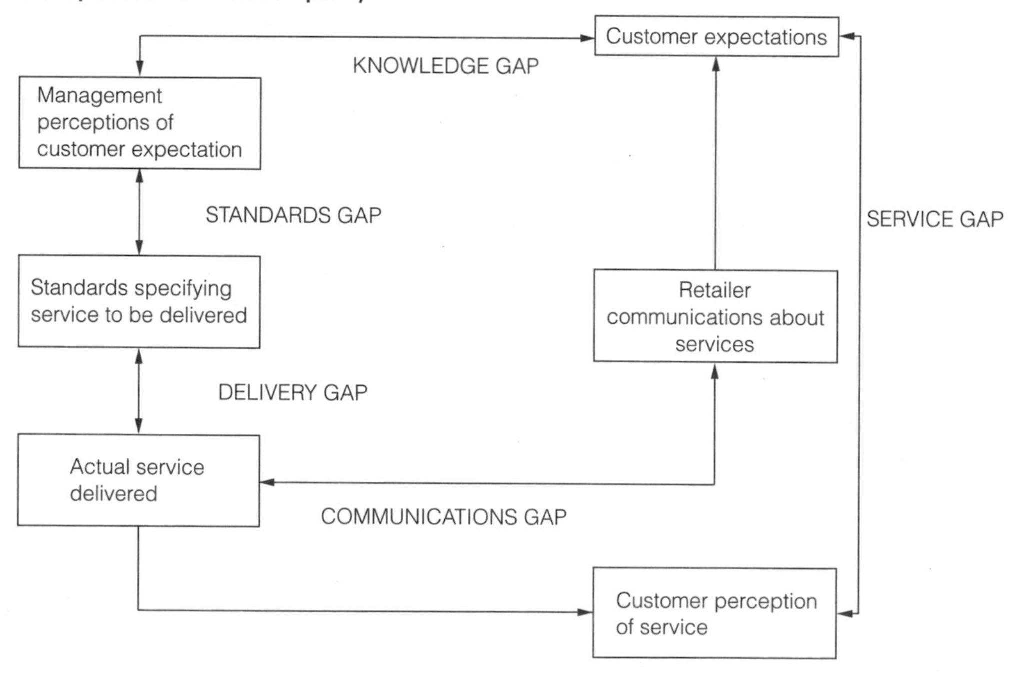

Source: Hoffman & Bateson (1997). Reprinted with permission of South-Western College Publishing, a division of Thomson Learning.

1 *The knowledge gap*—the gap between customer expectations of service and management perceptions of these expectations. This gap occurs when what management believes customers expect is different from what customers really expect. For example, the program manager of a community sport centre might believe that players expect hour-long games of netball when they would instead prefer the opportunity to play shorter but additional games.

2 *The standards gap*—the gap between management's perceptions of customer expectations and the organisation's service quality specifications. This gap occurs when the organisation does not have the resources to deliver what the customer expects, or when management is indifferent to providing the expected levels of service. For example, the marketing manager of a professional basketball team may be aware that season ticket holders expect opportunities for more interaction with players but not see this as a priority. Alternatively, the marketer may be fully cognisant of the season ticket holders' expectations but have difficulty meeting them given the numerous other commitments of the players.

3 *The delivery gap*—the gap between the organisation's service quality specifications and actual service delivery. This gap occurs when quality specifications are not met, and is typically due to a lack of willingness or ability of the service personnel. For example, even though an aquatic centre's service charter may stipulate that its service staff be friendly, courteous and helpful to customers at all times, its staff may be either unwilling to go this extra distance for customers or simply not have the customer service and interpersonal skills enabling them to do so.

4 *The communications gap*—the gap between actual service delivery and external communications about the service. This gap occurs when the organisation promises more in its advertising and other communications than it can actually deliver. A classic example would be a professional sport club's advertisements promising its supporters a win at the next home game. (A basic premise of sport marketing is that winning is one thing that you can never guarantee and that you therefore shouldn't promise!)

In summary, sport marketers need to be cognisant of each of these gaps and how they contribute to spectators and participants getting what they expected and consequently their evaluations of service quality. Sport marketers will be able to improve the quality of their services by identifying and then closing each of the knowledge, standards, delivery and communication gaps.

Measuring service quality: SERVQUAL

Just as Parasuraman et al. (1985) developed the original gap model, depicted in a modified format in Figure 8.2, to enable us to better conceptualise the service quality process, they also later developed the most popular measure of service quality, SERVQUAL. The SERVQUAL instrument is based on the disconfirmation of expectations paradigm and the five service quality dimensions of tangibles, reliability, responsiveness, assurance and empathy (Parasuraman et al. 1988: 23):

- tangibles—physical facilities, equipment, and appearance of personnel;
- reliability—ability to perform the promised service dependably and accurately;

- responsiveness–willingness to help customers and provide prompt services;
- assurance–knowledge and courtesy of employees and their ability to inspire trust and confidence;
- empathy–caring, individualised attention that the firm provides its customers.

The SERVQUAL instrument comprises two sections. The first is an expectations section, containing 22 statements to measure customer expectations of excellent firms in a specific service industry (e.g. the professional sport industry). Each of these statements pertains to one of the five dimensions mentioned previously (i.e. tangibles, reliability, responsiveness, assurance, empathy). The second is a perceptions section, containing a matching set of 22 statements to measure customer perceptions of the particular organisation within the service industry being evaluated (e.g. Collingwood Football Club).

Customer expectations are measured on a seven-point scale, anchored by the labels of 'not at all essential' and 'absolutely essential'. Customer perceptions are also measured on a seven-point scale, anchored by 'strongly agree' and 'strongly disagree'. The results of the expectations and perceived performance sections are then compared to determine the 'gap scores' for each of the five dimensions. Large gaps indicate poorer than expected service and hence low service quality. The smaller the gap, the higher the evaluation of service quality and therefore the better. As with the 'very satisfied-very dissatisfied' approach to customer satisfaction measurement, the SERVQUAL approach enables researchers to assess service quality at the micro-level (e.g. ticketing procedures), the broader dimension level (e.g. tangibles) and the macro-level (e.g. the entire sport product).

Although SERVQUAL is the most popular service quality measure, it has attracted some criticism. The most common criticism is that the instrument's five dimensions (tangibles, reliability, responsiveness, assurance, empathy) can often not be replicated in different industries. In other words, the dimensions are relevant to some industries but not others. However, most researchers accept that SERVQUAL remains an important diagnostic tool for evaluating an organisation's service quality performance. Furthermore, and as indicated by its developers, SERVQUAL is an instrument that can help service organisations improve their service by better understanding the expectations and perceptions of its customers. As when measuring customer satisfaction, when using SERVQUAL sport marketers are advised to seek additional qualitative information from spectators and participants, including why they evaluate the service the way that they do and how the service might be improved.

Measuring sport service quality: TEAMQUAL and QUESC

Given the generic nature of SERVQUAL, its developers readily acknowledged that it should be modified to accommodate the peculiarities of certain industries. Examples of modifications of SERVQUAL in the context of sport are many and varied, including McDonald, Sutton and Milne's (1995) TEAMQUAL instrument for spectator sport and Kim and Kim's (1995) QUESC instrument for sport centres. These studies provide evidence of how SERVQUAL, although not perfect, is a good starting point for sport organisations wishing to evaluate service quality.

McDonald et al. (1995) modified SERVQUAL to accommodate the professional team sport spectator service. Specifically, they incorporated additional items into the instrument to account for the multiple-encounter nature of the spectator service (e.g. encounters with ticketing staff, concessionaires and merchandisers). Examples of some of the items pertaining to ticketing staff included ushers giving prompt service, ushers being consistently courteous, and ushers having the knowledge to answer questions. Developed in the United States in the context of professional basketball, their final instrument, TEAMQUAL, comprised 39 items grounded in the five SERVQUAL dimensions.

Kim and Kim (1995) developed their 33-item service quality instrument, the QUESC, in the context of Korean sport centres. Although they used the five SERVQUAL dimensions as a starting point for their research, their final results identified eleven distinct service quality dimensions (i.e. ambiance, employee attitude, employee reliability, information available, programs offered, personal considerations, price, privilege, ease of mind, stimulation and convenience). The dimensions they identified support the industry-specific nature of the service quality construct and should serve to remind sport managers of the necessity of accommodating the uniqueness of their particular service in service quality evaluations and research. Some of the items comprising the QUESC pertained to the variety of sports on offer, instructions for accessing or using facilities, and privacy.

Expectations: a better understanding

Having read the previous sections of this chapter, you should now realise that a sport customer's expectations play an important role in his or her evaluations of quality and satisfaction. The centrality of expectations to both constructs merits further discussion.

Just as it is accepted that expectations are the standards customers use to compare product performance in order to arrive at a level of satisfaction, so is it accepted that the disconfirmation of expectations process is key to determining perceptions of service quality. What is believed to differentiate the service quality process from the customer satisfaction process, though, is the type of expectation used.

Miller (1977) acknowledged four different types of customer expectations in his research. These included ideal (can be) expectations, expected (will be) expectations, minimum tolerable (must be) expectations, and deserved (should be) expectations. Ideal expectations operate at a wished-for level (e.g. *I expect my tennis coach to help me perfect my serve in one lesson*). Expected levels of performance are much more realistic, and reflect the probable or most likely performance (e.g. *I expect my tennis coach to help me improve my serve after several lessons*). Minimum tolerable expectations reflect the minimal level of performance that will be tolerated or considered acceptable (e.g. *I expect my tennis coach to improve my serve to the point where I can at least get the ball over the net on most attempts*). Finally, deserved expectations reflect the performance to which customers believe they are entitled given their inputs or investments (e.g. *I expect my tennis coach to help me greatly improve my serve after several lessons as long as I put in plenty of practice by myself too*). Another type of expectation falling somewhere between ideal and deserved expectations is what the customer desires.

Service quality studies in accord with the conceptualisation of quality in terms of excellence typically use ideal expectations. Customer satisfaction studies traditionally utilised predictive (will be) expectations (Oliver 1993; Parasuraman et al. 1988), although studies employing higher-level expectations such as deserved expectations (e.g. Patterson 1993) and desired expectations (e.g. Swan & Trawick 1980; Swan, Trawick & Carroll 1982) are

FIGURE 8.3 **Disconfirmation of expectations model (DEM) of customer satisfaction featuring low 'will be' expectations**

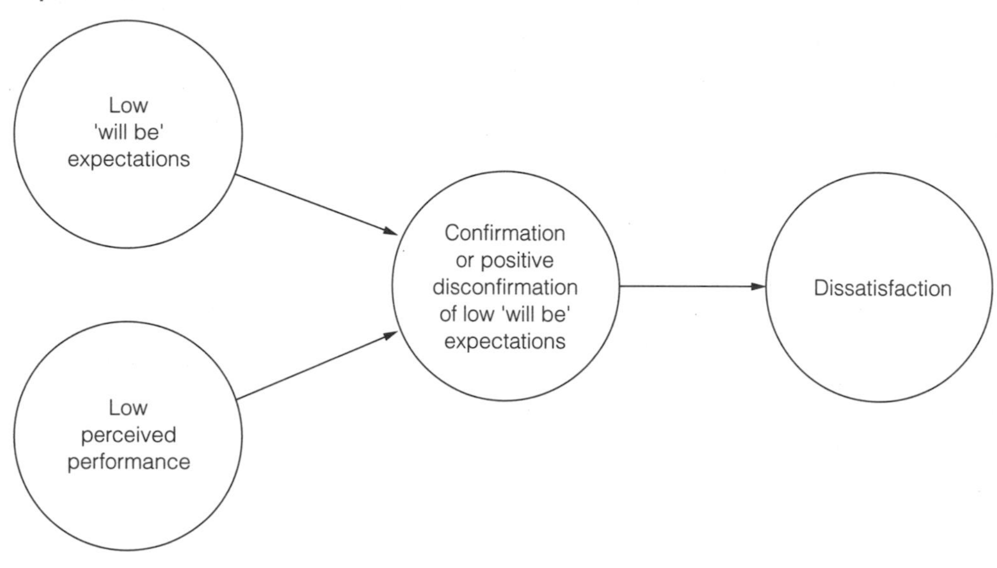

increasingly common. This trend towards higher-level expectations was necessary because the DEM posits customer satisfaction as the outcome of confirmation and positive disconfirmation but fails to account for the possibility of very low expectations. Yet it is possible that dissatisfaction as opposed to satisfaction, as depicted in Figure 8.3, may result when very low predictive expectations exist (Oliver 1997; Swan et al. 1982).

It does not make sense that customers would be satisfied if they anticipated a poor service experience and received exactly that. Consider the example of a spectator who watched her favoured team lose the National netball grand final by 27 goals when she had already anticipated that such a loss was likely (i.e. confirmation of low 'will be' expectations). Nor does it make sense that customers would be satisfied if they received only a slightly poor service. Consider the case of the lap swimmer who arrived at the aquatic centre on Boxing Day to find his favourite lane crowded but not quite to the extent he'd imagined (i.e. positive disconfirmation of low 'will be' expectations). In these examples, irrespective of the service being equal to or better than expected, it was still nothing to be really satisfied with. In brief, the use of higher level expectations diminishes the possibility of dissatisfaction arising from confirmation or positive disconfirmation.

Irrespective of the type of expectations spectators and participants hold and the relationship of each to service quality and customer satisfaction, it is important for sport marketers to understand the influence they have over what their customers expect. Expectations are influenced by many factors, several of which are under the control of the sport organisation, including (a) promises made by the sport organisation, for example through advertising and other communications; (b) tangible cues in the physical environment, predominantly the sport facility itself; and (c) pricing.

Given the centrality of expectations to service quality and customer satisfaction and the influence that sport organisations can exert on their customers' expectations, it is essential that sport marketers learn to manage what it is that their customers expect from them. Sport marketers must not promise more than their organisations can realistically deliver. They should ensure that the physical environment with which their customers interact is of the highest possible standard in terms of aesthetic appeal and cleanliness. Likewise, they should ensure that product prices are commensurate with product quality.

Summary

This chapter explored customer satisfaction and service quality. The provision of high-quality and subsequently satisfying sport services was linked to organisational success through a number of positive consequences for the sport organisation, one of the most important being customer retention.

Customer satisfaction and service quality were described as types of evaluations. It was noted that these evaluations can be of the overall spectator or participant service, as well as individual aspects of each service. Given the sheer breadth of the sport service, it is necessary for myriad factors to be successfully managed in order for customers to enjoy the sport experience and thus evaluate it positively. Due to the uncontrollability of the core product, though, sport marketers must realise that they have minimal influence over perceptions of quality and feelings of satisfaction arising from the game itself. As such, sport organisations must focus on ensuring that the product extensions are of the highest possible standard.

This chapter also outlined ways in which customer satisfaction and service quality can be measured. It is recommended that sport marketers ask their customers not only how satisfied they are and how high they perceive the quality of the spectator or participant service to be but also why they perceive the service the way they do. This combined approach enables sport marketers to identify things their organisation is doing particularly well, together with those things that need improving. When measuring customer satisfaction and service quality it is important to note that sport marketers should not be complacent about less-than-excellent levels of customer satisfaction and service quality. Suboptimal evaluations often present opportunities for competitors, especially when the sport customer is not an avid fan.

In addition to emphasising the importance of identifying the extent to which customers are satisfied and perceive the service to be of high quality, the chapter described the processes by which customers arrive at their satisfaction and quality judgements. Customer satisfaction was shown to arise from disconfirmed expectations of the sport service in accordance with the DEM, with the customer's disconfirmation being the key influence on whether he or she was satisfied or dissatisfied. Alternatively, service quality was modelled in accord with Parasuraman et al. (1985), who conceptualised it in terms of a number of 'gaps' (i.e. service, knowledge, standards, delivery, communications) between the expectations and perceptions of customers, management and employees.

In closing, the chapter drew attention to the centrality of customer expectations to both customer satisfaction and service quality. Sport marketers need to acknowledge that customers can hold several different types of expectation and that evaluations of satisfaction and quality will vary with the expectation type used. More importantly though, sport marketers must understand those factors that influence the expectations held by spectators and participants and learn to manage them successfully. Through identifying, understanding and managing expectations, sport organisations will be better placed to provide high-quality and thus satisfying sport services which in turn may provide them with a competitive advantage in the quest for the sport customer's dollar.

CASE STUDY

A problem of quality

The Springdale Indoor Sports and Aquatic Centre (SISAC) opened nine years ago and has made a reasonable profit ever since—that is, until recently. Six months ago another centre, offering many of the same services as SISAC, opened not more than 4 km away.

Up until the opening of the new centre, SISAC typically operated at peak capacity. Community sport groups regularly booked all of the courts, the three pools were always busy, and you could barely squeeze another fitness enthusiast into the gymnasium or aerobics classes. The snack bar and sports shop also enjoyed healthy patronage.

Although the manager, Ritchie Sotiriadou, anticipated that some SISAC customers would inevitably be lost to the new centre, he had no idea that the extent of customer attrition would be so huge. Member retention for the once lucrative fitness centre was down by 38% and new member sales were at an all-time low, despite resources being heavily expended on several promotional campaigns. Meanwhile, the resident masseuse had walked out due to lack of customers and the swim school had moved to another pool. Furthermore, the new centre had lured the ever-popular netball competition away and it looked as though the basketballers were set to pack their bags and follow suit.

Ritchie shook his head in despair as he reflected on the centre's lost customers, lost sales and subsequent financial difficulties. Given the similarity of the two centres' services he simply couldn't comprehend why SISAC's customer base was continuing to shrink while his competitor was going from strength to strength. He believed that the novelty of the new centre should have long since worn off and that business at SISAC should be back to normal. In particular, Ritchie couldn't understand why many of SISAC's previously loyal fitness centre members of three and four years had left. Nor could he understand why the community sport groups that organised the netball and basketball competitions, as well as the owner of the swim school, could so easily turn their backs on what he'd considered successful and rewarding relationships with his centre.

Sure, there had been customer complaints over the years, sometimes quite a few, but Ritchie believed that some people were just born complainers and it was impossible to please everyone all the time. The problem with customers, he often told himself, is that they expect too much. He did acknowledge that the junior staff at the reception counter were to blame for some of the complaints. Nevertheless, he refused to employ more experienced and expensive staff, as he reasoned that all his existing employees had to do was stick to what was outlined in SISAC's customer service and policy manual. Anyway, as far as he could determine, many of the complaining customers had just kept coming back and spending money, so what was the point of listening to them in the first place? Irrespective of customer complaints, including those due to his staff, Ritchie had always been adamant that he knew his job and he knew what the customers wanted. Indeed, with years of experience under his belt Ritchie figured that market research was a waste of resources, especially when money was tight and he was expected to turn a profit.

The devastating loss of customers, however, was eating away at Ritchie's confidence, not to mention SISAC's bottom line, and it was blatantly obvious to him that something had to be done—he just didn't know what. He didn't want to engage in a price war with his new competitor, nor another expensive advertising campaign, but saw no other option. As he sat at his desk contemplating the implications of introducing a new pricing strategy, Rosanne Taylor, his newly appointed marketing assistant, walked into his office and asked the question that would eventually help him solve the centre's problem. 'Ritchie', she said, 'what do you know about service quality?'

Questions

1. What do you think Ritchie's answer was?
2. How satisfied do you think SISAC's customers are? Why?
3. What evidence is there that SISAC provides poor service quality?
4. Which of the service quality gaps exist at SISAC, and what evidence is there of these gaps?
5. What actions would you recommend that Ritchie take to narrow the service gap?

9

The sport promotion mix

Stage 1—Identification of marketing opportunities

▼

Stage 2—Strategy determination

Step 5—Determine core marketing strategy

Marketing and service mix—sport product, pricing, place (physical evidence, people, process), customer satisfaction

Promotion mix—sales promotion

Step 6—Determine tactics and performance benchmarks

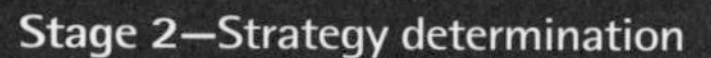

Stage 3—Strategy implemention, evaluation and adjustment

CHAPTER OBJECTIVES

Chapter 9 introduces the sport promotion mix. This chapter provides a model of communication that underpins the communication process and is driven by the AIDA buyer readiness model. The traditional elements of the promotion mix are discussed, including advertising, public relations and publicity, and sales promotion. In addition, elements special and important to sport are added, including sponsorship and promotional licensing. Many of the components of the sport promotion mix are the subject of separate chapters. This chapter introduces these elements and specifically examines the types of promotion and product demand, as well as concentrating on the importance of sales promotion for sport.

After studying this chapter you should be able to:

1 Understand the communication process and the buyer readiness model AIDA.
2 Articulate the concepts related to promotion strategy.
3 Recognise the components of the promotion mix.
4 Establish procedures for selecting the correct promotion mix.
5 Develop strategies to determine the applicability of personal selling.
6 Comprehend the importance of the escalator principle.
7 Develop programs and techniques to increase sales.

HEADLINE STORY

The money-back guarantee

> Bill Veeck, the great pioneer in North American sport marketing during the 1940s and 1950s, always argued that promotion must be more than simply amusing or entertaining...it had to create conversation. His contention was that when a fan left the ball game he had to talk about what he had seen. To this end he offered 'the money back guarantee'. (Veeck & Linn 1962: 119)

In what was a complex world, Veeck articulated three simple principles that set him apart from other sport promoters. He insisted that a city owed nothing to a baseball (sport) team; that baseball (sport) was not a civic monument and had to be hustled; and, most importantly, that 'every day was Mardi Gras and every fan was King'. In the process of expressing these three principles Veeck recognised three major dimensions of sport: the fans, the game and the periphery. Furthermore, while acknowledging the importance of a winning team, he argued that the game itself had to be attractively packaged and aggressively promoted, and that the comfort and satisfaction of the fan had to be ensured.

Nevertheless, Kahn (1972) argues that more than anything Veeck liked to win. He contends that Veeck's objectives were to have a winning team and great promotion—failing that, a winning team and poor promotion, and if all else failed a losing team with great promotion. The fundamental belief in this instance was that great promotion would assist in maintaining consumption or minimise supporter drop-off during on-field decline.

In the Australian context, World Series Cricket during the 1970s, Australian Rugby League (ARL) in the 1980s, the ARU in the 1990s and the Australian Football League throughout the 1990s and into the new millennium not only heavily promoted their respective core products—they also increasingly highlighted the product extensions. While superstar athletes, media-created celebrities, entertainment, excitement and glamour may have resulted in a different type of fan consuming sport products, the success of night and midweek contests suggests that sport promoters tapped into an emerging sport spectator trend: a trend where the athletic contest is only part of the total entertainment package.

In an era when contemporary sport consumers are derided by long-suffering traditional fans as 'theatre goers', it is clear that sport events are no longer confined to the playing field with the spectators 'looking in from the outside'. Fans are now part of the event and construct the spectacle while simultaneously consuming it. The 'Mexican wave', various team chants, the interaction of team mascots with the crowd and the use of contemporary music are all examples of the nexus between on-field and off-field activity. Promotion is now an integral and vital part of the sport experience. How the sport marketer and promoter manipulate the promotion mix will be vital to the success of the game and even the long-term viability of the sport.

Promotion strategy defined

Broadly, a promotion strategy is a controlled, integrated program of communication designed to present an organisation and its products or services clearly to prospective customers. Furthermore, it communicates needs-satisfying attributes in order to facilitate sales. This in turn contributes to long-term profits. Underpinning promotional strategies is the communication process, and an understanding of such processes is required to enable the formulation of relevant strategies. Communication occurs when an individual attends to a message and attributes importance to it. Once information processing occurs, communication is said to have taken place (Cravens 1994). Sportview 9.1 is an example of broad promotional strategy.

SPORTVIEW 9.1

The Souths revival

The promotional strategy to revive the fortunes of the South Sydney Rugby League Club (the Rabbitohs) is an example of a concentrated multifaceted promotional campaign that led to stunning results. Briefly, rugby league was established in Australia in 1907 with the South Sydney Rabbitohs admitted to the competition in 1908. Historically it has been one of the more successful teams in the competition, with 20 championships over its 94-year history. However, in 1999 the National Rugby League announced that it would exclude the Rabbitohs from the 2000 season as it did not meet the criteria established for inclusion in the competition in the post-Superleague era. The decision was based on home and away crowds, gate receipts, sponsorship and profitability. While other clubs in a similar position decided to amalgamate, South Sydney rejected this solution and as a result was expelled for the upcoming season, but in 2002 the Rabbitohs were welcomed back to the competition.

While the courts eventually made the decision that allowed the Rabbitohs to re-enter the competition, a sustained promotional effort by those associated with the club resulted in the adoption of a belief by the public that Souths had been an unnecessary victim of a capricious NRL. Furthermore, the dissemination of this belief was unprecedented in modern sporting history.

Fundamentally, for Souths to be readmitted to the competition they had to plead their case before the court. This would involve a substantial sum of money, which was beyond their current financial capacity. One arm of the strategy was to recruit high-profile individuals (e.g. radio personality Andrew Denton, movie star Russell Crowe) to support the cause. Grassroots support was also solicited. In 1999, 40000 people attended a 'Reclaim the Game' rally, and $300000 was raised at an auction to provide a fighting fund for the upcoming court battles. In 2000/01 street marches took place in Sydney with in excess of 80000 in attendance. The trade union movement also rallied to the South Sydney cause.

While the decision to return South Sydney to the elite competition was made in the Federal Court, it was the result of a sustained campaign aimed at promoting the history, tradition, viability and community nature of the game and team.

DeVito (1999: 5) notes that 'communication can vary from self-thought through to that which may involve millions of people'. For example, think of the number of spectators that watched the 2000 Olympic Games or the 2002 World Cup Football on television. Also think of that individual in front of the television willing his team/athlete to be victorious. The spectator is engaging in intrapersonal communication at the same time as experiencing very public communication.

Conceptually, communication involves the message context and source, the intended receivers, the encoding and decoding processes, message pathway and interference (or noise), and the outcomes. However, as these variables are broken down the true complex nature of communication is realised.

Devito (1999: 9) suggests that 'there are four contexts for communication and they are the physical, cultural, socio-psychological and temporal'. Significantly, all are relevant to the sport experience. The physical context refers to the space in which the communication takes place. An example of this is the difference in crowd behaviour at various sporting contests. The spectators at a Super 12s game at Aussie Stadium in Sydney will be far more vocal during the play than a tennis crowd in Melbourne during a final of the Australian Open. While it is perfectly acceptable to abuse the referee, albeit in a witty manner, at a football match, the same cannot be said for tennis. Similarly, different cultural groups may require, and exhibit, different communication processes. Witness the differences between the motorcycle fan at Phillip Island and the polo spectator at Werribee. In both instances the communication process may alter according to other variables, such as the closeness of the score, injury or even changes in the weather. This exemplifies the social-psychological context. Finally, the temporal context relates to the position of the message in time and space. A winning performance is likely to result in other patterns of communication than losing. A favourite team or athlete winning would be the cause for celebration, whereas a loss, especially an unexpected one, could result in sadness and a desire to be alone.

Once the context has been established, any resultant message is both encoded by its source and decoded by its receiver. Messages do not always need to be verbal, as non-verbal cues are often more powerful. The use of a previous elite performance to promote an upcoming event is an example of this. In the lead-up to the Commonwealth Games in Manchester in 2002 the Seven Network highlighted the earliest performances of contemporary elite athletes, which conveyed the message that the Games might be the birthplace of new Australian champions—hence their viewing should not be missed. However, it is important when messages are encoded, whatever the medium, that they are not so abstruse as to confound the intended receiver. Reebok's clever yet somewhat mystifying television ad in the late 1980s which featured the slogan UBU left many viewers scratching their heads. This advertisement was eventually pulled, as the message of individuality, non-conformity and independence was lost on the intended audience. DeVito (1999: 9-11) suggests that 'understanding how communication works (communication competence); cultural specificity, acquired knowledge and previous experience are all critical to an appropriate encoding/decoding process'.

The greatest inhibitor to successful message conveyance is 'noise'. Noise can be physical, psychological, or simply an unintended interpretation or decoding of a message. The effective sport promotion uses a simple, non-confronting, unambiguous message to highlight a service or product. Nike's 'Just Do It' is probably the most obvious example of this.

Finally, the intended consequence of the communication process is to produce a change in behaviour. In most instances it is to predispose the intended recipient towards the product or service featured in the message. Ultimately, the desired outcome is usually the consumption of the product or service.

A response model

As well as understanding the communication process, it has become increasingly apparent that there is a need to comprehend the buyer readiness model that essentially drives the communication process. Whereas communication models are generally driven from the producer, buyer readiness models are end user-driven. According to Belch and Belch (2001), there are three main categories of response models: traditional response hierarchy models, alternative response models, and integrated information response models. Within each category there are a numbers of subcategories. This section focuses on the AIDA model, which is one of the four traditional response hierarchy models. All four models comprise a cognitive, affective and behavioural stage, with AIDA an acronym for attention, interest, desire, action. In this instance the promotion aims at getting the consumer's attention, creating an interest in and a desire to purchase the product or service, and finally engaging in an exchange process, which usually involves the actual purchase.

In 2002 Foxtel added a dedicated Australian Rules football channel to its cable network. The Network cleverly adopted an AIDA-type model in encouraging uptake by potential subscribers. Well before the channel actually appeared on the screen, other cable stations promoted the day on which the new channel would become live, hence generating *attention*. During the initial phase broadcast was provided free to existing cable subscribers, thus generating *interest*. In this initial telecast, phase highlights packages were shown which demonstrated the more sensational aspects of the game. Moreover, promises were made that each week every game would be telecast. Consequently, it did not matter which team was supported, the fan would get to see that team's game on television. The result was that a *desire* was created. Finally, to encourage the fan to take up the package, special financial inducements were offered for early *action* relating to subscription to the service. The AIDA model was clearly in effect in this instance.

Promotion and product demand

As previously indicated, the ultimate goal of promotion strategy is to stimulate demand for a particular product. However, before strategies are developed there is a need to understand the type of demand that exists, which may be:

- generic; or
- brand; and
- direct or indirect.

Generic demand is the demand for a particular product category. At a national level, a government policy may promote sport and recreation as a means of raising health and fitness levels among the population at large. In this case tennis clubs, fitness centres, sports stores, and recreational and tourist accommodation can all benefit from the generic campaign. Occasionally a market leader unilaterally engages in generic advertising when industry sales are down.

At a league, competition or association level, sport marketers engage in promoting the sport or competition while leaving clubs to their own marketing devices. For example, during the Australian Open, Tennis Australia will create a generic demand for tennis by promoting the sport in general. It is then up to local clubs and associations to establish localised promotion strategies allowing them to tap into the generic demand.

Most consumer promotion is directed towards boosting brand demand. The Sydney Swifts, the Adelaide Thunderbirds and the Queensland Firebirds of the National Netball League (2002 Commonwealth Bank Trophy) all adopt specific promotion strategies in an attempt to encourage consumption and support of their particular teams–the brands. In the process, the demand for the generic product (i.e. the national league) is increased. Occasionally brand switching may occur when for example a Melbourne Phoenix fan becomes a Melbourne Kestrels fan, but in the main the promotion strategy results in better industry (i.e. national league) sales, or in this case an increase in the number of fans attending women's netball games.

The majority of consumer promotion is an attempt to stimulate direct demand for a specific product. Sporadically, a manufacturer may promote an element of a product, which may stimulate demand for that component, which in turn may directly stimulate indirect demand for a particular brand. For example, lycra manufacturers promote the attributes of lycra, which indirectly stimulates demand for products made using the substance, such as fitness and cycling apparel.

Irrespective of the type of demand, the audience targeted by the promotion strategy invariably remains the same. Current and future customers, stockholders, the public at large and special-interest groups are all existing or potential consumers. However, responses to promotion strategies will vary based on myriad consumer behaviour factors (discussed in chapter 3) and models of response such as AIDA. Acknowledging such differences, sport promoters need to tailor marketing strategies in order to attract specific consumer groups. This is done by fully comprehending the stages in promotion strategy development and then manipulating the promotion mix.

Stages in promotion strategy development

In establishing promotion strategy development, an organisation needs to undertake the following steps.

As Figure 9.1 shows, first an initial analysis of the specific situation is required, when the following questions should be addressed: What is the general direction of the firm in the prevailing social and economic climate? What are the product or service's strengths and weaknesses compared with those of the competition? Are there legal, technological or distribution issues that need to be factored into the decision making?

Once an analysis of the situation has been undertaken, objectives need to be developed. Consideration here should the composition of the target market, what the sales objectives are and, equally importantly, the message to be communicated.

Once the objectives are known, programs need to be established that will enable the objectives to be accomplished. These may include the creative and media strategies to be employed, the sales promotion to be utilised, reseller support programs, and the budget that underpins the breadth and scope of the programs.

FIGURE 9.1 **Stages in promotion strategy development**

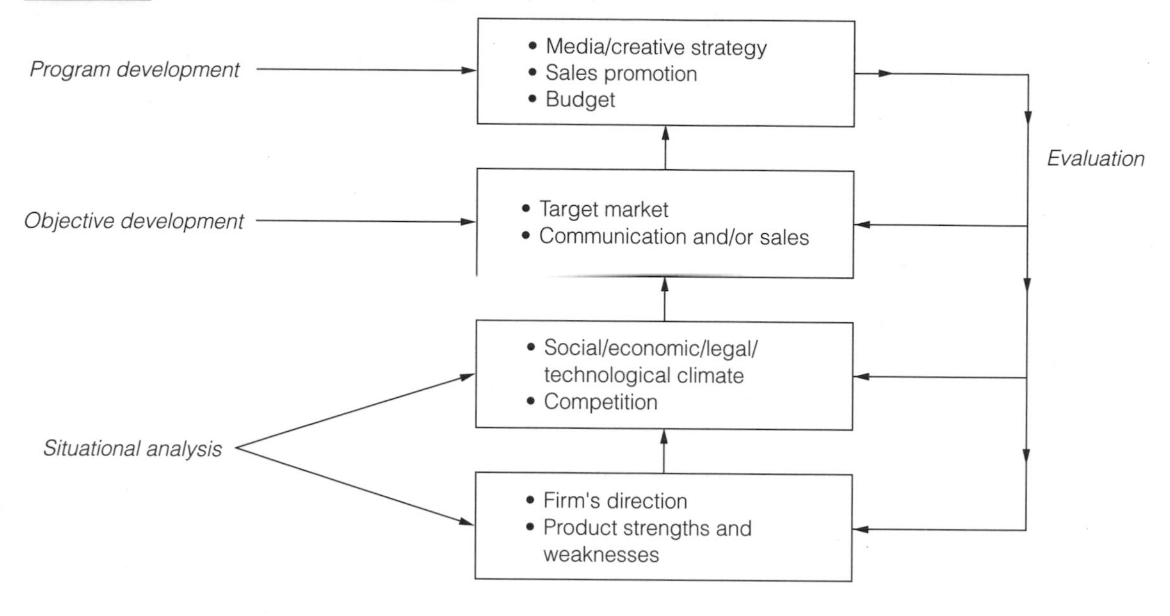

Concurrently with program execution, a system of evaluation, or for monitoring the effectiveness of such strategies, needs to be rigorously implemented. These evaluative mechanisms need to be specifically linked to the stated objectives. By clearly defining the stages in promotion strategy development, an organisation not only establishes a framework for future activities but also, by constantly using it as a reference source, creates an excellent evaluative mechanism.

Defining the promotion mix

The growth of World Series Cricket in the late 1970s provides one example of the multifaceted nature of the promotion mix. Sportview 9.2 shows how one-day cricket was positioned as an alternative form of the game and how it was promoted.

SPORTVIEW 9.2

World Series Cricket: the watershed in sport promotion

In the late 1970s, the establishment of World Series Cricket was an excellent example of a controlled promotion strategy. During the period 1977–79, the World Series was positioned as an alternative to the traditional game. In the process, it not only used the best athletes the sport had to offer, it also radically altered the tone of cricket by creating stylistic changes in the game's production and presentation. In numerous ways the sport was repackaged as a television spectacle to captivate the home viewer. Multiple camera angles, coloured uniforms, on-screen graphics and various auditory devices were introduced, which elevated the entertainment level of the game. Sport and entertainment fans in general, not only cricket devotees, were captivated.

Simultaneously, other promotion strategies were implemented—at the ground, on television, on radio, in newspapers and magazines, and in department stores and supermarkets across the country—which resulted in multiple layers of cricket consumption. World Series Cricket sold books, fruit, paint and even lunchboxes, as well as cricket apparel. Furthermore the catchy song used to promote World Series Cricket ('C'mon Aussie, C'mon') became one of the most popular songs on Australian radio. Commenting on the song, Haigh (1993: 220) indicated 'top rating [Sydney] radio station 2SM played "C'mon Aussie C'mon" until its needles were blunt'.

The message World Series Cricket communicated through its promotional strategy was one tinged with excitement, glamour, aggression, superstars and non-stop entertainment. Judging by the numbers that turned up to see World Series Cricket limited overs games, it is obvious in hindsight that the successful promotion strategy adopted by the organisation for cricket worldwide also marked a watershed in sport marketing in Australia.

The promotion mix consists of advertising, public relations and publicity, sales promotion, promotional licensing and personal selling, which includes sponsorship and telemarketing. How these elements are combined, and in what measure, depends on the target market, the organisational objectives and the promotion strategy that is to be utilised.

Advertising

Advertising is a non-personal communication by an identified sponsor. This is the most obvious form of sport and event promotion. On a regular basis, sport producers such as the NRL, the NBL and the ARU advertise their products on television and/or radio, as well as in the daily newspapers, with the intent of informing potential consumers and shaping their choices. In regard to events this information would contain the names of the sponsoring organisation and the organisation paying for the advertisement, the time and place of the event, the featured acts, sports or athletes, perhaps cost and, invariably, a telephone number for further information. Advertisements for a fitness centre could include information as to the range of services offered. Advertisements for sport equipment such as tennis racquets could include the particular facts of the equipment and also, for specific versions, technical specifications.

The major advantage of advertising is that the advertiser can control the time, placement and content of the advertisement. The major disadvantage is cost per exposure per consumer, especially with mass advertising. An expanded analysis of the role of advertising in sport marketing is presented at length in chapter 10.

Public relations and publicity

Two other forms of communication are public relations (both proactive and reactive) and publicity. Public relations is discussed at length in chapter 15.

Publicity is a non-personal communication that is neither paid for nor sponsored by a promoting organisation. The best example of this is the amount of copy, space and time given to sport and related activities in the media. The various football codes dominate the back pages of newspapers during the winter, while cricket predominates during the summer. Less regular publicity is given to sports like basketball, netball, motor racing, hockey and bowls. Activities such as golf, tennis and horseracing may attract significant publicity at specific times of the year. The tennis Grand Slams, major international golf tournaments and the Melbourne Cup all feature heavily at the appropriate time. Moreover, similar scenarios occur whether on television or radio or in the newspapers.

The major advantage of publicity is that it is free. However, the disadvantages can be numerous. The relevant sporting body cannot control the time and placement of the story, nor can it control the slant a particular journalist or writer will place on a story. Undoubtedly, publicity can be either positive or negative, and it is thus up to sports to promote the former and minimise the latter. Similarly, it is incumbent on sport promoters to have a public relations strategy in place to negate the effects of adverse publicity. The need for publicity is also discussed in chapter 15.

Sales promotion

Sales promotion is the set of promotion activities that stimulate and support advertising, personal selling and publicity. Usually such activities are temporary in nature and may involve price or non-price strategies. For a non-price strategy, see Sportview 9.3.

SPORTVIEW 9.3

What if you held a promotion and nobody came?

One of the more bizarre sport promotions was reported in the *Sydney Morning Herald* on 10 July 2002 and featured a minor league team from Charleston, South Carolina—the Charleston Riverdogs. Apparently the organisation took the unprecedented step of locking everybody out of the stadium in an effort to record the lowest attendance at a professional baseball game on record. The gates were padlocked and only organisation employees, scouts and media representatives were permitted inside Joe Riley Stadium.

So what of the hundreds of fans that turned up to see the game? They were kept outside the stadium until the game was recorded as official (after the fifth inning) and only then were they let into the park. In the meantime they were provided with food and beer at a party thrown by the organisation.

For the record books, the attendance was recorded as zero and the Columbus Red Stixx beat the Charleston Riverdogs 4–2. Unfortunately for the fans, all the runs were scored before they were admitted to the venue. Only in America!!

Source: Adapted from *Sydney Morning Herald*, 10 July 2002.

Sales promotion based on price invariably involves 'two-for-one' deals, group discounts or, in some circumstances, 'half-price tickets', which is a popular concept in the theatre industry. In July 2002 the NRL reduced game ticket prices for the remainder of the season in an effort to swell crowds at rugby league games. Promoted on the basis of making the game more affordable for the family, by illustrating pricing comparisons with its major competitors, the promotion was an instant success, with bigger crowds for the ensuing games.

The use of give-aways, such as caps, drink bottles, posters or sport memorabilia, is an example of non-price promotion. Although such promotion can occasionally offer an adult premium, more often than not it is directed towards children, which in turn influences family attendance and consumption. Spolestra (1991: 12) contends that:

> for a premium to excite fans enough for them to buy tickets, the premium needs to have a perceived value equal to the price of the tickets.

Irrespective of whether the sport marketer chooses to run with a price or non-price promotion, Spolestra also argues that energies should be directed not to increasing average attendances but to increasing the number of sold-out games, which will boost average attendances.

Personal selling

Personal selling is paid personal communication by an identified sponsor. It uses oral presentation to prospective consumers or purchasers. Evans and Berman (1987) suggest that the key features of personal selling are:

1. identifying prospects;
2. determining the customer's needs;
3. selecting a sales strategy;
4. communicating with the buyer; and
5. evaluating the sales strategy.

The two most obvious varieties of personal selling are the 'face-to-face' presentation and the increasingly common telemarketing.

Face-to-face presentation

Face-to-face presentation is most closely related to sponsorship, and the growth of this component of the promotion mix in the sport marketplace was exponential over the latter half of the 20th century. This is evidenced by corporations such as McDonald's, Coca-Cola, Qantas or Telstra, which are prepared to invest a significant part of their marketing budget in direct sport sponsorship. The fundamental underpinning of this position is the belief that sport, especially on television, delivers a captive audience to the company. As a result, organisations are prepared to pay large sums in an effort to connect with clearly segmented consumer markets. This issue of sponsorship is discussed in depth in chapter 13.

Telemarketing

Telemarketing is not as advanced in sport in Australia as it is in North America, but the concept is well known. Insurance companies, credit card organisations, banks, telecommunications agencies, the tourism industry and general market research firms are constantly in phone contact with Australian homes, day and night. By accessing existing databanks the telemarketer usually has some knowledge about the potential client's consumption patterns. In North America the selling of season tickets and requests for alumni contributions to universities are clear examples of telemarketing. There, representatives of the respective organisations phone previous or current consumers (i.e. fans or students) in an attempt to either initiate or elevate patterns of consumption. Relevant information is held in existing databanks.

In the case of university students, alumni are asked to recall their positive experiences with the university and then requested to pledge a donation, either one-off or continuing, to one or a number of universities. At the forefront of many such requests are college athletic programs. Such donations may assist capital works programs, student athlete scholarships, or ongoing awards and honours. Whatever the case, the donation, gift or commitment is usually solicited by telephone and relies on known information about the client.

Similarly, with season tickets, at the end of one season an organisation's telemarketers quickly need to swing into action for the next. Existing season ticket holders are quizzed as to their future intentions, and lapsed members and season ticket holders can once again be reminded of membership benefits. Both current and previous consumers should be well known to the organisation through in-house databases. By pre-selling a large percentage of seats, merchandise and services, an organisation establishes its product as a premium article, which assists not only in sponsorship development but also in future pricing strategies.

While the former are examples of telemarketing at a macro-level, this promotional tool also has strong relevance to community sport. Local recreation centres can canvass former clients as to the reasons for their failure to continue to use the facility's services and, in the process, discern how their needs are currently being met. The benefits of doing this are numerous: the centre can be made aware of service shortfalls, and it may also be apprised of changing demographics or psychographics within the catchment area. Conversely, it may stimulate reconsideration of facility use, and useful information may be provided to frame future marketing strategies.

Likewise, information regarding the facility's services can be provided to local industry with the intention of assisting the latter to conduct its business. This can take the form of offering group or corporate rates for specific programs or services, conducting 'contra' arrangements where relevant expertise or products are exchanged, or even providing on-site consultancy and health, fitness and wellbeing services. In many cases it is the function of the telemarketer to initiate interest and, if appropriate, instigate some action.

Finally, the local junior sporting club engages in a form of telemarketing when it contacts parents and interested individuals to assist in the operation and organisation of the club's affairs. Money is not always the focal point of the request: more often than not it is labour, time and expertise. Nevertheless, conceptually it is the same as telemarketing for season tickets, for alumni support, or for tracking information on fitness centre defection. In each case there is an exchange process taking place with the intention of creating a win–win situation. The exchange may not always involve physical goods, as feelings, perceptions or beliefs can form part of this process. Nevertheless, benefits and costs are clearly established and comprehended by both parties to the agreement. If this happens, the telemarketer has done his/her job well.

Promotional licensing

According to Irwin, Sutton and McCarthy (2002: 242), promotional licensing 'is the act of granting a second party permission to use a mark, name, symbol or likeness'. Interestingly, the authors believe, and provide evidence, that 'promotional licensing as a promotion strategy may have reached its zenith in the mid 1990s with a 100% increase in sales of major US sport merchandise between 1990 and 1994 but with only 5% increase in sales in the ensuing 5 years' (2002: 242–3). Nevertheless, officials of the Atlanta organising committee for the 1996 Olympic Games suggested that corporations paid as much as US$50.7 million to have an official association with the Games.

Licensing can involve the use of a logo, an association, the right to designations such as 'official', the right of service, or the privilege to conduct promotion activities. Merchandise examples of sport promotional licensing are numerous. Caps, shirts, windcheaters, jackets, scarves and keyrings are merely the tip of the iceberg in licensed goods. Products on supermarket shelves, in service stations and in hardware stores often carry the name of a sport, team or athlete, which on sale will return a percentage to the licensing agent.

There is no doubt that the growth in promotional licensing over the past decade has been prolific. However, in some instances it has created dissent as to use of trademarks, images and logos. These issues, and others, are discussed at length in chapter 16.

Selecting the promotion mix

Selecting the correct promotion mix is potentially one of the more difficult decisions facing the sport promoter. As is the case when selecting the appropriate marketing mix, the blend of promotion activities engaged in to entice the consumer must reflect the type and nature of the product or service and the specific characteristics of the consumer. Not only would a billboard on a major freeway for a marginal sport or niche product be inappropriately placed, the expense involved would be disproportionate to the 'cost per exposure'. A combination of selected advertising in a sport-specific magazine, publicity in local or community newspapers, and telemarketing using in-house databases would be a more appropriate way of connecting with potential consumers. Conversely, national sporting organisations employ promotion strategies such as national advertising on radio, television and newspapers; they promote sport-specific magazines; they are the beneficiaries of a colossal amount of publicity across all media; and they engage in telemarketing and personal selling to boost attendances at events. Here the use of billboards on major arterial routes would be most appropriate, especially if a significant event in the sport were about to occur, such as a final, a playoff, a State-of-Origin or a blockbuster match-up.

Yet it is equally important for local, community and regional clubs and organisations to establish an appropriate promotion mix. Moreover, while the scope and size of their mixes may be vastly different from those experienced at national or professional level, conceptually they are very similar.

Sales promotion, ticketing and participation

In 1995, the Sydney Swans chief executive officer undertook a series of research projects that enabled the organisation to formulate a promotion strategy aimed at 'selling' the team to what the chief believed to be a potential AFL spectator base in Sydney of 650 000. In June 1996, Smith reported that (1996a: B6, 1996b: 42):

> from this research the club launched a series of acquisition, retention and cross selling programs that led to a 50% increase in membership, the development of a solid database, a strategic alliance with East's Rugby League Club, Swan-link–a transport joint venture with the NSW Department of Transport, and a four-fold increase in the sale of Swans merchandise.

The impact of the promotional activities undertaken by the Sydney Swans on match attendance and club membership is one of the success stories in Australian sport. In 1997 a record crowd of 46 168 witnessed the last home game of that season, and in 1999 the club had an unprecedented 31 000 members.

By undertaking this research and implementing a number of key recommendations, the Swans management demonstrated a fundamental knowledge of the attendance frequency escalator principle discussed below, and instigated programs and techniques to boost sales.

The attendance frequency escalator

One of the key issues facing the sport industry is how to encourage existing consumers to elevate their levels of involvement at the same time as introducing new consumers to sport products and services. This is as true for recreational activities and merchandise as it is for professional sport.

The consumption of sport was initially thought to be analogous to a staircase. Consumers would make an initial foray into the product by purchasing a single game ticket or buying a single piece of apparel or merchandise. The consequences of an incorrect choice would not be great. Once the consumer was happy that the right decision had been made, they would increase their level of consumption to a degree with which they were comfortable: in other words, they would take a number of steps up the sport consumption staircase. Marketing was focused on the new consumer, ignoring the contribution that an existing member, fan or participant could make to the sport or organisation. (Potentially, the satisfied customer is an organisation's best salesperson.)

While the staircase analogy may have had initial applicability to the sport industry, the sheer complexity of potential sport consumption choices created the need for a framework that exhibited greater flexibility and fluidity. Furthermore, the initial staircase structure did not allow for non-direct consumers or non-consumers. The frequency escalator provides a mechanism for tackling such shortcomings.

Mullin (1985) contends that the distribution of existing consumers 'is a continuous series of steps on an escalator that runs from one through to the number of games in a season'. Conceptually, this can be applied not just to the sport spectator but also to the snow skier, fitness centre member, tennis player or golfer, who may indulge in their activity of choice from infrequently to daily. When these are combined with pre-consumers, who are divided into non-consumers and indirect consumers, the possible levels of consumption are vast. Hence the escalator principle recognises both the fluid nature of consumption and the increasing levels at which consumption is possible. To explain the process Mullin (1985) created the categories shown in Figure 9.2.

The frequency escalator for sport attendance and participation FIGURE 9.2

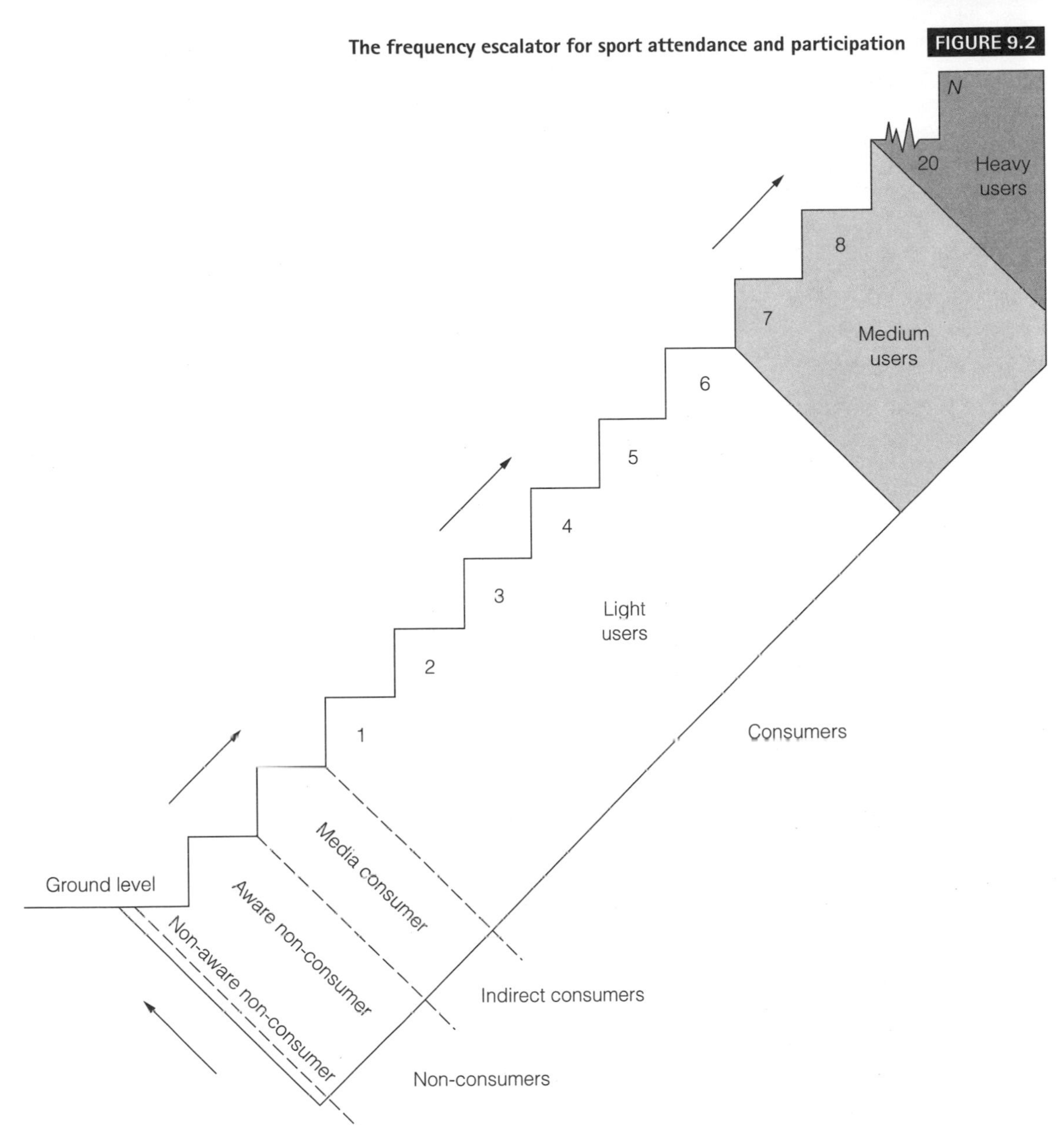

Source: Mullin (1985:163). Reprinted with the permission of Michie, Charlottesville, VA, in conjunction with LEXIS-NEXIS.

Non-consumers

While non-consumers may be divided into aware and non-aware categories, establishing promotion strategies aimed at such groups is problematic. The sport promoter either does not know the constituency of the group or realises that a conscious decision not to consume the sport offerings has been made. While advertising campaigns that both inform and educate may have some success in introducing new consumers to a product, such strategies are little more than one part of an extensive promotion campaign. Nevertheless, non-consumers are now a significant part of the sport consumption process and need to be acknowledged accordingly.

Indirect consumers

Indirect consumers listen to sport on the radio, watch it on television, read about it in the newspapers, and discuss it with friends and colleagues. In all respects this group is extremely important. If fans refused to listen to or watch the game, buy the merchandise, or associate the sport with a particular manufacturer, the potential for corporate involvement in sport would be severely limited. Only 16 000 tennis fans can watch the ladies' and men's final of the Australian Tennis Open live, but many millions can be transfixed by the event on television.

Here it is the task of the sport marketer to attempt to convert the indirect consumer to one who purchases the live or actual experience or commodity. Given that in most instances such consumers are predisposed towards the sport product, the inducements that can be utilised to offer the 'one-off' experience are numerous. Moreover, if such inducements are tied to an appropriate advertising campaign, the potential to add to the direct consumer base is enhanced. Nevertheless, it should be recognised that indirect consumers are an integral part of any attendance or participation act, and as such their level of commitment must be appreciated and acknowledged. Moreover, strategies should be implemented that ensure their ongoing support at the level with which they are comfortable. Junior supporters' clubs on television, sport-specific magazines and home pages on the World Wide Web all provide for a specific level of sport consumption.

Direct consumers

Direct consumers are categorised into light, medium and heavy users, and promotions should be designed to encourage consumers to move towards the heavy end. Shilbury (1994) suggests that sport marketers should initially aim for a 60% heavy, 10% medium, 30% light combination of consumers, and this idea has merit. The selling of 60% of tickets pre-season enables early financial strategy and fiscal planning, while the 10% allocated to medium users, or mini-season ticket holders, provides a mechanism for light users to elevate their level of consumption without making the leap to a full season ticket. This is especially important in sports such as basketball, where the season is invariably long and many games are played. By reserving 30% for the walk-up crowd the sport marketer ensures access to infrequent game attenders, first-timers and fans who want to see an individual game due to a strong match-up, star players or game promotion.

The advantage of this ticketing strategy is that it allows for fluidity in fan movement. The suggestion inherent in the sport attendance frequency escalator is that the consumer is moved by the sport or organisation towards higher levels of consumption. It also argues that, given the variety in light, medium or heavy use, the movement from one category to the next is rather seamless, with a relatively ill-defined transition phase. This is in contrast to the sport participation staircase, where the consumer makes a conscious decision to move to the next consumption level. In this case, stages are discrete and may be mutually exclusive. The key issue related to the sport attendance frequency escalator is: How do sports encourage higher consumption levels? Strategies and programs need to be developed that will not only enhance awareness of the benefits resulting from additional investment on the part of the consumer but also result in increased sales.

By encouraging different levels of participation and hence segmenting the market, the sport marketer strives to ensure maximum consumption of the event–the sellout. It should not be forgotten that the first objective of sports attendance is to sell out the stadium. The second objective is to repeat the first as often as possible. Spolestra (1991) argues that it is much more fun to go to a sold-out event than one that is only half-sold. Sellouts create premium tickets, which in turn elevate the profile of the event. This in turn enhances the desirability of the product, which itself leads to increased sales. Once an event has been sold out, the sport marketer can focus attention on providing excellent service to the fans on hand.

However, the sport marketer should not create a perception of a sellout merely in an attempt to create premium tickets. In the early 1990s the Sydney Kings organisation had to work assiduously to combat the notion that their basketball games were always sold out. Although this was not the case, basketball fans, believing this to be true, often stayed away from games when excellent seats were still available.

Programs and techniques to boost sales

The four major areas that need to be concentrated on with respect to sales are:

- indirect consumers;
- light users;
- medium users; and
- heavy users.

While the first three groups are encouraged to elevate their usage level, anti-defection programs need to be implemented for the heavy usage category in an attempt to prevent them from 'falling off' the escalator.

Indirect to light

Converting indirect consumers to light users is not so difficult and is best accomplished using advertising and sales promotion. These consumers have already shown a predisposition towards the product by being media fans or purchasing related merchandise. What needs to be done is to provide them with an incentive to walk into an arena and see first-hand what has previously been mediated for them. The number of possibilities here are endless. The most obvious is providing a tangible connection between the products consumed at home and the event itself. Media competitions, game-redeemable coupons and event-associated product purchases all provide an attractive entry into the initial consumption experience.

Light to medium

Moving the light user to the medium user category can be achieved through sales promotion and personal selling. Consumers at this stage are still predominantly price-sensitive, so offering reduced prices for bulk purchases and discounts on selected associated goods will often encourage light users of the product. Given that there are various levels of medium usage, designated seating, newsletters and invitations to pre- or post-game functions and special events may be appropriate incentives.

Medium to heavy

Encouraging the medium user to become a heavy user is rather more difficult than the previous scenarios, as more often than not medium users have reached saturation level in terms of their personal consumption. This may not be a problem if the season is not excessively long or expensive. To encourage heavy usage, organisations need to make this individual feel very special. Here the emphasis should be on personal selling and premium sales promotion. While group-specific deals and give-aways can be negotiated for this group, these may be only the start of the service offered. Sport promoters need to think about the range of value-added extensions that can extend the heavy user's enjoyment of the product, such as valet parking, special dining, boxes and access to play-off or finals tickets. They also need to be aware of those club resources which may facilitate the heavy users' or members' conduct of their own business. These may include the use of athletes to promote facets of the members' business, the use of organisational space and expertise to conduct business seminars and workshops, or even the provision of networking opportunities across this category of membership. All participants should be working towards a win-win situation.

Anti-defection programs

Although all products and services have natural attrition rates, this does not mean that defection should be meekly accepted. Programs aimed at minimising defection should be firmly entrenched and constantly evaluated in any promotion strategy. By being aware of the client's purchase and usage habits through constant monitoring of databanks, changes in patterns of behaviour may quickly be noticed. Immediately a decline in usage is evident, sales staff or other appropriate individuals need to contact the client quickly to discern the reasons for consumption fall-off. By responding to consumer issues and concern in a prompt manner, organisations are more likely to maintain their heavy usage consumers.

Summary

Establishing promotion strategies is a complex yet exciting task. Advertising, public relations and publicity, sales promotion, personal selling, including sponsorship and telemarketing, and promotional licensing are crucial to the success of any sport product, event or service, and as such are vital to the promotion mix. Furthermore, the sport marketer not only needs to be fully conversant with the components of the promotion mix but also needs appropriate application skills for any given situation.

Once the promotion strategy has been established, it is incumbent on sport marketers to analyse consumers within the framework of the frequency escalator to monitor ongoing consumer behaviour. Programs and techniques to boost sales and prevent defection need to be established and implemented, to ensure continued consumption of the product and to extract maximal gain from the specific promotion activity. Contemporary sport marketers also need to be able to offer the 'money-back guarantee'.

CASE STUDY

Auckland's adolescents and the Anna Kournikova factor

'Thanks Mum,' shouted Auckland teenager Lewis Sinclair as he and three of his 14-year-old mates spilled out of his mother's car. The four teenage boys hurried their way through the turnstiles, taking in the shimmering surfaces of the still vacant outside courts. Jubilant yells greeted them from the practice doubles match on Court 6 along with the low hum of the brightly attired crowd meandering its way to Centre Court. Clutching their $35 uncovered stand tickets, they dodged and weaved their way through the crowd, anxious to get to their seats before the start of the biggest extravaganza in New Zealand's women's tennis. Why were these four teenage boys at an ASB Bank Women's Tennis Classic Tournament in Auckland, New Zealand, on this beautiful summer's day? In two words: Anna Kournikova.

Anna Kournikova, with her athletic figure and alluring looks, has long been a popular cover girl for general, sporting and certainly tennis magazines. Although her world tennis ranking has slipped to 71 following an injury-marred 2001, she had previously risen to No. 8 in the world after enjoying a top 15 ranking throughout 1999 and 2000. Her annual earnings have been estimated at $NZ37 million, an amount surpassed in the world of tennis only by Martina Hingis and Andre Agassi. However, whereas Agassi and Hingis derive large amounts of their income from prize money, it is estimated that 90% of Anna Kournikova's income is a consequence of her endorsements. Adidas alone is reputed to pay her $NZ12 million annually, while Terra Lycos (Internet company), Yonex (sports equipment), Berlei (sportswear) and Omega (watches) all sponsor Kournikova.

Attracting this tennis star kept Richard Palmer, the ASB Bank Women's Tennis Classic Tournament director, on tenterhooks for weeks as Palmer and his fellow organisers were conscious of not exposing Auckland's tennis clubs to a loss-making event. Luckily, Kournikova's performance on court helped reduce this risk. However, as might be expected, Kournikova's presence didn't come cheap. Once her entry was confirmed, prices were set 15–20% higher than previously positioned. In addition, a volume ticketing strategy supported this premium pricing strategy. As a consequence, patrons who bought tickets for the Second Round, when they were sure to see Kournikova's first match (she had a First Round bye), were committed to buying a ticket for the following day. This ensured that the tournament came close to covering its costs by end of play Wednesday. Moreover, the previous weekend's qualifying matches, supplemented by the drawcard of Kournikova's practice sessions, allowed a $10 daily entry charge when previous years' qualifying matches had been free of charge.

Undoubtedly, Anna Kournikova was the major focus of the tournament, despite the organisers working hard to try and shift some of the attention on to other players with better records and higher rankings. The crowd thinned noticeably once Kournikova left the court. One might ask then, were tennis fans denied the opportunity of seeing the tournament, and its main drawcards, Anna Kournikova and Conchita Martinez (former world number 2 and former Wimbledon champion)? 'No', said tournament director Richard Palmer. 'Prior to tickets going on sale to the general public all tennis club members in Auckland Tennis's affiliated clubs received a two-week preferential period for ticket purchase.'

After the dust had settled and the enthusiasm for Anna Kournikova's presence at the Women's Tennis Classic had subsided, the question that needed to be asked was, how successful was the tournament? Auckland Tennis reported that Auckland's tennis clubs, along with their professional coaching staff, were once again looking forward with optimism. Post-tournament interviews with several Auckland tennis coaches reported unprecedented interest in tennis from all age groups. Court usage was up and membership attrition appeared to have been arrested. Of course, the challenge to Auckland Tennis and its affiliated clubs was to convert this initial wave of enthusiasm for tennis, particularly women's tennis, into ongoing commitment and sustained growth.

ASB Bank remained tight-lipped about the returns from its sponsorship of the tournament. ASB Bank is Auckland's biggest sponsor of sport and sport events, meaning that isolating the effect of one event from the overall impact of the bank's sponsorship portfolio is impossible. However, anecdotal evidence suggested that it had received approximately three times the media coverage of past tournaments. Moreover, with Stanley Street Courts holding 3000 fans per day (including the corporate box crowd), and a Monday–Saturday main draw, there were 18000 ticketing opportunities. The official attendance figure, including practice days and spectators in corporate boxes, was 22400. It could be argued that exposure for ASB Bank in this instance was excellent.

EziBuy, the tournament's secondary sponsor, indicated that it was well pleased with its first major foray into event sponsorship. Co-owner Peter Gillespie suggested that, 'EziBuy used the Women's Tennis Classic to showcase their brand to the Australasian market', at the same time as providing an excellent platform to further build the brand. Prior to the tournament, EziBuy bought the customer database of Australasia's leading direct mail clothing company, Myer Direct, which added another 2.3 million potential customers (almost all of whom live in Australia) to its existing customer base. Gillespie further opined that the 'move to sponsor [the Classic] was a strategic one and women's tennis was ideal for EziBuy to put its name to as it was synonymous with women's apparel'. Hence they were gratified with the outcome, which was 28 hours of live television coverage and quarter of a million exposures of prominent signage.

Finally, Kournikova used the Women's Tennis Classic to launch her Adidas YOC (Youth On Court) range of tennis wear. The collection was based on Ursula Andress's trend-setting bikini from the James Bond movie *Dr No*. The pro-tennis shop on Stanley Street sold large quantities of the aqua-belted shorts and tops during the tournament.

All things considered, Anna Kournikova's presence at the Women's Tennis Classic resulted in a resounding success for the tennis tournament itself, New Zealand tennis in general, the ASB Bank, Ezibuy, Adidas and undoubtedly Lewis Sinclair and his three mates.

Source: Adapted from a case provided by Lesley Ferkins (UNITEC) and Ron Garland (Massey University). Reproduced by permission.

Questions

1 What are the main lessons from this successful promotion?
2 What are the potential short- and long-term limitations of such a promotion?
3 What are some of the mechanisms by which New Zealand club tennis could leverage this promotion?

10

Advertising

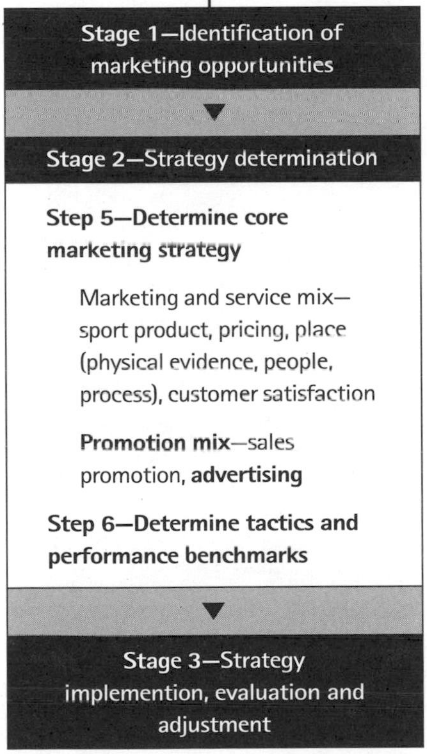

Stage 1—Identification of marketing opportunities

▼

Stage 2—Strategy determination

Step 5—Determine core marketing strategy

Marketing and service mix—sport product, pricing, place (physical evidence, people, process), customer satisfaction

Promotion mix—sales promotion, **advertising**

Step 6—Determine tactics and performance benchmarks

▼

Stage 3—Strategy implemention, evaluation and adjustment

CHAPTER OBJECTIVES

Chapter 10 introduces advertising as a component of the sport promotion mix. Advertising is a non-personal paid message aimed at creating awareness about a product or idea. This chapter examines some of the ways in which advertising is used in sport to promote sporting contests and events. The types of advertising are also described, as are the creative techniques used to develop ideas and communicate them to the public.

After studying this chapter you should be able to:

1. Articulate the concepts related to advertising.
2. Recognise the message capabilities of various media.
3. Establish procedures for selecting appropriate media.
4. Establish strategies for selecting the appropriate media mix.
5. Develop mechanisms for measuring advertising effectiveness.

HEADLINE STORY

Athens opts for old-fashioned values

On 14 February 2002 *SportsVine*'s Justin Collins reported:

> the 2004 Athens Olympic Games has launched the first phase of its advertising campaign conveying the message 'Unique Games on a Human Scale'. The stated intent of the organising committee through the advertising campaign was to 'restore the human being as the center of the Olympic celebration, projecting its values and its competitive spirit'. Only time will tell whether the stated aim is achieved, however Athens 2004 clearly articulated the advertising theme to be adopted leading up to the games. Contrast this with Sydney 2000 who constantly used upbeat advertising to sell 'the games of the new millennium'. The distinction between Sydney and Athens exemplifies how sport advertising is contextualised within an organisation's, industry's or in this instance country's historical and cultural development. While Sydney is a young vibrant city of the future, Athens is a city steeped in tradition. This has been reflected in the advertising campaigns of SOCOG and Athens 2004 respectively.
>
> The intent of advertising is to provide a message in such a way that a potential consumer is predisposed towards the message and by extension the product. The success of advertising campaigns very much depends on the manner in which it resonates with the intended viewer. While the triumph of the Sydney Olympic Games has now been consigned to sporting history only time will tell what part the Athens 2004 advertising campaign will play in their attempt to replicate Sydney's success. (Collins 2002)

Apart from the advertising related to the 2000 Olympic Games, possibly the two most successful Australian sport advertising campaigns were the 'Simply the Best' campaign for the New South Wales Rugby League in the late 1980s to early 1990s featuring Tina Turner, and the 'C'mon Aussie, C'mon' cricket campaign of the late 1970s. In fact, the momentum gained by both campaigns pushed them beyond the boundaries of sport and into a wider cultural milieu. In both cases it could be claimed that the advertising campaign ensured the medium-term success of the sport and established new market segments for the respective games.

Although the 'Simply the Best' and 'C'mon Aussie' campaigns are obvious success stories, they are by no means unique. Australian corporations, and multinational organisations with an Australian arm have been prepared to make a significant investment in Australian sport. Some examples are the Australian Football League (AFL), the Australian Tennis Open, the Australian 500 Motorcycle Grand Prix, the Formula 1 Grand Prix, surf lifesaving, cricket and basketball, both men's and women's. In all instances this capital involvement is leveraged through significant advertising campaigns.

Mullin et al. (2000) suggest that a major problem in advertising is perceptual distortion or noise, and Irwin, Sutton and McCarthy (2002: 145) contend 'breaking through the noise is becoming increasingly difficult'. However, Sutherland (1993) says that how advertising works is something of a mystery given that consumers tend to believe it has no effect on them personally; the fact that advertisers keep advertising means that something is working on someone. It is the who and how that need clarification.

> The dilemma for sport marketers is that, while they are firm in their belief that advertising their goods and services boosts sales, or at least results in a predisposition towards their product, questions related to the media to be used, target markets to be engaged, cost per exposure, messages to be communicated and the creative component all need to be addressed. While the act of advertising is relatively simple, the construction of effective advertising is quite complex.

Relationship between advertising and product life cycle

Before making decisions as to the appropriate media to be used, sport marketers need to understand the relationship between advertising and the phases of the product life cycle, discussed in chapter 5. During the goods or services introductory phase, advertising should be informative. Here the advertisement should provide all the salient information about the product. This may include special features, relevant technical specifications, pictorial or illustrative representations, place of purchase and/or consumption, and even price. Basically, the sport promoter is stating what the goods or services are and where they can be obtained.

During the growth and maturity phases, advertising should be persuasive in nature. Consumers should be reminded of the benefits and/or the desirable attributes that can be gained by consuming the product.

During the decline phase, reminder advertising should be used. The intent behind this is to provide impetus for consumers to reconsider purchase options or, if the event is cyclical, to remind past consumers that the event will return at some stage in the future and to keep that time free.

Annual events such as the various motor vehicle grand prix are a good example of this process. Initial advertising emphasises information as to event location, date, ticket options and purchase sites, and promoter. As the day of the event approaches, advertising promotes the participants or stars, becomes more subjective and develops emotional overtones. The 2001 Qantas Australian Motorcycle Grand Prix used the advertising slogan 'You can't beat the world's best', while the 2002 Skyy Vodka Australian Motorcycle Grand Prix used the advertising slogan 'You can't beat 317kpm'. The Australian Formula 1 Grand Prix held in Melbourne during March 2002 simply proclaimed 'The World According to Formula One'. Intermittent advertising takes place through the year, usually associated with similar events, providing fans with broad details of the next race.

Purpose of advertising

Stanton et al. (1995) state that advertising is the activities associated with presenting a paid, sponsor-identified, non-personal message about an organisation and/or its products, services or ideas. While advertising can take many forms, it is basically constructed around a message that is designed to build audiences and promote sales. Joel Hochberg, president of DDB Needham Worldwide, believes that (*Marketing News* 1988: 3):

> an ad that doesn't sell product has no purpose. To work in the marketplace it must have relevance, originality and impact. If it is not relevant it has no purpose, if it is not original it will not attract attention and if it does not have impact it will leave no lasting impression.

Hence it can be argued that, irrespective of context, the foundation of successful advertising is the ability to communicate. The willingness of organisations to part with large sums of money to use sport to communicate messages to consumers is evidenced by Sportview 10.1.

SPORTVIEW 10.1

The ball keeps on rolling, and the $$ keep on flowing

According to Michael McGuire (2002), 'televised sport was the only sector that escaped the advertising recession' and 'in the midst of what some have described as the worst advertising recession since the end of World War II sport continues to exert a fascination over the public and advertisers alike. Consumers keep watching and advertisers keep spending'. Noting that CUB spends 60% of its yearly $25 million advertising budget on sport, Carlton and United Breweries' Paul Kennedy suggests that given that 18+ males are high watchers of sport, sport advertising is a cost effective vehicle to link product with potential consumers.

McGuire suggests that despite the attractiveness of televised sport to potential advertisers, actually working out how much is spent on television is not easy to determine and suggests that best 'guestimates' range from $300 to $400 million per year. However, it is thought the football codes attract in the region of $150 million worth of advertising, with the AFL accounting for approximately half that amount, cricket $30 million, tennis $20 million and motor racing in excess of $10 million. Finally, McGuire asserts that the Seven Network acquired $100 million worth of advertising relating to the 2000 Olympic Games. For the 2002 Winter Olympic Games, Seven attracted advertising from Westpac, Subaru, Lexus, retail giant Harvey Norman and the NRMA. Selling the 2002 Commonwealth Games to potential advertisers is not difficult as one-off sporting events, especially in a sports-fixated country like Australia, always commands a premium.

Source: Adjusted from McGuire (2002: M01).

O'Hara and Weese (1994: 9) establish a framework to 'better communicate product and service offerings to target groups'. Entitled the 'advertising management process', this five-step program incorporates research, campaign planning, creative development, media planning, and implementation and evaluation. The process is schematically illustrated in Figure 10.1.

The process is a simple yet effective way of establishing sports advertising strategy, as it links the five components of advertising management in a sequential manner. Following the data collection or research, a campaign is planned around a major theme. At this time, how that theme will be creatively developed, and how it will be produced and presented

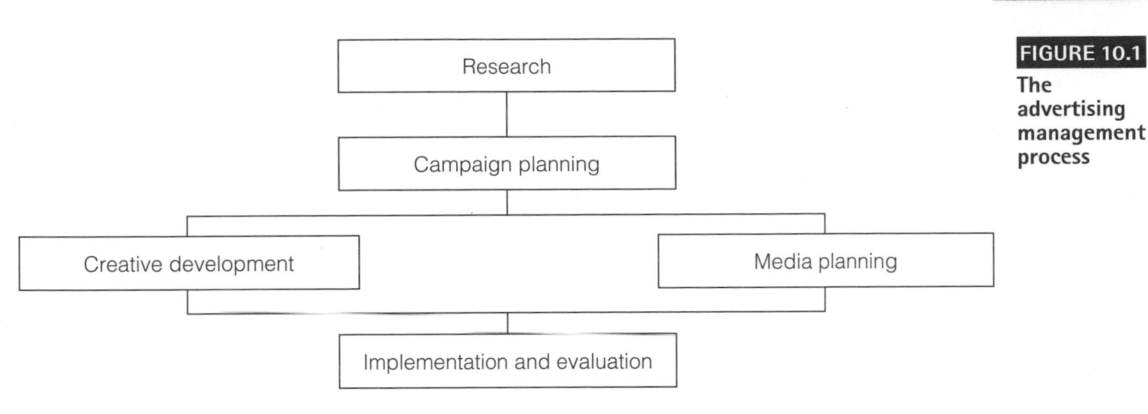

Source: O'Hara and Weese (1994: 11).

FIGURE 10.1 **The advertising management process**

for different media are simultaneously established. During implementation, an evaluative mechanism is established to ascertain the effectiveness or lack thereof of the campaign.

O'Hara and Weese contend that advertising must create exposure, generate processing and lead to long-term communication effects such as attitude and awareness. The comment by Andrew Hipsley, director of marketing for McDonald's Australia, that McDonald's is 'looking for a platform that would make an Olympics marketing program relevant and meaningful to consumers over a four year period' (Shoebridge 1996: 75), is a tangible example of the O'Hara and Weese framework.

Quite simply, the purpose of advertising is to influence consumers to respond positively to products or services. While this can best be achieved by establishing advertising campaigns that are linked to prior experience and are strategically focused, there are no fail-safe mechanisms to ensure success. While some advertising campaigns have been abject failures, others have had outstanding success. Moreover, not all are contemporary. Sportview 10.2 provides evidence of sport advertising in Sydney in 1925.

SPORTVIEW 10.2

Olympia Motor Speedway

Over the past 20 years a number of venues in Australia have become synonymous with motor vehicle racing. Bathurst in country New South Wales, Eastern Creek Raceway on the Western fringes of Sydney, Calder Raceway on the outskirts of Melbourne and possibly the best known, especially for motorcycles, Phillip Island in Southern Victoria, have all showcased the highs and lows of this exciting and sometimes dangerous sporting activity. However, there was one track that has long since been overtaken by the Sydney residential sprawl—the Olympia Motor Speedway at the beachside suburb of Maroubra.

In a story entitled 'Speed freaks' in the *Sydney Morning Herald*, columnist James Cockington contends that on a sultry afternoon in December 1925, more than 70000 people, the largest crowd ever attracted to any sporting event at that time, turned up at Olympia Speedway to watch the motorcycles race.

What encouraged so many paying patrons to turn up at the speedway, as well as non-paying patrons to take up various vantage positions on the surrounding sand hill? Advertising. Cockington suggests that the spectators 'were lured to the barren swampy area by an extensive advertising campaign promising that Olympia Motor Speedway represented the new bold future of sport'. The hyperbole ran: 'if you are a sportsman with a drop of red blood in your veins come to Maroubra on December 5th'. As history notes, they came in their droves.

Unfortunately for the promoters, the opening-day crowd was a 'one-off', and neither the original nor subsequent management organisations could replicate the initial success. Eventually the huge concrete bowl was covered in and now forms part of the Coral Sea Park. In 2001, digging in the area uncovered part of the original concrete bowl and interest in the site, especially in motor racing enthusiasts, was rekindled.

As an example of sport advertising there is no doubt that the 5 December 1925 Olympia Motor Speedway campaign was an effective strategy. The fact that the initial success was not replicated is not a reflection on that strategy but rather an indictment of the product offered.

Source: Adjusted from Cockington (2002: 5).

Advertising strategy

In establishing an advertising strategy, the following issues need to be considered:

- Has the target audience been identified, and can it be described?
- What part does advertising play in relation to the totality of the promotional strategy?
- Are the objectives sales- or communication-related, and how does this affect both the media and creative strategy to be used?
- Have instruments for monitoring and evaluating effectiveness been established, and are they in place?
- What is the advertising budget?

It is important that the answers to all these questions be known before embarking on an advertising campaign.

Similarly, both the size of the community and the size of special-interest groups or target audiences in the market can affect advertising strategy. However, despite any benefits one advertising medium may have over another, a mix of several is often the best strategy. Even the use of just two media, such as print and radio, can result in an interaction that makes each more effective.

The major issue facing the sport marketer's use of advertising is whether to stress reach or frequency. Reach refers to the identification of potential consumers, and frequency relates to the number of exposures required to access the consumer. Both are critical to a successful advertising strategy. When determining reach, the advertiser must decide which consumers are being targeted. When determining frequency, the advertiser must decide how many exposures are necessary to reach the prospective consumer. Here factors such as price, stage in the product life cycle, purchase frequency and competitive advertising need to be addressed. It should be remembered that it takes a number of exposures to communicate a specific message, as there are always communication barriers to overcome.

Reach should be stressed over frequency when a product is being introduced or has a large target market. Frequency should be stressed over reach when products are often bought and brand switching may take place, when the target market is relatively small, or when the message is difficult to explain and repetition is important in communicating the advertising idea.

Advertising objectives

Advertising objectives can be either sales- or communication-related.

Communication objectives endeavour to provide messages that are understood by consumers about the product or service as a result of the campaign. This type of advertising is predominantly used when a change of image is desired or there is an attempt to build or strengthen a particular demographic. It may also be appropriate if an organisation wishes to generate community goodwill or there is a need to counter a competitive campaign thrust. Advantages of adopting an advertising strategy based on communication objectives are:

- It encourages the identification of process goals and requires that the campaign be evaluated in terms of those goals.
- Communication goals are less likely than sales objectives to be affected by other variables such as price or availability.

One disadvantage of communication objectives is:

- Attitude may be unrelated to purchase intention.

It could be argued that, given that the fundamental basis of advertising is to communicate, objectives should be communication-linked.

Sales objectives indicate a target level of sales to be achieved as a result of the campaign. Advertising of this type is used when the desire is to encourage membership, audience or product consumption. The obvious advantage of this type of advertising is:

- Sales are a result of purchase behaviour, which is the ultimate goal of the advertiser.

The main disadvantages of basing campaigns purely on sales objectives are:

- The number of sales alone rarely provides much in the way of decision-making guidance.
- Advertising often has a lagging effect on sales; hence past, not present, advertising may influence current sales.
- Changes in competitive decisions may cause changes in current sales.

For the 2002 World Cup in Korea and Japan, Reebok decided not to follow the path of Nike in the leveraging of the World Cup in order to grab a slice of the $9.2 billion sportswear market. The Nike World Cup marketing campaign enlisted the services of Terry Gilliam to produce its television advertising while supporting the campaign with an online dedicated football website. Head of interactive Reebok Nigel Hill suggested that, given the money others were spending on 'flashy campaigns', the value was not really there. He further suggested that Reebok might have 'fun with the brand and engage in viral or guerrilla type campaigns. Hill argued that it was a 'relatively inexpensive way to raise brand awareness' (*Sydney Morning Herald* 2002: 25).

When determining advertising objectives, the issue of timeframe is critical. On some occasions sport marketers are limited in scope because the event, product or service, like the 2002 World Cup, is a 'one-off' experience. Conversely, it may be part of a long-range plan, with various steps along the way. Here advertising strategies can build on previous campaigns. Timeframes can also influence the advertising media to be used, as some can be used with little advance notice while others require lead-time. In general, for immediacy, nothing is better than television; and for mass distribution, newspapers are excellent.

Advertising budget

Costs distribution

In determining how the advertising budget should be allocated, the decision needs to be made whether the budget strategy should be massed or distributed.

When adopting a *massed* strategy, the advertising budget is used heavily at the beginning of a campaign and falls away quickly as the weeks pass. The percentage of advertising recall is initially high but then drops off quite quickly. This is an appropriate strategy to adopt for annual events, the commencement of seasonal or holiday activities such as snowskiing, or the introduction of a new product or model into the marketplace.

With a *distributed* campaign, the advertising budget is used evenly throughout the year for a predefined period. The percentage of recall is initially low, but recall elevates with repeated weekly exposure. Activities such as professional sports, which are constant, result in a playoff period and have a limited off-season, mainly use a distributed advertising budget. It should be remembered that all advertising campaigns have time limits in terms of effectiveness. However, eventual advertising wearout can be delayed by introducing variations on the theme. The time will come, however, when the advertising campaign has no effect or, more significantly, a negative impact on sport consumption.

Cost intensity

Irrespective of whether a massed, distributed or combination advertising strategy is adopted, the advertising budget should be determined by the importance of the campaign, which in turn should be based on expected returns from the investment. While some types of advertising are cost-intensive, others are labour-intensive, and available resources need to be taken into account when establishing strategy. Radio, television, newspaper, magazine and supplement, outdoor advertising, direct mail, posters and premiums or give-aways are cost-intensive, in that they require more in terms of money than staff time. Conversely, press releases, contact with special-interest groups, personal contact with business and community leaders, speakers, personal appearances, special-event stations, involvement in community events and promotion stunts are labour-intensive, in that they require more in terms of staff time than money.

Advertising sport services

According to George and Berry (1981), advertising services is quite different from advertising goods, and they articulate six guidelines for advertising services. They contend that performance is inextricably linked to consumer perception of a service; hence the service has to be sold to employees before it can be sold to consumers. Sporting organisation employees must not only be educated, motivated and encouraged to communicate the benefits of the service being offered–they must also inherently believe in its quality.

Likewise, positive word-of-mouth communication, the provision of tangible clues such as the facility in which the service is provided, making the sport service comprehensible by linking it to tradition and history, and establishing continuity of advertising through the use of constant themes and images, are all designed to establish a background against which the service can be assessed.

The final guideline of advertising sport services, promising only what is possible, is potentially the most crucial for the sport marketer. Although Bill Veeck offered the 'money-back guarantee', in many cases this is not possible. In the lead-up to the 1996 Olympic Games, Australian swimming coach Don Talbot expressed in quantitative terms the anticipated level of success for the Australian swimming team. When this was not forthcoming, the Australian public believed that the Australian swimming team had not delivered on the promises made by Talbot. The result was a vigorous and sometimes acrimonious public debate that raged between the athletes, coaches, press and sport media consumers. Sport marketers should take the lesson of Atlanta on board and only ever promise what they know they can deliver.

Types of advertising

When establishing advertising strategies, sport marketers have a twofold task. Initially, a creative strategy must be implemented, which should be a response to the following questions:

- What is the purpose of the advertising?
- Who is it aimed at?
- What is promised?
- How will it be delivered?
- What will be the 'personality' or the essence of the product?

Next an organisation needs to establish a media strategy, which determines the best media for the message.

Hochberg (cited in *Marketing News* 1988) contends that all these questions have to be answered in conjunction with each other. However, for the purposes of this chapter, mechanisms for establishing a creative strategy will be noted before potential media strategy is examined.

Creative strategy

The task of the creative strategy is to develop message ideas and execute them effectively. Effective message ideas should be based on consumer research findings, fit the overall marketing strategy, be appropriate for the target market, be simple or basic (one major point), and be developed so they are most resistant to counter-attack. It should be remembered that if an organisation's *unique selling proposition* (USP) is price, it is very easy for competitors to attack in the marketplace. While creativity is usually situation- or even person-specific, and hence highly individual, there are a number of more general creative approaches that organisations can utilise.

Umbrella advertising relies on an established brand name. This is most appropriate when the brand name is well established. Major sport codes will advertise the league, sport or competition rather than the specific clubs. The Australian Football League (AFL), Australian Rugby Union (ARU) and the National Basketball League (NBL) all use umbrella advertising to promote the sports of Aussie Rules, rugby and basketball respectively. They are secure in their knowledge that umbrella advertising will promote consumption of their specific products. However, organisations such as the Women's National Basketball League (WNBL) or the National Soccer League (NSL) may find it better to advertise their product, women's basketball and soccer, through individual teams such as the Sydney Flames or Perth Glory, rather than the league itself.

Honest twist advertising relies on surprising the intended recipient, and is often associated with humour. Football heroes, often from a bygone era and from different codes, using comedy to promote an inexpensive clothing chain is one example of this. Similarly, Peter Sterling, former Parramatta Eel and more recently with the Nine Network, is supported by 'an elephant' to promote a particular swimming pool manufacturer.

Demonstration advertising shows the product in use. This is applicable when potential consumers are unfamiliar with the product or how to use it. While the obvious example is the raft of celebrity-endorsed home fitness equipment that appears during late-night 'infomercials', it also has applicability to sporting events. Demonstration games can both inform and persuade consumers, especially if associated with lifestyle. Prior to the 2000 Olympic Games, beach volleyball was not a high-profile sport in Australia. Via demonstration advertising, beach volleyball rapidly evolved from a summer sand activity to an extremely popular Olympic sport.

Testimonial advertising involves an actual user of the product serving as a spokesperson. Past athletes are often used to promote sport and related products by organisations that believe that former champions strike an accord with older market segments. This in turn may encourage them to consume the current offering. During the 2002 Football World Cup, Brazilian soccer star Pele, arguably the world's most famous athlete, appeared nightly in a television advertisement extolling the virtues of treatment for erectile dysfunction. While this may lend a perceived credibility to the product and its use, the 'reality' touch does have its downside. Former New York Jets quarterback Joe Namath regularly appeared in advertisements for a liniment company, suggesting that its application was just the thing his aching arthritic knees needed after years of NFL football. Unfortunately, the advertisement was still appearing on US television after Namath had had both knees replaced.

Slice-of-life advertising uses some aspect of daily life as a part of the advertisement. The intent behind this approach is to communicate messages and images to consumers that they can relate to. This approach is probably most appropriate when it connects fans with their past, usually their youth. While this belief is a fundamental underpinning of Major League Baseball (MLB) in North America, it has real relevance in most sport settings. Hence, when cricket advertisements feature children in backyards hitting 'sixes' over the neighbour's fence, then transform that action to the final of a day/night match in front of 90 000 at the Melbourne Cricket Ground, consumers readily see the connection between the two.

Lifestyle advertising operates on the basic tenet that the use of a product or service will result in the user accessing a particular lifestyle. Although this type of advertising has obvious relevance to the health and fitness industry, both horseracing and harness racing have adopted this type of advertising in recent years in an attempt to entice groups to the track. In an increasingly hectic environment, sports that can incorporate family lifestyle in their advertising may find themselves well placed in the sport marketplace.

Announcement advertising provides information about a new brand, product, package, design or formula. The most common examples of this type of advertising happen when sports apparel companies introduce new models into the market. In most cases the release is accompanied by a new advertising campaign. Sporting organisations use announcement advertising to inform their consumers of changes that they need to be aware of to ensure their enjoyment of the event. Event timing, parking conditions, public transport facilities and member information related to event entrance are just a few of the instances that warrant announcement advertising.

Imitation or symbolic association advertising attempts to associate attractive personal qualities with ownership or use of product. This approach is often connected to celebrity endorsement. Here the advertisement suggests that adoption of a particular product or service will infuse the consumer with desirable traits. Gatorade tapped into this advertising vein successfully when it ran the 'I want to be like Mike' advertisements. Canon also tried it with its 'Image is Everything' campaign featuring Andre Agassi, which was less successful. Moreover, this campaign allowed a numbers of other firms to adopt humorous parodies of the Canon approach, which were better than the original. Issues such as these are elaborated on in chapter 13.

Media strategy

Before establishing guidelines that help decide the advertising strategies and media to be used, it is making a number of general observations about key advertising media.

Media alternatives

Newspapers are current and relatively inexpensive, and reach a mass audience. In deciding to advertise using newspapers, sport marketers need to provide copy that is eye-catching and succinct. It is also important to be aware of the section the target audience reads. The business sections of daily newspapers are increasingly becoming a repository for sport advertising.

Magazines invite leisure readership, as they invariably lie around the house or business for an extended period. Similarly, the one issue is often read, or at least browsed through, by potentially quite different consumer groups. Here, appearance and layout designs are of paramount importance. Sport-specific magazines such as *Inside Sport* or *Sports Illustrated* provide obvious examples of sport advertising

Outdoor advertising, in the form of billboards or fence signage, involves the presentation of an uncomplicated message. Usually just a logo or a few words predominate, which the advertiser hopes will trigger recognition of a much more complicated message. Signage advertising major sport events such as the Australian Tennis Open, the Formula 1 Grand Prix and the 500 Motorcycle Grand Prix regularly appears at the appropriate time on central-business-district buildings and freeway billboards. Such displays usually feature the major slogan or logo, event date and ticket availability. This information is then reinforced and elaborated on in other media.

Radio advertising relies on recall in a heavily cluttered marketplace, so frequency is critical. Radio's advertising advantage lies in the fact that, given its lack of visual images, the imagination of the listener may be stimulated by suggestive advertising. As a result, event promoters can create advertising around the sounds of the ski slope, the beach and summer or the city, while at the same time creating an element of mystery.

Television advertising exists in an extremely cluttered marketplace, although there is little doubt that television advertising reaches the largest possible audience. Moreover, the use of visuals plus sound provides the most effective mechanism for presenting specific information. One problem facing television advertisers is how to stand out in an increasingly crowded marketplace. Humour, celebrity advertising or contemporary music are usually effective, as is 'black-and-white' or retro advertising. In 2002 the AFL used music from one of Australia's greatest rock bands, Hunters and Collectors, to encapsulate its season. The images attached, linked to the song 'The Holy Grail', featured Australians from all walks of life and from all points of the compass converging on AFL stadiums. Other television advertisements that appear to captivate audiences are those presented in the form of an unfolding tale. An interesting clothing firm advertisement in 1995 incorporated visuals without sound. When this advertisement played, detached viewers paid attention to their television thinking that there was something amiss with their equipment. The relationship between sport, advertising and television is discussed at length in chapter 11.

Brochures, flyers and *posters* usually combine the features of billboards plus newspaper and magazine advertising. The advantage of this type of advertising is that it can segment the market very well.

The Internet, especially the World Wide Web, has become a major source of information and opportunities for both organisations and individuals. While business, government and educational institutions are the major users of such technology, sporting organisations are increasingly turning to the Internet to conduct their business. Comprehensive websites have been established by the Australian Sports Commission, Tennis Australia, the NRL and Athens 2004, the official website of the 2004 Olympic Games. Myriad unofficial home pages also exist. Lee (1996: 86) contends that organisations:

> are seeing the promotional and marketing value of being on the net. Not only does it provide up-to-date information for followers of a particular sport here and abroad, there is the potential to capture the interest of children and others tapping into the web.

Other advantages of the Internet include the ability of sponsors to use the home page of a particular sport or organisation to provide a link to the sponsor's site, where further information can be gathered on the sponsor's products and services. There is little doubt that this expanding technology is providing information to organisations on a scale previously not possible. Moreover, the use of e-mail and bulletin boards has dispelled the isolation previously experienced by sport managers of small organisations.

Timing and cost

Two additional factors that need to be considered, irrespective of the media alternatives, are timing and cost. The dual questions related to timing are how soon the advertising goals need to be achieved and how the advertising mix is established to gain optimal support and recognition. Cost is usually determined as cost-per-thousand, or CPM. Here it needs to be ascertained how much it will cost to make impressions on 1000 people. The formula is:

$$CPM = \frac{Cost}{Reach} \times 1000$$

For example, if a radio commercial costs $200 and is estimated to reach 175 000 listeners, the CPM is $1.14.

Media selection

The criteria for media selection depend on the factors previously discussed. Elements such as budget, sales or communication objectives, and target audience are, in the main, internal to the organisation. However, there are a number of qualitative and quantitative media factors that need to be considered.

While television advertising can be strong in terms of its total population reach, uniform coverage, emotional stimulation, and ability to use slice-of-life and humour, it is rather weak with respect to upscale selectivity, positioning and the predictability of audience levels. Marginal sports such as polo would be better advertised in other media, such as magazines, whereas television is a perfect outlet for the various traditional summer and winter sports.

Radio's advertising strength lies in its young adult selectivity, its CPM, and its ability to exploit time-of-day factors and to stimulate the imagination. The downside of radio is its lack of uniform coverage, its lack of depth in demographics and its inability to conduct product demonstrations or exploit attention-seeking devices. Demographic-specific activities that have been appropriated by identifiable consumer markets would be well served by using radio. An upcoming skateboard exhibition, surfing contest or harness race meeting could be better served by advertising on a niche-market radio station than on television.

The potency of newspaper advertising lies in its capacity to select local markets, to exploit day-of-week factors, and to convey detail and information. The downside of newspaper advertising relates to its lack of national coverage (except for national newspapers), its general inability to negotiate rates and its inadequate ability to intrude. For sport marketers, newspapers are best used for providing fixture information and updates.

Finally, magazine advertising is appropriate if market selectivity, frequency control, advertisement positioning and prestige of the medium are important. It is difficult to stimulate emotion or imagination, negotiate rates, use slice-of-life or, once again, be intrusive when using this medium. Noting magazines' strength, sport advertisers would be well served by advertising in their sport-specific magazine.

Measuring advertising effectiveness

The components of a successful advertising-testing program are many and varied. The successful advertising campaign must not only be clear and objective and aid in the decision-making process–it must also offer good value and be valid and reliable as well as practical and defensible. Finally, it should produce understandable results.

The sport marketer should expect that the organisation's advertising is both seen and heard, communicates messages and/or creates impressions, associates brands with images, is persuasive and sells. To ensure that this is the case the organisation needs to engage in copy testing. This action has the potential to minimise risks and marketing mistakes, maximise budget efficiency, and move the product or service ahead in the marketplace.

The two major testing programs are recall and recognition. Recall requires respondents to remember a particular advertisement (aided) or an advertisement within a product category (unaided). Recognition involves showing the respondents the advertisement. Chapter 13 develops the concepts of recognition and recall in detail.

The current industry trend in advertisement testing uses the recall method. The philosophy behind this methodology is that if people can remember a commercial, its intended message and the brand name, there is a better chance that persuasion will occur and the brand will sell. The most common recall-testing method used in television is the day-after-recall (DAR) interview, which is conducted within 24 hours of the advertisement's display. This interview establishes respondent type, programs viewed, whether or not the respondent recalls the advertisement and the components recalled. With respect to the print media, the Starch Readership Test also examines recall. Less than 17% related recall is regarded as low and anything above 32% as high. It should be ascertained through additional questioning what respondents were doing during the advertising period and what media they were attending to.

To perform well in a test of recall, a commercial must cut through the clutter of the medium and the apathy of viewers and gain attention, which in turn maximises the audience for the message to follow. This has tended to lead to loud and flamboyant commercials. The ARU, the National Basketball League (NBL) and World Series Cricket have adopted stunning visuals, usually augmented by rock'n'roll, to advertise their respective products.

Although there is no guaranteed formula for success, effective advertisements usually exhibit the following traits:

- They identify the brand early.
- They are simple, yet interesting and involving.
- They adopt audio and visual reinforcement.
- They link the brand to the image created.

Once an advertising campaign has been tested, the results obtained can give rise to different courses of action. An organisation may:

- give an unreserved green light to the campaign;
- alter the media mix;
- alter timing based on demographic information; or
- if the advertisement is not communicating the intended message to the correct demographics, decide to start the process again.

Summary

Sport advertising is now a multi-billion-dollar industry and has as its prime purpose the influencing of consumers to respond positively to products or services. The foundation of successful advertising is the ability to communicate, and this can be conducted through various media using vastly different strategies. Newspapers are current and relatively inexpensive and reach a mass audience, while magazines invite leisure readership. Radio can bring the imagination into play, while television unquestionably reaches the largest possible audience. Outdoor advertising involves the presentation of an uncomplicated message, while brochures, flyers and posters effectively segment the market. The Internet is increasingly being used to provide information and links to sponsors' home pages and to conduct sport business. Two additional factors that need to be considered, irrespective of the media alternatives, are timing and cost.

Media selection depends on elements such as objectives, whether they be sales or communication, budget and target audience. However, there are a number of qualitative and quantitative media factors that need to be considered. The successful advertising campaign must not only be clear and objective and aid in the decision-making process–it must also offer good value, be valid and reliable as well as practical and defensible, and produce understandable results.

Advertising services is different from advertising goods. However, through advertising to employees, realising the value of word-of-mouth, providing tangible clues, making the service comprehensible, ensuring continuity in advertising themes and images and, most importantly, promising only that which can be delivered with total certainty, the potential impact of intangibles on service can be reduced and, to a lesser extent, controlled.

Recognising that creativity in advertising is very much a matter of individual choice and perception, this chapter has focused on the strategies that can be adopted to inform the creative underpinnings of sport advertising. A thorough understanding of the objectives of, and the budget allocated to, a sport advertising campaign will in part dictate the type of campaign to be run and the media to be used. Once these decisions have been made, the creative component can be established within a well-defined structure. A clear indication of the effectiveness of the strategies can be obtained through ongoing monitoring of the advertising campaign.

CASE STUDY

The Australian Motorcycle Grand Prix

'I am delighted to say that the Fosters Australian Grand Prix has been voted the best GP in the world by riders, managers, the media and others,' said the NSW Minister for Sport and Recreation Chris Downy in a media release on 8 December 1993. Speaking at the launch of the 1994 Grand Prix, Mr Downy further suggested that a 1991 study of the economic impact of the Grand Prix at Eastern Creek showed that visitors had spent almost $13 million at the event.

The 1994 Fosters Grand Prix, promoted under the banner 'Come on feel the noise', offered 37 hours of action and entertainment, which included 500 cc, 250 cc and 125 cc bike races, rock concerts, and four support-class races with Big Bangers and Harley Davidson twin sports. Footraces, the RAAF Roulettes, the Red Beret parachute team, a motorcycle stunt team, the Bridgestone Holden Precision Driving Team, a Touring Car grudge match and activities for children were all part of the day's entertainment. However, the hoped-for numbers of spectators were never achieved.

When Barry Sheene took over the running of the 1995 Grand Prix for IMG he became the third promoter in five years for the event. His charming, affable manner was ever present in all the television advertisements as he asked the question 'But are you going to be there?', but little changed in 1995. Although spectator attendances increased slightly each year, not enough spectators attended to make the race an economic windfall. By 1996 attendance had subsided and the event was headed for its previous home at Phillip Island in Victoria in 1997.

Potential consumers were targeted through a variety of advertising media, but in the main they failed to hit the mark. Radio advertisements on Triple M, and television advertising featured the lead riders, spectacular crashes and loud noise, appeared regularly in the days and weeks leading up to the event, especially on Channel Nine sport programs. Similar advertisements were played in Sydney cinemas. Newspapers, magazines and billboards on Parramatta Road all advertised the upcoming Grand Prix. However, in most instances the impact was minimal.

The results from a survey conducted for the 1994 race indicated that, although nearly 20% of respondents found out about the Grand Prix from either television or via word-of-mouth, cinema, newspapers and radio appeared to have minimal reach. While word-of-mouth was the main source of Grand Prix information for women, the print media had a greater reach with older respondents and the electronic media with younger. It was also found that advertising had a greater impact on purchases of single-day tickets as opposed to three-day passes.

The results from a survey conducted for the 1995 race indicated the following rates of exposure:

- Channel Nine 15.67%
- Triple M 3.23%
- AMEN 2.53%
- Advertisements/billboards 1.76%
- *Two Wheels* 1.67%
- *Telegraph Mirror* 1.18%

In both years the category 'word-of-mouth' was significant.

Source: Adjusted from Quick (1994, 1995).

Questions

1. What are some additional creative twists that could be used?
2. Which media would you use with which target markets, and what would be the communication message?

3. How would you recify the lack of response to radio, newspaper, cinema and magazine advertising?
4. When conducting research on advertising, how do we resolve the 'word-of-mouth' issue?
5. What advice would you give future promoters of the Grand Prix in terms of advertising?

11

Sport and television

Stage 1—Identification of marketing opportunities

▼

Stage 2—Strategy determination

Step 5—Determine core marketing strategy

Marketing and service mix—sport product, pricing, place (physical evidence, people, process), customer satisfaction

Promotion mix—sales promotion, advertising, **television**

Step 6—Determine tactics and performance benchmarks

▼

Stage 3—Strategy implemention, evaluation and adjustment

CHAPTER OBJECTIVES

Chapter 11 examines the television–sport nexus. Specifically, it describes how television generates its principal source of revenue through advertising and how this revenue determines the level of television rights paid to sporting organisations. This chapter also describes how program popularity is measured, and the link between this system of measurement and how advertisers assess the value of their advertising investment. Pay-television is also discussed.

After studying this chapter you should be able to:

1 Identify the nature of the sport–business–television relationship.
2 Understand the commercial basis on which television operates.
3 Identify why sport programming is so attractive to television networks.
4 Understand and apply the terminology used to measure television audiences.
5 Recognise issues associated with determining advertising effectiveness.
6 Explain the new dimension that pay-television brings to the sport–television relationship.
7 Calculate advertising revenue generated from sport programming.
8 Convert advertising revenues to the relative worth of sport television rights.

HEADLINE STORY

If it's on television, it must be more sport

It is the armchair 'winter Olympics'. Starting with the French Open in late May and going through to the Pan Pacific Swimming Championships at the end of August, hardly a day will go by this winter without some live or delayed coverage of a major sporting event on free-to-air television. In the past week Nine had most of the top-rating sporting events, yet still wasn't the 'sportiest station'. That title clearly went to SBS which devoted more than 43 hours or almost a third of its schedule to the Soccer World Cup. There was almost 33 hours of live or delayed sport on Nine, 19 on Ten, six on the ABC and just five-and-a-half hours on the former 'home of sport', Seven. This is one of the most intense periods of top-quality sport that Australia's ever seen, particularly because it's the first time the World Cup has been played in an Australia time zone.

Last year six of the top ten rating programs were sport events: the number one was the men's Wimbledon Final, when more than 3 million people in Australia's five major capital cities stayed up to watch Pat Rafter lose a thriller to Goran Ivanisevic. With Rafter out of contention for Wimbledon this year, the tussle for the top ratings spot is likely to be between the AFL Grand Final on Ten, the World Cup final on Nine and the Commonwealth Games on Seven. But no one expects even the biggest of this year's events to get near Seven's record-breaking ratings at the Sydney Olympics. More than 10 million Australians watched the opening and closing ceremonies, while almost nine million cheered on Cathy Freeman's gold-medal-winning 400-metre run. (Minchin 2002: 9)

In an unprecedented rush to secure the television rights to a succession of major events, Australian broadcasters understand the importance of major sporting events to the mix of programming, and their capacity to sell advertising inventory during these events. For the broadcaster, it is simply good business. Each broadcaster anticipates recouping its investment through strong advertising and sponsorship sales during major events such as the Soccer World Cup, Wimbledon, US Open (golf), Tri Nations rugby union and the Commonwealth Games. The World Cup in particular provides four weeks of premier programming, during which the networks will sell advertising inventory at peak rates. Given the time zone compatibility with Australia, many matches were shown in prime time viewing.

The Sydney 2000 Olympic Games, like all recent Olympic Games, relied on substantial revenues from broadcast rights. For example, the IOC (2002a) reports that Sydney 2000 generated US$1.3 billion from the sale of its television rights worldwide. The Sydney Olympic Organising Committee was allocated US$800, the International Agency against Doping US$25 million, the IOC itself retained US$130.9 million, International Federations received a share of US$189.7 million and National Olympic Committees shared US$185.9 million. Television coverage garnered during Sydney 2000 included 220 countries that televised the event, a global (unduplicated) audience of 3.7 billion, global coverage of 27 600 hours and total viewer hours estimated at 36.1 billion viewers (IOC 2002a). By contrast, Salt Lake City in 2002 attracted 2.1 billion viewers with 160 countries televising the winter Olympics, and total viewer hours were estimated at 13.1 billion (IOC 2002b). Finally, for the networks, programming of this profile provides the opportunity for pre-emptive promotion of forthcoming station programs to a large and captive audience. In essence, the networks capitalise on the opportunity to boost the ratings of future programs, further enhancing the value of major sports event programming.

Television and sport marketing

The purpose of this chapter is to explore the sport-television relationship. Clearly, it is a business relationship and one that has grrown in importance throughout the world. For many sports, including the National Basketball Association (NBA) and National Football League (NFL) in the United States, cricket and the Australian Football League (AFL) in Australia, and soccer, golf and tennis worldwide, television rights provide a substantial source of revenue. (A summary of some of the world's major professional sport television rights is given in Appendix 11.1 on p. 206.) Television networks now demand more from their right to broadcast than in their previous passive business partnerships with various sports. To ensure that networks maximise their revenue and profits, program directors and television executives are increasingly influencing the scheduling of games and events. The balance between playing at times conducive to optimum athletic performance and playing at times best suited to optimum ratings is one aspect of the sport-television relationship that creates tension. This tension has the potential to upset the mutually beneficial relationship currently in existence.

Figure 11.1 displays the principal players in the sport television business. Fundamentally, the business of the commercial television industry is the sale of airtime to advertisers. The price at which commercial TV airtime is sold is a function of a number of factors, the most important of which are the number of television viewers, and the price and availability of advertising space on suitable alternative media. Commercial television uses programming to influence the size and profile of its viewing audience, which is measured by independent ratings (ANZ McCaughan 1993: 9):

> The principal profit equation for commercial television is to ensure that the revenue generating capacity of a schedule of programming sufficiently exceeds both its cost of production or acquisition as well as associated overheads, to produce a reasonable return on investment for the broadcaster.

To achieve a reasonable return on investment, the networks rely on programming that has the ability to capture and captivate an audience. The series of relationships shown in Figure 11.1 is driven by the middle circle–the system of measuring the number of people watching specific programs. The currency used to measure the success of television programming is a rating point. These rating points, as is shown later in this chapter, determine the success or failure of programs and, as a consequence, network profitability.

The advertising agency shown in Figure 11.1 acts as a broker or 'middleman' between corporate clients purchasing advertising time and the networks. In general, advertising

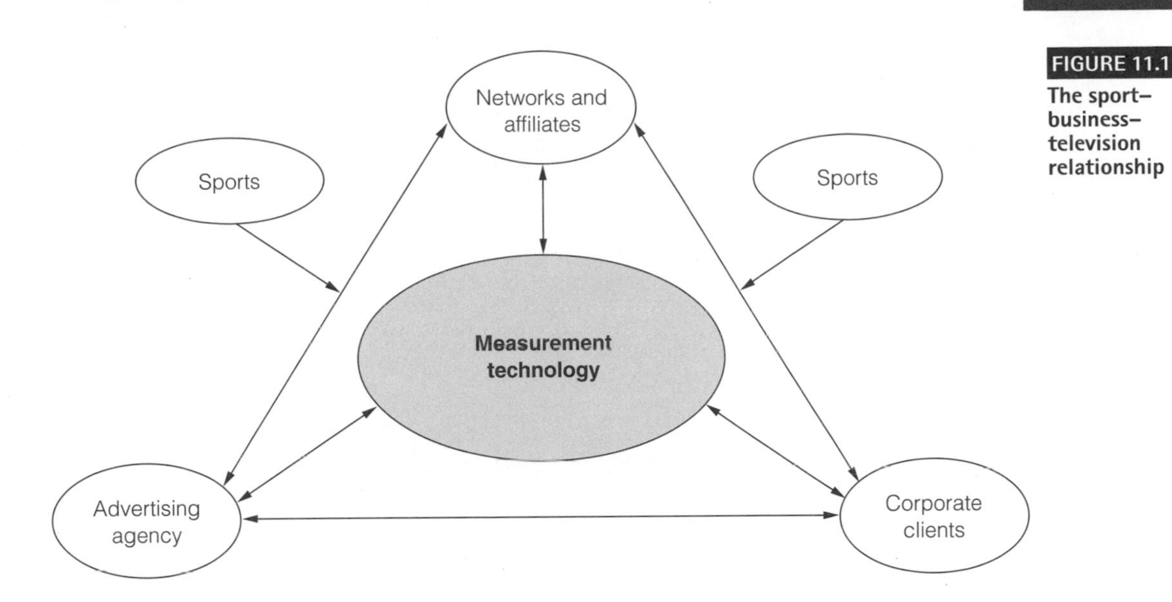

FIGURE 11.1
The sport–business–television relationship

agencies form buying groups, allowing them to obtain discounts on advertising rates from the networks. These discounts are obtained due to the high volume of advertising inventory purchased by the advertising agency, a volume that corporations individually cannot match. Corporate clients at times also negotiate directly with networks, although this is less common because of the ability of the advertising agency to negotiate more favourable rates due to the volume of inventory being purchased.

Advertising agencies also offer expertise in recommending the most efficient forms of advertising or media buys for a particular product. A media buy refers to the range of advertising spots purchased across a variety of networks and programs. In its broadest sense, a media buy also includes other avenues for advertising, such as radio, newspapers, magazines and outdoor billboards. A spot refers to the purchase of advertising inventory on television, usually in the form of a 15-, 30- or 60-second placement of an advertisement during a program. The costs to purchase these spots during sport programming are considered later in this chapter.

Sport programming

The importance and significance of the sport-television relationship are indicated by the rapid increase in sport programming in Australia since the inception of television in 1956. In Sydney in 1958, just over twelve hours of sport programming went to air during the week commencing 1 September. Ten years later during the week commencing 31 August, four stations showed a total of 22 hours of sport programming. Channels Seven and Nine covered Australian Rules and rugby league, with ten one-hour boxing and wrestling programs also shown. By 1978, in the week commencing 2 September, 33 hours of sport programming were shown in Sydney, and by 1988 five channels showed 43 hours of sport during the week beginning 15 August (Jarratt 1988). In Melbourne during the week beginning

26 May 1996, free-to-air sport programming had escalated to 79 hours. By 2002 in the week commencing 16 June, the five free-to-air networks showed just under 100 hours of sport programs. In addition, pay-television providers offer three channels dedicated to 24 hours of sports programming. The increase from 1996 is largely, but not solely, attributable to the extended period of major sports events noted in the headline story. During 2002 Australian pay-television services underwent a rationalisation, with Optus Vision withdrawing its sports content channels, and opting to develop an alliance with Fox Sports to deliver Fox Sports channels.

These results suggest, as did the headline story, that sport programming is a ratings winner. Networks would not schedule so much sport programming if it were not profitable to do so. Why then is sport programming so attractive? Klattell and Marcus (1988: 4) summarise the intrinsic value of sport programming to television:

> At its best, television sports is the finest programming television can offer. In many respects, sports may be the quintessential television program format, taking fullest advantage of the role TV plays in our daily lives. Sports on TV have visually attractive elements–splashy colours, attractive locations, motion and movement galore. They have expansive vistas, exquisite details, and larger-than-life images . . . There is drama, tension, suspense, raw emotion, real anger, unvarnished joy, and a host of other responses. Most of all you are watching real people compete for real, as unsure of the outcome as the viewer. In sports TV the 'bad guy' of the script often wins, unexpected things happen, virtue doesn't necessarily triumph, and goodness is not always rewarded.

The features of sport programming described by Klattell and Marcus underpin the reasons why sport is so attractive to television. They also explain why the networks are prepared to pay large fees to obtain the exclusive rights to broadcast a competition such as the AFL or cricket, or a major event such as the Olympic Games.

How is the IOC able to command these fees, and how do sports such as cricket, rugby union and tennis command significant revenues from the sale of these exclusive rights? Calculation of fees is based on the projected advertising sales and profit derived from the exclusive broadcasting of an event such as the Olympic Games. The value of advertising is determined by the system of measurement used to determine the popularity of programs or, more specifically, how many people watch.

Measuring the television audience

The size and composition of television audiences are measured by ratings services. Ratings are collected by using the 'people meter', an electronic measuring device that records what programs are being watched. This device also has the capacity to record who is watching, which provides important demographic information to networks and advertisers.

Measurements made

The following terminology is used in relation to measuring television audiences.

TABLE 11.1 **Top 20 programs, 2–8 June 2002 (total people)**

	Rank description	Ch.	5 city total	5 city total TARP (%)	Sydney (000s)	Sydney TARP (%)	Melbourne (000s)	Melbourne TARP (%)	Brisbane (000s)	Brisbane TARP (%)	Adelaide (000s)	Adelaide TARP (%)	Perth (000s)	Perth TARP (%)
1	National Nine News Sunday	9	2 030 627	15.30	538 537	12.80	732 753	18.70	351 590	14.90	220 887	17.40	186 859	12.40
2	World Cup Soccer Group Match 23	9	1 888 176	14.20	621 796	14.70	542 731	13.80	272 686	11.50	189 981	14.90	260 982	17.30
3	State of Origin Rugby League Qld v NSW	9	1 686 521	12.70	877 573	20.80	88 994	2.30	664 206	28.10	23 545	1.80	32 203	2.10
4	2nd Big Brother Double Eviction	10	1 660 466	12.50	480 393	11.40	478 671	12.20	292 541	12.40	190 228	14.90	218 633	14.50
5	National Nine News	9	1 647 972	12.40	440 593	10.40	574 312	14.60	345 680	14.60	166 967	13.10	120 420	8.00
6	Harry's Practice	7	1 630 639	12.30	462 462	11.00	547 483	14.00	290 439	12.30	156 077	12.30	174 178	11.60
7	60 Minutes	9	1 627 097	12.20	518 219	12.30	532 550	13.60	264 911	11.20	151 657	11.90	159 760	10.60
8	Ground Force	7	1 615 467	12.20	465 381	11.00	530 503	13.50	220 859	9.30	188 419	14.80	210 305	14.00
9	A Current Affair	9	1 584 959	11.90	461 260	10.90	568 421	14.50	305 656	12.90	138 704	10.90	110 918	7.40
10	Hot Auctions	7	1 554 112	11.70	362 831	8.60	601 329	15.30	176 761	7.50	198 658	15.60	214 533	14.30
11	National Nine News Saturday	9	1 551 224	11.70	407 317	9.70	571 495	14.60	296 550	12.50	141 169	11.10	134 694	8.90
12	Nine's Friday Night Football	9	1 538 176	11.60	461 141	10.90	489 336	12.50	322 223	13.60	181 827	14.30	83 649	5.60
13	E.R.	9	1 532 053	11.50	427 737	10.10	513 811	13.10	292 895	12.40	143 672	11.30	153 938	10.20
14	All Saints	7	1 518 866	11.40	463 653	11.00	468 497	11.90	259 310	11.00	168 401	13.20	159 004	10.60
15	Who Wants to be a Millionaire?	9	1 513 964	11.40	519 558	12.30	516 742	13.20	240 004	10.10	128 867	10.10	108 793	7.20
16	Big Brother Live Nomination	10	1 499 187	11.30	436 268	10.30	351 023	9.00	257 905	10.90	182 226	14.30	271 765	18.10
17	Better Homes and Gardens	7	1 491 713	11.20	460 026	10.90	425 530	10.80	283 276	12.00	180 958	14.20	141 922	9.40
18	Location, Location	9	1 478 951	11.10	523 124	12.40	498 808	12.70	265 578	11.20	191 441	15.00	130 037	8.60
19	Getaway	9	1 471 432	11.10	450 411	10.70	466 073	11.90	262 460	11.10	162 450	12.80	151 675	10.10
20	CSI: Crime Scene Investigation	9	1 466 231	11.00	470 629	11.20	456 911	11.60	250 602	10.60	136 415	10.70		

Source: OzTAM, (2002b), reprinted by permission. Copyright OzTAM.

Homes using television

Homes using television (HUT) is the number of homes where at least one television set is switched on at any point in time. For example, in 2002 there were 1.47 million households (HH) in Sydney with a television and 1.37 households in Melbourne. In excess of 4.75 million households use a television in Sydney, Melbourne, Brisbane, Adelaide and Perth (OzTAM 2002a). In relation to households with pay-television, OzTAM (2002a) estimates show 412 000 in Sydney and 316 000 in Melbourne, with a five-city aggregate of just over 1 million households.

Program ratings

Program ratings are the percentage of households that are tuned to a particular station at a particular time. The top-rating shows in Melbourne for the week ending 8 June 2002 are shown in Table 11.1, with both the total people watching and the total audience rating points (TARP) percentages. OzTAM and the television networks are interested in the specific rating points for those programs, which are derived using the following formula:

$$\text{Rating} = \frac{\text{HH tuned to program}}{\text{Total HH}}$$

As indicated at the start of this chapter, during the month of June 2002 a number of major sports events were telecast, and you will note the World Cup figures prominently in the top 20, together with the rugby league's second State of Origin match and Nine's Friday Night Football (AFL). Note the variance in Table 11.1 in people watching from state to state depending on the event and the other programs that feature in the top 20.

Audience share

Audience share is the percentage of the total viewing audience in a given period tuned to a particular station. This is an important figure, because it considers the number of televisions actually in use and the total size of the potential audience. The number of televisions in use is likely to be fewer than the total number of households with televisions. Audience share is calculated by dividing the number of households watching a program by the number of households using televisions:

$$\text{Share} = \frac{\text{HH tuned to program}}{\text{HUT}}$$

Target audience rating points

Target audience rating points (TARPs) are the audience at a given point in time expressed as a percentage of the potential audience available. Table 11.2 illustrates the cumulative nature of TARPs in relation to 2001 Friday night NRL telecasts. Table 11.2 shows the average Friday night TARPs for the duration of the NRL season. Also shown are the various demographic groups typically used in the analysis by advertisers, networks, corporations and sporting organisations. Corporations are often more interested in the detailed demographic data, as these relate to the groups most likely to purchase the firm's product. In other words, if Coca-Cola advertised during the rugby league telecast, the company might be more interested in the number of people in the 16–24 age group watching Friday night matches, as this might represent an important buying group.

TABLE 11.2 Friday night NRL average ratings

	TCN 9 Sydney		QTQ 9 Brisbane	
	Average homes rating		Average homes rating	
	6.30–7.30pm		5.30–7.30pm	
	24 weeks		24 weeks	
		TARPs		TARPs
Total households	245 975	17.30%	138 161	16.20%
Total individuals	417 851	10.00%	215 880	9.30%
All people 18+	351 661	11.00%	190 478	10.90%
Men 18+	203 278	12.90%	105 428	12.30%
Men 16–24	25 269	9.30%	9 189	6.00%
Men 16–39	89 929	11.30%	39 533	9.50%
Men 18–39	83 136	11.30%	36 851	9.60%
Men 40–54	59 805	13.60%	36 613	14.90%
Men 55–64	30 251	16.00%	14 043	13.10%
Men 65+	30 086	14.30%	17 921	14.80%
Women 18+	148 383	9.10%	85 049	9.50%
Women 16–24	13 911	5.30%	6 757	4.50%
Women 16–39	64 616	8.30%	31 965	7.60%
Women 40–54	34 106	7.80%	27 463	10.90%
Women 55–64	18 842	10.30%	10 934	10.40%
Women 65+	33 039	11.90%	16 861	11.00%
Ppl AB	70 846	9.70%	31 553	9.40%
GB	157 342	11.00%	88 095	10.30%

Source: GTV Nine, (2002).

Gross rating points

Gross rating points (GRPs) are another cumulative measure representing the sum of TARPs for a given schedule, often referred to as total TARPs. Cumulative ratings such as GRPs and TARPs are usually calculated for a week or month and, as noted by Buzzard (1992: 40), are often 'used as a comparison to circulation figures in the print media. It measures the station's overall effectiveness, or the total number of different people who saw a program or commercial'. Reach is a measure of the number of different people watching, and frequency is the number of times a person or household watches the same program, commercial or station. A total television buy of 240 GRPs could be calculated as follows:

$$\frac{\text{GRPs}}{240} = \frac{\text{Reach}}{80} \times \frac{\text{Frequency}}{3}$$

Average audience

Average audience is the estimated audience over a stated period, usually 15 minutes. This figure is usually expressed in thousands. Examples are given in Table 11.2.

People meters

The method used to collect ratings data has changed during the past fifteen years. Up until 1991 the diary was used. This required randomly selected households to fill in their viewing patterns during a two-week period, usually referred to as the ratings period. At the end of the two weeks, the diaries were collected and analysed to determine program ratings. The method by which this information was collected, collated and interpreted was rather slow and cumbersome, compared to the use of the people meter.

In 1989 the first trials began with ACNielsen's people meter. The most significant change as a result of using the people meter was that data could be collected for 52 weeks of the year, thereby removing the tendency of networks to schedule major programs during known ratings periods. A major advantage of the people meter technology is its capacity to download the results of the previous day's viewing by nine o'clock the next morning, providing television executives with immediate feedback on the success of their programs. In 2002 ACNielsen's people meter service was replaced in the metropolitan area by OzTAM, which is a joint venture between the three main commercial broadcasters in Australia. OzTAM subsequently appointed Advanced Television Research (ATR) as the ratings provider, or in other words the agency responsible for data collection. What then is the people meter, and how does it work?

The people meter is a small eight-button unit placed on top of the television set. Each member of the household is assigned a button number, and their names are printed above their assigned button number. There is a set of red and green lights on the front of the unit to indicate whether selected people are in the viewing audience. Green indicates viewing; red indicates no viewing. Household members indicate their viewing by pushing their assigned button on either the people meter or the remote control, changing their light from red to green. There is a button labelled OK that must be pressed when all viewing entries have been made. When a household member leaves the room, he/she must again press a button to indicate no viewing and press the OK button to signify a change in audience. When visitors come into the room, they must indicate their presence by pushing a visitor button on the unit placed on the television. Visitors will be asked their sex and age.

Data collected from people meters are downloaded to a central computer, and it is from here that the various rating figures are generated. As can be seen from the need for visitors to input their basic demographic information, detailed reports are possible for every program. Indeed, detailed reports are possible for every minute of the day for every program. Typically, data are reported in 15-minute blocks.

People meters are an improvement on the diary system, where the accuracy of data reported by households was often suspect. Household members often forgot to complete the diary daily, relying on their memory to fill it in at a later date. Of course, people meters rely on household members diligently turning their green and red lights on and off as they cycle in and out of watching television.

The other major weakness of the people meter is that it cannot detect whether household members are actually watching television, even though they are recorded as being in the room. Remember, this is important because the advertisers assume that people recorded as being in the room actually watch the program and register or acknowledge the advertisements shown. Whether this is the case is examined later in this chapter.

Audience sampling

People meters are not installed in every house using a television. This would be too costly and time-consuming. To obtain reliable data a random sample of the population is taken. The objective of the sample is to install meters in a random, representative and projectable sample of households for the defined market. At present OzTam uses a sample of 3000 metropolitan households randomly selected, including 750 from Sydney, 700 from Melbourne, 600 from Brisbane, and 475 each from Adelaide and Perth. These 3000 homes determine the success and failure of television programs and in turn the value of advertising. Regional and pay-television ratings data are collected by ACNielsen. To ensure a valid sample, there must be a genuine representation of the population within each city or regional area. Factors taken into account include postcode, size of household, number of television sets, age of the grocery buyer, presence of children and claimed reception of TV stations (OzTAM 2002a). Households not eligible for the sample include:

- non-private dwellings–hospitals, prisons, schools etc.;
- households without a television;
- households of people working in the television, market research or advertising industries;
- households moving within the next three months; and
- households occupied for less than nine months a year.

Advertising during sport programming

Super Bowl XXXVII (2003) advertising inventory is expected to sell at just over US$2 million per 30-second spot. Friedman (2002: 3) notes that 'Walt Disney Co. has taken the unusual step of selling Super Bowl inventory much earlier than usual, making the game broadcast on ABC part of an unprecedented deal with OMD USA, New York that exceeds $1 billion. OMD has agreed to buy about one third of the inventory in the Super Bowl–around 20 30-second commercials'. Although OMD will probably secure these spots for less than the anticipated US$2 million due to volume purchase, it nevertheless is still a significant sum of money to pay for advertising during sports programming. The Ten Network, broadcasters of the 2002 AFL Grand Final, one of the biggest TV-watching days of the year in Australia, were hoping to attract advertisers nationally across the network at $60 000. Individual markets ranged from $30 000 per 30-second spot in Melbourne to $6000 in Brisbane. In the 2001/02 summer of cricket, advertising rates peaked at $16 000 for the first and second one-day finals played in Sydney and Melbourne. Test Matches played against New Zealand in 2001/02 attracted advertising rates of $2900, rising to $4800 for Test matches against South Africa. Interestingly, 30-second spot rates for the Perth Test match televised in the eastern states during prime time (three-hour time difference) rose to $10 000.

An example of the strategy used to sell advertising inventory by the networks is seen in Figure 11.2. Some of the sales data for the 2002 Australian Formula 1 Grand Prix in Melbourne are shown, along with ratings data for the 2001 event, telecast schedules for 2002, the cost of television sponsorships of the event and the cost of 30-second spot packages. National sponsorships of such sporting events usually offer more to the corporation than traditional spot advertising. In this example, television sponsorship benefits included:

- specially produced opening and closing and internal billboards;
- promotion–sponsor will receive logo association with telecast promotion;
- ten 30-second spots spread through all telecasts on all Nine Network stations;
- placement–4 × 30 seconds on Saturday and 6 × 30 seconds on Sunday.

FIGURE 11.2 *Wide World of Sports* **Telecast Guide for the Australian Formula 1 Grand Prix, Melbourne 2001**

The Formula One Series will hit Melbourne in February–March for the 1st round of the FIA Formula One Championship at Albert Park.

11 Formula One teams, 22 Formula One drivers, and hundreds of thousands of fans will flock to the Albert Park circuit.

The 2002 Qantas Australian Grand Prix will be held from 28 February to 3 March and promises to be one of the most tightly fought championship contests in years.

Nine's *Wide World of Sports* cameras will be on hand to provide a comprehensive coverage of the weekend's racing, coverage that has earned the FOA award for best telecast worldwide, five times.

Once Melbourne has been decided, the circuit will continue on its journey around the world in 16 different countries. Monaco, Imola, Magny Cours, Spa Francorchamps and Monza are just a few of the exotic locations.

The Nine Network will take you along for the ride as we buckle up for another year of high-octane action, only on the *Wide World of Sports*.

Average Rating for Sunday, 3 March 2001

	TCN-9 Sydney		GTV-9 Melbourne		QTQ-9 Brisbane		NWS-9 Adelaide		STW-9 Perth	
	000's	TARP %	000's	TARP %	000's	TARP %	000's	TARP %	000's	TARP %
Homes	176 588	12.40	364 228	27.10	146 578	17.20	89 936	18.10	67 925	12.60
All people	272 337	6.50	612 924	15.90	203 600	8.80	144 993	11.40	94 880	6.40
Child 5-12	18 961	4.40	42 009	10.40	12 992	5.20	11 954	9.30	2099	1.30
Teens 13-17	7843	2.90	38 280	15.30	386	0.20	4388	5.20	4066	3.70
All people 18+	231 590	7.20	514 019	17.30	184 453	10.50	122 276	12.50	88 051	7.80
Men 18+	157 875	10.00	289 191	19.90	114 696	13.40	75 920	16.00	56 182	10.10
Men 18-24	25 197	11.70	20 129	9.80	10 542	8.80	6584	10.60	4289	5.20
Men 25-39	56 911	10.90	123 888	26.60	41 294	15.70	22 337	16.30	23 097	13.50
Men 40-54	37 629	8.50	91 303	22.90	30 292	12.30	22 901	16.80	15 527	9.60
Men 55-60	21 371	11.30	26 302	15.20	18 483	17.30	10 622	17.70	7708	11.20
Men 65+	16 767	8.00	27 569	13.30	14 083	11.60	13 477	16.70	5561	7.70
Women 18+	73 715	4.50	224 827	14.80	69 757	7.80	46 356	9.20	31 868	5.60
Women 18-24	10 624	5.10	13 318	6.70	6823	5.70	3650	6.10	4913	6.20
Women 25-39	26 448	5.10	86 936	18.50	16 942	6.30	15 960	11.80	10 848	6.50
Women 40-54	14 716	3.40	50 399	12.40	18 105	7.20	16 044	11.40	10 363	6.30
Women 55-60	8801	4.80	47 051	26.90	11 619	11.00	4576	7.40	2251	3.40
Women 65+	13 126	4.70	27 123	10.00	16 268	10.60	6125	5.70	3497	3.70
Grocery buyers	97 867	6.90	220 274	16.30	80 321	9.40	59 531	12.00	40 363	7.50
SE AB	54 389	7.50	88 841	14.70	18 420	5.50	20 261	11.90	11 281	5.00

2002 TELECAST SCHEDULE

	Saturday, 2 March 2002	Sunday, 3 March 2002
TCN-9 Sydney	12.30pm–4.00pm	10.30am–4.30pm
GTV 9 Melbourne	12.30pm–4.00pm	10.30am–4.30pm
QTQ-9 Brisbane	11.30am–3.00pm	9.30am–3.30pm
NWS-9 Adelaide	12.00pm–3.30pm	10.00am–4.00pm
STW-9 Perth	9.30am–1.00pm	7.30am–1.30pm

Television sponsorship

National sponsorship of the telecasts of the Melbourne Grand Prix is available and provides association with this unique sporting event.

Sponsorship benefits include:

- Billboards—Opening, closing and internal.
- Promotion—Sponsors will receive logo association with telecast promotion.
- Spot package—10 × 30 seconds per network station.
- Placement—Saturday 4 × 30 seconds
  Sunday 6 × 30 seconds

*Only sponsors receive airtime in actual race—2 × 30 seconds

The price of this National Sponsorship is:

TCN-9 Sydney	$ 40 000
GTV-9 Melbourne	$ 95 000
QTQ-9 Brisbane	$ 25 000
NWS-9 Adelaide	$ 25 000
STW-9 Perth	$ 20 000
Network	$205 000

SPOT PACKAGES

Spots can be purchased through all telecasts on all stations or in any specific telecast on individual stations or in any combination.

	Saturday, 2 March 2002	Sunday, 3 March 2002
TCN-9 Sydney	$2500	$4000
GTV-9 Melbourne	$6000	$10 000
QTQ-9 Brisbane	$1000	$2200
NWS-9 Adelaide	$1000	$2200
STW-9 Perth	$600	$2000
NETWORK	$11 100	$20 400

Source: GTV Nine (2002).

Sponsoring an event like the Grand Prix is obviously more expensive than simply purchasing a series of 30-second spots, as is indicated in Figure 11.2. Most coverage of major sporting events includes television sponsorship opportunities. Sales of advertising time and television sponsorships are the precursors to determining the worth of television rights purchased by networks. It is important for sport managers to value the potential revenue to networks from televising their sport. Sportview 11.1 illustrates how revenue generated from advertising during sport programming can be calculated. It is this calculation that leads to determining the television rights paid by networks for exclusive broadcasting of sporting events.

SPORTVIEW 11.1

Calculating the worth of AFL television rights

The first live telecast of Australian football occured in 1957. The popularity of these broadcasts resulted in the Victorian Football League (VFL) charging £500 per station to televise football in 1958. The television station that has remained most closely aligned with football is the Seven Network. In 1976, Channel Seven paid $3 million over five years. Channel Seven has retained the rights until 2002 except season 1987. In 1988, the Seven Network paid $30 million for the seasons 1988 to 1992. In 1991, the Seven Network renegotiated the rights for $47 million for three years to the end of the 1995 season. A further $10 million in free advertising was also negotiated during rights deal with the Seven Network for a figure reported to be $90 million for the three years 1996 to 1998. Another new contract was established for the period 1999 to 2001 and was negotiated in 1995. This latest deal also included an agreement between the Seven Network and pay-television operator Optus Vision to telecast all AFL games during the 1996 season. Mostly, these games were replays, with a handful shown live.

Data collected during the 1995 season showed how much revenue advertising during AFL programming on the Seven Network generated. The information shown in this sportview was collected during telecasts of Rounds 21 and 22 and the first final round of the 1995 season. Content analysis of the sport programming shown in Melbourne revealed 860 minutes of AFL programming shown during Round 21 870 minutes in Round 22 and 570 minutes during the first week of the finals. The purpose of this investigation was to determine the worth of advertising during these matches to the Seven Network. The table below shows the amount of actual football shown (F), advertising time (Ad) and time given to station promotions (Ch 7).

AFL programming on the Seven Network, Melbourne, 1995 (minutes)

	Round 21			Round 22			First week finals		
	F	Ad	Ch 7	F	Ad	Ch 7	F	Ad	Ch 7
Friday night	132.7	22.2	5.0	146.5	30.0	3.5	155.5	20.5	4.0
Saturday replay	69.75	17.25	3.0	69.5	17.5	3.0	68.0	19.0	3.0
Saturday night	153.0	33.0	4.0	146.5	29.75	3.75	153.0	22.0	5.0
Sunday game day	46.0	12.0	2.0	46.0	12.0	2.0	45.25	12.75	2.0
Sunday live	297.5	55.0	7.5	294.0	59.5	6.5	46.0	12.0	2.0
Total	699.0	139.5	21.5	702.5	148.7	18.75	467.5	86.25	16.0
Percent	81.3	16.2	2.5	80.7	17.1	2.2	82.1	15.1	2.8

On average, 81.6% of telecast time was devoted to football. The remaining 18.4% of the telecast featured non-program material of which 15.9% was devoted to advertising and 2.5% to Seven Network promotions. The total potential revenue generated through sale of advertising was determined by multiplying the rate for a 30-second commercial by the number of advertisements that appeared throughout the telecast. A 60-second advertisement was simply credited with two commercial placements and a 15-second advertisement with half a commercial placement. The cost to advertise (30-second spot) ranged from $1500 for Sunday game day to $4000 for Saturday night replay, Saturday and Sunday night live, and $4800 for Friday night.

From calculating the worth of time dedicated to advertising, revenue to the Seven Network during each weekend of the broadcasts was worth in excess of $1.2 million. Over the three weekends $3 854 000 of advertising inventory was available. Actual revenue generated was $3 307 850, which represents inventory available minus Seven Network promotions.

The Seven Network paid approximately $13.5 million for the rights to the 1995 season. Based on a 22-week home and away season, and three rounds of finals (total 25 weeks), there was a capacity to generate advertising revenue in excess of $32 million (averaged over 25 weeks at $1 284 700 per week) in the Melbourne market. Other special events during the season included State-of-Origin, the Brownlow Medal count and the Grand Final, which would generate significantly more advertising revenue and value to the advertiser.

Numerous methods exist enabling advertisers to measure the cost efficiency of their advertising in terms of number of people reached. These methods utilise the value of gross rating points, total audience rating points, cost per rating point and cost per thousand. To obtain a measure reflecting the needs of advertisers, the cost per thousand (CPM) was used to determine advertising effectiveness (i.e. homes reached). CPM is defined as 'how much it costs to advertise to reach 1000 homes or viewers' (Buzzard 1992: 42). The formula for determining CPM is the cost of the buy divided by the average households or persons reached, per average minute or quarter-hour, multiplied by 1000.

Average household ratings for each segment were obtained for each telecast and converted into the total number of Melbourne households (1 118 000) tuned into the telecast. The cost to reach 1000 Melbourne homes ranged from $14 to $29 over the review period of the telecast. The range in Round 21 was $15 to $22, in Round 22 $14 to $19 and in the first week of the finals $14 to $29. Using the Friday night Round 21 fixture as an example, the calculation of the CPM is obtained by taking the advertising rate of $4800 and dividing by the average homes viewing (220 000, rating 18.9). This figure is then divided by 1000, providing a resultant figure of 22, indicating that it cost the advertisers $22 to reach every 1000 Melbourne homes during Round 21 Friday night game. These figures indicate a good return on investment to advertisers in terms of audience reach. In essence it cost advertisers 22 cents per home.

Results achieved from this study indicate that the Seven network seems to be performing extremely well in recouping its investment in football. Revenue exceeding $1 million each weekend for 10–15 hours of telecast equates to in excess of $27 million for the season, solely from the Melbourne market. These figures are achieved despite the Seven network forgoing $4.5 million of potential revenue each season in order to promote its own programs.

The Seven network incurs production costs as well as its outlay to the AFL for the rights, and these production costs reduce the revenue generated from sale of advertising time. Production costs usually assume approximately 20% of the network's total outlay. Considering the cost of the rights paid to the AFL ($500 000 per weekend) and including costs of production (assuming costs in the region of $100 000 per weekend), the revenue obtained from the Melbourne market appears to indicate a very healthy return on investment. Income exceeding $1.1 million each weekend, minus expenditures of $600 000 for production and station promotions, provides a weekly profit in excess of $500 000. Over a 25-week period this represents profits exceeding $25 million.

Lawrence (1995) indicates that in 1994 the rights fees were worth between $15 million and $17 million and the revenue generated from sales of aadvertising was worth $35 million. Based on the figures obtained from the analysis of three rounds of AFL extrapolated over 25 weeks, it would seem that a large proportion of this $35 million would be generated through the Melbourne market alone, highlighting the strategic significance of the Melbourne television audience to both the AFL and the Seven Network.

Source: Adjusted from Turner and Shilbury (1997).

Advertising effectiveness

Nakra (1991: 217) notes that:

> commercial avoidance and audience erosion are two interrelated problems that marketing executives and media planners have been aware of for more than 30 years. With the rapid advancement of technology the problem of 'zapping' has become even more predominant.

Zapping involves viewers rapidly changing channels in order to avoid commercials. It also involves video-recorded programs, where viewers simply fast-forward past the advertisements. Zapping therefore represents a fundamental challenge to the basis of the television advertising formula, which assumes, as indicated earlier in this chapter, that viewers recorded as watching a program also watch and acknowledge advertisements. A difference can exist between exposure to the program and exposure to the commercial messages. It is likely that further advances in technology will improve the ability of the viewer to zap commercials.

Central to this issue of zapping is the cost-effectiveness of advertising. The best-known method for establishing the cost-efficiencies between program buys is cost per thousand (CPM). An example of the use of CPM is shown in Sportview 11.1. This method has been widely used to show 'audience or target size counts, which may or may not accurately represent the number of people viewing the program, segments of it, or the commercials' (Lloyd & Clancy 1991: 34). Lloyd and Clancy posit three questions in relation to their suggestion for the use of a measure known as cost per thousand involved (CPMI):

1 Do individual programs differ in their ability to involve viewers?
2 Just how closely related are CPM and CPMI for the same set of programs?
3 In other words, would media planners and buyers make the same or different media buys if the decision were based on CPM versus CPMI?

The answers to these questions are based on the extent to which the media environment affects, tempers or moderates the nature of the advertising response. Two hypotheses have emerged from research investigating these questions. The first asserts that the more involved viewers are in a program and the more they like it and are engaged by it, the weaker will be the advertising response. Proponents of this hypothesis maintain that commercial breaks represent an unnecessarily intrusive element in an otherwise enjoyable viewing experience. As a consequence, the advertisements are filtered out, perceived negatively or simply avoided. The second hypothesis adopts the opposite view. It suggests that characteristics of the program, as subjectively perceived by the involved viewer, produce efforts to minimise surrounding distractions and cause an enhanced orientation towards the program and source of the stimulus (Lloyd & Clancy 1991). Enhanced involvement prompts the viewer to remain activated, producing a more positive impact on advertising effectiveness. Implications of these hypotheses are:

- to develop appropriate ratings indexes to determine program involvement; and
- to factor these indexes into CPMI measures.

At present, no research is available indicating the level of involvement that sport programming generates. However, sport programming for cricket, for example, where only one short commercial can be shown between overs, may have an advantage in ensuring that viewers watch and acknowledge the commercial (i.e. do not zap). Australian Rules football may also have a similar advantage, as commercials are shown after a goal is scored and are typically last just 30 seconds before play recommences. Sports such as golf, basketball and car racing may provide viewers with the opportunity to leave the room, knowing that a series of four to five commercials will be shown.

This also raises the question of advertisement placing in programs. Typically, first-in and last-out commercials are considered more valuable, as viewers see the first before leaving the room and the last when returning after the commercial break. Interestingly, networks often use the first or last advertisement for their own station program promotion purposes.

All of these factors impinge on the effectiveness of advertising during sport programming. Little research has been conducted on sport programming to shed more light on the answers to the questions raised in this section. There is little doubt, however, that these issues form the basis on which networks set advertising rates and, as a consequence, the amount in television rights they are prepared to pay sporting organisations.

Pay-television

Another player has recently entered the sport–business–television relationship. Pay-television was introduced to Australia in 1995. It is slowly becoming available worldwide, contributing to the globalised economy and in particular the familiarity of sport.

The business basis on which pay-TV is predicated is fundamentally different from that of the free-to-air networks described in this chapter. So far we have described how free-to-air networks rely on advertising as their primary source of revenue and profit. Free-to-air networks are in the business of reaching the widest possible audience, hence the term broadcasting. Free-to-air television is popular and generally taken for granted as an everyday part of life. Pay-television, on the other hand, requires the payment of subscription fees to receive programming. The basic operating premise on which pay-TV exists is known as narrowcasting, and its revenue base is sourced from subscription fees. Unlike with the free-to-air networks, advertising is not the predominant revenue source.

Pay-television in Australia at present is not as freely accessible as the free-to-air networks. It is assumed that this market will expand over time. Initially, advertising on pay-TV was banned for a period of five years, although in mid-1997 advertising became legal, diversifying revenue opportunities and more closely aligning pay-television with the free-to-air networks. Logically, this will intensify competition for advertising revenue in the television industry.

Legislation governing the introduction of pay-TV in Australia prohibits major sporting events being shown solely on pay-TV. For example, the AFL Grand Final, Melbourne Cup, major golf and tennis events, and the Olympic Games are subject to anti-siphoning laws designed to ensure that the majority of the population retains the ability to see these sporting events. Pay-TV represents further opportunities for sports with their marketing, promotion and revenue-generating strategies. The sport channels, in concert with the movie channels, are pay-TV's greatest strength in terms of attracting subscribers. The opportunity therefore presents itself to an increasing range of sports to obtain some exposure via pay-television.

In terms of extracting rights revenue from pay-TV operators, the same principle applies as for free-to-air operators: to determine how much revenue the sport contributes to the network. The difference is that it is not so easy to calculate this contribution. Free-to-air networks, as shown earlier in this chapter, can simply calculate the total advertising time in dollar terms, thereby determining how much direct value sport programming represents. It is more difficult to determine how many subscribers subscribe solely or predominantly because a specific sport is shown on a pay-TV channel. In some cases, major sports such as cricket, the AFL and rugby league clearly add to the likelihood that subscriptions will grow due to their availability on a pay-TV channel. The AFL, for example, has a dedicated channel on Fox Sports at an extra cost of approximately $8 per month. Rugby league is also shown extensively on Fox Sports, exemplifying the impact of the major sports as a strategic source of programming.

Fundamentally, sports not already receiving extensive free-to-air coverage will want to obtain exposure on pay-television. In the end, for some of these sports, the benefits may be the exposure via programming rather than any financial gains via television rights for exclusive coverage. This highlights the important role of television in the overall marketing and promotion of sport. Some sports, as demonstrated in this chapter, have the capacity to gain financially from television broadcasts; others do not have this capacity. For some sports, the opportunity to gain exposure through programming without receiving any financial incentive is another important consideration when developing promotion mix decisions. It is also possible that some sports will have to pay to have their sport shown on either pay-TV or free-to-air television. In this case, the decision to spend money will come from the promotion mix budget. Television therefore is an important consideration when framing promotion mix decisions.

Another question that arises is what sport managers need to do to enhance the attractiveness of a sport for television. There is no easy answer to this question. Some sports have used rule changes to make the game more attractive; other sports have changed the uniforms worn by players to make them more appealing; still other sports have simply paid for airtime until their sport has become well recognised and people want to watch it on a regular basis. Whether it is pay-TV or free-to-air television, the formula does not change. Television executives will want to know how much revenue and subsequent profit the sport will attract for the network before they agree to show it on television. It is possible that pay-TV offers slightly greater opportunities in the early years, as there will be pressure to fill programming, particularly on all-sport channels.

One thing is certain: the complexity of the sport-business-television relationship is intensifying in terms of attracting revenue sources and viewers. What has not changed is that programming is designed to capture a market of viewers, to either expose them to advertising or to get them to subscribe to a pay-TV operator's range of channels.

Digital television

Fancy using your television to order a pizza, enter a competition or change the narration on a documentary? Digital television promises such features, but Australians are far from being able to take up the advantages. Not so in Britain, where 39% of the population has access to interactive TV—compared with 35% who use the Internet—allowing them to control which court they watch during Wimbledon, for example, or to order food while watching a Pizza Hut ad (Hickman 2002: 6).

This is the brave new world confronting the television executive and ultimately the sports consumer and sport marketer. Imagine being able to choose your preferred match and court at Wimbledon, or the golf hole or players you, the sports fan, would actually like to watch during a golf tournament. This may be possible with the onset of digital television during the next decade. The implications for sport broadcasting are significant. Digital television's introduction to Australia has commenced–albeit in a rather uncertain environment, as it relates to standards and protocols for the delivery of digital services. Nevertheless, during the next decade high-definition television services will become available, and with them the potential for interactivity, such as that described by Hickman.

Although pay-TV has brought a greater number of channels to consumers worldwide, this is nothing compared to the capacity of digital television, which has the potential to unblock the content bottleneck through the provisions of hundreds and hundreds of channels. In the traditional analogue format, delivery was restricted by television's large usage of spectra or frequencies available to broadcast. Digital transmission is expected to improve quality and allow interactivity and consequently, greater control by sports consumers of the type of programs watched, and the cameras and angles used. At the heart of this technological revolution is bandwidth: 'Bandwidth refers to the capacity to distribute content... Digitized information can be made to take up much less space than analog signals. In a process known as compression, unnecessary information can be removed from video signals.' (Todreas 1999: 79)

The opportunities to arise from technological developments such as digital television need to be carefully considered by sport-marketing managers. The implications extend beyond the value of television rights to sporting organisations, but also to where the control starts and stops for the provision of services to sports consumers. Recent issues surrounding virtual advertising, essentially made possible by digital technology, highlight the complexities new technologies create for sport managers and television executives. For example, virtual advertising can be incorporated in a telecast without disrupting the view to the spectators. However, these images can be set to block out existing ground signage, which would cause some obvious problems (individual corporations pay for the right to display ground signs knowing that television will pick up these signs as part of the broadcast). Perhaps the most interesting potential usage of interactive television is shown in Sportview 11.2.

SPORTVIEW 11.2

Di3: Sky Gamestar invests in interactive TV software for World Cup 2002

Sky digital viewers can join in this year's biggest sporting event and manage their own international football team in a new interactive World Cup fantasy football game, using software developed by Di3.

Launching this May, Sky's World Super Manager is available to internet users around the world via the Sky Sports website at www.skysports.com and to over 15 million digital satellite viewers in the UK via Sky Gamestar—Sky's dedicated TV games portal.

The game allows budding Sven Goran Erikssons to pit their sporting wits and select and manage a team of international players from the 32 football World Cup squads. Di3's back-end database management and scheduling technology does all the maths, allowing players to monitor their team's performance from the comfort of their armchair as the tournament unfolds.

Di3's interactive games engine was first used by Sky for Sky Sports Super Manager—the UK's first cross-platform fantasy football game. The existing software has now been enhanced by Di3 to handle transfers throughout the FIFA World Cup competition and prompt swapping of eliminated players after knockout phases. Registered users of Sky Super Manager will be able to transfer their existing username and password to the World Cup competition.

Adrian Pilkington, Head of Games at BSkyB, commented: 'Fantasy Football has been a tremendous success so far with over 70,000 Sky Gamestar teams registered since launch in November. The Sky World Manager version lets players compete nationally for the glory of becoming the ultimate Manager—all through their Sky remote control'.

Mark Hughes, managing director, Di3, explained: 'Sport has already proved to be an extremely popular genre for contextual interactive TV services. For the sports fan, iTV enhances the viewing experience by adding a new entertainment dimension. For the content provider, it attracts increased revenues and generates viewer loyalty'.

Di3 designs game engines and other iTV software that can be extended to serve a number of platforms and a variety of payment mechanisms. For example, online players pay a registration fee via a secure server while set top box players pay via a premium rate telephone number. New games and genres can also be added cost-effectively.

Source: Extract from M2 PressWIRE, 2002. Reprinted by permission, M2 PressWIRE, www.m2.com.

Summary

This chapter attempted to demystify the sport-business-television relationship. Television rights to sporting events are one of the most visible and talked-about components of sport marketing. The networks of the world pay exorbitant sums for the exclusive rights to broadcast sporting events such as the Olympic Games and World Cup soccer. These sums merely recognise the number of people watching such events. Sporting events at varying levels—some worldwide, some nationally—deliver audiences to advertisers via programming, which in turn delivers revenues to sport in the form of rights fees and profits to television networks via the sale of advertising inventory.

The people meter is the electronic device used to measure the success of television programs. The people meter collects ratings, which measure how many people with televisions are watching a particular program. Audience share and TARPs also measure the success of television programs, providing detailed and specific information about who is watching. It is not enough simply to identify how many people with televisions are watching a program: it is also important to know the demographic profile of these viewers. Advertising rates are based on ratings figures, and the income derived from advertising determines what rights fees can be paid for the exclusive broadcast rights to sporting events.

Some sporting organisations have been slow to awaken to the value of their product. In marketing terms, many sports have not maximised their revenue opportunities through television, primarily through not understanding how the worth of television rights is calculated. As the sport sector professionalises, this is changing, as evidenced in the escalation of rights fees during the past decade.

The other major marketing benefit to be gained from television is exposure. Indirectly, televised sport has the potential to attract viewers to the live event, thereby contributing to the revenue generated via gate receipts. In many ways this is a vicious circle. Televised sporting events can contribute to reduced attendances, explaining why sport programming is often 'blacked out' in the city where the event is being staged. Television therefore is an important consideration when framing marketing and promotion mix decisions.

Pay-television contributes to the exposure sporting organisations may gain from television. The relatively recent introduction of pay-TV to Australia has meant exposure for sports not normally shown on television. Pay-TV is beginning to offer reasonable exposure because the subscriber base is steadily growing. Therefore, only the major professional sports have demonstrated the capacity to attract revenue from pay-TV providers. Over a period of time, however, it might also offer some revenue-generating potential for smaller sports. This chapter showed that the principal source of revenue for pay-TV operators comes from individual household subscriptions; however, pay-TV operators are also allowed to show advertisements, thereby diversifying sources of revenue. This revenue source is not anticipated to be large in the short term, but will create some discomfort for the free-to-air networks.

The various business relationships described in this chapter are neither mysterious nor surprising once the commercial basis on which television operates is understood. What is interesting is the complex set of relationships developing between sport and television as both endeavour to maximise the revenues and profits from their respective product offerings.

CASE STUDY

OzTAM and ACNielsen TV ratings services

It is not surprising that Australia's big advertisers and media buyers are feeling exasperated. With the close of the first official television ratings week of 2001 on Saturday, February 17, the audience measurement figures have created nothing but confusion and bad feeling between the metropolitan commercial networks and the advertisers who pay about $2.5 billion to them each year (*Business Review Weekly* 2001).

The reason for the conflict can be traced to the three commercial networks' decision to jointly form a company to undertake the important task of measuring audiences watching television programs. OzTAM, jointly owned by Nine, Seven and Ten, is responsible for providing to the networks daily measurements garnered from service provider Australian Television Research (ATR). The decision to form OzTAM meant that ACNeilsen, the company previously responsible for data collection and reporting, was replaced, although it maintained responsibility for regional television audience measurement.

The source of the conflict between the advertisers and networks was a result of measurement discrepancies reported by both OzTAM and ACNielsen. The latter continued to report its rating results after the contract had expired. Meade (2001: 8) reported, for example, that 'ratings figures from OzTAM reveal the Nine Network medical drama *ER* to be the no. 1 program for last week, with a total of 1.8 million viewers nationally. Nine's other hit show, Friends, came ninth with 1.6 million viewers. But ACNielsen data for the same week has the US sitcom taking out the top position with 1.9 million viewers'. With so much advertising money contingent on ratings points, a few points' variance can be costly for both network and advertiser. Bryden-Brown (2001) confirms the industry-wide criticism OzTAM was confronting due to the acute differences in rating data between OzTAM and ACNielsen.

The reason there is so much difference between OzTAM and ACNielsen is the size of the sample and its location. As it is too costly and impractical to measure the viewing habits of every household with a television, the measurement agencies employ a sample of the five major cities in Australia, the formation of which is based on statistically accepted procedures. However, there remains the potential for sample bias and sample error. The importance of obtaining an accurate and objective sample lay at the heart of the dispute between advertisers and networks, and between the networks themselves. Independent New Zealand auditor Professor Peter Danaher, who was recruited by OzTAM and ACNielsen to analyse and explain the reasons for the differences between television ratings data (Meade 2001), noted that: 'Since both ATR and ACN operate a sample of homes, the ratings they report are subject to usual sampling errors. For the Sydney market ATR has about 1900 panellists, while ACN has about 1400 panellists. For samples of this size the respective maximum sampling errors are 2.3% and 2.7%. Therefore, all rating comparisons must be put into the perspective of an expected sampling error band of the order 2 to 3 per cent. That is, two ratings are significantly different only if they differ by more than 3 rating points. For the smaller panels in Brisbane, Adelaide and Perth, this tolerance level is up to 3 to 4 rating points'. (OzTAM 2001)

Wilmoth (2001: 2) reports that Danaher found that 'the "weighting" system used by Australian Television Research, the company that collects ratings for OzTAM, meant a greater proportion of young people's viewing habits had been recorded. It found that the disproportionate weighting in OzTAM's audience sample clearly needed attention, especially in Melbourne, where over half the survey groups were badly under or over-represented'. The report, covering 18 March to 7 April, found that on 30 March one panellist had a 'weight' of 20000 people and that this accounted for half a rating point, which was estimated to be worth approximately $12.5 million in adverting revenue (Wilmoth 2001). Danaher also found that about 85% of the ratings reported by OzTAM and ACNielsen were within the statistical tolerance that is expected of a sample survey. Other important issues included the number of age categories used, establishing the correct proportion of single-person homes, and thus finding the right balance of older people, younger people and homes with children. Also the length of time people have been on the panel and panel fatigue can influence results. The people meter system relies on the diligence of panellists to register their viewing by pushing the buttons that control the people meter.

Finding the right statistical balance will always be a challenge for whatever company is responsible for collecting and interpreting television ratings data. As long as it is too costly to measure all households, it will remain important to accurately and independently measure television audiences. The agency responsible for measurement is also an issue.

Tensions between the networks in the early stages of OzTAM's entry to the market created an interesting situation, as each network was a part-owner in the company responsible for reporting audience measurement. The Nine Network, in particular, was strident in its criticism of the new measurement systems, with Schulze (2001: 3) observing that 'Nine Network chief executive David Leckie must be thinking it's better the devil you know'. Nine had been the initial loser in the new system, with Wilmoth (1991: 2) noting that 'When OzTAM first published its ratings in January (2001), the Seven Network took the lead from Nine for the first time in many years, causing alarm at Kerry Packer's TV stations'.

With a half a rating point worth approximately $12.5 million per anum to a network, it is no wonder that the Nine Network was concerned about the system responsible for knocking it off its position as the number 1 network in Australia, albeit temporarily.

Questions

1. Why is OzTAM a joint venture of the three Australian commercial networks? Comment on the ethical dimensions of the three networks' decision to jointly organise for the supply of television audience measurement.
2. Why is the sample error important in understanding rating measures? How do the differing sample sizes used by ACNielsen and ATR affect sample error?
3. Why is it important to attain a representative sample from various demographic groups? Explain, using specific television shows you watch or know about, how the under- or over-representation affects the sale of advertising inventory for television programs.
4. Explain why the ACNielsen and ATR systems produced different ratings data.
5. What is panelist fatigue? How might panelist fatigue affect ratings measurement?

Appendix 11.1—Worldwide television rights

US PROFESSIONAL SPORTS

NFL	US$ million	Network	Baseball	US$ million	Network
1978–81	646	ABC, CBS, NBC	1980–83	46	ABC, NBC, USA
1982–86	210	ABC, CBS, NBC	1984–89	183	ABC, NBC
1987–89	1430	ABC, CBS, NBC	1990–93	365	CBS, ESPN
1990–93	3650	ABC, CBS, NBC, ESPN, TNT	1994	85	The Baseball Network (joint venture ABC, NBC) ESPN
1994–97	4388	ABC, Fox, NBC, ESPN, TNT	1996-2002	2331	Fox, NBC, ESPN
1998–2005	17 600	Fox, CBS, ABC, ESPN	2003-2008	3 300	Fox, ESPN

NBA	US$ million	Network	NHL (in USA)	US$ million	Network
1982–86	27	CBS, TBS, USA	1987-88	8	ESPN
1986–90	66	CBS, TBS	1988-89	15.9	SportsChannel
1990–94	219	NBC, Turner	1989-90	16.8	SportsChannel
1994/95–1997/98	1 292.05	NBC, Turner	1990-92	23.3	SportsChannel
1998/99–2001/02	2 640	NBC, TNT,	1992-94	29.5	ESPN
2002/3–2007/8	4 600	ESPN, ABC (Walt Disney Co.) TNT, TBS America Online (AOL Time Warner)	1994/95–1998/99	216.5	Fox, ESPN

Source: USA Today (1994); Hirsley (1998); Zbar (2002); Mermigas (2002).

OLYMPIC GAMES

USA Summer	US$ (million)	Venue	Network	USA Winter	US$ (millions)	Venue	Network
1980	85	Moscow	NBC	1980	15.5	Lake Placid	ABC
1984	225.6	Los Angeles	ABC	1984	91.6	Sarajevo	ABC
1988	300	Seoul	NBC	1988	309	Calgary	ABC
1992	401	Barcelona	NBC	1992	243	Albertville	CBS
1996	456[a]	Atlanta	NBC	1994	295	Lillehammer	CBS
2000	705	Sydney	NBC	1998	375	Nagarno	CBS
2004	793[a]	Athens	NBC	2002	545[a]	Salt Lake City	NBC
2008	894[a]	Beijing	NBC	2006	613[a]	Turin	NBC

Australia Summer	US$ (million)	Venue	Network	Australia Winter	US$ (million)	Venue	
1984	10.6	Los Angeles	10	1984	1	Sarajevo	7
1988	7.4	Seoul	10	1988	1.1	Calgary	7
1992	34	Barcelona	7	1992	8.5	Albertville	9
1996	30	Atlanta	7	1994	5	Lillehammer	9
2000	45	Sydney	7	1998	9.3	Nagano	7
2004	50.5	Athens	7	2002	11.8	Salt Lake City	7
2008	63.8	Beijing	7	2006	14.8	Turin	7

Notes: [a]Includes profit sharing.
Source: International Olympic Committee (1996b).

12

Sport and the Internet

Daniel Evans

Stage 1—Identification of marketing opportunities

▼

Stage 2—Strategy determination

Step 5—Determine core marketing strategy

Marketing and service mix—sport product, pricing, place (physical evidence, people, process), customer satisfaction

Promotion mix—sales promotion, advertising, television, **Internet**

Step 6—Determine tactics and performance benchmarks

▼

Stage 3—Strategy implemention, evaluation and adjustment

CHAPTER OBJECTIVES

Chapter 12 considers another critical relationship—the Internet–sport nexus. The Internet is a powerful communications medium that has the ability to influence sport organisations in a variety of ways. This chapter discusses the Internet in the context of communication. Initially, an example of the network of relationships that can be created for sport on the Internet is provided. The ability of the World Wide Web (WWW) to be assimilated into organisational operations and inform both internal and external stakeholders is then demonstrated. The concept of online communities is subsequently reviewed, as is the ability of the medium to reach consumers at all stages of the buyer readiness continuum. In conclusion, the chapter describes how sporting organisations are using the Internet to generate revenue at the action stage of buyer readiness.

After studying this chapter you should be able to:

1 Recognise potential web linkages between sport organisations and their stakeholders.
2 Comprehend the concept of information technology (IT) assimilation.
3 Understand the importance of community building through an Internet strategy.
4 Identify the impact of the Internet at different stages of buyer readiness.
5 Identify revenue-generating opportunities via the Internet.
6 Understand the overall role of the Internet in organisational communication.

HEADLINE STORY

Sport spiders patrol the web

Broadcast rights holders are hiring web sentries to scour the Internet for marketing predators. UK-based Sports Marketing Surveys (SMS) is one of the new 'black widows' of world sport, sending its sentinels to monitor the World Wide Web for unauthorised Internet broadcasts. Both intentional and inadvertent infringements of expensive broadcast rights for events such as the 2000 Olympics and Soccer's 2002 World Cup are causing organisations to employ 'web cops' to police these breaches. With up to 15 people raking the World Wide Web during these events and sending 'real time' video clips of infringements directly to legal departments for immediate attention, sports broadcast rights holders are getting serious about protecting their investments. (Britcher 2001: 16)

That sport organisations are going to such lengths to safeguard their Internet interests demonstrates the industry's regard for its value. This chapter examines the growing use of the Internet in sport business, and sport's affinity with the medium. The impact of television on sport is clearly demonstrated in chapter 11, and many people believe the Internet will be similarly tied to the future of sport. US National Football League (NFL) commissioner Paul Tabligue noted that the web is as important to contemporary NFL teams as network television and its revenues were to teams in the 1960s (Wilner 2000).

The Internet is clearly a powerful communication channel that provides sport marketers with an effective tool. As the threads of the World Wide Web stretch further into global society, more and more people are relying on the medium to perform daily tasks. With this in mind, sport marketers who are better able to leverage the core strengths of the Internet are creating significant competitive advantage.

According to Porter (1985), a systematic review of the important activities within an organisation's value chain is a critical element in the ongoing search for competitive advantage. To this end, Figure 12.1 provides an example of the network of relationships that can be developed through the Internet between sporting organisations and their stakeholders, and the subsequent functionality that can add value.

The central component in this generic model is the particular sport organisation to which the model is being applied. In practice, therefore, the sport organisation could be a professional club or a national governing body. The inner web captures eight typical stakeholder 'branches' for sporting organisations, while the outer web holds three examples of Internet-based functionality that relate directly to each stakeholder. The entire network is connected by the World Wide Web in a process known as IT assimilation, which is represented by the black 'threads' connecting the sporting organisation with the individual elements of the chain.

The relationships and activities captured in Figure 12.1 provide an example of what Westland and Clark (2000: 141) describe as 'examining (the) value chain to understand how processes can be changed or augmented using information technology to improve efficiency, reduce cycle time, and improve services provided to customers'. To further explain this relationship, one branch of the model is highlighted in Figure 12.2.

The 'league/central body' branch within a sporting organisation's web relationship is emphasised in Figure 12.2. As stated, this branch is, along with the other seven, interconnected

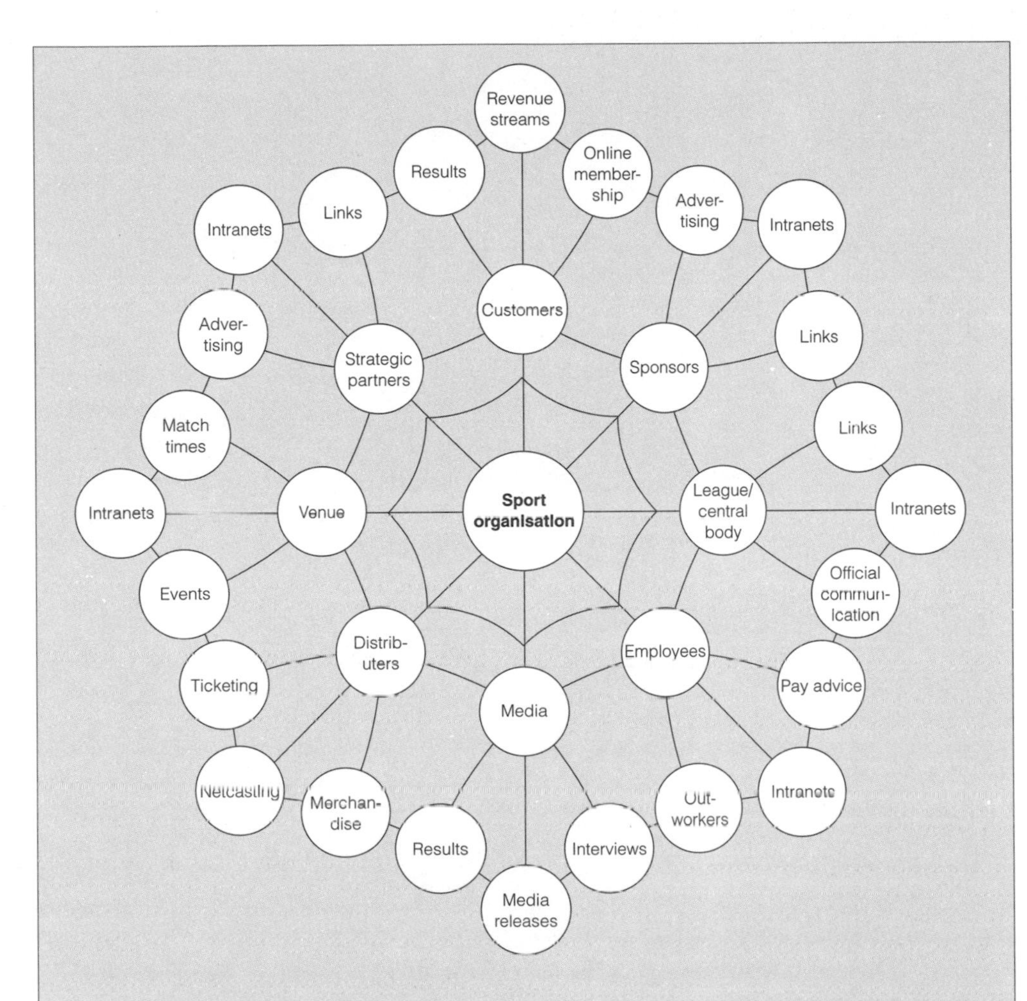

FIGURE 12.1 **The World Wide Sporting Web**

with every element of the model through the process of IT assimilation; however, it can be considered independently. If the model were being applied to the Sydney Swans football club, the 'league/central body' stakeholder would be the AFL. The Swans may consider numerous types of Internet functionality to improve their relationship with the AFL, including providing links for web users with league sponsors, allowing access to both athlete and customer databases for market research (via an intranet), and streamlining official communication. Similarly, if the model were being applied to a State Sport Organisation (SSO), the 'league/central body' stakeholder would be the National Sport Organisation (NSO), and similar functionality could be employed.

Each of the stakeholder branches can be examined by sport organisations in an effort to fully utilise the competitive power of the Internet. Sport marketers in particular need to

FIGURE 12.2
The 'league/central body' branch of the web

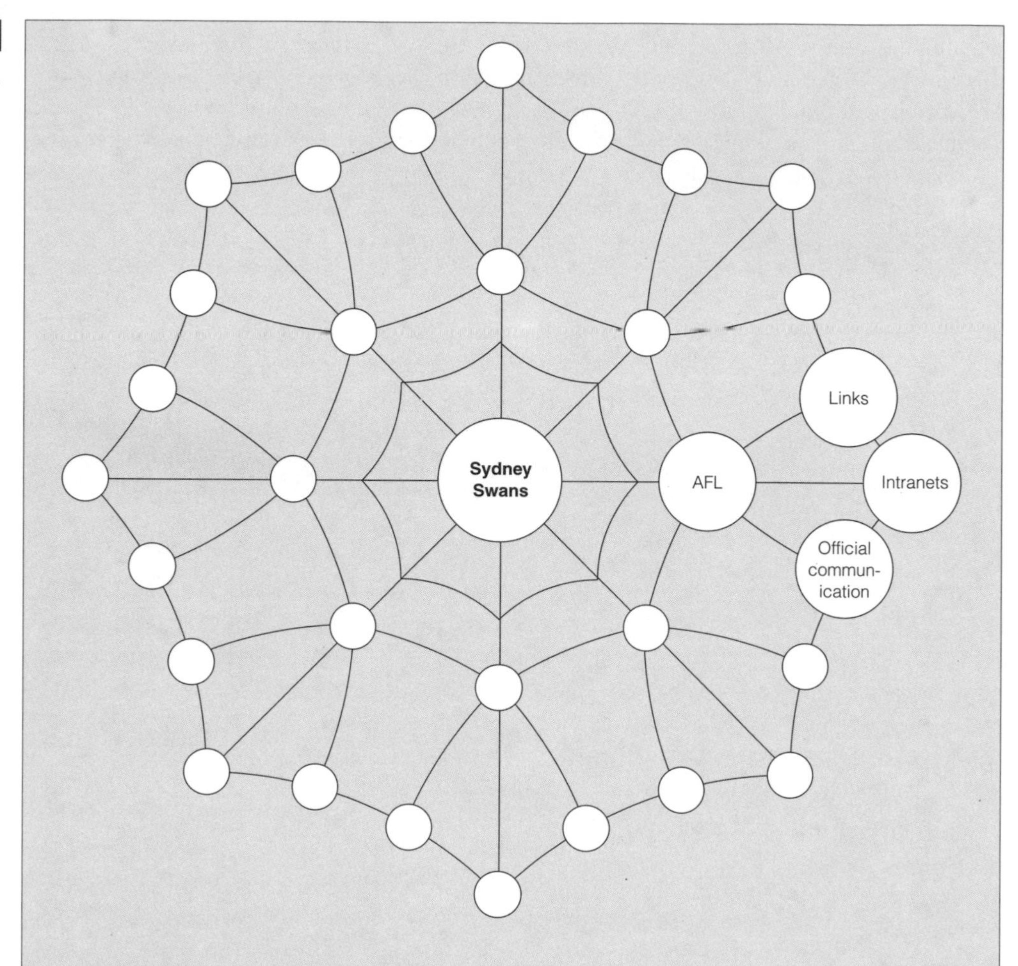

identify the myriad ways they can use the Internet to gain an advantage. Many of these opportunities are described in this chapter, with Figure 12.1 providing the framework for the discussion.

Chapter 9 reviews consumers' buyer readiness within four stages: attention, interest, desire and action. The Internet provides alternative opportunities to influence consumers in each of these stages, especially through the establishment of online communities. The concept of the online community is discussed later, as is the impact of the Internet on each stage of buyer readiness. First, however, the concept of IT assimilation is reviewed.

IT assimilation

The concept of IT assimilation is reflected in Figure 12.1 through the black threads that link every element of an organisation's operations. There is growing recognition of theories that recommend that the Internet be considered in a holistic manner by organisations. These theories can be generally described as IT 'assimilation theory'. Assimilation theorists include Armstrong and Sambamurthy (1999), El Sawy, Malhotra, Gosain and Young (1999), and Raghunathan and Raghunathan (1994). They conclude that the greatest benefits to organisations via the Internet occur when merging IT strategies with the overall strategic thrust of the firm (Raghunathan & Raghunathan 1994) and incorporating IT into the entire spectrum of organisational activities. In other words, the emergence of the electronic economy has provided a business environment in which the Internet permeates every aspect of an organisation.

This understanding affects the Internet strategies employed by sport organisations. Although generating revenue is rightly the key consideration in Internet strategies, value can be created in a number of other ways. Cutting costs and improving customer service are not as noticeable as large rights deals, but are important elements of a holistic Internet strategy. Similarly, keeping stakeholders informed is important in a professional business environment, and can be achieved readily via the Internet. In fact, IT assimilation refers to the myriad ways that the Internet can be incorporated into an organisation, with the sum of these applications representing potential competitive advantage.

There are countless other IT applications that fall under assimilation theory. E-mail, for example, has revolutionised many business activities, and intranets allow staff and stakeholders to access internal information. The opportunity for staff to work from outside the office as 'outworkers' has also been facilitated. In short, assimilation theorists call for organisations to examine their entire operation in search of opportunities for improved performance via the Internet. Three such opportunities are:

- disintermediation;
- knowledge management; and
- customer service.

Each of these examples of assimilation opportunities is now reviewed.

Disintermediation

Standing (2000: 4) describes disintermediation as encompassing the process by which 'middlemen' companies are being 'bypassed by the Internet revolution as more companies that create the goods and services interact directly with the consumer without the aid of intermediaries'. In other words, the Internet can enable organisations to create the type of vertical integration opportunities discussed in chapter 7.

The three functionality opportunities stemming from the 'distributors' stakeholder branch in Figure 12.1–ticketing, netcasting and merchandising–all offer disintermediation opportunities. Both ticketing and merchandising can be performed through a virtual store, and represent disintermediation prospects. For example, an organisation's ability to sell match tickets online, and subsequently to reduce or eliminate the commissions paid to ticketing agencies, represents a disintermediation possibility. Such opportunities are related to revenue-generating strategies, and clearly affect bottom-line profits through cost-cutting. Virtual stores provide a similar example of potential disintermediation benefits, with the elimination of the need to pay commissions to merchandise wholesalers improving profits above and beyond the revenue associated with additional merchandise sales.

The growing use of the Internet for audio and visual game broadcasts represents a further, significant opportunity for disintermediation. Clubs may be able to bypass traditional broadcasters altogether, and package their own product for advertisers. The potential of such netcasts is explored more fully later in this chapter, but in terms of disintermediation, each of these three examples has presented opportunities for sport organisations to use the Internet to eliminate 'middlemen' and their margins and to interact directly with their customers.

Knowledge management

According to the *Harvard Business Review on Knowledge Management* (1998), the way companies generate, communicate, and leverage their intellectual assets is an important source of competitive advantage. The Internet is a dynamic tool that has created a number of ways for sport organisations to improve organisational learning.

In terms of knowledge generation, the compilation and electronic storage of information on athletes, business activities, and in particular supporters, is growing. A key component of strategies to generate supporter information is the development of online communities (discussed later in this chapter). The communication and leveraging of this knowledge can be facilitated by intranets, the importance of which is evidenced by their inclusion in Figure 12.1 as a functional element of several stakeholder branches.

Internally, knowledge management techniques include intranets for the 'employee' stakeholder, which allows them access to job-relevant data. For example, coaches, doctors and nutritionists could have remote access to the ever-growing athlete files, recruiting data and relevant reports in order to improve on-field strategy and performance. Similarly, management-related information that accumulates over time can be made available to off-field employees such as marketers.

Externally, the relationships with 'sponsors', 'league/central body', 'venue' and 'strategic partner' stakeholders can all be leveraged with strategic intranets based on knowledge (refer to Figure 12.1). For example, the ability to grow, access and utilise market information over time, and across geographical boundaries, is a significant resource that will generally be extremely appealing to sponsors, leagues and strategic alliance partners. The marketability of such databases as a revenue source is also considered later, as part of online community development. For 'venue' stakeholders, the ability to access 'to the minute' ticket sales information, for example, can assist in timely seating configurations that maximise prearranged capacity, proximity, safety and functionality trade-offs. In short, effective knowledge management is a significant source of competitive advantage that can enhance numerous aspects of operations for sport organisations.

Customer service

The customer is identified in Figure 12.1 as a key stakeholder of the sport organisation. Therefore, improved customer service via the Internet is a potent value-adding opportunity for sport organisations. The importance of service quality opportunities is identified in chapter 8. Figure 12.1 also displays three examples of customer functionality in the outer web, with 'results' and 'online memberships' discussed here and 'revenue streams' covered later in the chapter.

A website can provide customers with timely and accurate information and results, and the ability to conduct transactions online. These types of services are essential to maintain high-level customer service, and ultimately affect the organisational bottom line. Creative, value-added services like club screen savers and links to other useful sites are also part of improved customer service. In addition, sport organisations are increasingly offering high-service Internet memberships that provide customers with 'gold service packages', including privileged news releases.

Sport organisations can conduct market research to assess each of the activities their customers engage in, and identify where they can assist via the Internet or improve the overall customer experience. These services can be particularly helpful in the case of international sports where geography restricts customers, and their implementation helps to build community feeling among supporters, the latter another essential component of Internet strategy.

The implementation of IT assimilation strategies offers numerous competitive advantage opportunities for sport organisations. Before considering the impact of the Internet on the four stages of buyer readiness, we look at the concept of online communities. A critical element of online success in any industry, sport has an inherent advantage in the creation of this valuable commodity.

Online communities

According to Martin (1997: 44), 'digital communities are the future lifeblood of the net'. They are the Internet version of the loyal audiences eagerly sought after by newspapers, trade publications, interest-based magazines and television stations. The ability to hold an audience is crucial to success in these businesses, with product sales and advertising revenue inexplicably tied to consumer numbers. Online communities in the sporting environment are simply those customers who regularly visit the organisational website. These customers may seek information, interaction or services and, if they can be fostered, provide enormous opportunities for organisations.

While the Internet does indeed alter the way organisations and marketers reach their customers, it is also demonstrating its ability to provide new channels for achieving this objective. Online communities are a natural evolution from a medium built on networks, both technical and human. Simeon (1999: 298) observes that 'many commercial Web sites have moved from providing basic company and product information to becoming an integral part of product and service launch strategies'. She goes on to identify some of the dynamic website features capable of developing online communities, including bulletin boards, chat rooms and audio and video capabilities.

The 'culture' of sport provides its businesses with an arguably unequalled head start in this element of online success. Providing customers with a forum to 'meet' like-minded individuals, and encouraging and supporting conversation, is crucial in the development of an online community that, according to Judson and Kelly (1999: 154), 'may spur sales of high-margin peripheral items related to the product'. This process is somewhat easier when the product around which the community is being built is highly involved. In this respect the sport industry makes the leap into cyber community building, with a product arguably generating higher levels of consumer passion and desire to be associated with the product than any other. Online communities are difficult to manufacture for fast food or whitegoods. They are, however, a natural progression for the sports product and its traditional membership base.

Manchester United, the Los Angeles Lakers, the New Zealand All-Blacks and the Collingwood Football Club are all in a commanding position to manufacture an online community, because for many consumers their product is highly involved. The ability to provide access to chat rooms, regular feedback, interesting competitions, up-to-date information, as well as tickets, merchandise and broadcasts, makes customers want to return to a place they feel part of. The website also provides an opportunity for clubs to promote athlete-supporter interaction in a safe environment via chat rooms, which clubs can ultimately leverage. Sport organisations can use these types of strategies to build a large, loyal, online community, unrestricted by geographical boundaries.

In some cases the online community is also evolving into a 'virtual home'. For NBL club the Melbourne Tigers (considered later in Sportview 12.1), the closure of the historic Albert Park home base to make way for a golf course created something of an identity crisis–a situation familiar to a growing number of 'homeless' sporting organisations. The Internet has presented a cost-effective meeting point for the organisation and its supporters and other stakeholders.

The advantages of a large and loyal online community for a sport organisation are substantial, and can be both assimilation- and revenue-related. Customer service can be drastically improved, and increases in revenue occur through primary and associated products: for example, the emergence of a new demographic attractive to sponsors and the development of a group of human advertisements for a business are significant benefits associated with online communities. Bishop (1998: 77) concurs with this evaluation, promoting organisational strategy that both expands and enhances the richness of customer databases. Bishop adds: 'as it becomes larger and more useful, [a customer database] will help increase sales and, if appropriate, can become an asset you can sell or rent to other organisations'.

Having constructed an online community, sport organisations are in a position to move these cyber consumers through the different stages of buyer readiness, and ultimately into buyer action! This process, described in chapter 9, is looked at below in relation to the Internet.

Buyer readiness and the Internet

Like the process of building an online community, customers can be systematically moved through the buying process of AIDA (attention, interest, desire, action). Sport marketers can utilise a number of Internet features to facilitate this process and ultimately improve revenue streams. Each of the four elements of buyer readiness is now reviewed in relation to Internet marketing strategy.

Attention

The promotion of a web address and its features through traditional media or sales promotions is an important part of the promotional mix, and plays a vital role in generating attention for the site. Indeed, a cursory review of sports advertising on television and in newspapers demonstrates the increasing importance of promoting websites. However, using the Internet as an independent communication channel, sport organisations can be proactive in grabbing the attention of sport consumers through such strategies as the manipulation of search engines and databases.

Sport organisations need initially to consider their actual web address, the key words they link to their site, and the search engines they register with. These decisions affect traffic to the site. In addition, strategically identified databases can be targeted for e-mail advertising and promotions. Tactical alliances with related organisations that provide mutually beneficial web links can also increase traffic, as demonstrated in Figure 12.1, where strategic links are identified as important functional components for three stakeholders: 'sponsors', 'league/central body' and 'strategic partners'.

By maximising the likelihood that web users will find their site, and electronically promoting the site through appropriate databases and the strategic use of web links, sport organisations can draw significant attention to their website.

Interest

Having got the customer's attention, Internet sites must generate an interest in staying. This important element of buyer readiness requires the high involvement of the sport-marketing department. Websites should be clear and well designed, and convey as closely as possible the culture of the organisation. This can be achieved through consistent use of corporate colours and logos for example, and here the input of professional graphic designers is as critical to websites as any other communication channel. Ease of navigation and speed are as important as 'look and feel' in retaining customer interest, and should be a priority for web designers. This phase of buyer readiness is also an integral part of community building, in that it influences a customer's inclination to return.

Desire

At this point a successful Internet strategy will have attracted potential customers to the site, and sparked their interest with a speedy, easy-to-navigate site that has a unique 'look and feel'. The next step is to stimulate a desire to become more highly involved. Sport marketers are now limited only by their imagination. The Internet can facilitate all of the traditional sales promotions, trials and giveaways associated with arousing purchase desire, and the unique features of the Internet make it suitable to any number of novel marketing strategies. Promotions can be both truly global and interactive. Again, as with community building, the highly involved nature of the sport product places it in an enviable position. Sport marketers are well placed to leverage the 'sexiness' of their athletes and the public desire to associate with their success and athleticism, via both traditional and innovative online sales promotions.

Action

Online purchasing by consumers is the ultimate aim of a well-executed Internet strategy from the sport organisation's point of view. The ability to facilitate action is what the buyer-readiness sequence is all about, and revenues being generated online are already significant. Church (2000) reported that 1999 revenues from advertising on sport sites amounted to US$612 million. This figure, however, pales in comparison to her projections of US$6.27 billion for advertising through the same channels by 2005. Similarly, notable estimates were made for 2005 sales of online sport merchandise (US$5.8 billion) and ticketing sales

(US$2.9 billion). In Australia, the AFL signed a five-year Internet rights contract with Telstra in 2002 for a reported $30 million.

These massive figures indicate why online revenue strategies are critical to the future of sport organisations. Revenue streams emanate from various customers, and take pride of place at '12 o'clock' in Figure 12.1. Having generated 'attention', 'interest' and 'desire', providing suitable online products that consumers are able to access via the organisational website is paramount. Online revenue-generating schemes are limited only by administrators' imagination; however, six typical revenue streams are reviewed below:

- virtual stores (including merchandising and ticketing);
- online advertising;
- netcasting;
- online memberships;
- online gaming; and
- online gambling.

Virtual stores

With customers' growing propensity to make purchases online, revenue from virtual stores is a growing concern for sport organisations. Generally, a sport organisation's online store is simply an electronic version of a traditional outlet, and will contain all of the items typically available from such channels, such as merchandise, memorabilia and match tickets. Importantly, the Internet's ability to overcome geography also presents sport organisations with an effective opening into the global marketplace. Organisations like the Los Angeles Lakers and Manchester United, for example, which have large followings outside their national borders, can now efficiently tap that market via their virtual stores.

As explored earlier, there are also potential disintermediation advantages generated through the use of virtual stores. Sporting organisations have traditionally distributed merchandise through a combination of privately run stores and licensed retailers. Virtual stores, however, have few of the typical overheads and costs associated with 'actual' stores, and can bypass the commissions payable to licensed retailers.

Online advertising

There are a number of reasons for sporting websites being among the most attractive available to advertisers. According to Church (2000), the typical online sports visitor has a higher net worth and propensity to buy online than visitors to other sites. In addition, the 'stickiness' of sports sites (or their ability to hold a visitor for longer) makes them more attractive to advertisers and sponsors. The growing popularity of online gambling and the power of major sports to attract global audiences are also contributing to the propensity for advertisers to be interested in sports sites. Table 12.1 supports these observations, showing that the profiles of the typical Internet user and the typical sports fan are almost a perfect match.

Sports-related websites are already making a significant impact online. We have already noted the US$612 million spent on advertising on sports-related sites in 1999, and the projections of US$6.27 billion for advertising through the same channels in 2005. Online advertising, therefore, will presumably form an important part of Internet strategy for sporting organisations.

TABLE 12.1 Demographics of Internet users and sports fans

	Internet user	Sports fan
Male	70%	64%
Female	30%	36%
Average age	32.7	34.0
Median income	US$50 000–US$60 000	US$50 000+

Source: Delpy & Bosetti (1998). Reprinted by permission of Fitness Information Technology.

Netcasting

Using the Internet to compete with television's dominance of broadcasting is perhaps the most exciting development presented by the medium. Netcasting is much cheaper than launching a television channel, and users can log in from any computer and, increasingly, from mobile telephone devices. With the steady penetration of broadband cabling, netcasting is increasingly being considered the platform for media ownership by sport organisations. Manchester United supporters, for example, can currently watch delayed highlights of any of their club's games from the past 10 years for £25 a year, or £3.99 a month.

As sports audiences on the Internet grow, organisations are assessing their ability to use disintermediation and bypass television broadcasting. The number of sporting events being broadcast on the Internet is certainly growing, the medium's global access and interactivity being highly attractive to sponsors and marketers. Although the rewards associated with Internet broadcasting are compelling, the path forward is not completely clear. Table 12.2 displays the major benefits and disadvantages aligned to Internet broadcasts of sporting events

Table 12.2 presents a range of considerations for sport in terms of netcasts, with the equation readily applicable for further illumination to actual examples. GazeTV is the netcasting component of www.gaze.com, created by Melbourne Tiger and Australian Boomer Andrew Gaze (considered as part of Sportview 12.1). GazeTV can offer sponsors a global audience and is well placed to incorporate interactive technology. In addition, the service has the potential (subject to contractual agreements) to offer packages similar to those provided by Manchester United, or even to provide live coverage, and already enables supporters not present to feel a part of home games. Given GazeTV is a relatively low-cost production,

TABLE 12.2 The Internet and sport broadcasting

The equation	
Benefits for sponsors/marketers	**Disadvantages for sponsors/marketers**
Global access	Slow international take-up of broadband
Interactivity with fans/customers	Consumers' reluctance to pay for content
Ability of clubs to retain revenues	Inability to deliver high-quality video
Development of niche sports	Uncertain financial returns
Potential for revenue generation	Consumers' concern over security of e-commerce
Opportunity to promote brand	

Source: Adapted from Walmsley (2001).

with similarly low levels of e-commerce, the major query here would involve video quality. A visit to www.gaze.com relieves this concern, with the site currently providing high-quality live-action footage, which, in terms of the overall sport broadcasting equation presented in Table 12.2, is a good sign for Australia's Sydney 2000 flag-bearer.

At present the broadcasting status quo is precarious. The benefits associated with Internet broadcasts are significant, and the disadvantages, while present, are far from insurmountable. Improving technology and society's growing use of the Internet for both communication and financial transactions is going a long way to overcoming its disadvantages. For sport marketers, the implications of a significant increase in Internet broadcasting are momentous.

Online memberships

Sport organisations are also moving towards generating revenue through the sale of online memberships that provide subscribers with access to exclusive information releases and value-added services. AFL clubs experimenting with the concept in 2001 had positive experiences, with at least one club boasting an online membership in excess of 1000. Multiplied by the $25 fee, the preliminary results augur well for this Internet-based revenue stream in the future.

Online gaming

As distinct from online gambling, various small payment games available to sports enthusiasts such as fantasy leagues, tipping, or variations of the traditional 'spot the ball' competitions, are having considerable success online. These interactive types of gaming both generate revenue and assist in the formation of online communities. As such they are an important element of Internet strategy for sport organisations.

Sportview 12.1 examines the website of one of the NBL's premier clubs, the Melbourne Tigers, which has incorporated examples of many of the strategies discussed so far in its 'virtual home'.

SPORTVIEW 12.1

Melbourne Tigers and Andrew Gaze: all net!

According to its website, the Melbourne Tigers is Australia's premier basketball brand and has been in existence for nearly 70 years. During that time the club has become the most widely known and supported basketball club in Australia, and is captained by the country's best-known basketball commodity—Andrew Gaze.

The combination of a rich club history and the country's most marketable basketball star makes the Melbourne Tigers an attractive prospect for marketers via any channel. In recent years, however, the club has focused on the Internet as a means of reaching its community and providing a vehicle for sponsors. Tigers CEO Nigel Purchase is quick to emphasise the growing importance of the Internet to the organisation: 'As the Australian basketball community embraced the Internet, the functionality of our web site became a necessity. It is a cost effective method of communicating with the supporters, and is increasingly becoming a valuable revenue stream'.

The Tigers' site, www.tigers.com.au, currently contains numerous online community building tools including a tipping competition, polls, question and answers with players, and the 'Tiger Beat', an electronic update service for supporters, sponsors and business partners of the organisation. In addition, club sponsors feature prominently, and a link is available to strategic partner 'Sportal'.

Andrew Gaze has also entered the cyber world. His own website, www.gaze.com, contains similar interactive functionality, and registers thousands of unique users every day. The site contains a variety of news, shopping, coaching and competitions, and includes GazeTV, a popular online broadcast service that shows live-action footage of interviews, highlight packages and fan feedback. The five-time Olympian and seven-time NBL most valuable player recollects the strategy behind GazeTV: 'We were always conscious of making this site appealing on as many levels as possible. The TV program gives fans a real feeling of the atmosphere courtside. I just love that!'.

For the Tigers and Andrew Gaze, the Internet is now a critical part of their business strategies. While sport organisations and their stars are now virtually compelled to have an Internet presence, the Tigers and Gaze have become online pioneers in the Australian professional basketball market. Both on and off the court their future is, in basketball and cyber parlance, ALL NET!

Online gambling

The final element of online revenue to be considered is online gambling. Investment bank Merrill Lynch expects e-sports betting to rise, from its current US$142 million, to US$2.8 billion by 2015 (Gerlis 2001). Some industry experts feel this to be a very conservative estimate. In fact, it can be argued that, with the development of wireless Internet access (through mobile devices), online gambling will become so 'instant' that it can be done anywhere, anytime, anyway. Savvy sport organisations will incorporate strategies to gain a share of this significant market.

Australia is a key market within an online sport betting industry that investment bank Merrill Lynch recently predicted would be worth US$173 billion by 2015. Although Australian online gambling legislation is currently quite restrictive, it seems inevitable that AFL clubs will one day follow the 'leed' of sporting clubs like Premier League soccer club Leeds United.

Leeds supporters can currently use a Leeds United-branded mobile phone to access unique mobile content from the official Leeds website–and to place a bet on their team! Having signed a revenue-sharing deal with Wap Integrators, a technology company with a UK betting licence, Leeds is well placed to benefit from online gambling as part of a wider Internet strategy. Leeds followers in Australia and globally can get the Leeds URL and pay a local phone rate for bets, or order tickets, merchandise or even travel (Gellatly 2001).

Summary

Chapter 12 was framed by the World Wide Sporting Web portrayed in Figure 12.1. This illustration presents the Internet as a marketing tool that, according to assimilation theory, has the ability to permeate an entire organisation. The model depicts the online relationships between stakeholders and the organisation, and presents examples of Internet functionality. Assimilation opportunities for sport organisations such as disintermediation, knowledge management and improved customer service were discussed.

The concept of online communities has emerged as critical to the success of sport organisations' online sorties. For the sport marketer, the successful manufacture of these audiences represents an exiting new market ripe for exploitation.

The Internet was also considered in terms of consumer buyer readiness, as discussed in chapter 9. Creative sport marketers have the opportunity to influence consumers as they move through the buying process of attention, interest, desire and, crucially, action. Six distinct types of online revenue streams were considered that in combination have the capacity to radically alter the sport business landscape.

Although rhetoric surrounding the global potential of the Internet abounds, there is growing evidence that, for the sport industry in particular, the World Wide Web offers marketers unique opportunities. Indeed, for sport, the Internet has rapidly moved from the ranks of a potential marketing channel to a critical nexus–the Internet-sport nexus.

CASE STUDY

www.daviscup.com

Davis Cup tennis is an institution. Dwight Davis commissioned the Davis Cup trophy in 1899, with the USA defeating the British Isles 3–0 in Boston in 1900. Australia joined in 1905, and by 1970 the tournament boasted 50 participating nations. In 2002 the Davis Cup had continued its remarkable growth and become the largest annual sports competition in the world, with 142 nations participating in 80 ties per year.

By any measure, the Davis Cup is a massive event. In 2000, the yearly attendance was well in excess of 500 000, with a global television audience of over 612 million people watching the event during 1645 broadcast hours. The culmination of a remarkable year came in December 2000, when a phenomenal 47.6% of the Spanish television-watching public tuned in to see Juan Carlos Ferrero secure victory for Spain over Australia.

Controlled by the International Tennis Federation (ITF), which represents member national associations, tennis is an intense sport, with worldwide participation and sexy stars. The unique format of the Davis Cup, with its national, team-based competition, generates pride and passion from players and supporters alike. Despite the fact that players receive no payment for their efforts, 18 of the world's top 20 players took part in the tournament in 2001.

Naturally, sponsors have clamoured to be involved with an event with the global reach and relevancy of the Davis Cup. Paris-based bank BNP Paribus took over the title sponsorship in 2002, with other sponsors including Wilson Racquet Sports, Hugo Boss and Heineken (through the popular 'Heineken House'). With sell-out crowds and worldwide exposure, the ITF has identified the Internet as a critical component of its strategy for further development. Its web presence has already proven fruitful.

The tournament website, www.daviscup.com, is powered by the ITF and its partner, NEC. In 2001 the site attracted well over 50 million page views, including 16 million during semi-finals week alone. Delivering point-by-point live scores from Davis Cup ties worldwide, live radio commentary for selected ties, and on-site live cameras, daviscup.com has been immensely popular. Team news and player biographies also feature on the site, which boasts the world's largest tennis results database, going back 100 years and covering both small satellite events and Grand Slams.

There is no disputing the quality of the information being provided by the ITF via daviscup.com, nor the traffic being generated by its broadcasting and results during selected ties; however, it seems that the ITF has yet to realise the potential of the site to become the pre-eminent global tennis community. Tennis buffs can subscribe to a free newsletter containing up-to-date information, but the site offers few opportunities to tennis followers to become actively engaged, communicate with like-minded tennis 'nuts' and get involved in other forms of community development. In addition, there is no attempt at all to generate revenue. Given the auspicious initial online venture in terms of traffic, the ITF is eager to further leverage the Internet for competitive advantage, and is currently considering its cyber strategy for daviscup.com in the future.

Source: Adapted from *Sport Business International* (2001), no. 64, pp. 2–7.

Please go to the Davis Cup home page at www.daviscup.com and answer the following questions.

Questions

1. How do you rate the 'look and feel' of the site's home page?
2. Can the ITF build an online community? If so, how?
3. Based on Figure 12.1, who are the major stakeholders of the ITF?
4. What type of strategic intranets could the ITF consider?
5. The site does not currently have any revenue streams. Who are the ITF's customers? What functionality would you recommend to generate revenue?

13

How to attract and implement sponsorship

Stage 1—Identification of marketing opportunities

▼

Stage 2—Strategy determination

Step 5—Determine core marketing strategy

Marketing and service mix—sport product, pricing, place (physical evidence, people, process), customer satisfaction

Promotion mix—sales promotion, advertising, television, Internet, **sponsorship**

Step 6—Determine tactics and performance benchmarks

▼

Stage 3—Strategy implemention, evaluation and adjustment

CHAPTER OBJECTIVES

Chapter 13 introduces the concept of sponsorship. Sponsorship is one of the most visible elements of the sport promotion mix. In this chapter, a framework for how to create win–win relationships is presented. Celebrity marketing as a special case of sport sponsorship is discussed and the chapter finishes with overviewing some trends that drive the future of sponsorship.

After studying this chapter you should be able to:

1 Describe sponsorship as a distinctive element of the promotion mix.
2 Create a win–win relationship between a sponsor and a sponsee.
3 Identify some of the trends that drive the future of sport sponsorship.
4 Describe the basics of implementing and leveraging a sponsorship arrangement.

HEADLINE STORY

Boosting sales, raising awareness or philanthropy?

> I was always very conscious of the fact that we weren't able to offer our sponsors anything specific in return for their support . . . The obvious way of raising money by doing deals was just not available to us. I wanted to make sure that the Sydney bid was never criticised if we lost; that no-one could say we didn't look after the people who had given us money. So I worked hard at trying to give all our sponsors value for their money. (McGeoch & Korporaal 1994: 114)

In these few lines, Rod McGeoch, chairman of the Sydney 2000 bid committee, succinctly describes the sponsorship dilemma. One organisation needs sponsorship to reach its goals; another expects to benefit from sponsoring an organisation or individual. How can sponsorship be made to work? When is the sponsor satisfied? Can the effectiveness of the sponsorship be measured? Is sponsorship more effective than, for example, advertising? These questions can be answered only if a clear understanding of the goals of the sponsoring organisation exists. Does it want to boost sales or raise awareness, or is the chief executive officer simply a philanthropic follower of the team or sporting code?

This chapter defines and discusses the concept of sponsorship from both the sponsor's and the sporting organisation's points of view. It is important to understand which other organisations are competing with sporting organisations for limited sponsorship dollars, so a brief overview of the market for sponsors is provided. Sponsorship as an integrative tool of the sport promotions mix is discussed when goals of sponsorship are considered, followed by the advantages and disadvantages of sport sponsorship. The second part of the chapter presents a sponsorship framework and discusses how to create win–win situations. Win–win situations are created when all parties entering into an agreement benefit from it. Sponsoring individual athletes, as an area of special interest in the sport industry, is considered next. The benefits for both the sponsor and sponsee should be taken into consideration when wanting to create a balanced win–win situation.

The third part of the chapter takes us beyond the basics of sponsorship. To take a really integrated marketing approach, sponsorship support activities and tie-in promotions need to be initiated.

What is sponsorship?

Historically, sponsorship has often been associated with charity and altruism. The *Penguin Pocket English Dictionary* still defines sponsorship as 'somebody who pays for a project or activity'. In today's (sport) business environment, however, nothing is less true. As an important marketing tool for many organisations, sponsorship involves a reciprocal relationship. One party puts something in and the other party returns the favour. Sleight (1989: 4), in his pointed definition of sponsorship, acknowledges the importance of the reciprocal relationship. His definition is used in the remainder of this book:

> Sponsorship is a business relationship between a provider of funds, resources or services and an individual, event or organisation which offers in return some rights and association that may be used for commercial advantage.

In marketing it is common to look at the different marketing tools, like sponsorship, from an applied point of view. In other words, how can we use this tool (i.e. spend money, resources or services) to reach sales-related goals? This is the *sponsoring* organisation. From the sporting organisation's point of view, the main goal of sponsorship is not sales-related. Sporting organisations or athletes mainly use sponsorship to accumulate funds, resources or services. These funds, resources or services are then used to run the operations of the organisation. This is the *sponsored* organisation. We further discuss the business relationship between sponsor and sponsee later in this chapter. Application of the sponsorship tool is not limited to sporting organisations, as is shown in the next section.

The market for sponsors

A market, as a collection of buyers, consists of all those organisations and individuals in need of something. The collection of organisations and individuals in competition for sponsors (funds, resources or services) therefore makes up the market for sponsors. Expenditure in this market worldwide needs to be considered in light of the global growth of sport sponsorship, growing in value from US$1.5 billion in 1989, US$5.5 billion in 1996 and US$10 billion in 1999, to an extrapolated value of approximately US$20 billion in 2005. The United States alone would account for almost half of that amount, of which 85% would be sport-related sponsorship (SportBusiness 2000: 58; Boyle & Haynes 2000: 49). According to Sport and Recreation Victoria (2000), A$429 million was spent in Australia in 1996, growing to A$519 million in 1998, A$1.16 billion in 1999, A$1.252 billion in 2000, and plateauing at A$1.248 billion (approximately US$700 billion) in 2001 (O'Riordan 2002: 48). This 'plateau' can largely be attributed to the fact that Australia hosted the 2000 Olympic Games. Obviously, sponsorship investments of Australian companies increased dramatically in relation to the Games, returning to more 'natural' levels in 2001. Figures for the United Kingdom indicate a sport sponsorship expenditure of US$500 million in 1998, with expectations that the UK will hit the US$1 billion mark somewhere around 2003.

Although these figures are only estimates, it can be argued that this is a huge pool of potential funds for sporting organisations. There are two major trends that have to be taken into consideration before we arrive at a final conclusion about available funds:

1 the move to big event sponsorship; and
2 the growing competition for sponsorship dollars.

As stated earlier, the Sydney Olympic Games exemplified the move to big-event sponsorship in 2000. The Sydney 2000 Games needed to attract close to A$500 million in sponsorship. Local sponsors accounted for A$300 million; the worldwide International Olympic Committee (IOC) TOP sponsors contributed the rest. During the Olympic Games period, local (Australian) companies redirected their sponsorship dollars from local, regional or national sporting organisations to the Olympic Games. This drained sponsorship budgets of Australian sporting organisations. This happens also with other media-attractive events (e.g. Grand Prix, World Swimming Championships) that are able to attract mass television audiences. In other words, a relatively large portion of sponsorship funds goes to relatively few organisations. Although it will be shown later that even global corporations increasingly attempt to apply their sponsorship locally, it remains a fact that much of the attraction of the sponsorship opportunity lies in its media attractiveness, with the bigger events being the more likely beneficiaries. As a matter of fact, Westerbeek and Smith (2002) observed that 'Sponsors will simply not spend such amounts of money without the committed support of major broadcasters to the event. It is unsurprising therefore that sponsorship of youth sporting events accounts for as little as 0.5% of all sport sponsorship'. The Commercial Economic Advisory Service of Australia (CEASA) found that the top five sponsored sports in Australia are motor racing, Formula One, Australian Rules football, rugby league and horseracing, in that order (O'Riordan 2002). Figure 13.1 shows the top five sponsored sports in the world.

In the market for sponsors, competition is also increasing. Global figures indicate a rise in sponsorship expenditure with most funds being channelled into sport (85%), but the picture in Australia is much more sobering. Sport and Recreation Victoria (2000) figures indicate that as much as 67% of all Australian-based sponsorship funds in 1996 were spent in industries other than sport.

Although expenditure on sponsorship is still growing, the increasing dominance of big sporting events and powerful sporting organisations, and increasing competition from organisations other than sport, are making it more difficult for many (smaller) sporting organisations to attract funds, resources or services through sponsorship. The relative distribution of the top five industries that sponsor sport worldwide is presented in Figure 13.2.

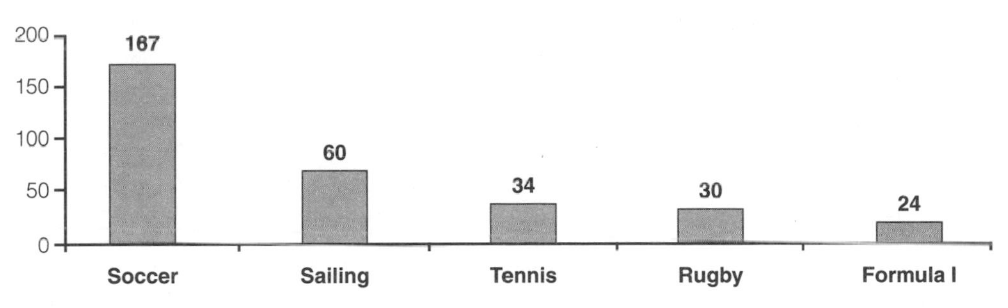

Source: Adapted from *SportBusiness* (2000: 58).

FIGURE 13.1 Top 5 sponsored sports based on number of deals in 1999 (minimum value US$75 000)

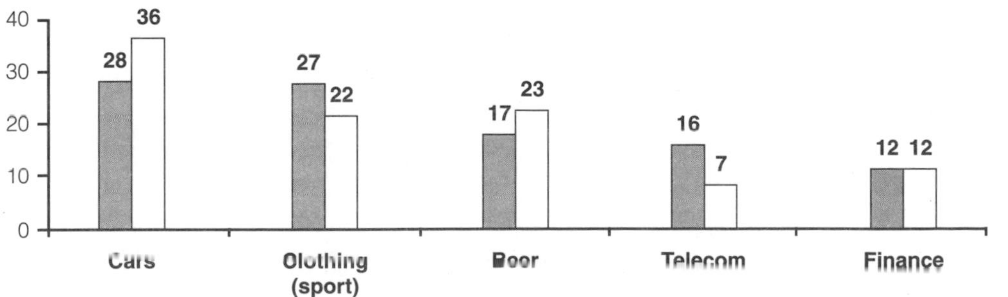

Sources: Adapted from *SportBusiness* (2000: 58); Sport and Recreation Victoria (2000: 5).

FIGURE 13.2 Relative comparison (%) of top five industries that sponsor sport in Australia and worldwide

For example, of all the sponsorship deals in the top five, 28% are car industry-related. Figure 13.2 also shows that the number of sponsorship deals with the automotive industry in Australia is relatively higher than in the rest of the world.

Sponsorship goals: the right to associate...

Historically, the sponsorship tool can be seen as a derivative of either advertising or public relations, as elements of the promotion mix, or a combination of the two. Throughout the past decade, however, sponsorship has developed as an independent and important element of the promotion mix. In other words, sponsorship clearly stands apart from other promotion mix elements, potentially to be considered as the dominant promotional tool in a marketing communications program.

In chapter 10, advertising is defined as a non-personal communication by an identified sponsor. From the sponsor's point of view, the difference between sponsorship and advertising is the actual message communicated, and how the message is communicated. In advertising, the content of the message and the moments of communication are determined by the paying organisation. When using sponsorship, however, the sponsor provides financial or material support for what are often independent organisations, individuals or activities. Less control can be exercised over the communication through these entities, and the timing of communication cannot be controlled. Although indirect (through the sponsored organisation), the actual message is often communicated at a more personal level (e.g. to people visiting an event). These points are returned to when discussing the advantages and disadvantages of sport sponsorship.

Public relations goals such as 'earning understanding and acceptance' and 'creating goodwill' can be sponsorship goals as well. The fact that the organisation has to pay for the association with the sponsored organisation, and that communication takes place through an independent organisation, distinguishes sponsorship from pure public relations. The sponsored organisation is used as the means of communication, which in effect can make sponsorship a public relations tool.

A general goal of sponsorship is described by Wilmshurst (1993: 377). Elements of both advertising and public relations can be found in this goal, which reads:

> sponsorship is usually undertaken to encourage more favourable attitudes towards the sponsoring company or its products within a relevant target audience, such as consumers, trade customers, employees or the community in which it operates.

Earlier in this chapter we described the difference in goal orientation between the sponsoring organisation (sponsor) and sponsored organisation (sponsee). Because the sporting organisation most of the time is the sponsee, neither advertising nor public relations goals seem to fit! In order to obtain sponsors, it is important to know about the sponsor's goals, but sponsee goals are often different. Table 13.1 presents an overview of different sponsor and sponsee goals–goals that have to be matched when a sponsorship framework is created.

It can be argued that the sponsor goals listed in Table 13.1 need to be categorised, for example, under headings such as corporate, marketing and media objectives. Strategic, tactical and operational would be another possible categorisation, as is the distinction between direct (sales) and indirect (exposure) marketing objectives. The reality of the sponsorship

TABLE 13.1 Sport sponsor and sponsee goals

Sponsor goals	Sponsee goals
Image creation or improvement	Obtaining *funds*
Business relationship marketing	Obtaining *resources* (goods)
Media realtionship marketing	Obtaining *services*
Employee relationship marketing	Raising awareness
Community relationship marketing	Brand positioning
Business development	Raising credibility
Increasing sales	Image creation or improvement
Brand positioning	
Raising awareness	
Corporate responsibility	
Targeting new market segments	
Developing new distribution channels	

opportunity, however, is that what is really bought by the sponsor, as outlined in our definition at the beginning of the chapter, is the right to 'associate'. In other words, the sponsor attempts to forge a connection between the sponsorship property (i.e. event or athlete) and the company or brand. The assumption is that a value transfer from the event or athlete to the company or brand occurs, in the process achieving sponsorship objectives. (We will further introduce this 'image transfer' concept later in this chapter when discussing celebrity marketing.) Using the 'buyer readiness sequence' (attention, interest, desire, action) presented in chapter 9, rather than categorising sponsorship objectives according to their functional or hierarchical intention, perhaps best describes sponsorship objectives. For example, a high-profile event can best be used to attract attention to a new brand, a high-profile athlete to generate further interest, a special niche event (e.g. Xtreme Games) to create 'desire' to own the product and, finally, a community-based event to make people buy the product in a convenient and comfortable environment. In other words, sponsorship, when applied to different properties, can be used to achieve a wide range of objectives. (We use the AIDA model again in chapter 14 when we discuss measuring the effect of sponsorship programs.)

Advantages and disadvantages of sport sponsorship

It was shown above that sponsorship has distinctly different characteristics from other elements of the promotion mix such as advertising and public relations. Sponsorship in a sport context allows the sponsor to communicate more directly and intimately with its target market (in this case the people interested in the sporting organisation and its products).

In chapter 1 some unique characteristics of the sport product are listed. Some of these are applicable when discussing the advantages of sport sponsorship. First, sport consumers tend to identify themselves personally with the sport, which creates opportunities for enhancing brand loyalty in products linked to the sport. Sport evokes personal attachment, and with this the sponsor can be linked to the excitement, energy and emotion of the sporting contest. In other words, sport has the potential to deliver a clear message. Sport has universal appeal and pervades all elements of life (geographically, demographically and socioculturally). This characteristic presents the opportunity to cross difficult cultural and language borders in communication, enabling the sponsor to talk to a (global) mass audience. At the same time the variety in sports available makes it possible to create distinct market segments with which to communicate separately. The universal appeal and strong interest in sport give sport a high media exposure, resulting in free publicity. Free publicity can make a sponsorship deal very cost-effective. Thousands of dollars in advertising expenditure can be saved when a sporting organisation or athlete attracts a lot of media attention. This makes many organisations want to be associated with sport. Also, because of the clear linkage of the sponsor to a sporting organisation or athlete, sponsorship stands out from the clutter, contrary to mainstream advertising, in which people are bombarded with hundreds of messages each day.

With so many advantages, why do organisations not simply spend their complete promotional budget on sponsorship? Well, there are some disadvantages to be considered before entering into a sponsorship agreement. In ambush marketing (discussed in chapter 14), non-sponsors take advantage of the efforts of real sponsors in that they try to be associated with the sponsored organisation, event, product or athlete. Lack of control over media coverage is another disadvantage of sport sponsorship. Also, the media are sometimes reluctant to recognise the sponsor's name when reporting on events or the achievements of athletes. Achievements of teams or athletes are another area that cannot be controlled. A non-performing team or athlete will have direct influence on the perception the public holds of the sponsor. The implications of this for the sponsorship of individual athletes are considered later in this chapter.

Creating win–win situations

If both sponsor and sponsee have to benefit from a cooperation, certain goals of both need to be satisfied. The main question that sponsor and sponsee have to ask themselves is: How can we successfully reach our own goals by assisting the sponsor/sponsee to reach their goals? The sponsorship framework in which win-win situations are created is conceptually quite simple, and is presented in Figure 13.3.

The assumption in the framework is that certain benefits will satisfy certain goals. Those benefits can be delivered only by an entity other than the organisation. If two entities, both in search of benefits to satisfy their own goals, are able to deliver the benefits needed by the other entity, they can become engaged in an exchange of benefits. By exchanging benefits, both organisations 'benefit' from the cooperation; therefore, a win-win situation is created.

It must be noticed though that in today's sporting environment it is often not enough to 'create' a win-win situation and leave it at that. It is rapidly becoming common practice for sponsor and sponsee executives to organise regular strategic-planning meetings, in order to maximise the effectiveness of the sponsorship. During these meetings it is evaluated whether the goals of both the sponsor and sponsee are being reached and whether any new insight and ideas can increase the effectiveness of the sponsorship. More and more, executives discuss new business opportunities beyond the scope of the (current) sponsorship through which the actual sponsorship can lead into a strategic alliance. A strategic alliance

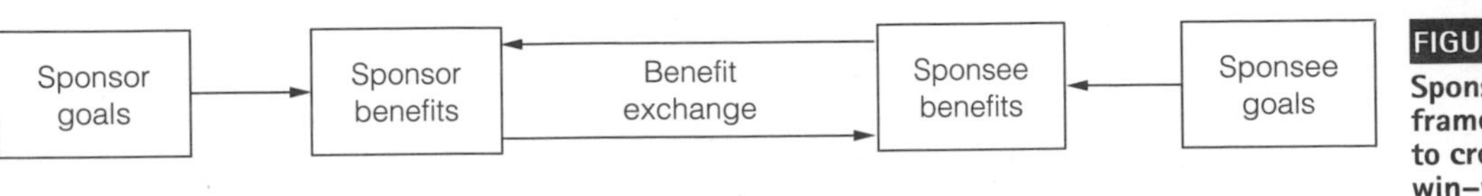

FIGURE 13.3 **Sponsorship framework to create win–win situations**

is a commitment and relationship between two organisations from which both organisations hope to benefit.

It is now time to examine the conceptual sponsorship framework in practice. Table 13.1 presented possible sponsor and sponsee goals. Table 13.2 expands on this to include the operationalised benefits needed to reach the listed goals, and provides an example. The goals of a sponsor (beer brewer Heineken) and a sponsee (a sporting organisation) are shown in bold type. The benefits needed by both organisations to reach their goals are shown in bold type as well. If both organisations are willing and able to provide the benefits needed by the other organisation, a win-win situation can be created. The example is summarised at the bottom of the table.

There are a variety of issues to consider before a deal can be closed and a win-win situation is created. How to write a sponsorship proposal and how to enhance the value of a sponsorship are covered in the this chapter's case study. Now we take a closer look at a typical sport industry sponsee: the individual athlete.

Sponsoring individual athletes and celebrity marketing

Belch and Belch (1998) suggest that when communicating a message the credibility and attractiveness of the source are of particular importance. Credibility and attractiveness are therefore the concepts to consider when organisations choose to use athletes as their source of communication. Consider this example (Beydemuller & Fiedler 2001: 29):

> After his third world championship title, Michael Schumacher is established as a cult figure among his fellow countrymen. He has become a license to print money. His incomparable driving skills alone are worth a fee of 46 million Euro per year to the Ferrari team. In addition he earns an estimated 22.5 million Euro from advertising contracts and merchandising. Renowned companies (DVAG, L'Oreal, Omega, Nike, Hilfiger and RTL among others) are investing about 15,300 Euro in the smart smile of the man from the Rhein–per second of each commercial.

Credibility and attractiveness

Why is Michael Schumacher so successful in conveying the message of so many companies? Why is he such a powerful source? Are there limitations to the credibility and attractiveness of sporting celebrities like Schumacher? To answer these questions, it is first necessary to elaborate on the concepts of credibility and attractiveness. A simplified model of the communication process, including these concepts, is presented in Figure 13.4. The model shows that when a source is credible and attractive, the message will become more powerful and will have a higher impact on the receiver of the message. This in turn will lead to a positive association with the source and message, eventually leading to a planned change in the perception, awareness or buying behaviour of the receiver. If the source is not credible and attractive, the opposite is more likely to happen.

TABLE 13.2
Exchanging benefits to satisfy goals of sponsor and sponsee

Sponsor goals	Sponsor benefits	Sponsee benefits	Sponsee goals
Image creation or improvement Business relationship marketing Media relationship marketing Employee relationship marketing Business development Increasing sales **Brand positioning** Raising awareness Corporate responsibility Targeting new market segments Developing new distribution channels	**Television exposure** **Print media exposure** Access to sporting organisation's mail-outs Naming rights Logo use Signage **Advertising rights** Merchandising rights Product exclusivity Sampling opportunities Athlete use **Hospitality opportunities** Access to database (addresses etc.)	**Dollars** Goods **Services** Exposure Affiliation	**Obtaining funds** **Obtaining resources** (goods) **Obtaining services** (Raising awareness) (Brand positioning) (Raising credibility) (Image creation or improvement)

Heineken Beer Breweries' goal	Heineken Beer Breweries' benefits	Sports organisation benefits	Sporting organisation goals
Brand positioning	Television exposure Print media exposure Advertising rights Hospitality opportunities	\$25 000 Fully created party for sporting organisation members	Obtaining funds Obtaining services

According to Belch and Belch (1998), a source is credible when it has expertise about the message. When Michael Jordan endorses the sport drink Gatorade, he is a more credible source than golfer John Daly endorsing basketball shoes. It is more likely that Jordan has expertise about the sport drink than that Daly has any about the shoes. A source also becomes more credible when it is trustworthy. Brazilian soccer star Rivaldo will probably be more honest and believable in supporting the wellbeing of the Amazon rainforest than in endorsing the benefits of being a member of the Turkish Automobile Club. Information from credible sources will influence the receiver in that the message communicated will become the opinion of the receiver. This opinion will have an influence on the (buying) behaviour of the receiver.

A source becomes more attractive when there is a similarity between the source and the receiver. The more similarities a person can (or wants to!) identify between the athlete and him/herself, the more likely that person is to be influenced by the message of the athlete. Many juniors aspire 'to be like Mike'. Linking this message to drinking Gatorade, Michael Jordan successfully influences the buying behaviour of many juniors around the world. Likeability is another determinant of attractiveness. Sporting celebrities are admired for their performances and become well known to the public, given the high visibility and hence media coverage of sport. Rather than a plain advertisement, Ferrari uses Michael Schumacher to draw attention to its message, in order to stand out in the very cluttered advertising media.

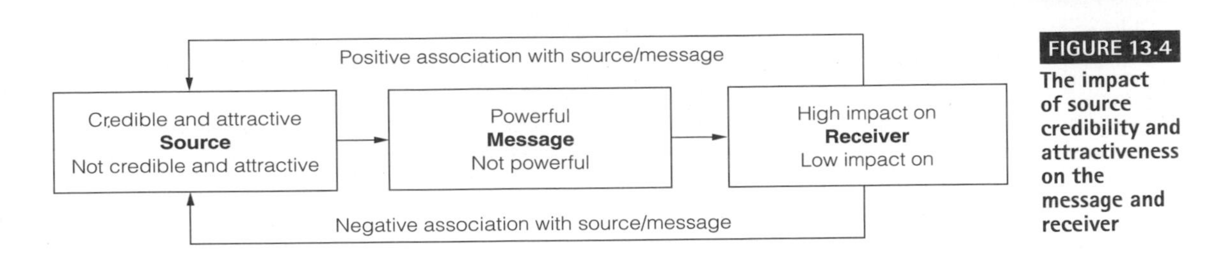

FIGURE 13.4 **The impact of source credibility and attractiveness on the message and receiver**

How important the attractiveness of an athlete is to organisations associated with the athlete is exemplified by golfer Tiger Woods. When the American PGA renegotiated its television contract, it agreed on a new four-year deal worth US$870 million, some US$90 million per annum up from the last deal. It has been argued that Tiger Woods single-handedly is accountable for this rise, and the proof is in the pudding. Sport television ratings in 2000 in the USA showed the PGA tour to be up 22% over the 1999 season. This increase is even more spectacular when compared to the 2000 ratings of the NFL (down 7.2%), Nascar (down 7.3%), the NBA (down 11.9%; Jordan was still in retirement) and the MLB (down 22.2%) (Wilner 2001a).

Credibility and attractiveness, however, are influenced by other factors when using an athlete celebrity.

Considerations when using athlete celebrities

Using a single athlete, as opposed to a sporting organisation, team or event, brings with it advantages and disadvantages.

The single athlete can stand out in myriad advertising messages, especially when performance is high. Nike athletes like Andre Agassi and Richard Krajicek, both considered huge tennis talents, did not perform up to the expectations of the general public over the longer period. Agassi's world ranking fell to as low as 30, and Krajicek never seemed to perform when it really mattered (in Grand Slam tournaments). Nike even considered discontinuing the agreement until Agassi, with a new coach, became number 1 in the world and Krajicek won Wimbledon in 1996.

Another uncontrollable factor is the personality of the star athlete. Athletes who find it hard to control themselves when they lose, say things to the press they regret later or always seem to run into trouble are risky investments for organisations trying to build a consistent image or sell more products.

More recently, Nike seemed to have hit the mark again when Australian tennis star Lleyton Hewitt reached the number 1 position in the world and then won Wimbledon in 2002, after much publicised difficulties controlling his on-court temper and initial struggle to building rapport with audiences. 'Winners are grinners' and, although the performance and personality of athletes cannot be controlled, it can heavily influence their credibility.

Organisations also have to realise that young people are more likely to be influenced by athlete celebrities than older people. Therefore the target publics that organisations want to communicate with by using athlete celebrities have to be carefully selected.

When using high-profile celebrities, organisations run the risk that the message or product they want endorsed will be overshadowed by the celebrity. Because high-profile celebrities are attractive to a mass audience, many organisations want them to endorse their messages. This can easily lead to overexposure of the athletes, which will make the messages they communicate less credible. Overexposure is noted when it becomes too obvious that the celebrities are being paid to endorse the message, and the public can become very sceptical.

Sportview 13.1 gives examples of these considerations.

SPORTVIEW 13.1

Marketing Michael

According to *Forbes* magazine, in 1995 Michael Jordan received more than US$40 million for endorsing such products as Nike basketball shoes, Big Macs, Gatorade, cars for Chicago-area Chevy dealers, basketballs for Wilson, lottery tickets for the state of Illinois, calendars, school supplies and greeting cards for *Cleo*, underwear for Hanes and Oakley sunglasses (part of this deal with Oakley was a seat on the board).

His alignment with Wheaties is so strong that the cereal's manufacturer, General Foods, has printed a special edition Wheaties box with Jordan and the Chicago Bulls on the cover. When the Bulls won the NBA title in June 1996, Michael Jordan Wheaties boxes were in supermarkets within hours. It seems Wheaties needs Jordan more than he needs the cereal. Its share of the $US7.9 billion ready-to-eat cereal market is only 1.6%. The idea of having to do without Jordan is a nightmare for General Foods. Jordan's endorsement power, which barely waned during his two seasons of retirement, continues to grow. *Forbes* estimates that since 1990, when he started getting major product endorsements, he has earned $170 million as a 'pitch man' (Hay 1996: 18).

David Falk, Jordan's marketing agent from ProServ says, 'we haven't packaged Michael Jordan, we have done a good job exposing who he is and what he is to corporate decision makers. Once they saw what he was firsthand, the rest flowed from there'. It was clear from the beginning that Jordan was a made-for-the-media athlete. He had natural ability to communicate, to provide intelligent answers to questions, to delicately handle the tough questions. The 1984 Olympic gold medal enhanced Jordan's image as an all-American kid, and unlike other Olympic heroes, his star only has risen from there. His visibility was a key factor in reversing the declining fortunes of the NBA in the 1980s and when Nike and Jordan developed the first Air Jordan basketball shoes, Jordan told his former roommate at the University of North Carolina to 'better get some Nike stock; they are going to make a shoe for me, these Air Jordans, and someday it's going to be worth a lot of money'. At Nike the director of design, after releasing the Air Jordan No. 6 says, 'one of the things about Michael Jordan is we can take incredible risks in the product because his wearing them validates it. The fact that Michael Jordan is wearing this plain-toed shoe will make it all right for a lot of people'.

Jordan's fame presents him with a range of moral dilemmas. In 1989, kids began murdering one another for the $115 sneakers that bore his name. Jordan was first informed about sneaker violence by *Sports Illustrated* reporter Rick Telander, whose

May 14, 1990, cover story 'senseless' helped focus attention and sharpen debate on the issue. 'I thought I'd be helping out others and everything would be positive', a visibly shaken Jordan told Telander. 'I thought people would try to emulate the good things I do, they'd try to achieve, to do better. Nothing bad. It is kind of ironic, though, that the press builds people like me up to be a role model and then blames us for the unfortunate crimes kids are committing'.

Although Jordan's image has suffered some minor damage in 1993, when rumours regarding selfishness, aloofness and serious gambling problems surfaced, David Falk remains confident his client will remain among the few celebrity legends, who will not lose their public appeal. Although Michael will lose the principal platform from which he addresses the public, he will not fade into obscurity. 'It is assumed that when you stop playing the impact dramatically goes away. Quickly because you are not in the public eye. In his case I don't think that is going to be the situation at all. I think he is going to be very much before the public eye, and he is still going to be doing Nike commercials and other commercials. (Naughton 1992: 11–29)

In the NBA of 2002 though, Michael is still pulling in the crowds and his consistent high performance keeps him at the top of the list of the most ubiquitous endorsers of our time. Michaels' new team, the Washington Wizards, suddenly sell out all their matches, both at home and on the road, and 'before Jordan's return became official, NBC [television] didn't have the Wizards on their schedule, and Turner had Washington just once. Now, the Wizards plan to make the maximum number of appearances on both networks—11 on NBC, 15 on Turner—with NBC actually planning to shuffle its entire schedule and occasionally televise Jordan and the Wizards in prime time. (Wilner 2001: 15)

Sources: Excerpts from Hoy (1996: 18); Naughton (1992: 11–29); Wilner (2001b: 15).

The integrated marketing approach

Sponsorship support activities complement the sponsor's goals. Given the sponsorship framework, the sponsee can either supply support activities or participate in support activities in order to ehance the value of the sponsorship for the sponsor. Examples of different sponsorship support activities are given below. Fuji Xerox Australia, as an Olympic sponsor, serves as a case example, presented from the sponsor's point of view.

Sponsorship support activities

A personal letter (direct mail) notified business relations that, on 5 September 1995, Fuji Xerox Australia would host a special Olympic event in the central business district of Melbourne. The media were informed through a press release (publicity), and around 400 general managers and marketing managers of a variety of organisations were invited to the Victorian Arts Centre to witness and participate in Fuji Xerox's Olympic sponsorship launch. A well-organised introductory show, in which the Olympic flame was lit, led into a video presentation of Australia's Olympic achievements throughout the years. The motivator of the Australian Olympic team, Mr Laurie Lawrence, followed the video presentation and entertained the crowd with sport stories in which the importance of teamwork was stressed. Fuji

Xerox's marketing manager then highlighted his organisation's commitment to the Olympic team, enabling Australian athletes to represent their country. Four Olympic athletes were honoured and awarded before a variety of new Fuji Xerox products were introduced. Guests were invited to take drinks and food after the formal presentation and to see the new products in action in the different demonstration areas (personal selling). Different Olympic prizes were given away by the present Olympic athletes, and every guest deciding to buy Fuji Xerox products in the following weeks automatically entered the draw for a trip to the Atlanta Games in 1996 (sales promotion). Opportunities for interviews and photo sessions were given after the event (public relations). In the months following the Olympic launch several television commercials and newspaper advertisements backed up the Olympic sponsor involvement of Fuji Xerox.

Sponsoring (inter)nationally but making it work locally

Cousens and Slack (1996) state that sport sponsorship can be a very effective tool to enhance corporate image at the (inter)national level. However, consumer awareness of the fact that McDonald's was the sponsor of the 1994 World Cup of the World Soccer Federation (FIFA) might not have been enough to strengthen consumer demand at the local level. McDonald's franchisees needed to have the opportunity to leverage the sponsorship to make it work in their local store. For example, McDonald's, as the sole retail sponsor of the World Cup, was able to feature the games in its restaurants. It organised local franchise-backed soccer tournaments and hosted local McKicks mobile soccer clinics. Although optional for franchisees, these local tie-in promotions proved to be very successful in boosting sales, developing relationships with the local community and targeting new market segments.

An Olympic sponsor since 1986, VISA has gained a reputation as one of the most successful sponsors of sport in the world. The credit card business is extremely fragmented when considering the face-to-face communication with customers. VISA has 1.2 billion cardholders worldwide, who obtain their cards through one of the 21 000 member financial institutions. VISA is responsible for some US$2 trillion in business. As an Olympic sponsor it has to create alliances with local partners in order to talk to (potential) customers, both on the Olympic site and through the various media outlets. In Salt Lake City, VISA created partnerships with the Salt Lake Visitors and Convention Bureau as early as 1996. It further aligned with the local Chamber of Commerce, Ski Utah, Park City, Deer Valley and the USA ski team. Many banks have historically not been involved with the Olympic Games, yet VISA managed to convince twelve of the USA's largest banks to become active Olympic VISA marketers, representing 80% of the financial market in the USA: 'Throughout the world, thousands of member banks are running marketing programs which utilise Olympic branding and messages. Millions of VISA cards now bear the famous five rings and the presence of Olympic branding at point of sale further cements the relationship' (Roberts 2002: 22–3). Smaller sponsorships (e.g. the local bakery sponsoring the local hockey club) can be leveraged according to the same principle: tie-in promotions making customers aware of the association between sponsor and sponsee.

The above examples show the importance of leveraging the sponsorship through support activities and tie-in promotions. If sponsorship is seen as a single, separate tool, benefits resulting from it will be much less. Leveraging the sponsorship is as much in the interest of the sporting organisation as it is in the interest of the sponsor. An unsuccessful sponsorship deal is less likely to be renewed, leaving the sporting organisation without a sponsor. When the sporting organisation is able to supply or participate in support activities, sponsorship will more successfully operate as part of the total promotion and marketing plan. This ultimately will lead to a win-win situation.

To distinguish a win situation from a not-win situation, it is important for the sport marketer to measure the effectiveness of sponsorship, largely the topic of chapter 14. Now we take a brief look at some of the current trends in relation to sport sponsorship.

Current trends in sport sponsorship

The first sport sponsorship trend is the move from sponsoring the big, established sports to the new, exciting, up-and-coming sports. For example, extreme sports such as skateboarding, inline skating, surfing and snowboarding offer affordable sponsorship opportunities, especially when compared with the established global sports. The 'new' sports also boast a highly identified and segmented following. In other words, 'niche' sports offer excellent opportunities for sponsors to talk one-on-one with a target market, because the segmentation information that is available about the target market is much more specific than the bigger sports mass market segments.

The extension of exploiting 'niche' market opportunities through sponsorship relates to another interesting trend, so-called sponsor-funded programming. The increasing demand for quality content by broadcasters has been identified as a new opportunity for sponsors. Rather than broadcasters funding and producing sports programming, sponsors become partners in this process. For example, the Trans World Sport program, often screened as part of in-flight entertainment, is now called Samsung World Sport. One of the major disadvantages of sponsorship—the perceived lack of control over the sponsored property—can now largely be overcome because the sponsor becomes a co-producer. It has even been suggested that a consortium of sponsors may become involved in the bidding process for broadcast rights in order to obtain complete control over the production of their sponsored property (*SportBusiness International* 2002).

Another important generic marketing trend that is emerging is the move from 'commercial' marketing approaches to 'cause-related' marketing approaches. This trend may be considered in the 'ethics' or 'corporate social responsibility' framework, briefly outlined in chapter 1. In the context of sponsorship, the move to cause-related marketing is critical for sport organisations in particular. Big corporate sponsors increasingly are looking for opportunities to show to their customers that 'they care', especially after corporate scandals such as Enron and Worldcom in the United States, or the corporate collapses of insurer HIH and Ansett Airlines in Australia. The general public demands evidence of corporations (sponsors and sponsees!) that they are 'good corporate citizens', that they behave ethically, and that they give back to the communities they receive from. Sport organisations should therefore carefully balance their on-the-field ambitions with those in the world outside the arena. On-field success requires significant resources to pay the superstars responsible for victory, in turn raising the price for fans at the gate and through pay-television subscriptions. The latter may damage the public's (fans') opinion about the sport organisation, ultimately leading to a decline in attractiveness as a vehicle for sponsorship because the sport organisation is not viewed as an exemplar of community friendliness. Hence, sponsors may direct their marketing resources to organisations such as the Salvation Army or UNICEF. In other words, sport is no longer the natural 'number 1' choice of sponsors.

Finally, some soccer clubs in Europe are exploring new opportunities through the application of virtual advertising technology to shirt sponsorship. Some of the clubs that have signed players from different continents are keen to offer virtual shirt sponsorships to different markets. Viewers in Asia will see Feyenoord's Japanese star player Shinji Ono promoting a Japanese brand (in Japanese writing), whereas hometown fans were exposed to the current sponsor, a local insurance company. According to the experts, though, the technology needs at least a few more years of maturing before it is ready to be exploited through virtual shirt sponsorship (Hancock, 2001).

Summary

This chapter showed the strategic importance of sponsorship for sport organisations. For both sponsor and sponsee, sponsorship can be used to satisfy multiple goals, particularly advertising- and public relations-related for the sponsor and fundraising-related for the sponsee. The relationship between the goals of sponsor and sponsee were shown in the sponsorship framework for how to create win-win situations. Relationships between sponsor and sponsee can even lead to a strategic alliance between the two organisations. Sponsorship as a tool of the promotion mix is still growing in popularity because it is generally seen as a cost-effective manner of achieving the sponsor's communication goals.

Because of the high visibility and attractiveness of sport as a communication medium, many sporting organisations tend to overemphasise the importance of sponsorship as a potential source of income. Sporting organisations should be aware that this 'sponsorship myopia' can lead to an underusage of the other elements of the marketing mix in developing a broad-based marketing program. From the sponsor's point of view, sponsorship alone will not satisfy the communication goals set. A comprehensive set of sponsorship support activities and tie-in promotions is required to optimise the sponsorship effort and make the sponsorship as successful as possible in the overall marketing effort.

Sponsoring individual athletes has distinct advantages and disadvantages. The sponsor-athlete relationship is similar to the sponsor-sporting organisation relationship in that both involve mutual commitment and obligations. Sponsorship support activities need to be considered in both relationships. How we can measure the effectiveness of the sponsorship is further explored in chapter 14.

CASE STUDY

Attracting a naming sponsor for the local badminton club

This case study is purely fictional. The persons and organisations in the case are non-existent.

Simon Huttle, president of the local badminton club, was enjoying an after-the-match mineral water with his fellow board member, Robert Acket. Simon was particularly pleased with himself, because he had won the match against his ten-years-younger treasurer.

Robert, being quite embarrassed about his loss, tried to direct the conversation away from their game, asking Simon, 'What's the state of affairs in renewing the contract with our current naming sponsor, Simon?'

Simon's smile disappeared. 'Two weeks ago I got the news that they're not willing to renew. They'll cease the agreement at the end of this financial year. I wanted to wait till our board meeting tomorrow night to tell you this, but now you're asking...'

'Why?' Robert responded in a sudden state of shock. 'We've done everything we can to make them happy. Their name is on the racquets, we tell our members to fill up their cars with their fuel, and we invited their local employees to our general assembly. And how can we possibly field a team in the regional competition without the support of a naming sponsor?'

'Well, I was going to ask you that question, Rob. You're the treasurer. You should be able to answer that question better than me. But for your information, a friend of mine is in the advertising business. His name is Jim Beam and his company has been involved in sport sponsorship as well. I've asked him to prepare an outline for a sponsorship proposal. He'll present it tomorrow night.'

Disappointed with this news on top of his earlier loss, Robert drank his water and grabbed his gear. 'Well, catch you tomorrow night then,' he said and went home.

Question 1: Given your knowledge of sponsorship after reading this chapter, can you detect any information explaining why the sponsor decided to cease the agreement?

When Robert drove home, he tried to think of reasons why an affluent sponsor like theirs would choose not to continue the very pleasant relationship they had built through the years. He decided to prepare some questions to ask Jim during the board meeting the next night.

When Robert arrived at the board meeting the next night, his colleagues and Jim Beam were already there. Simon welcomed Robert and started the meeting.

'Welcome, fellow board members. As you can see I've invited a guest tonight. I'd like you to welcome Jim Beam from A.M. Bush Advertising. I have a special reason for inviting him. Two weeks ago our sponsor of five years gave me a call to tell me that unfortunately they were not in the position to continue their association with our club.'

'What!' Pamela Rush, the secretary, cried out. 'They can't do that. And by the way, why didn't you tell us earlier, Simon?'

Simon ignored her second question and continued introducing Jim. 'I've asked Jim to prepare an outline for a sponsorship proposal, in order to prepare ourselves as soon as possible and find a new sponsor for the new season.'

'You still haven't answered my question, Simon,' Pamela interrupted. She rephrased her second question.

Question 2: By telling the other board members earlier, could they have done other things before calling in the advertising expert?

'I don't know, Pamela,' Simon responded, slightly irritated, 'but the fact is that we have a problem, and I took the liberty to initiate action to solve it!'

Robert came to Simon's rescue by asking Jim what he thought of the situation. Simon looked gratefully in Robert's direction for a moment and finished his introduction of Jim. 'Can you present us your suggested sponsorship proposal outline Jim?'

'Yes, thank you, Simon, for your kind words and your invitation... Dear board members, the outline I will present to you is very brief. I deliberately left blank spaces in order to give you the opportunity to actively contribute. Every heading of the outline is accompanied by one example,' Jim said.

Question 3: Contribute examples and possibilites in the context of your organisation for every heading in Jim's outline:

Suggested sponsorship proposal outline

- Executive summary.
- Organisation/event/athlete history and present situation
  —achievements of the club in the competition they played in.
- Target audiences (for sponsor and sponsee)
  —sponsee target audience: families with young children.
- Sponsorship track record
  —five years of successful sponsorship with last sponsor.
- Period of association for the proposed sponsorship
  —a period of three years with annual options to renew after that.
- Benefits on offer
  —sponsor's name on the racquet.
- Benefit valuation (capitalisation)
  —sponsor's name on the racquet of all teams: $1000.
- Packages
  —signage package: court 1, 2 signage, sponsor's name on first-team shirts.
- Sponsorship support activites
  —local paper advertising.
- Ambush prevention strategy
  —exclusive sponsor rights.
- Effectiveness measurement
  —recall measurement among members.

Question 4: Are there any elements missing in this outline? Are the listed elements presented in the right order?

Robert decided that it was about time he asked one of the questions he had prepared on the way home yesterday. He was wondering how they could avoid contracting a sponsor with whom there obviously wasn't a 'fit'. He still could not figure out why the current sponsorship did not work out.

'Jim, why do you think our sponsor wasn't interested in continuing the relationship?' Robert asked.

'That's a good and vital question, Robert. I think we are dealing with a classic case of incongruity of goals.'

'Can you explain that in plain English?' Robert responded.

'Of course. Both the sponsor and the badminton club have certain goals they want to achieve with the sponsorship, right? Well, in this particular case, it's likely that the sponsor was able to satisfy your goal, which was supplying you with an amount of money, but the club wasn't able to let the sponsor effectively communicate with their potential clients', Jim said.

'Effectively, in that other organisations or events were more related to their products?' Pamela contributed.

'Exactly!' Jim said. Pamela smiled in Simon's direction and Jim continued. 'By linking the sponsor goals to tangible benefits, you, as an organisation looking for sponsors, can identify whether you're in the position to supply the desired benefits. If this is the case you have prepared a potential "fit" between your organisation and the sponsor. In other words, you need to do a bit of work before you send out proposals!'

'But Jim, if we go through all of this, and we actually have a sponsor, how can we make sure we hang on to that sponsor?' Sandy Mash, the vice president of the club, involved herself in the discussion.

'You mean, how can we increase the value of the sponsorship?' Jim replied. Sandy nodded and Jim grabbed an overhead and put it on the projector. 'Here are a few hints for how you can do this, Sandy. The list is not complete, but it is a helpful tool in intensifying the relation with your sponsor.'

The overhead showed the following list:

How to increase the value of a sponsorship

- Keep the sponsor informed.
- Remain informed about the sponsor.
- Promote the sponsor in the organisation and develop a sponsor culture.
- Create media alliances and involved the sponsor in them.
- Offer exclusivity.
- Maintain personal contact with the sponsor.
- Deliver *more* than promised.
- Acknowledge the sponsor in all communication.

'I want to suggest the following,' Jim Beam said to the board members. 'I've given you some information now.'

Question 5: Follow Jim's suggestions and take some time to prepare a draft proposal for your club, directed to a sponsor that fits your organisation.

'I think that's a good idea, Jim,' Simon said. 'Let's close the meeting here. I invite you all for drinks, and to meet again next week to discuss our proposals.'

The rest of the meeting agreed, and after thanking Jim Beam, they went off to the bar to enjoy a good whisky.

14

Measuring the effectiveness of sponsorship

CHAPTER OBJECTIVES

Chapter 14 further explores the concept of sponsorship. Where in chapter 13 we examined the key success factors in attracting and implementing sponsorship, here we introduce the different methods that can be used to evaluate the effectiveness of sponsorship. It needs to be noted that the chapter is written from the perspective of the sponsor: that is, we consider the effect of sponsorship in regard to the goals set by the sport sponsor. Beyond effectiveness, we also explore the concepts of ambush marketing and location dependency of sponsorship. In this chapter, we have integrated an extended case study. This means that the questions at the end of the chapter relate to all components of the case study presented throughout the chapter.

After studying this chapter you should be able to:

1. Describe different methods of measuring sponsorship effectiveness.
2. Understand the relationship between effectiveness measures, sponsorship objectives and the buyer readiness continuum.
3. Understand the principles that underpin ambush marketing tactics.
4. Understand the relationship between 'exposure' and 'impact' in regard to which sponsorship property is chosen by the sponsor.

Stage 1—Identification of marketing opportunities

▼

Stage 2—Strategy determination

Step 5—Determine core marketing strategy

Marketing and service mix—sport product, pricing, place (physical evidence, people, process), customer satisfaction

Promotion mix—sales promotion, advertising, television, Internet, **sponsorship**

Step 6—Determine tactics and performance benchmarks

▼

Stage 3—Strategy implemention, evaluation and adjustment

HEADLINE STORY

Introducing the case study: We've signed the deal! but how do we make it work?

From season 2001–02 the English Premier League changed its name. What was the Carling Premier League will for the next three years be known as the Barclaycard Premier League. As the title sponsor of the world's most prominent and successful domestic soccer competition, Barclaycard pays the League US$70 million for the privilege. With the League being covered on television in 142 countries around the world, this investment may turn out to be one of the best sport sponsorship ploys of the decade.

Throughout this chapter we introduce the different organisations that are involved in making the sponsorship work for Barclaycard, as part of the case study that underpins and is developed during the chapter.

When the complete sponsorship program is put into action, it is important for both sponsor and sponsee to measure its effectiveness. We show that sponsorship objectives cover the whole spectrum of the 'buyer readiness continuum', a tool that demonstrates the stages through which consumers proceed before undertaking a transaction. As briefly discussed in chapter 13, we recognise that sponsorship objectives can be categorised under headings such as corporate, marketing and media objectives, or as strategic, tactical and operational objectives. The real distinction is between direct (sales) and indirect (exposure) marketing objectives. We argue that the sponsorship opportunity is really about the right to 'associate', the forging of a connection between the event or athlete and the company or brand. This right to associate is then translated into potential communication outcomes, and they can be plotted along the buyer readiness continuum, or the 'attention–interest–desire–action' sequence. The relationship between objectives, buyer readiness and effectiveness measurement is visualised in a model in the second part of this chapter. Effectiveness can also be diminished by the practice of ambush marketing, a topic also discussed here.

SPORTVIEW 14.1

Case study Part 1

We've signed the deal! But how do we make it work?

The sponsor

Barclaycard, a fully owned subsidiary of Barclays, announced title sponsorship of the Premier League only eight weeks before the start of the new season. They surpassed companies like Budweiser, Coca-Cola and Vodafone in the betting stakes to become the new sponsor of the League. Sponsoring the title of the League has a distinct advantage over, for example, buying advertising time around football programming. It stands out from the clutter, and the association is with a 'living and breathing' entity. The credit card business has grown dramatically over the past decade, and Barclaycard as a market leader needed to step up to the international challenge. The principal company objective is to double profit in the entire business every four years. The sponsorship of the Premier League is anticipated to assist the company in making the brand better and more widely recognised; and, by being associated with such an emotional product, the brand will become more human, passionate, tangible and spirited. With coverage in 142 countries Barclaycard's ambitions are truly international. From its position as the leading credit card in the UK, the only expansion opportunity lies internationally.

By the way, it is not that Barclaycard, through the sponsorship, has spent an additional US$70 million on marketing. Much of the funds spent on sponsorship come from a decreased expenditure on advertising, clearly indicating that sponsorship is perceived to be a superior means of marketing communication. That space is now filled by Coca-Cola, which bought the broadcast sponsorship of the ITV flagship program *The Premiership*. One could argue that Coca-Cola has obtained the perfect ambush position.

Source: Based on Gillis (2002).

Measuring sponsorship effectiveness

As we have already indicated, how effective a sponsorship is, or has been, depends on the goals the sponsor and sponsee have set before they enter the sponsorship agreement. For example, Heineken has different goals when sponsoring the Australian Open Tennis Championships from those when sponsoring the Heineken Classic golf tournament. The goal at the tennis is global attention-related, whereas the goal at the golf is more related to direct sales—through, for example, business relationship marketing activities. How the public perceives the association between sponsor and sponsee determines what can be measured as the effect of the sponsorship. If, for example, the public links the name of the sponsor only to the event, and does not change its buying behaviour, it makes little sense to measure after-sponsorship sales. In this section, it is assumed that the overall effectiveness of the sponsorship is based on the achievement of the sponsor's goals. Achievement of sponsee goals are partly met at the agreement of the sponsorship (i.e. receiving funds, goods or services). Other goals, like brand positioning, can be measured in a similar fashion to the sponsor's goals.

Hansen and Scotwin (1995) identify four levels of measuring sponsorship effectiveness:

- exposure;
- attention;
- cognition; and
- behaviour.

As is shown in the case study, exposure is the broadest measure of sponsorship effectiveness. It measures how many times (in seconds on television, or number of columns and photographs in print media) an organisation or brand is observable. Television exposure, for example, is measured by multiplying seconds by the number of viewers; hence exposure is expressed in 'exposure per 1000 viewers in 30 seconds'. Exposure value can be compared with advertising value by multiplying seconds (30) by advertising rates for 30-second commercials. The resulting value presents the sponsor with the money figure that would have been paid had the sponsor invested the money in 30-second commercials. However, there are significant problems with these measures of effectiveness. For example, how do we know that viewing a 30-second commercial equals the value of viewing 30 seconds of scattered brand exposure throughout an event broadcast? This problem is compounded when one realises how hard it is to accurately measure the number of viewers. These problems relate to the fact that exposure is one thing, but what really matters is the impact of exposure.

In other words, volume of exposure is only the start of measuring the effect of sponsorship. A better measure of impact is how much attention people pay to a brand or an organisation. Attention can be measured in terms of changes in recall or recognition by individual target-market members. Recall is the more powerful measure of effectiveness in that research subjects are not aided in recalling sponsors' names. In recognition, subjects are asked to choose from a list of possible sponsors. The benchmark for attention measures has to be the recall or recognition measure before entering the sponsorship agreement. This may be achieved through pre-testing. Otherwise, changes in recall or recognition cannot be measured.

Cognitive effects also can be measured in individuals who are part of the target market(s) of the sponsor. The association between a car manufacturer and a car racing event evokes a stronger cognitive effect than the association between a car manufacturer and a tennis event. The car manufacturer–car race link is logical and requires little explanation. The car manufacturer–tennis event link is expected to evoke a more general association, and tries to link the image of the event to the image of the car. Both effects are often measured in associative tests. For example, given the Australian Open tennis championships, the question 'Which sponsors do you associate with this event?' can be asked. One can even consider using research techniques that compare attitudes people have about different brands, including the brands that compete with the sponsor. Tracking studies, where factors such as the brand image are researched over an extended period of time, also fit the category of measuring cognitive effects. Cognitive tests are better described as qualitative research techniques because they deliver information that allows the researcher to explain consumer behaviour, rather than the quantified measures that result from media monitoring. Cognitive research becomes more important towards the 'desire' and 'action' stages of buyer readiness.

The most direct measure of sponsorship effectiveness is buying behaviour. What are the effects of the sponsorship on attitudes towards buying, or even the direct sales figures or turnover of the organisation, or the sales figures of certain product lines? In this case, the benchmark for measurement has to be set before the sponsorship. Behavioural measurement of sponsorship has often been criticised because of the difficulties in isolating the effects of sponsorship on sales and turnover from those of other promotion mix tools. Experimental research designs or historical analysis of prior promotion impact may help the researcher to isolate the impact of sponsorship investment.

Measurement of sponsorship effectiveness is a difficult issue. How effectiveness is measured strongly depends on the goals of the sponsor, and even then many variables can influence effectiveness. One of the most important variables to influence sponsorship effectiveness is the choice of the sponsored object or sponsorship property.

SPORTVIEW 14.2

Case study Part 2

We've signed the deal! But how do we make it work?

The sponsorship research firms

IPSOS UK conducts sponsorship effectiveness research on behalf of all major brands in football. According to spokespersons of the organisation, there is still much confusion about the right approach to conducting useful research. Effectiveness research consists of both quantitative and qualitative approaches. As a matter of fact, IPSOS interviews some 20 000 individuals per annum, enabling it to both quantify and qualify the movement of perceptions and attitudes. IPSOS' director of sponsorship research, Mike Jackson, argues that effective sponsorship is underpinned by extensive pre-testing of what the sponsorship can do for the brand, which rights are obtained through the sponsorship, and how these rights can be exploited throughout the whole company. It took Barclaycard three months to achieve a desired level of association, what it would have expected to take at least two years. A majority of keen football fans, three months into the sponsorship, spontaneously associated Barclaycard as a leading brand within the Premiership.

It is interesting to note that the research industry seems to develop along two distinct lines. One branch of the industry focuses on media evaluation, assessing the amount of exposure, whereas 'effectiveness' research aims to qualify the impact of exposure—impact that can, according to Jackson, be greatly improved if the sponsor realises that buying the rights is only the first step in the process of achieving an effective sponsorship.

Source: Based on Gillis (2002).

The sponsorship properties: events and athletes

It can be argued that there are literally hundreds of sponsorship opportunities, including sponsoring the name or title of an event or stadium, broadcast sponsorship, location sponsorship (e.g. the fifteenth green), leader board sponsorship, corporate hospitality suites, athletic outfit sponsorship (e.g. shoes, apparel)—the list goes on. It is largely up to the creativity of sport marketers to come up with new ways of packaging 'rights to associate with' for sponsors to buy and use. Irrespective of how this is done, the majority of sponsored properties in sport can be categorised either as events or athletes. As we noted earlier, what principally determines the success of the sponsorship is the amount of exposure received, and the impact exposure has on the sponsorship objectives. Figures 14.1 and 14.2 provide insight into the most marketable Australian athletes and events.

In Table 14.1 'exposure' is mapped along the lines of geographic distribution and the geographic diffusion of the sport property. Geographic diffusion of the sport property really relates to the diffusion of appeal of the sport: in other words, do a broad selection of people know about and like the sport, or is the potential audience narrowly defined? Geographic distribution and sport diffusion are used as the key drivers of (potential) sponsorship

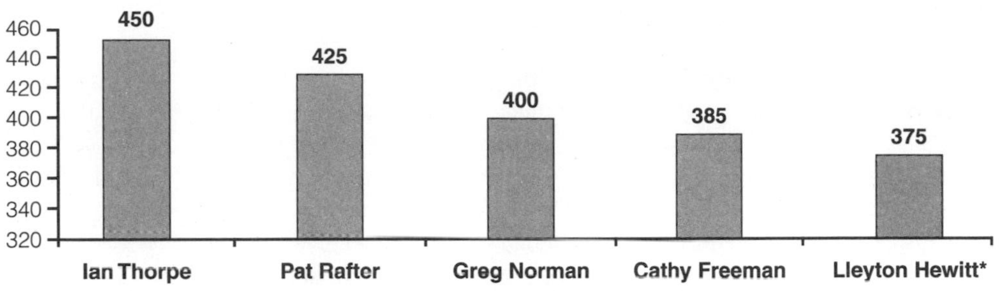

FIGURE 14.1 Top five most marketable Australian athletes (× A$1000 in sponsorship per annum)

* Hewitt has most likely taken over the number 1 spot after his 2002 Wimbledon victory.

Source: Adapted from Beikoff (2002).

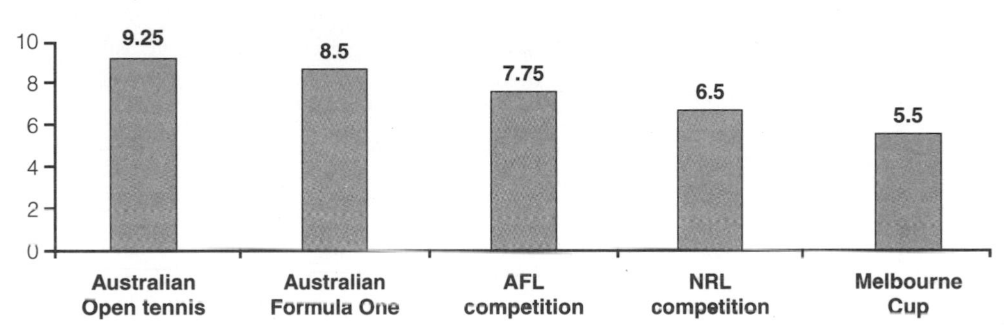

FIGURE 14.2 Top five most marketable Australian events (× A$million in naming rights sponsorship)

Source: Adapted from Beikoff (2002).

exposure. Or, stated differently, generic global sport offers potentially greater exposure than local niche sport–hence, the latter presents more affordable sponsorship opportunities. Again it needs to be stated that, after picking the right property, success is largely determined by leveraging activities (impact) executed by the sponsor and its support agencies.

SPORTVIEW 14.3

Case study Part 3

We've signed the deal! But how do we make it work?

The sponsorship consultants

In order to capitalise on all opportunities that the football industry has on offer, Barclaycard has employed Arena as its sponsorship consultants. Arena provides the link between the sponsorship and the football industry, and in the process offers Barclaycard access to an impressive network of football's stakeholders. It manages the Barclaycard player-of-the-month award, which involves coordinating a comprehensive panel of experts who vote on a monthly basis. Every month negotiations take place with the respective club of the 'player of the month' in order to maximise exposure and impact. For example, Arena always makes sure the player is photographed with the trophy on Friday night so the papers can carry the picture in the Saturday's lead-up to the round of football over the weekend. A Barclaycard director hands over the trophy and the broadcaster gets a shot of the action to include in its late-night reports. Next to this operational activity, Arena also provides top-end strategic branding advice. Sean Jefferson, CEO of Arena, argues that his job is all about creating a new sub-brand. The Barclaycard Premier League did not exist before June 2001, so a lot of hard and smart work needs to go into building this brand for the benefit of the company as a whole. Ultimately, successful creation and leveraging of the sub-brand 'Barclaycard Premier League' needs to result in a new brand image for Barclaycard as a company.

At present, however, Jefferson is dealing with a rather exciting operational problem. With the Premiership race as close as it has been in years, five clubs are still in it with a chance. With all challengers at home in the final weekend, Jefferson is considering preparing a mobile 'Cup presentation unit' in a helicopter. Making the sponsorship work is hard yakka, right down to the wire!

Source: Gillis (2002).

The SPONSEFFECT model

In both this chapter and chapter 13 we have discussed the range of issues that are important in regard to attracting, implementing and measuring the effect of sponsorship. It has been noted that the formulation of specific sponsorship objectives is critical when selecting the right sponsorship entity, in turn affecting the different measures to be used when assessing the effectiveness of the sponsorship partnership. We have also argued that both objectives and effectiveness measures are strongly linked to the buyer readiness sequence.

TABLE 14.1
Exposure of selected sport properties

	Local	Regional	National	International	Global
Niche sport narrow audience	Mount Buller snowboarding championships			Gianni Romme (speedskating world champion)	Xtreme Games
		James Hird (Aust. Rules football player)	Australian National hockey championships		
Wide audience		World Masters Games		European soccer championships	David Beckham (soccer player)
Generic sport	Metropolitan school cricket championships		Chinese National table tennis championships		The Olympic Games

TABLE 14.2
The SPONSEFFECT model

Main sponsorship objectives	Buyer readiness stage	Main effectiveness measures	Most likeley sponsored property*
• Image creation or improvement • Brand positioning • Raising awareness • Develop new distribution channels • Target new market segments • Community relationship marketing	**Attention**	• Audience numbers (on site, ratings) • Recall/recognition • Surveying (pre/post) • Media monitoring	• Global event • International event • International athlete
• Business development • Brand positioning • Image creation or improvement • Media relationship marketing • Community relationship marketing	**Interest**	• Attitudes • Recall/recognition • Number of inquiries • Preference testing • Surveying (pre/post)	• Global event • International event
• Business relationship marketing • Increasing sales • Brand positioning • Employee relationship marketing • Target new market segments	**Desire**	• Intentions to purchase • Brand preference • Brand image monitoring	• Regional event • Special (niche) event • Local event • National athlete • Local athlete
• Increasing sales • Employee relationship marketing • Business relationship marketing	**Action**	• Purchase from product sales tracking • Historical analysis of prior promotion impacts • Experimental designs	• Local application of all types of events • Local customisation of all types of athletes
• Relationship marketing	**Post-purchase**	• Repeat purchase • Attitudes • Brand preference • Comparative brands	• Continued sponsorship of those events and athletes that have proven successful

* It is recognised that potentially a wide range of events and athletes can be used to achieve the sponsorship objectives; however, we have chosen to list only a limited number of better-suited entities.

The practical value of the AIDA model lies in its strong focus on moving consumers from being unaware of a product to buying it. Ultimately sponsorship is about only one thing–bringing as many customers to the sponsor's company and enabling them to buy as many products as possible, preferably many, many times! In reality, the stages of attention, interest and desire are therefore quite awkward. We don't want consumers to be in those stages for too long. As can be observed from the model, it is much harder to define clearcut objectives and sponsorship properties for the interest and desire stages than it is for the attention and action stages. It is therefore very important to remember that the mid-stages of buyer readiness are transitory.

In the SPONSEFFECT model (Table 14.2), all these issues are summarised. The model can be used by sponsors and sponsees to assist them in planning and executing sponsorship agreements. We briefly introduce the concept of ambush marketing here, because it may strongly influence the effectiveness of the sponsorship deal, from the perspective of both sponsor and sponsee.

Ambush marketing

The Australian *Trade Practices Act 1974* defines ambush marketing in an indirect manner under Section 53 as follows:

> A corporation shall not, in trade or commerce, in connection with the supply or possible supply of goods or services or in connection with the promotion by any means of the supply or use of goods or services: (c) represent that goods or services have sponsorship, approval, performance characteristics, accessories, uses or benefits they do not have; (d) represent that the corporation has a sponsorship, approval or affiliation it does not have.

Ambush marketing is a problem for the sponsor in that funds or services are invested in an association with a sporting organisation of which non-investing organisations reap the benefits. Ambush marketing is a problem for the sponsee in that the effectiveness of the sponsorship will diminish and a prolonged business relationship with the sponsor will be put in jeopardy. More and more, sponsors are demanding that sponsees take precautions to prevent ambush marketing. In servicing the sponsor, sponsees should therefore take a proactive stance in preparing for potential 'ambushers'.

A proactive strategy can consist of the following actions:

- identification of potential ambushers (these are often potential sponsors the sporting organisation did not sign up);
- identification of the commercial value of the sponsorship (which benefits the sponsee can deliver, and how potential ambushers can obtain these benefits without being involved as an official sponsor);
- detailed contracts (including exclusivity rights, detailed descriptions of what is being considered as conflicting signage/advertising, sponsor/sponsee obligations to prevent ambush marketing); and
- joint sponsor/sponsee counteract strategies (which determine how sponsor and sponsee will react in terms of public relations, advertising–for example buying 'strategic' media time during potential 'ambush time slots'–or public appearances when commenting on an ambusher's actions).

This is a limited and certainly not complete list of actions to prevent ambushers from taking advantage of a sponsorship relationship. Although ambush marketing can never be eliminated, solid preparation can assist sport marketers in servicing the sponsor to the best of their ability. It needs to be noted that ambush marketing, in the context of 'ethics' in sport marketing, increasingly is an activity that is viewed as unethical behaviour. As described at the end of chapter 13, consumers are increasingly aware of and sensitive to 'corporate abusive practices', ambushing being an obvious example. In the very near future 'to ambush' may not be worth the effort. Behaving in a societally responsible manner may prove to be the best marketing medicine of them all. Sportview 14.3 is an example of some historic ambush marketing during the 1988 Winter Olympics in Calgary, Canada, contrasted with recent moves by the IOC to implement 'ambush prevention strategies'.

SPORTVIEW 14.4

Ambush marketing at the Olympics

The Olympic Games attract global interest and can deliver tremendous exposure. Billions of spectators watched the combined 1988 Summer and Winter Olympics and many corporations would therefore like to benefit from the exposure of being associated directly or indirectly with the Olympic Games.

Research evaluating the effectiveness of sponsorship and ambush marketing at the 1988 Olympic Winter Games investigated the recall and recognition of official sponsors, ambushers and other organisations. The large drawing power of the Olympics was evidenced by the fact that 82 per cent of the people surveyed watched some part of the Olympic telecast. Of the respondents, 41.4 per cent were light viewers (watched one to four days), 27.2 per cent were moderate viewers (five to nine days) and 31.3 per cent were heavy viewers (ten to sixteen days).

Overall, 20 per cent of the respondents correctly recalled the official sponsors, with recall varying by product category: from 50 per cent correct for credit cards to 7 per cent for airlines. Recognition (choosing from a list with names) of sponsors was higher, with 39 per cent of respondents correctly recognising offical sponsors. Recognition also varied by product category, from a high 59 per cent for fast foods to 25 per cent for hotels.

To determine the effect of viewing the Olympic telecast on consumer perceptions, the three viewer groups were used to analyse sponsor awareness. The ability to both recognise and recall sponsors varied directly with viewership: light viewers averaged 18.9 per cent correct recall, moderate viewers 33.5 per cent and and heavy viewers 37.5 per cent. For recognition, the numbers ranged from 37 per cent to 46 per cent to 52.2 per cent.

Ambush marketers attempt to avoid the up-front high investment of sponsorship while gaining the glamour and benefits of an Olympic tie-in; their hope is that consumers associate their products with the Olympic Games and thus weaken any major advantage of their competitors who paid for official sponsorship. To determine the effect that ambushers had on sponsorship awareness, the number of correct sponsor identifications were compared with the number of ambushers as sponsors. Seven product categories, each with one official sponsor and one major ambusher, were chosen. The results for recall and recognition were aggregated. Across the overall sample an average of 2.57 official sponsors were correctly identified (out of a possible seven). In comparison, on average 1.43 ambushers were identified as official sponsors. Ambushers were significantly less recognised as official sponsors.

A closer look at these data by product category, however, leads to some interesting cautions for advertisers. In only four out of seven product categories studied were the correct official sponsors identified more than the non-sponsors (ambushers and others). In the other three cases the sponsor was not number one when it came to sponsor identification; in two of these three cases the official sponsors, while engaging in other promotional activities, were not major advertisers on the Olympic telecast, and in the third case (cars), the ambushers were engaged in very heavy advertising (Ford and Chrysler bought all available advertising time for domestic cars). This might indicate that to achieve any benefits from being a sponsor it is necessary not only for a company to sponsor an event such as the Olympics but to heavily advertise the fact that they are *official* sponsors. Buying the right to be an "official sponsor" may, in reality, only be buying a licence to spend more money!

Atlanta 1996 Olympic sponsors did everything within their power to combat the ambush strategies of competitors. But it seems that ambushers are always one step ahead of their 'official partner' competition. Nike, as the pre-eminent ambusher in Atlanta, achieved great exposure through building-high billboards and 'precinct theming', to the extent that parts of the inner city were transformed into Nike town suburbs. Although Nike was gladly accepted into the Olympic sponsorship family of Sydney 2000 when Reebok decided to discontinue its relationship with the five rings, the IOC had learned its lesson the hard way. The Salt Lake City Organising Committee (SLOC) installed a 'Brand Protection Program', obtaining a permit from city authorities to close all streets directly connected with the Salt Lake Ice Centre and the Olympic Medals Plaza. The streets of Salt Lake became an Olympic venue in their own right, 100% controlled by SLOC. To prevent ambushers from using tall buildings as advertising banners, the SLOC launched a 'Cityscape Program'. Through negotiations with building owners, nominal fee contracts were drawn up allowing the SLOC to completely wrap the buildings in Games-related imagery. If space could not be leased, the contract stated that building owners would not lease the space to anybody for the duration of the Olympic Games. Life for an ambusher is becoming increasingly difficult!

Sources: Excerpts from Sandler & Shani (1989: 9–14); based on Naidoo and Gardiner (2002).

Location dependency of sponsorship

In this final section it is appropriate to reflect on the increasing specialisation in regard to sponsorship as a promotional tool. Here we would like to introduce the concept of 'location dependency' as a special characteristic of sport sponsorship. Westerbeek (2000) tested the hypothesis: 'revenue maximisation of tenants of sport facilities is dependent on geographical location of the facility (location of distribution)'. Revenue maximisation was operationalised pertaining to sponsorship. A survey instrument was sent to all sponsors of a Melbourne-based football club. Sponsors were grouped as location-dependent and location-independent based on the location of their head office and financial turnover achieved in the area around the sport facility. The survey collected information on three different steps in the sport consumption process, including 'coming to the sport facility', 'being in and around the sport facility' and 'being serviced in the sport facility'. Indicative evidence was found in support of the general hypothesis. Smaller, low-spending sponsors with an important percentage of turnover in the area around the sport facility were less likely to move with the football club to a (remote) new facility. In relation to sponsors' objectives, it was found that objectives of location-dependent sponsors are directed more towards direct sales, whereas location-independent sponsors' objectives seem to be indirectly related to sales and more towards obtaining exposure.

In a follow-up study, Westerbeek and Smith (2002) found that location-dependent organisations had fewer employees, and spent less on sponsorship, and on sponsoring sport in particular, than their location-independent counterparts. Where location-dependent organisations predominantly operated in metropolitan or state territories, location-independent organisations operated largely on a domestic or international level. Location-dependent sponsors perceive issues in relation to 'location' of the sport facility (such as an attractive environment, close proximity to head office, distribution outlets and major residential areas) to be significantly more important than do location-independent sponsors. Location-independent sponsors perceive 'corporate exposure' issues (such as quality television coverage of the game, frequent telecasts from the stadium and excellent corporate hospitality facilities at the stadium) to be significantly more important than do location-dependent sponsors. The location dependency of sponsorship shows that the complexity of effectiveness measurement will only grow, when sponsors become aware of how they would like to maximise their sponsorship investment.

Summary

In this chapter we have extended our thinking about sponsorship as a concept. Whereas in chapter 13 we predominantly looked mainly at the relationship between the sponsor and the sponsee, in this chapter we advanced that relationship to the audience that is most important to the sponsor—the (potential) customer. A range of measures that can be used to measure the effectiveness of sponsorship were introduced, discussed in direct relation to the sponsor's objectives, and placed in the buyer readiness continuum. Following the measures of effectiveness it was argued that the amount of exposure and the potential impact of this exposure will make sponsors decide which sponsorship properties they can consider purchasing. Ultimately, sponsorship effectiveness is a combination of choosing a suitable sponsorship propery, setting specific objectives that can be fitted to the buyer readiness continuum and linking this to the appropriate qualitative or quantitative effectiveness measures. In order to further protect the sponsorship rights, ambush marketing opportunities need to be detected in order to prepare for potential ambushers taking advantage of the sponsor's rights. Location dependency, as a special characteristic of sport sponsorship, was discussed as an example of the increasing complexity of the sponsorship effectiveness measurement environment. In the case study it is shown that the public relations support function is paramount when aiming to maximise sponsorship benefits.

SPORTVIEW 14.5

Case study Part 4

We've signed the deal! But how do we make it work?

Bringing it all together: the PR consultants

Hitting the right tone with all the people involved in football, from the fans to the clubs and from the sponsors to the broadcasters, was the task at hand for Barclaycard's PR consultants Lexis, eight weeks from signing the contract in June to the start of the Premiership in August. Because of the huge cultural significance of football in day-to-day life in the UK, you don't just sponsor the Premier League: you have to earn the right to sponsor it. Showing that you understand and respect the game, and the ways in which the game is being delivered to all its stakeholders, is the way to do this, and requires constant creativity. At Lexis, the Barclaycard team meets every morning to have a brainstorming session on what is happening in football that day. Tim Adams, chairman of Lexis, says that 'it is part of our job to act as an intermediary between the company and its outside audiences, creating campaign themes and spotting new opportunities'. Next to this strategic input, Lexis runs close to 3000 ticket competitions a year in order to sustain the sponsor's profile. In the end, Adams vehemently agrees that effectiveness research is also the key to PR success, stating that 'IPSOS research is a key measure of how we are performing and what comes through is that the sponsorship is working and the PR initiatives have a major part to play in that process'.

Source: Based on Gillis (2002).

Questions

1. In your opinion, how likely is it that Coca-Cola will take a genuine ambush approach in that it will try to steal Barclaycard's glory as the official sponsor of the Premier League?
2. Over the three years of the sponsorship deal, determine which sponsorship objectives will be set for each of the years.
3. In the first year of the sponsorship, which stage of buyer readiness will dominate sponsorship planning? Justify your answer.
4. What will make Barclaycard decide to renew the sponsorship deal after successful completion of the three years of the contract?
5. If you were asked to measure the effectiveness of the sponsorship at the end of year three and you were given the choice of three effectiveness measures, which would you choose? Justify your answer.

15

Public relations

Stage 1—Identification of marketing opportunities

▼

Stage 2—Strategy determination

Step 5—Determine core marketing strategy

Marketing and service mix—sport product, pricing, place (physical evidence, people, process), customer satisfaction

Promotion mix—sales promotion, advertising, television, Internet, sponsorship, **public relations and publicity**

Step 6—Determine tactics and performance benchmarks

▼

Stage 3—Strategy implemention, evaluation and adjustment

CHAPTER OBJECTIVES

Chapter 15 introduces public relations as an element of the sport promotion mix. The public relations process, applied both proactively and reactively, is examined in this chapter, which notes how sporting organisations have been required to take a more active role in managing their public relations. How to execute a public relations program is discussed by examining the various stages of communicating with different media. Special attention is paid to publicity as an important component of the overall public relations strategy. Sportviews are replaced with an extended case study. This means that the questions at the end of the chapter relate to all components of the case study presented throughout the chapter.

After studying this chapter you should be able to:

1. Identify critical activities of the public relations process.
2. Create an extensive list of sporting organisation publics.
3. Distinguish between proactive and reactive public relations strategies.
4. Link the public relations strategy to the promotion and marketing strategy.
5. Develop a comprehensive set of public relations actions in order to generate publicity.

HEADLINE STORY

Introduction to the case study

A case of racial vilification

On Anzac Day, 1995, a capacity MCG crowd witnessed one of the greatest battles of recent time. After two hours of hostilities, and a struggle for power, not a single point separated Collingwood and Essendon. However the battle aptly fought on a landmark day in Australia's war history was remembered for more important reasons. Michael Long recounted the event: 'We wrestled each other to the ground near the Members' wing and it was while I was getting up he called me a black bastard. There were other players around us who heard the words so I asked the umpire why he didn't report him.' (Warren & Tsaousis 1997: 38)

Almost daily, news in relation to drug use in sport, major injuries, signing of high-profile athletes or, indeed, racial abuse appears in the papers or is broadcast on television or radio. Sporting organisations or athletes without problems are rare. Perhaps sporting organisations have more problems than other organisations, but more likely the reason is their high visibility in society. This chapter deals with the management function of public relations, showing how public relations can be helpful in solving a crisis such as the headline story. It is also shown that public relations can be used in a planned and positive way.

Public relations is one element of the promotion mix. Many people show considerable interest in the fortunes of sporting organisations and their athletes. A high interest results in a high visibility, and therefore sporting organisations have relations with many publics. A public is a group of people who share an evaluation of specific problems or issues. This justifies special attention to public relations in the context of the sport industry. Being part of the promotion mix, public relations deals with communicating with the target audiences or, better, publics of the organisation. To understand better how, when and with whom to communicate, it is first necessary to define the concept.

Defining public relations

Griswold (1995: 7) defines public relations as:

> the management function which evaluates public attitudes, identifies the policies and procedures of an individual or an organisation with the public interest, and plans and executes a program of action to earn public understanding and acceptance.

Three critical activities can be derived from this definition:

- evaluating public attitudes;
- identifying the policies and procedures of an individual or an organisation with the public interest; and
- planning and executing a program of action.

These three activities form the basis of this chapter.

Evaluating public attitudes

In chapter 4 we discussed the process of marketing research. Marketing research techniques are also used in identifying and evaluating the attitudes that publics have towards the sporting organisation, its products and its employees (often the athletes). In order to communicate effectively, however, it is important not only to identify public attitudes but also to convey these attitudes to the management of the organisation. Management can then adjust organisational strategies to more effectively influence public attitudes. If, for example, the local soccer club is suddenly losing members, attitudinal research might find that members did not understand why the club sold the league's top scorer to a rival club and sebsequcntly cancelled their memberships. With this information, management of the soccer club could put public relations strategies in place to improve members' understanding of this decision.

Public relations objectives and their relationship to promotion and marketing objectives

Because public relations is part of the promotion mix, and the promotion mix is part of the marketing mix, it is obvious that marketing objectives are the basis for both promotion and public relations objectives. Returning to the soccer example, one of the club's marketing objectives might be to boost memberships by 10% in the next year. A promotion objective to support the marketing objective might be to sign up at least fifteen new youth members during a weekend shopping-mall promotion. This objective could more easily be achieved if the club had a favourable image over three other soccer clubs in the area. A public relations objective therefore might be to become the preferred soccer club in the area with 75% of the population. If this percentage were not reached (e.g. as a result of selling the top scorer), a public relations program of action might help the promotion and marketing activities to become more successful.

In general, the following broad public relations objectives can be formulated to support promotion and marketing objectives:

- earning understanding and acceptance for organisational activities;
- explaining certain behaviour;
- educating and informing publics;
- raising awareness for the organisation or new products;
- creating trust (in the organisation or its products); and
- creating goodwill.

These objectives show that most public relations objectives, and hence activities, will not be aimed directly at increasing sales or, in the soccer example, increasing memberships. Linked to the other marketing functions in the organisation, public relations becomes part of an integrated marketing approach. This integrated approach should lead to a more efficient and effective achievement of overall marketing objectives.

To know where to start, the organisation needs to be aware of public opinion about the organisation and its product range.

Public opinion

Evaluating public attitudes has been defined above as one of the critical activities of the public relations function. Seitel (1995: 52) defines an attitude as 'an evaluation people make about specific problems or issues'. A public then is a group of people who share an evaluation about specific problems or issues. When certain group attitudes become important and strong enough, they turn into opinions. Opinions about certain issues can lead to behaviour. It is the opinion of the larger public that influences the buying behaviour of target markets. Consider the following example by Rhoden (1993: B11):

> By the summer of 1993, Michael Jordan, the most widely recognised athlete in the world, had begun to develop serious public opinion problems. After leading the U.S. Dream Team to an Olympic victory and then his Chicago Bulls to an unprecedented third straight National Basketball Association title, Jordan was the focus of nasty rumours regarding selfishness, aloofness, and serious gambling problems. Then, late in the summer of 1993, tragedy struck. Jordan's father, James, was found murdered in his car. The nation mourned with Michael. Scarcely two months later, in the midst of major league baseball's playoffs, Michael Jordan stunned the world by announcing his retirement from basketball. The news was so jarring that President Clinton even took time out to address a statement of support to Michael. In the space of one traumatic quarter of the year, Michael Jordan's public opinion ratings had rebounded from questionable to sky high.

It was in the commercial interest of the multiple organisations that Michael Jordan was associated with to turn the negative public opinion around. Since his second return to the game of basketball, not many people in cities other than Washington will become season ticket holders of the Wizards (they are a public, not a target market), but their opinion about Jordan and hence the Washington Wizards will influence Washington citizens to affiliate with the Wizards. Not many senior citizens will consider drinking Gatorade (a sport drink endorsed by Jordan) because Jordan does (they are a public, not a target market), but their opinion of Jordan will influence young people in their decision to drink Gatorade.

In other words, public opinion highly influences the buying behaviour of target markets and therefore becomes one of the primary areas of public relations activity. Reinforcing existing positive public opinions and changing negative public opinions are the underlying aims of all public relations strategies. Depending on marketing objectives and public opinion, certain publics will become the target audience for public relations activities. ANZAC Day 1995, as introduced in the headline story, was the catalyst for the AFL to recognise issues associated with racial vilification. It also understood that this was a significant social issue that had the potential to polarise the community. The AFL had to take action, and it had to work at shaping public opinion about the sensitivity of the issue and how it was to be managed. Sportview 15.1 continues this case, providing the background leading to the AFL's handling of racial vilification and the subsequent public relations issues.

Publics of sporting organisations

In other chapters the term 'target market' is used to define the group of people at whom marketing activities are directed. Target market implies a focus on exchange between the sporting organisation and its customers. It was shown above that publics have a much wider scope. The Michael Jordan example showed that the public at large can be the target audience of public relations activities without being a target market. In other cases, such as a product recall after a manufacturing mistake, the target market may be the target audience

SPORTVIEW 15.1

Case study Part 1

Public relations crisis management: a case of racial vilification

Identifying the key 'players'

Michael Long

Essendon player Michael Long through his weekly column in the *Northern Territory News* initially raised the case of racial vilification, the day after the event (Denham, 1995a). The article described the incident but did not directly refer to the person responsible for racially vilifying Long. Through exposing the case to the public in this manner, Long immediately drew community attention to the case and the greater issue. To further raise community awareness, in a front-page exclusive two days after the Long article was published, *The Age* reported that Long had experienced 'shocking' racist abuse. (Oldfield 1995: 1)

Damien Monkhorst

The Collingwood player handled the media quite differently from Long. At no point in the process did he seek media attention to debate the issue or plead his innocence. The first official response from Collingwood, ten days after the event, was from Collingwood solicitor David Galbally, who stated that the club had 'retained the services of Geoffrey Scher, QC, to act on Monkhorst's behalf should the AFL Commission find him guilty of racially taunting Long' (Linnell 1995a: 36). Collingwood supported its player and quickly set to portray him in the media as the innocent victim. Galbally commented (Linnel 1995a: 36):

> We [Collingwood] say that it's a great tragedy that it's come out in the public arena in the manner that it has because all the reputations can only be tarnished...Monkhorst was distraught over the allegations... [and] denied making any comments based on race. (Linnell 1995a: 36)

The Australian Football League

One of the first players to speak out against racial abuse experienced on and off the field was Aboriginal player Nicky Winmar, when he lifted his shirt and proudly pointed at his dark skin at Victoria Park in 1993. While at the time the AFL acknowledged the problem, little action was taken to seriously address the issue. The 1993 Grand Final, 'the day of Atonement, represented an attempt by the AFL to "celebrate" indigenous people in Australian cultural life and to portray this to an international television audience' (Warren & Tsaousis 1997: 37).

In 1995 the AFL, as the governing body of the competition, first had to resolve the conflict between Long and Monkhorst and, second, had to establish some guidelines for future action of this nature—in turn advocating the social rights of people of Aboriginal or ethnic descent in Australia.

The case of Michael Long highlighted inadequacies in AFL policy to deal with the race issue. The AFL had promised to implement a code of conduct two years earlier, resulting in 'vociferous calls directed at the AFL from certain sections of the Melbourne press, the football fraternity, and Members of Parliament, calling for regulation against racial sledging' (Warren

& Tsaousis 1997: 38). At this point the AFL was faced with a crisis. From a public relations perspective there was little need to evaluate public attitudes. The public, in many ways, had been very forward in expressing its views on the Long case.

Analysing the steps taken by the AFL

The first step taken by the AFL to address the issue of racial abuse was the implementation of the long-awaited code of conduct. The code was explained to the media through a press release and press conference, stating that it provided for 'fines of up to $5000 for offences such as racial abuse' (Connolly, 1995: 5) and was a serious measure by the AFL to stamp out racial taunts in football. Subsequent criticism that the code did not adequately tackle the real problems of racial abuse resulted in the AFL 'doing a backflip' to pursue mediation and education as its answer to the specific Long versus Monkhurst case. The first example of mediation could be witnessed publicly through a news conference:

> At a news conference called by the AFL, Mr Oakley [CEO of the AFL] sat between Long and Monkhorst, defending the league's mediation stance, while prohibiting the players from commenting... [Mr Oakley] described the result as the perfect solution. (Mithen 1995: 1)

The public reconciliation act staged by the AFL was clearly an attempt to establish credibility, targeting the largest AFL audience—the mass spectator market. Through this form of reactive public relations the AFL also attempted to address the case in light of the community issues it had raised. In summary, this action was performed to:

- define a stance for competition policy;
- define the position of the AFL on the community issue of racial vilification;
- demonstrate success at mediation in difficult issues and cases;
- declare the Long case over and done with;
- generate credibility for the AFL, protecting sponsors and other organisational stakeholders; and
- establish confidence in the AFL operations and policy development with government departments, and community and human rights groups.

The success of the AFL in resolving the Long case was short-lived, with criticism coming from all directions. Credible sources such as Essendon coaching legend Kevin Sheedy, also a close friend of Long, described the resolution by the AFL as a 'Clayton's decision' and 'ordinary'. The AFL responded through a press release stating that the AFL Commission had 'done more than any other code to counter racial abuse in football' (Smith 1995a: 1). Further critical commentaries resulted in the AFL redrafting its proposal on racial vilification. The new policy stated:

> Under the AFL's racial vilification rule, mediation is the preferred course of action for disputes. Should a satisfactory result not be achieved, the matter is then referred to the league's tribunal, which has the power to fine clubs up to $50,000 and suspend players. (Linnell 1995b: 42)

The policy represented a new process of education and mediation. The AFL marketed the new version to target audiences through a range of strategies that included:

- Mr Oakley being interviewed about the policy on 3AW;
- press releases and press conferences to publicise details of the new proposal;
- implementing a television advertising campaign aimed at racial abuse awareness (Mithen & Smith 1995: 36); and
- using Aboriginal footballers and other well-known sportspeople to visit schools and discuss racism (Richards 1995: 5).

as well. Often, public relations activities will go beyond direct communication with the target market, aiming to positively influence the wider public opinion.

Jefkins (1994: 97) lists the following basic publics that apply to most organisations:

- the community;
- potential employees;
- employees;
- suppliers of services and materials;
- the money market;
- distributors;
- consumers and users; and
- opinion leaders.

Jefkins shows that the public at large, organisational members, organisational stakeholders and customers of the organisation are all potential target audiences of the public relations function. These four headings are used in Table 15.1 to identify a range of more specific publics, most common for sporting organisations. Table 15.1 identifies the publics of sporting organisations.

When the publics of a sporting organisation are identified, and the sport marketer has knowledge of their opinions, the policies and procedures of the organisation can be linked to the public interest.

TABLE 15.1 **Publics of sporting organisations**

Public at large	Organisational members	Organisational stakeholders	Customers
Television representative	Voting members	Investors, lenders	Spectating members
Radio representatives	Voluntary workforce	Sponsors	Sponsors
Written media representatives	Voluntary board	Licensees	Fan club members
Local community	Professional administrative workforce	Sporting-governing bodies	Merchandise customers
National community	Professional playing workforce	Local government	Corporate guests
Global community	Coaches	National government	Casual visitors
Educators	Recruiting officers	Grassroots sporting organisations	Television audience
Schoolchildren			Radio audience
			Newspaper audience

Linking policies and procedures to the public interest

How can an organisation create a fit between what it does and what its publics are interested in? If people are not interested in buying an organisation's products, can it at least make sure that they have a favourable perception of the organisation? These are questions that need to be answered when trying to act in a positive way as perceived by the publics. The organisation can do this in a planned, proactive way but is sometimes forced to do it in a reactive way. Examples of both are given in the following sections. How far an organisation can go in manipulating public opinion is discussed under ethics; then media relations are considered.

Proactive public relations: why do we do the things we do?

Proactive public relations can be defined as a planned effort to influence public attitudes in order to create favourable opinions. Creating favourable opinions in order to boost sales, to enhance an image or to raise awareness for the organisation can all be the broad objectives of proactive public relations. The last part of the case study largely relates to proactive public relations in which raising awareness for a new policy was the aim of the campaign. The product launch is another good example of proactive public relations. As an integrated part of the overall marketing efforts of an organisation, it supports the achievement of marketing objectives. Sport, however, is much more familiar with reactive public relations. Sportview 15.2 extends the AFL racial vilification case, detailing the publics and target groups central to its public relations strategy.

SPORTVIEW 15.2

Case study Part 2

Public relations crisis management: a case of racial vilification

Why did the AFL choose to communicate the new racial policy to what can be identified as three main target groups? First, the press release and media conference were a means of educating the print media, often openly critical of the AFL's previous attempts to establishing racial policies. Patrick Smith (1995b: 55) commented that the 'rule to deal with on-field racial and religious vilification is responsible and strong administration at its very best'. Second the implementation of television advertisements accessed mass audiences (crucial to competition success), creating positive awareness about the new policy and serving as a mass educational tool at the same time. Third, schools were targeted to implement programs for children who, when not properly educated, represented the very beginnings of racial intolerance.

To summarise the public relations strategies of the AFL pertaining to this issue, comments made by Mr Ian Collins, General Manager of Football Operations, serve the purpose: 'the league was happy to be involved in the move, which was part of an AFL program to stop racism in football' (Richards 1995: 5). As operations manager of the AFL, his first comments on the race issue in football were recorded four weeks after the initial event. In terms of 'managing' the crisis, this clearly demonstrates that the AFL appreciated the gravity of the case and regarded the management of this issues crucial to its credibility. Using their CEO, Mr Ross Oakley, as spokesperson left personnel normally responsible for public relations of this nature, Mr Ian Collins and Mr Tony Peek (Communications Manager), 'unavailable for comment' (Richards 1995).

Analysing the key publics

It has been widely documented that the Michael Long case has had significant implications on and off the football field. In order to analyse such implications, the key publics involved in the case need to be identified. The following table defines the publics of the AFL applicable to the Long case.

Publics of the Australian Football League, applicable to the Long case

Publics at large	Organisational members	Organisational stakeholders	Customers
• Channel 7 • Local and national radio stations • Local and national newspapers, magazines, journals • Equal Opportunity Board • Commonwealth Human Rights Commission • Aboriginal Advancement League • National Multicultural Advisory Council • Aboriginal Education Association of Victoria • United Nations Association • Department of Education	• Member clubs • AFL Commission • AFL employees • AFL Players' Association • Individual players (Aboriginal and ethnic)	• Investors and lenders of finance • CUB, Coca-Cola, Ansett Australia • Licensees • MCC • Dept. of Immigration and Ethnic Affairs	• Casual spectators • CUB, Coca-Cola, Ansett Australia • AFL, MCC and club members • Channel 7 audience • Local and national radio audiences • Local and national newspaper, magazine and journal audiences

From viewing the table, it becomes evident that a number of subgroups will have had an impact or influence on the progression of the Long case. These groups include different government departments, community groups, the AFL Players' Association, public opinion leaders, sponsors, and a variety of customer groups. Sportview 15.3 investigates the role of these groups and the effect of the case on their role and cause with an analysis of groups within the context of the two major issues raised by the case: the on-field implications of the AFL policy, and the broader social issue of racism and the battle against it.

Reactive public relations: Why have we done the things we've done?

Reactive public relations actions are put in place when unplanned events occur that negatively influence the attitudes of the organisation's publics. Preventing the problem is always better than fixing the problem, but sometimes even careful planning does not prevent things from happening. Sporting organisations and their athletes receive high-level attention from the media and hence are more likely than other organisations or persons to become involved in crisis situations. Just consider the ongoing saga of the racial vilification case.

It can be argued that a crisis, like a positive drug test or racial abuse, might be expected and prepared for. During major events like the Olympic Games, national sporting bodies know that the chances of athletes being caught using banned drugs are much higher. How can a sporting organisation employ a proactive public relations strategy in preparing for a crisis situation? Sporting organisations cannot always prevent a crisis from happening, but anticipation and preparation will reduce the damage.

Ethics

Seitel (1995: 121) defines an individual's or organisation's ethics as the 'standards that are followed in relationships with others–the real integrity of the individual or organisation'. If one of the most important goals of the public relations function is to enhance public trust in an organisation, clearly the public relations professional must act in an honest and trustworthy manner. Linking the policies and procedures of the organisation to the public interest means that no other organisation or individual should be harmed by the actions of the organisation. Spreading rumours about rival athletes or clubs not based on facts, to enhance one's own image, is therefore unethical behaviour. Bribing the media to report favourably on important issues is also unethical behaviour. Much can be written about this topic. The bottom line is that, in the interest of the publics and the organisation, honest information and genuine procedures will benefit most in both the short and long run.

Media relations

Earlier in this chapter it was shown that public opinion is one of the most important forces influencing the buying behaviour of publics of sporting organisations. It is the task of the sport marketer to influence public opinion in order to create a favourable image of the sporting organisation. In this decade of globalisation and booming communications technology, the media, communicating to a global mass audience, are unequivocally the most powerful means of influencing the public opinion. This is both good and bad for sporting organisations: good because, as we discuss later in this chapter, sporting organisations receive a lot of free publicity; bad because the content and timing of this free publicity cannot be controlled. This makes sporting organisations dependent on the media.

This dependency, however, can be managed to a certain extent. This is done through fostering media relations. To create and maintain favourable media relations, three actions are important to consider:

- form;
- inform;
- be informal.

Depending on the type of sporting organisation and its strategies, certain media channels are more important than others. The local tennis club, for example, will benefit more from local newspaper coverage and local radio, whereas a Grand Slam tennis tournament will need global television and newspaper coverage to satisfy sponsor needs. That is why a comprehensive form of potential media outlets has to be put together. This form, or media database, will enable the sport marketer to inform the media. This is done through formal channels, but communication may also be successful if informal communication can be developed with media representatives. Different ways of how to form, inform and be informal are now discussed.

Planning and executing a program of action

Once the sport marketer has identified the attitudes of the sporting organisation's publics, and thought of ways of linking their interests to the activities of the organisation, it is time to develop a program of action. With the media as one of the sport marketer's most powerful means of communication, a large part of this section will be devoted to public relations communication through the media. To start this process, it is first necessary to know which media are available and how to get in contact with them.

Form—the media database

Helitzer (1996) lists three main sources that have to be included in the sporting organisation media database:

- the media that routinely cover sport;
- personal contacts; and
- media directories.

These sources have to be categorised in a logical order. This is, the media outlets and contacts must be ordered according to the most relevant publics for individual sporting organisations. Contact persons and addresses are vital and should be updated regularly. A simple example of a media database of a small professional soccer club is presented in Figure 15.1. The different forms per media outlet can range from one or two contacts to several hundred!

Form—the communications plan

Planning communications is nothing more (and nothing less!) than putting together a plan of what to tell which media when. As previously discussed, proactive public relations communications should support the promotion and marketing goals of the sporting organisation. In relation to setting goals for the organisation, public relations action plans can be put together and, with the help of the database, distribution of information can be planned. Returning to the soccer example cited earlier in this chapter, when aiming to become the preferred soccer club in the area with 75% of the population, the local television station, regional newspaper 1 and community newsletters can be selected as the preferred media outlets. The local television station is targeted (once) for the finals at the end of the season, regional newspaper 1 is approached every week in relation to the weekend's results, and the community newsletters are targeted at least twice during the season in every suburb,

FIGURE 15.1 **Media database of a local soccer club**

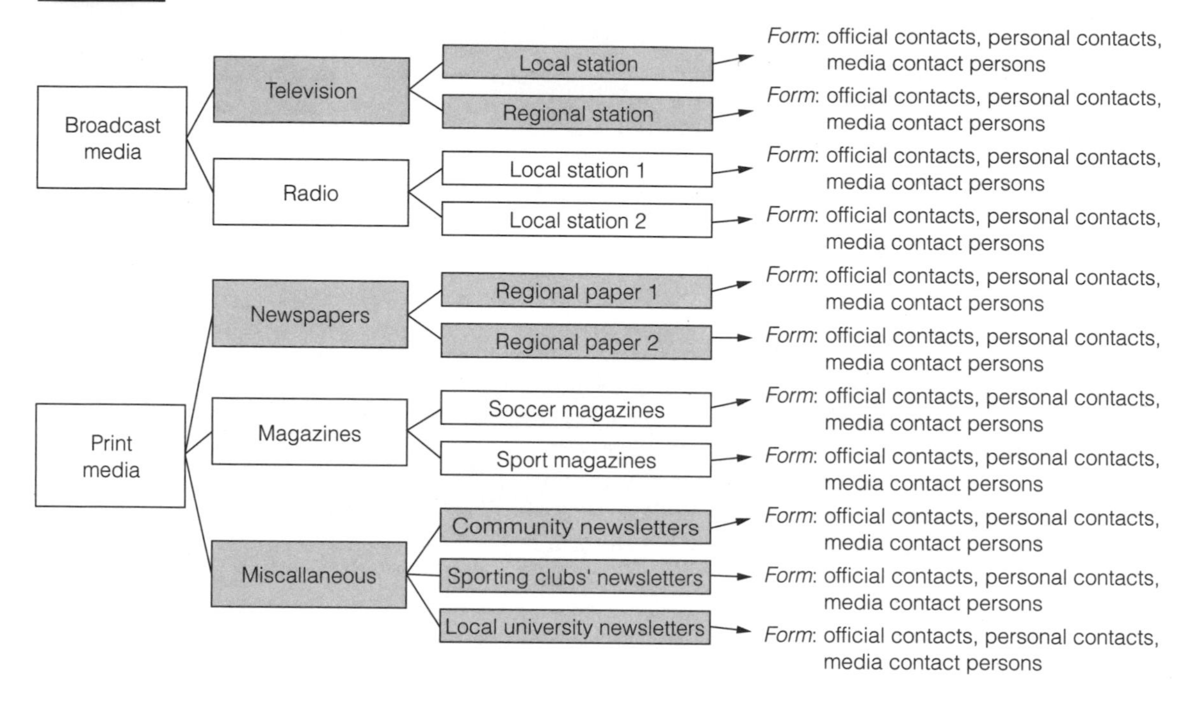

with information about youth activities at the club. Simple planning boards can be used to create a comprehensive annual overview of planned communications.

Inform—the press release

Press releases, as a means of informing the media, can be used for long-term proactive, short-term proactive and reactive public relations. Many organisations issue press releases on any topic of interest for one or more of their publics. The main goal of the press release is to inform the publics through the media in the way the organisation wants. Ideally, it will generate positive publicity for the sporting organisation or sport persons.

A few standard rules apply to the format of press releases:

- Use a catching and informative short title.
- Present the backbone information in the first paragraphs. Answer the questions who, what, when, where, why and how.
- Put facts first. Give accurate information. Use correct grammar.
- Include the name and address of a contact person.
- Use current media contacts and addresses when sending the press release.
- State the source of the press release, and date it.

The major causes of rejection of some press releases are:

- limited reader interest;

- poorly written;
- conflicts with media outlet policies;
- hard to distinguish from advertising;
- material obviously faked or exaggerated;
- apparent inaccuracies in story; and
- duplicates story previously used.

If an issue is important enough to create widespread media attention, a press release can be used to announce a press conference.

Inform—the press conference

A press conference presents the sporting organisation with the opportunity to inform all present media at once. Also, when media representatives consider the issue of the conference important enough to attend, it is very likely that some kind of publicity will be the result. When the media attend, they often use the provided information. Conference organisers should realise that, besides printed publicity, photographs and audiovisual information also will be collected by the media. This has implications for who the spokesperson will be, how he/she will dress, and how and where the names and logos of sponsors and the organisation will be presented.

Helitzer (1996: 179–81) states eleven reasons for sporting organisations to call a press conference:

- a major change in personnel;
- a major change in the status of a star player;
- an important event scheduled;
- a major investigation (e.g. into illegal drug use);
- a change in a major facility;
- award presentations;
- crisis developments;
- post-game interviews;
- the sport banquet speaker;
- the introduction of a new product; and
- a new rule that is complex or controversial.

A press conference should be called only when the general public or specific publics of the sporting organisation are interested enough to be informed. One of the above reasons might be applicable to a sporting organisation. If, however, the people or issues involved are still insignificant to the public, the media will not show up and the unsuccessful press conference will only damage the reputation of the organisation.

Inform and informal—interviews

Both a press release and a press conference can serve as an invitation for interviews. Interviews are one-on-one contact opportunities in which disseminated information can best be controlled. The interviewee has the opportunity to tell only what he/she wants to tell. However, conducting an interview and taking part in an interview are both skills in their own right. Poor preparation or failing to recognise an interviewer's leading questions can turn the opportunity into disaster for the organisation.

Helitzer (1996: 273) provides a list of the do's and don'ts of interviews:

- Don't permit off-the-record statements. Don't try to become a major part of the interview.
- Don't assume that every fact will be used.
- Don't complain if the result is not totally satisfactory.
- Do pick the best spokesperson.
- Do try to limit the subject to areas where your spokesperson is an authority.
- Do provide suggested quotes, anecdotes and statistics that can be used.
- Do rehearse fully!
- Do select the site where the spokesperson will be most comfortable.
- Do provide the press with full background.
- Do keep every promise to supply supplementary information.
- Do show your appreciation in a letter. It's even better than a call.

The interview presents the experienced sport marketer with an opportunity to use personal media contacts and disseminate information in an informal way. Informal contacts do not imply less care when supplying the information! The opportunity to talk informally to media representatives should not be turned into a disadvantage by accidentally releasing confidential information.

Form, inform and informal—publicity

Publicity, according to Belch and Belch (1998: 528), refers to 'the generation of news about a person, product, service [or organisation] that appears in broadcast or print media [at no cost to the organisation]'. Although not every public relations effort necessarily has to result in news appearing in broadcast or print media, it can be an effective and efficient means of public relations communication. As a subset of the overall public relations exercise, planning and executing a program of action (press release, press conference, interview) often lead to the generation of publicity. Mullin et al. (1993: 260) state that:

> sport is the most interesting specimen examined by the media...and it prospered because it received at no cost reams of publicity in daily and Sunday papers...This coverage, for which any other business would have had to pay, was given freely because of its entertainment value and because a newspaper that contained information about sport would sell more copies, creating both higher circulation and higher advertising rates.

Publicity is generated when the information has news value. Because the sporting organisation does not pay for the publicity, content is very hard to control. Also, the release time and accuracy of information are hard to control. But because the sporting organisation is not the direct source of information (other than in advertising or sales promotions), positive publicity can become very powerful and credible. Negative publicity, however, has the opposite extreme effect. In an integrated public relations strategy, the content, timing and generation of publicity are as much as possible controlled in the proactive strategy, and as much as possible prepared for in the reactive strategy.

Advantages and disadvantages of public relations

At the beginning of this chapter, public relations was introduced as one element of the promotion mix. Public relations has some distinct advantages over other elements when applied under certain conditions. Belch and Belch (1998: 524–7) list the following advantages:

- *Credibility*. Contrary to advertising, the source of the public relations message is often not the organisation itself, which makes the message more credible to the receiver.
- *Cost*. Apart from the public relations personnel cost, few other expenditures have to be incurred.
- *Avoidance of clutter*. Because many public relations efforts lead to news generation, information will stand apart from, for example, advertising or sales promotions.
- *Lead generation*. For example, when Tiger Woods–one of the longest drivers on the Professional Golf Association Tour–was seen using a Cobra golf club, the club manufacturer received inquiries from all over the United States, Europe and Japan.
- *Ability to reach specific groups*.
- *Image building*. Effective public relations programs lead to the development of a strong image, one that can resist negative publicity for a while.

The main disadvantage of public relations is the uncontrollability of publicity. When proactive or reactive public relations results in negative publicity, all potential public relations advantages turn into disadvantages. Negative information will hit more powerfully, and it will cost more to repair the damage. The avoidance of clutter, lead generation and ability to reach specific groups will now work against the organisation, damaging the favourable image.

Summary

This chapter described and discussed the promotion mix tool of public relations. This is an important tool for the sport marketer because of the high visibility and attractiveness of the sport product. Three critical activities were derived from a public relations definition in order to describe the main public relations activities:

- evaluating public attitudes;
- identifying the policies and procedures of an individual or organisation with the public interest; and
- planning and executing a program of action.

It is important for the sport marketer to know how the sporting organisation's publics perceive the organisation and its product range. Knowledge of public opinion and how to influence opinion is vital in order to create proactive public relations strategies. Therefore, public attitudes need to be evaluated. Proactive strategies enable the sport marketer to 'control and adjust' public opinion, whereas reactive strategies always require changing negative public opinions. Prevention is better than repairing damage.

As a very influential public of many sporting organisations, relations with the media were considered, and the public relations tools of press release, press conference and interviews were introduced. There are basically three things that need to be considered when communicating with the media. The sport marketer has to know with whom to communicate, what information to supply and how to maintain excellent relationships with media representatives. In sport marketing special attention needs to be given to the concept of publicity, as it is probably the most important means (and opportunity) of conveying information in the sport industry.

SPORTVIEW 15.3

Case study Part 3

Public relations crisis management: a case of racial vilification

Issue 1: the on-field implications of the AFL policy

AFL Players' Association

The AFL Players' Association (AFLPA) had a limited role in the debate surrounding the Long case. The confrontation between Long and Monkhorst (two players registered as AFLPA members) restricted the AFLPA's ability to act. On establishment of a policy and adequate resolution to the issue, the AFLPA provided support. The implications of this issue for the AFLPA could have been far-reaching if Long or a group of Aboriginal and ethnic players had instigated further action. However, this did not happen and it can be argued that the AFLPA was a benefactor of the policy being implemented. The Long case instigated an issue of particular importance to a selection of its membership and corrective action was initiated as a result of public pressures, without the AFLPA having to become a (political) player in the process.

Opinion leaders

In the Long case, opinion leaders (in and outside football circles, ranging from players, coaches and administrators to politicians and media representatives) had a significant influence on the awareness and opinions of AFL consumers about the racial vilification issue, mainly through print and broadcast media. While their activity did not highly influence the behavioural patterns of consumers, their visibility became a primary target for the AFL to control through a variety of public relations activities like press releases, news conferences, public statements and television commercials.

Sponsors

At first sight, the role of the sponsors in the Long case, as organisational stakeholders, was surprisingly low-profile. The major corporate sponsor of the AFL in 1995 was Coca-Cola, with Ansett Australia, CUB, Challenge Bank, Norwich Financial Services and Hungry Jack's as key support sponsors (AFL 1995: 5). During the case there was little to no public sponsor communication directly related to the issue. Only during the news conference at the AFL was the Coca-Cola logo evident as a backdrop. Sponsors, had they closely aligned or exposed themselves with the AFL during the period of wide and substantial criticism, could seriously have damaged their credibility and negated any positive exposure established through providing corporate support to the AFL as corporate or key support sponsors during this period.

Issue 2: the broader social issue of racism and the battle against it

Government departments

A number of federal and state government departments entered the debate of racial vilification in sport, encouraged by initial comments made by Mr David Shaw, Essendon president, who stated:

> The incident involving Michael [Long] had ramifications well beyond football...We have a responsibility and obligation to not only the club and football, but society in general, to try to do our part to get rid of racism in our society. (Denham 1995b: 1)

The AFL received public pressure from government bodies such as the Department of Immigration and Ethnic Affairs, the Department of Education and the National Multicultural Advisory Council. All bodies responded because issues raised in the Long case were representative racial issues experienced in society in similar fashion. To counter racial vilification in our society, a stand against this type of action needed to be taken.

Community groups

In a similar manner to government bodies, community groups took action to counter the broader implications of the issue. Initiated by the Aboriginal Advancement League, their response was directed at attempting to resolve the Long case and drawing attention to the broader social problems Aboriginals face in our society (Denham 1995b). Consultation by the AFL with the Human Rights Commission and the Equal Opportunity Commission demonstrated the legal implications of the Long case and the AFL's attempt to establish a racial vilification policy. The AFL effectively used the support of these bodies to launch its new education and mediation policy, demonstrating that it had 'underlined its commitment' to seriously address the problem within the AFL and in the broader community (Smith 1995b).

Assessment of crisis management

There is little doubt that the AFL found the Long case and its implications, in terms of establishing AFL policy and broader social issues, difficult to tackle. In turn it experienced difficulty controlling the quantity and quality of information communicated to one of the AFL's primary target audiences, the mass spectator's market, by print and broadcast media. Stapleton (1995: 69) stated that 'the AFL found itself uncomfortably holding a very hot political football—so hot they proceeded to drop it'.

In spite of these difficulties, the AFL implemented a number of public relations activities to communicate its message, including:

- press releases;
- news conferences;
- appearances by key AFL personnel (Oakley) on Channel 7 football programs;
- interviews on broadcast radio such as 3AW and 3LO;
- articles in AFL publications such as the *Football Record*;
- television advertisements;

- distribution of information booklets; and
- documentation in the 1995 Annual Report (Peek 1998).

Analysis of the breadth of communication tools utilised to inform target audiences indicates that the AFL was quite exhaustive in its efforts.

The AFL addressed the Long case through establishing an objective of developing a policy to counter racial abuse on the field. Criticism by the media of the initial policy release indicated that the AFL had not achieved its objective. It was clearly evident at this stage that the AFL had failed to appreciate the gravity and implications of the Long case. Measured through analysis of press reports, the AFL concluded that there had been negative audience reception and understanding of the case. However, following consultation with the Human Rights and Equal Opportunity Commission, the AFL drafted a policy that adequately covered the issues of the case. Through intense public relations activity the AFL then successfully communicated the policy and broader social message. (Parts of the 1996 policy are presented below.)

The AFL was fortunate that the issues underpinning the Long case had minimal influence on the perceptual or behavioural actions of AFL consumers. The changes resulting from the Long case, such as further acknowledgement of indigenous contributions to football and Australian society, significantly contributed to enhancing the quality of the AFL competition and its management of similar issues. The AFL has achieved this through effective public relations, particularly through cooperation with the Human Rights Commission and United Nations Association. The AFL Annual Report (1995: 36) noted:

> Racism in football was a major issue for the Australian Football League in 1995 culminating in the AFL receiving a special peace award from the United Nations Association for a number of initiatives to address the issue.

Further AFL actions in 1996 as a direct result of the Long case

The Long case refocused the attention of the AFL on dealing with racial and religious vilification, sparking the adoption of a new racial vilification rule by the Australian Football League Commission. The new rule was presented as part of a broader strategy designed to educate the football industry and wider community about why racial abuse is simply not acceptable. In communicating the rule to the public, the AFL stressed the importance of the involvement in and influence of various ethnic communities as well as Aboriginal and Torres Strait Islander athletes on the game of Australian Rules football. In an open letter to the public, through the AFL's own magazine, the *Football Record*, new initiatives to be implemented were communicated by the AFL's CEO, Ross Oakley (1996):

- A cross-cultural diversity program for AFL staff and senior AFL club officials. This program has been developed by the Victorian Aboriginal Education Association and will be held during late July. We will also be encouraging clubs to follow the lead of the West Coast Eagles and Footscray to run their own programs.
- Developing a proposal for consideration by the Federal Government for funding to assist the employment of Aboriginal development and liaison officers in each State. This would be similar to the employment of Gilbert McAdam as a development officer with the

Queensland Australian Football League whose job is jointly funded by the AFL and the Department of Employment, Education and Training.

- Developing a public education program, initially utilising a television commercial, to change the attitude and behaviour of spectators. The television commercial is being produced this week by our advertising agency, the Campaign Palace, and is expected to be on-air within two weeks. It will carry the tag line 'Racism: The Game Is Up'.
- In conjunction with the Australian Football Foundation, review the extent of football being played in Aboriginal communities throughout the country, what funding is currently available and how further junior development programs can be implemented in those communities. This is part of an overall review of football development around Australia.
- In conjunction with the Directorate of School Education in Victoria, the AFL has agreed to participate in a program designed to help combat racism in Victorian Government Schools. The program will involve Aboriginal players and other high profile athletes visiting schools to educate youngsters and talk about racism in sport.
- Each AFL coach has also received a letter from the AFL this week reinforcing the role they can play in stamping out on-field racial abuse which in turn will set an example for supporters off the field.

This case has presented a range of issues related to the participation of players of Aboriginal and ethnic descent resulting in racial taunts and vilification which unfortunately has been widespread throughout the AFL competition and (Australian) sport in general. Main case analysis was done from a public relations perspective, the Long incident raising a series of League related and community issues. As the governing body, the AFL was placed under significant pressures to act on behalf of Aboriginal players and the broader Aboriginal and ethnic community. The case addressed most of the issues in an effort to prepare a comprehensive paper for class analysis and discussion. (The case is in no way intended to illustrate academic (empirical) proof for either effective or ineffective handling of issues by persons or organisations described.)

Source: Ashley Wain originally wrote this case in 1998 as part of the Graduate Diploma of Sport Management at Deakin University. The case was updated, extended and edited for inclusion in this text by Hans Westerbeek and Ashley Wain.

Questions

1. The public relations crisis experience described in the case can be utilised to examine effective crisis management. A major contributing factor to initial action by the AFL was pressure to implement short-term public relations planning strategies. Considering this point, how can sport organisations more effectively devise PR policies under such time constraints?
2. The role Damien Monkhurst played in the case was low-profile. Do you think he made the right decision when deciding to stay away from the media, simply denying the racial vilification claims? Could he have handled the situation differently?
3. Can highly sensitive issues like racial vilification be used by certain interest groups to draw public attention to other causes of importance to them? Is this morally/ethically acceptable?

4 Can governing bodies like the AFL use negative publicity and turn it into positive publicity? How?
5 To be (or become) a good 'corporate citizen' is rapidly becoming an important strategic goal of many (multinational) organisations. In the context of this case, is 'corporate citizenship' an important (strategic) matter for sport organisations? Justify your opinion.

16

Promotional licensing

Stage 1—Identification of marketing opportunities

▼

Stage 2—Strategy determination

Step 5—Determine core marketing strategy

Marketing and service mix—sport product, pricing, place (physical evidence, people, process), customer satisfaction

Promotion mix—sales promotion, advertising, television, Internet, sponsorship, public relations and publicity, **licensing**

Step 6—Determine tactics and performance benchmarks

▼

Stage 3—Strategy implemention, evaluation and adjustment

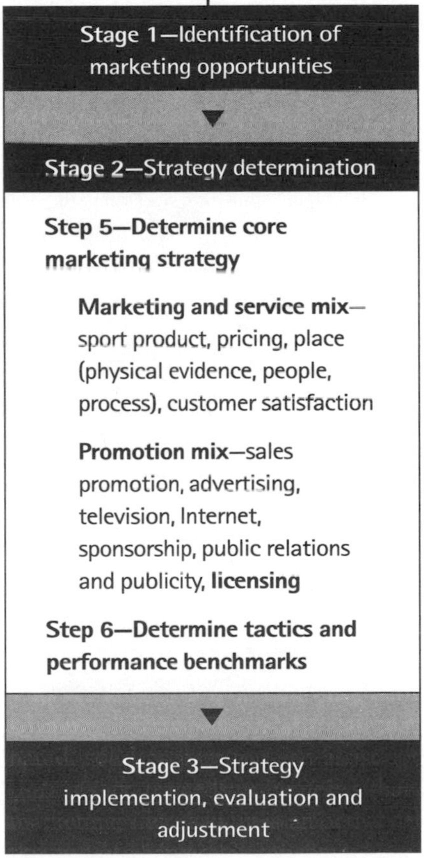

CHAPTER OBJECTIVES

Chapter 16 deals with promotional licensing as an element of the sport promotion mix. Promotional licensing involves developing a relationship between a licensor and licensee with respect to the right to use the name or logo of the sporting organisation. Terms such as licensor, licensee, royalty and trademark are introduced in this chapter. Related issues, including the role of licensing in raising revenues and branding, are also discussed.

After studying this chapter you should be able to:

1. Understand the importance of the (registered) trademark.
2. Identify the different steps in building a sport licensing program.
3. Identify licensor and licensee goals.
4. Describe the central role of branding in the sport licensing program.

HEADLINE STORY

Being Nick Faldo

> What's in a name? It's a question being tackled by many of sport's top stars as agents and sponsors ponder the value of image and intellectual property rights. Nick Faldo is embarking on a series of projects, which will establish his own answer to this question. His name, logo and image are soon to feature on a raft of new products ranging from wines to golf shoes, knitwear to sunglasses. These branded goods will stand alongside an ambitious portfolio of projects that include training schools, club shops and health spas. In addition, a golf-themed restaurant, the Jug and Jacket, named to commemorate Faldo's achievement of winning both the US Masters and the Open Championship in the same year, has an opening planned for this summer at a prestigious golfing location in Scotland. (Gillis 2002: 24)

Although the income from licensed merchandise for sporting organisations (in this case the Nick Faldo Golf Company) worldwide has increased enormously throughout the past 20 years, it has never been easy to put together a solid licensing program. How to build a sporting organisation's licensing program is discussed in the second part of this chapter. The first part discusses the different elements of the licensing concept. The different parties involved and terminology employed are defined and, where possible, placed in a sport context.

Licensing, as an activity, involves a licence, a licensor and a licensee: 'A licence is first and foremost the granting of an intellectual property right from the licensor to the licensee' (Wilkof 1995: 5). This means that the intellectual property right of a licensor must be valuable enough for a licensee to use and pay a royalty fee for. A royalty is a fee paid for usage of the intellectual property, and is often calculated as a percentage of the sales of licensed products.

As implied in the title of this chapter, promotional licensing can be seen as an element of the promotion mix. In the context of the sport industry it basically serves two purposes:

- promotion of the sporting organisation; and
- promotion of a third party or its products through use of the sporting organisation's name or logo.

In the latter case, the sporting organisation will derive royalty income from licensing the third party with the name or logo usage.

In the sport industry we are most familiar with the usage of names and/or logos (as the licensed property) of sporting teams or organisations printed on apparel (e.g. baseball caps, T-shirts) or other merchandise (e.g. pens, mugs, umbrellas). Names and logos of sporting organisations are intellectual properties, representing a certain or potential value. This value is built into the name or logo as a result of the organisation's sporting achievements and hence popularity, but also through (monetary) investment in the name or logo through the promotion efforts of the sporting organisation.

Not all sporting organisations, however, are in the position to license their name, logo or other properties to third parties. The name of the sporting organisation, or more broadly the brand, must be strong enough to generate interest and attention. Many sporting organisations set up licensing programs to receive royalties from the sale of licensed merchandise. However, without a strong brand name this makes little sense. Potential licensees are interested only if the name or logo can generate extra interest in, and demand for, the products that the name or logo is attached to.

A sporting organisation without a strong brand name can still become involved in a licensing strategy. The main aim of the licensing strategy is to increase awareness of the sporting organisation and indeed of its brand. The licensee, in turn, can use already strong sport brands in its own branding strategies, attaching the brand to newly introduced products, or products with a questionable image. The Australian Football League (AFL), for example, links its brand name to the products of tens of companies. On those products, the AFL logo and an 'approved product' sign are printed.

Branding is discussed in the third part of this chapter. First, it is necessary to discuss the basis for licensing in the sport industry: trademark licensing.

Trademark licensing

The Australian *Trade Marks Act 1995* defines a trademark as 'a sign used, or intended to be used, to "distinguish" goods or services of the plaintiff from those of any other person' (Section 17). A sign, then, includes the following, or any combination of the following: any letter; word; name; signature; numeral; device (i.e. symbol or logo); brand; heading; label; ticket; aspect of packaging; shape; colour; sound; or scent.

Trademark licensing is a multi-billion-dollar industry, and is defined by Wilkof (1995: 1) as 'an arrangement by which one party consents to the use of its trade mark in accordance with specified terms and conditions'. It is used in many industries for different purposes, which can be appreciated by considering the following examples:

- using the Calvin Klein clothing trademark to sell perfume (using the established brand/trademark to sell new products);
- Coca-Cola using an overseas franchisee to sell in new markets (using the established brand/trademark to sell in new markets);
- McDonald's using the Olympic rings to sell more hamburgers (using the established brand/trademark to boost sales); and
- licensing the sporting organisation's logo to an apparel manufacturer (building brand/trademark awareness and raising funds).

For a trademark to become the property of an organisation, it needs to be registered. When a trademark is registered, the owner will have the exclusive rights to:

- use the trademark; and
- authorise other persons to use the trademark (Section 20(1)).

Registration of the trademark is of extreme importance to the sporting organisation. Without this registration the original owner of the trademark has little legal protection when other organisations use the trademark in one way or the other. This point is reinforced by the Australian Olympic Committee's (AOC) decision to seek additional protection for its insignia. The *Olympic Insignia Protection Act 1987* (Cth) came into force in 1987 to enable the AOC to regulate the use of the Olympic symbol and other nominated Olympic designs. The Sydney Olympic Organising Committee for the Olympic Games (SOCOG) also sought added protection via the proclamation of the *Sydney 2000 Games (Indicia and Images) Protection Act 1996* (Cth) (repealed). Use of a trademark is important for an organisation in many ways. Some of the reasons are discussed in the next section.

Functions of a trademark

Wilkof (1995) identifies six different functions of trademarks. These functions developed over time, and hence the merchandising function incorporates elements of all other, earlier developed functions. The functions are:

- identification;
- physical source;
- anonymous source;
- quality;
- advertising; and
- merchandising.

Identification

The most obvious function of the trademark is to identify ownership or who is responsible for producing the product. When Juventus played Ajax in the European Champions League final, for example, soccer consumers knew that the 'black and white' Italians played the 'red and white' Dutchmen.

Physical source

Without being able to witness the production of certain products, the trademark can be seen as acknowledgement of the physical source of the purchased goods. The trademark serves as a stamp of approval. When licensing trademarks, however, the licensee is not the actual source of the goods. T-shirts with National Basketball League (NBL) logos printed on them are not produced by the NBL. Manufacturers are granted a licence to produce merchandise, and hence licensing seems incompatible with this function of the trademark. To reduce this incompatibility, it is important that the sporting organisation put in place stringent quality control procedures to ensure that products will be of a quality that the 'physical source' organisation would deliver itself.

Anonymous source

When the scope of production and marketing of an organisation expands, it becomes less likely that consumers of goods will know the actual name of the producer. The anonymous source function ensures that purchasers of goods or services with a given established trademark know that these goods or services emanate from a source that established those trademarks. In other words, the trademark products have proven their quality, validating their anonymous source. Large consumer good producers like Procter & Gamble and Unilever have hundreds of trademarks validating the 'anonymous source'. Sporting organisations are less likely to use this function of the trademark, although large entertainment companies involved in the sport industry actually do. For instance, sport properties such as the Mighty Ducks of Anaheim (National Hockey League) and the Anaheim Angels (Major League Baseball) not only are cartoon characters, they also are professional sporting franchises owned by the Disney Corporation. These sport properties are distributed through channels like ESPN, ESPN2 and ABC Sports, also owned by Disney. Disney also owns the names, logos and trademarks of all these organisational entities. In the case of the two professional teams–the Mighty Ducks of Anaheim and the Anaheim Angels–there are also licensing restrictions on the use of the logos and names placed by the National Hockey League (NHL) and Major League Baseball (MLB) as part of the franchise agreements.

Quality

Licensing of sport trademarks has become so popular because of the quality function of trademarks. If a trademark has the power to convey a quality perception, surely this perception can be transferred to products or entities linked to the trademark. From a legal perspective this concept changed the position of licensing. Provided that the licensor establishes sufficient quality control measures and procedures, it does not really matter whether the products emanate from the licensor (i.e. owner of the trademark) or another source. The quality level provided to the end consumer by the licensee should be similar to the quality level if the product had been provided by the licensor.

Advertising

Fuji Xerox using the Olympic rings, Heineken using Tennis Australia's logo and Vodafone using Manchester United's logo are all examples of trademark usage going beyond the creation of goodwill (as exemplified in the previous functions). Trademarks have become symbols with the power to sell goods and services. Although advertising can be criticised as an effort to manipulate the consumer's mind through slick, high impact campaigns, it does serve as a way to mass-communicate the source and quality of a product through the trademark. It complements the source and quality functions. The positive perception that consumers have of Manchester United, Tennis Australia or the Olympic organisation is transferred to the associated organisations and products, stimulating these consumers to use Vodaphone communication products, drink Heineken or use Fuji Xerox products.

Merchandising

The trademark becomes a product in itself when it is not serving to sell other goods or services but serving to sell itself. Examples are the teenage fans of a rock band buying all possible merchandise with the name of the band on it, or football fans buying shirts, mugs, jackets and pens with the name of their team on them. The consumer wants to be identified with the trademark organisation. Which merchandise they buy is secondary. Often, the only criterion is that it is visible to others, showing the consumer's allegiance to the trademark organisation.

Quality control

Quality control is a vital and integral component of trademark licensing. We have shown that the legal position of licensing changed when the concept of quality control was included. As long as the licensor establishes sufficient quality control measures and procedures, it does not really matter whether the products emanate from the licensor (i.e. owner of the trademark) or another source. The trademark identifies the source and distinguishes the products from those of others. The law loosely formulates standards for quality control in that the owner of the trademark should be capable of exercising control over the users of the trademark.

Wilkof (1995) distinguishes between two types of quality control: contractual and financial. *Contractual control* exists between two unrelated parties whose only mutual interest is the exploitation of the trademark. *Financial control* exists when two parties are related, in that one of them has an ownership relation to the other (e.g. a holding or subsidiary relation). Financial control is more stringent, as the aims of benefiting from the trademark are more likely to be in line with each other because of the ownership relation between the organisations.

In the sport industry, contractual control is the most frequently used type of quality control. A contractual specification of quality control terms and conditions should identify at least the following aspects of quality control:

- specification of standards;
- inspection of products and methods of production; and
- supply of samples.

The trademark licensing agreement

The trademark licensing agreement sets out the broader relationship between the licensor and licensee. Ownership of the trademark, who can use the trademark as the licensee and how the trademark can be used (contractual, i.e. quality control) are described first. Then the commercial and financial terms and conditions are described. Issues like how merchandise is going to be marketed and which royalties have to be paid by the licensee are described in this part of the agreement.

Sherman (1991: 330–1) describes several key areas that need to be addressed when preparing the trademark licensing agreement. In summary, the key areas are:

- scope of the territorial and product exclusivity;
- assignability and sublicensing rights;
- definition of the property and the licensed products;
- quality control and approval;
- ownership of artwork and designs;
- term renewal rights and termination of the relationship;
- initial licence and ongoing royalty fees;
- performance criteria for the licensee;
- liability insurance;
- indemnification;
- duty to pursue trademark and copyright infringement;
- minimum advertising and promotional requirements;
- accounting and record keeping of the licensee;
- inspection and audit rights of the licensor;
- right of first refusal for expanded or revised characters and images;
- limitations on the licensee's distribution to related or affiliated entities;
- representations and warranties of the licensor with respect to its rights to the property;
- availability of the licensor for technical and promotional assistance; and

- miscellaneous provisions, such as law to govern, inurement of goodwill, nature of the relationship notice, and force majeure.

It goes beyond the scope of this text to specify further the contents of the trademark licensing agreement.

Before taking a closer look at building the sporting organisation's licensing program, we outline the trademark licensing agreement briefly from both licensor's and licensee's perspectives.

Licensor's and licensee's perspectives

The trademark licensing agreement from the licensor's perspective should serve one most important goal. If the trademark is used by the licensee in any other manner than was intended by the licensor when entering the agreement, contractual arrangements must be in place to entitle the licensor to take action. Although this point is of obvious importance to the licensee as well, the focus of the licensee should be on the terms and conditions related to commercial and financial matters. This requires identifying the commercial possibilities of the trademark usage and how these may translate into a dollar figure. Sportview 16.1, adjusted from Schaaf (1995), exemplifies the licensor's and licensee's perspectives.

SPORTVIEW 16.1

The rugby union 'All Blacks/Wallabies/Springboks' video game

Sport Excitement Video Games (fictitious name) wants to create a game called 'The All Blacks/Wallabies/Springboks conquer the world'. The game will be marketed in New Zealand, Australia and South Africa. When sold in New Zealand, the game will be marketed as 'The All Blacks conquer the world', in Australia as 'The Wallabies conquer the world' and in South Africa as 'The Springboks conquer the world'.

Sport Excitement has several licensing considerations. The company needs to develop the actual game, which includes writing the software code for graphical display, play options, opponents and voice enhancement features (cost can go up to $400000). Sport Excitement also needs to pay the New Zealand, Australian and South African national governing bodies of rugby union their licensing fees. In this case all organisations have negotiated a minimum advance fee ($100000) plus a percentage of sales royalty fee (4%). On top of the licensing fees, Sport Excitement has to undertake the packaging, warehousing and shipping costs. Then it has to obtain the other necessary licences, from either the International Rugby Football Board (IRFB) or the Players Association, to feature indentifiable teams and/or players other than the three already identified. Next, Sport Excitement has to decide which game platforms it will develop for (e.g. Sega®, CD-Rom, Nintendo®). Depending on which platform the manufacturer develops, the cartridges will add extra costs.

An analyst calculates the revenue streams and forecasts the potential return on investment. The net revenue per platform for an average game is $32 per game *sold through*, meaning purchased at a retail outlet such as Target. The All Blacks royalty would likely be 4%

of that, less the advance. Therefore, if 100000 unit sold through, the All Blacks' royalties would amount to:

100000 (units) × (0.04)($32) – $100000 = $28000

In this case, the sporting teams are not the catalyst for the game. The developer seeks a category and the teams are merely the well-known vehicles to differentiate the product. In the competitive video-game development industry, the sophisticated marketplace will weed out poorly conceived games, and they will fail in spite of a fabulous licensor. Licensors, in this case, will help to sell the products, if those products are good!

Source: Adapted from Schaaf (1995).

How the general trademark licensing issues can be linked to a sporting organisation is explored in the next part of this chapter. Sportview 16.2 highlights some of the issues arising in using sport trademarks.

SPORTVIEW 16.2

Sport team logos are big business

'Have you ever considered using the logo of your favourite professional sports team in a promotional campaign? Did you know it would cost you? Apparently not all marketing professionals realise that sports teams, like other companies that produce products or services, own protectable trademarks that others may not use unless they first obtain the trademark owner's permission and usually pay a licensing fee.

'In a recent case, the Angels baseball team defended its trademark rights when it sued the Broadway department store after it ran an ad for women's dresses featuring three children wearing Angels uniforms. Broadway had failed to first obtain the requisite permission from the Angels and later refused to pay the Angels' requested licensing fee. Broadway claimed that it did not know it was supposed to pay a licensing fee, even though the Angels uniforms used in the ad contained registered trademark notations.

'Professional sports teams aggressively protect their trademark rights, which include its name and its logos. This is done by demanding licensing fees on other contexts which may, at first glance, appear worlds apart from the department store advertisement case. Recently, Major League Baseball has even cracked down on Little League and amateur adult teams that use major-league nicknames. Because Major League Baseball owns trademark rights in the names of all its teams when they are used in connection with baseball, it can legally require amateur teams using these names to wear only licensed apparel. This can add about $6 to the cost of each uniform.

'Trademark licensing increased the marketing opportunities for many companies. Instead of diversifying directly into a new product line, a trademark proprietor could license an existing producer in another industry to manufacture a line of goods under the licensor's trademark. This became very common, for example, between perfume companies and apparel manufacturers. It is now also common between professional sport organisations and apparel and novelty manufacturers.

'The sport organisation must specify the products on which any licensee is permitted to use the trademark, as well as supervise and control the quality of those products. The public will benefit because it will receive a guarantee that the sport organisation stands behind the goods bearing its trademarks. What would happen if Major League Baseball ignored the Little Leaguers' use of its nicknames? Major League Baseball could lose its trademark rights and that would mean the loss of millions of dollars a year in royalties from its extremely lucrative licensing business.

'Professional sport organisations have much to lose if they do not adequately control the use of their trademarks. In addition, it is safe to say that many consumers want to know that the products they buy are both high quality and "approved"'.

Source: Excerpts from Lans (1995: 6).

Building the sporting organisation's licensing program

An operational protocol

Irwin and Stotlar (1993) investigated the operational protocol employed by six major US sporting organisations in their sport licensing programs. The six organisations were Major League Baseball (MLB), National Football League (NFL), National Basketball Association (NBA), National Hockey League (NHL), National Collegiate Athletic Association (NCAA) and the US Olympic Committee. Table 16.1 shows the different elements of this operational protocol or, in other words, the activities that need to be executed in sport licensing programs. The number of organisations (out of six) actually using the listed elements of the protocol are given.

Table 16.1 presents a good overview of the operational activities that need to be considered when managing a sport licensing program. Before a sporting organisation can start managing a program, however, it has to be put together.

Key factors

Baghdikian (1996) has developed a model to assist the sport marketer in identifying the key factors (described below) when building a licensing program. The model is presented in Figure 16.1.

Organisational objectives

Like the other marketing tools discussed in this text, licensing should serve the broader purpose of achieving the marketing goals of the organisation, which in turn should support the achievement of overall strategic goals. In sport, licensing the organisation's trademark for merchandising purposes often aims to raise funds or to increase brand awareness. If

TABLE 16.1
Use of elements of an operational protocol for sport licensing programs

Operational element of program	Number of sporting organisations using the element (out of 6)
Program governance and leadership	
Internal licensing authority	5
Full-time principal licensing assignment	5
Direct reort to central administrator	5
Licensing policy committee assembled	3
Professional licensing agency assistance	1
Program protection and enforcement	
Legal specialist consultation	6
Majority of logos registered as trademarks	6
Licensee application and screening process	6
Licence issuance and renewal procedures	6
Non-exclusive basic agreement	1
Execution of joint-use agreements	5
Execution of international licences	5
Product sample required for quality control	6
'Licensed product' identification required	6
Counterfeit logo detection procedures	6
Counterfeit logo reduction procedures	6
Program promotions and public relations	
Proactive recruitment of licensees	5
Proactive recruitment of retailers	4
Licensee/retailer public relations program	6
Advertising used to promote products/program	6
Licensing program information published	6
Revenue management	
Advance payment required	6
Uniform loyalty charged on all products	2
Written royalty exemption policy	6
Royalty verifications routinely conducted	5
Royalty verifications conducted by specialist	5
Written royalty distribution policy	6

Source: Irwin and Stotlar (1993: 7–16). Reprinted with the permission of the publisher.

these goals fit the marketing strategy, the organisation can pursue finding a licensee or licensees.

Choice of licensee

In light of the functions of the trademark and the organisational objectives, it is important to find the right licensee. Pertaining to the functions of the trademark, the potential licensee should be capable of satisfying the quality control standards and should maintain the function of identifying the source of the products. From an organisational perspective it is

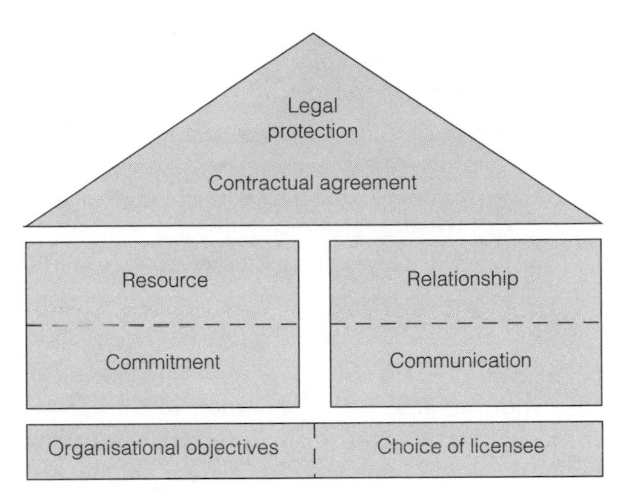

FIGURE 16.1 **Building the sporting organisation's licensing program**

Source: Baghdikian (1996: 39). Reprinted with the permission of the publisher.

important for the sporting organisation to find reputable partners with an ability to deliver quality on time with regular payments.

Commitment

Rather than leaving the work to the licensee and simply 'licensing' it to use the sporting organisation's trademark, the sporting organisation should commit itself to doing the preliminary market research and financial analysis. Baghdikian (1996: 38) states that:

> the San Jose Sharks, during their first season, compiled the worst on-field record in the National Hockey League (NHL). However, due to the organisations spending 13 months on consumer research, and planning a name and design that would create an exciting image in the market, the Sharks outsold all other NHL team-licensed products.

Resource

In investigating sport and collegiate licensing programs, Irwin and Stotlar (1993: 15) concluded that 'with nearly half of all colleges assigning program administrators less than 10% of their time to licensing, the complex administrative tasks associated with a licensing program cannot effectively be addressed'. Although the resources invested in managing a sport licensing program might be high, the resulting benefits are likely to be proportionately higher than the investment.

Communication

Although the licensing agreement (including contractual agreements) should serve as the basis for business communication, regular and open channels of communication should be established. A clear understanding of both parties' goals, the early detection of problems and effective quality control are the results of open and frequent communication between licensor and licensee.

Relationship

The more formal business communication described above can be complemented with more informal communication (e.g. between the two chief executive officers). An afternoon on the golf course with the aim of fostering personal relationships has often proven vital to the maintenance of business relationships.

Contractual agreement

The contract represents the written agreement that both licensor and licensee are legally obliged to fulfil. Examples of areas, suggested by Sherman (1991), to be included in a contract were listed earlier in this chapter. The contract is the agreement that licensor and licensee can turn to when they feel that one or the other party is not fulfilling the requirements of the agreement.

Legal protection

In chapter 14, ambush marketing is described as a business marketing its goods or services in a way that suggests that the business has a connection with a team, event or a competition, where there is in fact no connection. The practice of ambush marketing is of particular interest when considering the power of trademarks. Without the law and legal advisers, the sporting organisation has little to protect it from organisations ambushing its trademarks and other properties. The specialised nature of licensing in general, contracts, interpretations of law and the management of licensing programs requires the support and advice of legally qualified experts. For example, the Nick Faldo Golf Company has entered into a partnership with sports brand and business development consultancy WSM, which will police the licensing of his name (Gillis 2002). Figure 16.1 illustrates this by picturing legal protection as the 'roof' of the program.

Issues that can arise

The second part of this chapter has first provided a range of activities to be executed by sport licensing program managers and then the different steps that need to be taken when building the organisation's licensing program. Before we discuss branding in the context of the sport licensing process, Sportview 16.3 gives an insight into current issues relating to building a sport licensing program.

SPORTVIEW 16.3

Using the established brand to enter new markets

Although the market for licensed merchandise towards the end of the 1990s has experienced some difficult times, especially in the USA, the prospects for the future are bright. Partly due to the baseball strike and the NBA lockout in 1997/98, sales dropped dramatically towards the end of the 1990s. However, the NFL and NBA are revitalising and innovating the industry by entering previously untapped markets. For example, the NBA launched the Global Retail Environment Program through which they aimed to create 'unified NBA-branded visual impact zones at retail all over the world...looking at direct TV selling models, selling products in ad-spots during matches, and alternative retailing and merchandising, with the aim of getting the brand message at the point of sale' (Glendinning 1999: 10).

The Copyright Promotions Group (CPG), in their association with the 1999 World Cup Cricket in England, are a good example of licensing in the context of a one-off event. Of the five product categories that included apparel, toys and gifts, publishing, fast-moving consumer goods and promotions, 60% of revenue came from the apparel product category. The success of their licensing programs was based on their integral involvement in discussions that ranged from television rights to on-site sales of produce. This allowed them to come up with the best licensing strategies that not only protected and leveraged the rights of (often exclusive) licensees but provided the best possible value and return for the licensor as well. Even when fans are not able to attend the event or purchase memorabilia from event-specific merchandise stores, online shopping allows them to 'be part of the event' by ordering merchandise unique to the event (Westerbeek & Smith 2003).

With the opportunity that is the Internet, online sales of licensed merchandise may receive a welcome boost in the first part of the new decade. In particular, the market for soccer merchandise remains potentially very lucrative. Sales in relation to the Japan/South Korea World Cup were expected to generate US$1.5 billion, some 20% up from France 1998. The global opportunity presented to clubs such as Italian powerbrokers Juventus and Premier League giants Manchester United are there for the taking. Twenty per cent of the hits on the Juventus website are from Asia. The Asian opportunity consists of a potential 2-billion-person marketplace. The 'red devils' signed a new merchandising and licensing deal with Japan Sports Vision (JSV), the official World Cup distributor for Japan. JSV is a major client of Nike, and Nike in turn, has signed a 13-year deal with Manchester United, reported to be worth US$427 million, to become an official sponsor and the official merchandise partner of the club. By the way, Nike and its swoosh, as a strong yet vulnerable brand (and symbol) in its own right, have taken the 'unprecendented step of releasing a detailed report on its child labour policy. Its "Corporate Responsibility Report" offers an open assessment of the lobbyist's claims and details other ethical issues such as the effect of its activities on the environment and the company's involvement in local communities. Conscious of the impact even an isolated case can have on the image of the Nike brand—a commodity that has taken tens of millions of pounds to position.' (Clarke 2002: 26)

Only five years ago European soccer clubs handled most of their licensing programs in-house. Because the scope of merchandising operations was mostly domestic, many clubs felt that spending sparse resources on an outside licensing agency could not be justified. However, this attitude is changing rapidly. In order to maximise profiting from the club's brand equity, more and more clubs are selecting licensing agents. Chris Protheroe, director of the Copyright Promotions Licensing Group, argues that 'if they keep their merchandising rights in-house they avoid paying agency commission but they will naturally incur overheads of man-power, design, legal advice and accounting expenses' (Wallace 2002: 31). However, Edward Friedman of Zone Marketing thinks differently. He argues that 'licensing firms will never do as good a job as you can do yourself. A firm like Levi's, for example, wouldn't just hand everything over so why should football clubs?... You become only as good as the people who look after you.' (Wallace 2002: 32)

Branding

The branding process

Chernatony and McDonald (1992: 18) define a successful brand as:

> an identifiable product, service, person or place augmented in such a way that the buyer or user perceives relevant unique added values which match their needs most closely. Furthermore its success results from being able to sustain these added values in the face of competition.

We can all associate with the practical application of the brand concept. Powerful brands are immediately associated with the product or service they represent. Coca-Cola is a soft-drink, McDonald's sells hamburgers, Manchester United deals with soccer and the Indy 500 is about car racing. A brand represents the combination of the core product and the perceptions that consumers have about the product and its unique added values. Figure 16.2(a) shows what distinguishes a brand from the core product. In Figure 16.2(b) this is applied to a sport example.

FIGURE 16.2 Conceptual models of brand

(a) Brand = core product + perceived product

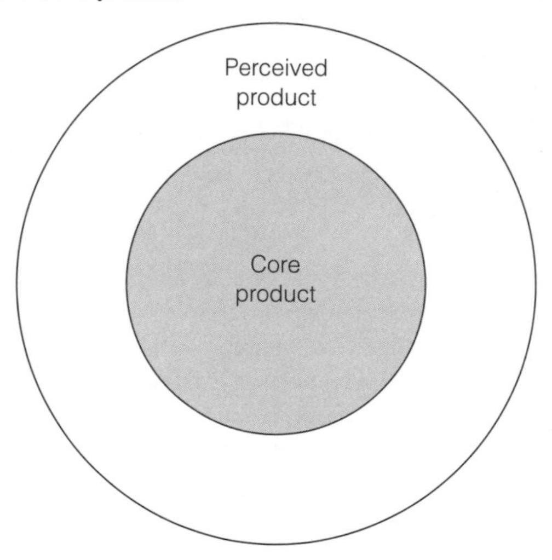

(b) A sport brand

Developing successful brands is important for organisations because the brand can be used as a means to communicate with consumers. Branding, as the process of developing and sustaining successful brands, has strategic relevance for the marketing function. In other words, the full marketing mix is used in the strategic branding process. The marketer tries to position the brand 'in the mind' of the consumer. Consumers start perceiving the brand as the symbolic total of the packaging, design, recall advertising, quality of product, price paid, and store or outlet where the product can be bought. This total brand perception enables the marketer to link mental visions to the organisation's branded products–expressing, for example, a lifestyle, a personality or a feeling. Powerful brands differentiate themselves from similar products of competitors and provide the opportunity to build long-term relationships with consumers, developing brand-loyal buyers. Brand equity, according to Gladden, Milne and Sutton (1998), is the combined tangible and intangible value of the brand, and can be broken down into four constituents: perceived quality (of the brand), brand awareness (recall, recognition), brand associations (in sport often emotionally loaded), and brand loyalty (the ability of the brand to retain customers). In the sport industry, the antecedents to brand equity are team-related (e.g. success, star players), organisation-related (e.g. reputation and tradition, overall entertainment package, service reputation) and market-related (e.g. media coverage and reach, competitive forces).

Table 16.2 describes eight different ways of using a brand in practice. Irrespective of which usage is chosen from this list, adding value, as perceived by the consumer, is the critical activity in the branding process. The marketer can use the brand as a symbol of, for example, prestige, status, lifestyle or personality, and can position the symbol in such a way that it expresses physical and psychological comfort to the target market.

If the sport marketer chooses to build the registered trademark into a brand, licensing in many ways can assist in achieving branding objectives.

TABLE 16.2 Different ways of using a brand in practice

Usage of brand	Why use it in that way
Brand as a sign of ownership	Buyer knows which organisation produced the product
Brand as a differentiating device	Buyer knows the product is different from comparable products
Brand as a functional device	Buyer knows why and how to use the product
Brand as a symbolic device	Brand communicates something about the buyer
Brand as a risk reducer	Brand communicates trust about the producer of the product
Brand as a shorthand device	Brand is a means to recall sufficient brand information from memory at a later purchasing time
Brand as a legal device	Trademark registration is legal protection from counterfeit production
Brand as a strategic device	Brand positioning is a means of ensuring a long term future for the organisation

Source: Adjusted from Chernatony and McDonald (1992).

Branding and licensing

In the first part of this chapter the relationship between the trademark of an organisation and the licensing process was explained. Trademark licensing, as an arrangement by which one party consents to the use of its trademark in accordance with specified terms and conditions, makes sense only if the trademark is in any way valuable to the potential licensee. The trademark can have value as an established brand, making it a powerful means of communication. If the trademark has the potential value of becoming an established brand, it has future earning power, making it an interesting investment. Sporting organisations can capitalise on this potential value by using other organisations to raise their own brand awareness. Table 16.3 provides an overview of the top five sport brands in the world. It needs to be noted that sporting good manufacturers are not included in the list. If they were, the big manufacturers would top the list, well ahead of the sport organisations presented in Table 16.3.

The potential power of sport brands

In chapter 13 we discussed the advantages of sport sponsorship. These advantages also explain why sport brands, or sport trademarks, are potentially powerful tools to add value. The advantages, explaining the potential power of sport brands, may be summarised as follows:

- Sport consumers tend to identify themselves personally with the sport, which creates opportunities for increasing brand loyalty in products linked to the sport.
- Sport evokes personal attachment, and with this the licensee can be linked to the excitement, energy and emotion of the sporting contest. In other words, sport has the potential to deliver a clear message.
- Sport has universal appeal and pervades all elements of life (geographically, demographically and socioculturally). This characteristic presents the opportunity to cross difficult cultural and language borders in communication, enabling the licensee to talk to a global mass audience.
- The variety of sports available makes it possible to create distinct market segments with which to communicate separately.
- The universal appeal and high interest that sport has in society give sport a high media exposure, resulting in free publicity. Free publicity can make a licensing deal very cost-effective.
- Because of the clear linkage of the licensee to the sporting organisation's trademark, the relationship stands out from the clutter, contrary to advertising, in which people are bombarded with hundreds of 'sender unknown' messages each day.

TABLE 16.3
Top five global sport brands

	Brand
1	Dallas Cowboys (American Football)
2	Manchester United (Soccer)
3	Washington Redskins (American Football)
4	New York Yankees (Baseball)
5	New York Knicks (Basketball)

Source: Adapted from Westerbeek & Smith (2003).

Earlier, this chapter presented some examples of how organisations use licensing and for which purposes. These purposes are repeated here in the context of the sport industry.

Using the sport brand to add value

Adding value, as the most important activity of creating powerful brands, can be done in many ways. It has been explained that branding is a strategic effort in that the marketer should use the whole marketing mix to build the brand. Using an established trademark or brand to add value to another brand is one means of applying the marketing mix. The Olympic sponsors are licensed to link the Olympic rings to their products. A varicty of consumer good licensees (e.g. Four'n'Twenty pies, Carlton Draught, Volkswagen) are licensed to use the AFL logo on their products. The potential licensees of Nick Faldo's name in the headline story use the brand equity he has built over the years to add value to already existing brands or general products.

More specifically, this added value is needed to fulfil one of the following purposes:

- to sell in new products using the established brand/trademark;
- to sell in new markets using the established brand/trademark; or
- to boost sales using the established brand/trademark.

The major aim of the sporting organisation in this process is to use its established brand/trademark to raise funds for the organisation. An extra bonus is the widespread attention that is given to its brand name through the promotional efforts of licensees. This is why careful selection of licensees is important, because the established sport brand should not be associated with a wrong or inferior product or organisation.

The branding process in a sporting organisation can be enhanced by using licensing as a means of raising brand awareness.

Using licensing to add value to the sport brand

If the sport brand is not established yet, but careful preparation and commitment have been put into preparing an appropriate and attractive brand name and symbols, licensing can be used as one way of informing consumers about the brand. The San Jose Sharks, used as an example earlier, raised their brand awareness and raised funds by offering a potentially profitable trademark to a selection of merchandise licensees. Using the marketing mix elements to integrate pricing, distribution and promotion of the merchandise, they successfully established the San Jose Sharks brand.

More specifically, licensing is used to fulfil the following purpose:

- licensing the unknown trademark to build brand/trademark awareness and raise funds.

The previous examples have shown that licensing plays a vital role in adding value to the licensor's, licensee's or both organisations' brands. The realisation that brands/trademarks are successful only if they add value to the product or the organisation, as perceived by the consumer, highlights the strategic importance of branding. Powerful brands can be developed only if the organisation views the branding process as integral to the marketing function, using all marketing mix elements to build powerful brands.

Summary

This chapter discussed the licensing of the sporting organisation's intellectual property (name and/or logo registered in a trademark) to a third party. It was shown that promotional licensing in the sport industry basically serves two purposes: promotion of the sporting organisation, and promotion of a third party or its products through use of the sporting organisation's name or logo. In the latter case, the major benefit the sporting organisation derives is a royalty fee, often calculated as a percentage of sales of licensed products.

The importance of registering a trademark was shown by discussing the different functions of the trademark. Registration of the trademark is always important because trademarks can become valuable organisational assets, namely brands. Through careful management, trademarks linked to products can be built into powerful brands. This was discussed in the last part of this chapter. A powerful sport brand is a valuable organisational asset because it has the power to represent multiple consumer perceptions. Consumers perceive a brand as a symbolic total of the organisation's product–in sport's case the excitement, speed and action orientation of the core product and its star players. Sport brands therefore are capable of linking powerful messages to other products through licensing.

The second part of the chapter discussed the process of building a sporting organisation's licensing program. This process was summarised in Baghdikian's (1996) model, but three issues were highlighted as being of particular importance. Operational activities in managing the program were presented, the minimum contents of a licensing agreement (as identified by Sherman 1991) were briefly summarised, and the importance of legal support and protection was emphasised. Promotional licensing is an expanding area in sport marketing and offers many sporting organisations potential for future income or growth, especially in the rapidly developing global sport marketplace.

CASE STUDY

Setting up a sporting organisation's licensing program

This case study was originally written by Eddie Baghdikian and is purely fictional. The organisations and persons in the case are non-existent.

In June 1992, Juan Garcia, director of hockey development at the South American Hockey Federation (SAHF), was approached by ALEGG Interdomestic Pty Ltd with a proposal promising to generate substantial revenue for the SAHF with no financial outlay required. ALEGG was proposing a licensing agreement by which the SAHF logo would be used to brand a wide variety of merchandise and these products would be marketed to SAHF members.

The role of the SAHF, as the central administrative body, is to manage, coordinate and unify the diverse facets of the sport of hockey in South America. This includes overseeing the development of grassroots programs, managing competitions and tournaments, and promoting hockey at all levels. As the representative body of all affiliated clubs and associations throughout South America, the SAHF ensures the commercial viability of hockey and seeks out and encourages sponsorship for hockey events on a national level.

The core product of the SAHF is essentially the development of the game of hockey. Until the approach by ALEGG, the SAHF had never undertaken any product extension strategies. ALEGG's proposal to enter into a licensing arrangement with the SAHF promised to develop and market a range of hockey merchandise and accessories aimed at SAHF members.

ALEGG was formed in late 1991 for the purpose of entering into licensing agreements with organisations such as the World Soccer Federation (FIFA) and other sporting bodies. The combined experience of its two directors and its South American general manager boasted more than 30 years knowledge in the areas of manufacturing, importing, wholesaling, retailing and marketing in a very wide range of consumer items. At the time of the approach to the SAHF, ALEGG informed Juan Garcia that as of February 1992 the company had entered into a merchandise licensing agreement between themselves and FIFA.

Juan did not believe that there was much of a market for SAHF-logoed products. He felt that there was no particular attraction or brand equity in the registered trademark of the organisation. However, with no financial outlay required, Juan also felt that he had nothing to lose if ALEGG thought that it could make the idea work.

The concept of a licensing program that to Juan represented no risk and no responsibility held considerable appeal, and so he and the SAHF ventured into the world of licensing.

The basis for the relationship

The negotiations began. Over the next four months the SAHF and ALEGG discussed the basis for the relationship that would ultimately lead to drafting the licensing agreement.

ALEGG would develop a range of SAHF merchandise known as the SAHF Members Collection. The range of licensed products would be entirely up to the SAHF. ALEGG would source the selected product line through its 'world-wide' manufacturing and supplier network, which was predominantly concentrated in the South East Asia region. All sourced products would be 'branded' as well as displaying the SAHF name and logo. The list of products included tracksuits, pens, keyrings, cufflinks, playing cards, calendar posters, diaries, umbrellas, T-shirts, sports bags, calculators and hats.

ALEGG would be primarily responsible for the promotion and distribution of all agreed merchandise, including a SAHF Members Collection brochure and other advertising material such as posters for all clubhouses. Coinciding with the marketing campaign, ALEGG would also have the entire range of goods made available at all major South American hockey competitions and have a salesperson to service this area. The SAHF would not be responsible for holding and purchasing stock.

The SAHF agreed to assist in the promotion of the merchandise through:

- *South American Hockey News* (communications newsletter for members);
- advertising;
- exposure at all SAHF events;
- regular mailouts to all clubs;
- a list of club secretaries to be provided to ALEGG; and
- general promotions mutually agreed on.

So far, the negotiations for the SAHF's first licensing program were going along well.

Estimating the projected income from the marketing program was not as important to Juan as the ability to make money out of something requiring no financial expenditure and with a minimal amount of resources required. In addition, the program would lift the profile of the organisation in the marketplace through the promotion of the SAHF name and logo. These were the broad objectives Juan set for the licensing program. In ALEGG's final proposal, Juan was also told that anticipated income figures in the first formative year would be exceeded significantly in subsequent years as the promotion programs gained momentum and the SAHF name and logo grew in recognition.

The licensing agreement

The 'exclusive licensing/marketing/manufacturing agreement' between the SAHF and ALEGG was drafted and arrived on Juan's desk. From this time onwards the normal printed ALEGG letterhead was no longer used and communications were now with ALEGG's international marketing director, and not the SAHF's usual ALEGG contact, the South American general manager—who seemed to have vanished.

ALEGG was to become the sole and exclusive producer, manufacturer, wholesaler and marketing representative of the SAHF. The agreement stated that the appointment of ALEGG was verbally formalised and agreed to on Thursday 8 October 1992 in order to permit ALEGG to incur expenditure in time and money to set up the logistical, administrative, and initial manufacturing and marketing requirements of the project. However, the three-year term of the agreement was to officially start on 1 January 1993, with a three-year option commencing on 1 January 1996, the three-year option being automatically renewable except for either party cancelling the agreement.

Cancellation of the agreement could be done only during the 30-day period in the month prior to the expiration of any three-year term of the agreement by giving eighteen months notice in writing. Alternatively, cancellation could be effected, by the SAHF only, during the 30-day period in the month prior to the expiration of any three-year term of the agreement by giving 90 days notice in writing and purchasing and paying the freight-on-board (FOB) price for all goods and/or services and/or work in stock and/or in progress for and on behalf of ALEGG in relation to ALEGG fulfilling its obligations and undertakings as part of the agreement. Payment then would have to be made prior to the expiration of the 90-day notice period. In fact, whether the SAHF or ALEGG breached any of the conditions of the contract, and cancelled, the SAHF would still be obliged to pay the FOB price under the terms of the agreement.

Juan pondered over this legal document. He did not like it in its present state. Even with his non-legal background and inexperience with licensing programs he figured that there was no 'out' clause without a substantial penalty to pay. He read on that ALEGG would pay the SAHF a licensing fee equal to 15% of the manufactured cost, paid at the end of each calendar month. ALEGG would also conduct the reconciliation and monitoring of all royalty payments.

Although there was the issue of the termination terms and conditions to resolve, the SAHF still thought that there was some scope for the program to work. Consequently, ALEGG was encouraged by the SAHF to reveiw the contract and keep working with the SAHF, even though an agreement was never signed.

Disjointed proceedings

The SAHF did not hear directly from ALEGG for some time. During the period up to May 1993, Juan heard that ALEGG had only made a few approaches at different SAHF-affiliated clubs. At this point Juan started to believe that the project had basically ended.

It was at this juncture that the SAHF changed its trading name to Hockey South America and embraced a new corporate logo. With the proliferation of initialled identities in the business world, the use of 'SAHF' was continuously being confused. The decision to adopt this new identity also brought the organisation in line with Hockey International, the controlling hockey body at the international level. Hockey South America, realising the importance of the role of marketing to its organisation and in line with the identity change, appointed a marketing and media officer in April 1993. This position, which reported to Juan, had as its primary objective the task of lifting the profile of the sport through the media and business world. Juan, who now was the director of development and marketing, decided to inform ALEGG of the changes.

On receiving the news, ALEGG advised Juan that it had more than $US400 000 of SAHF-logoed goods on order and approaching delivery, and further advised that the SAHF should consider not changing its name until 1994, to allow a stock rundown without financial loss to all parties concerned. In the same communication ALEGG conveyed that in the last few months it had been gearing for sales, through the 2931 affiliated clubs, to the 1 102 000 SAHF members.

The situation did not improve. The SAHF name change went ahead, and ALEGG kept struggling for credibility—without success. Juan rang FIFA to gauge the progress of FIFA's licensing agreement with ALEGG. He was told that FIFA was wanting to get out of the agreement. In September 1993, Juan wanted 'out' too. The last twelve months spent in attempting to develop a suitable merchandising relationship with ALEGG was sufficient time. Juan did not see evidence of any prospect for progress, now or in the future. Hockey South Amercia informed ALEGG in writing that it wished to terminate the proposed agreement and would deal with ALEGG only on a non-exclusive basis, as required by Hockey South America, the exclusive nature of the agreement also being part of the reason to terminate.

ALEGG had other ideas. It wanted to continue with the exclusive manufacturing and marketing licensing arrangement. It was committed to the three-year agreement with SAHF/Hockey South America. The subsequent meetings with ALEGG worried Juan. Present at these meetings was a person taking the minutes in shorthand. Anticipating the worst from an agreement that was not actually signed, and with no in-house expertise on these types of contracts, Juan sought legal advice.

In the meantime, ALEGG argued that the SAHF proposed to change its name to Hockey South America in or around July 1993 with little or no prior notice given. As a result, more capital investment and greater time allowance were now required. ALEGG also debated that it had outlaid in excess of $1 200 000 in time and money, all with a view to completing at least the first three years of the program, with an intention to ensure success so that the relationship would go beyond this initial three-year period.

ALEGG was determined to represent itself as a dedicated organisation with the right intentions to implement the letter of agreement, and to represent SAHF/Hockey South

America as the main cause of the current state of the project, through its lack of cooperation, commitment and communication. Nevertheless, ALEGG continued to have dialogue with Hockey South America on the 'new' line of merchandise and the 'new' 1993/94 catalogue/brochure incorporating the Hockey South America logo. ALEGG also discussed new club member updates, marketing strategy, and looked forward to receiving Hockey South America's positive response and full support.

Essentially, the response from the solicitors advised Juan to adopt a 'wait and see' posture—meaning, to await further approaches from ALEGG, hoping that, as a result of the lack of enthusiasm and support from Juan, the relationship would simply wither away. The solicitors also pointed out, however, that although Juan had not signed the proposed agreement with ALEGG there could be an enforcable agreement based on negotiations and part performance of the agreement.

Questions

1. Discuss the risks and rewards to an organisation of licensing its brands.
2. How well does the strategy of product extension, through licensing, fit the corporate objectives of the SAHF?
3. Identify the reasons why the licensing agreement between the SAHF and ALEGG failed.
4. What factors should Juan Garcia have considered in making his decision on whether or not to enter into the licensing agreement?
5. Juan felt that the SAHF logo had no inherent appeal or value. On what criteria should the marketer judge the equity in a brand and its suitability for licensing?

Source: Written by E. Baghdikian and not previously published. Printed with the permission of the author.

PART III

Strategy implementation, evaluation and adjustment

17

Coordinating and controlling marketing strategy

Stage 1—Identification of marketing opportunities

▼

Stage 2—Strategy determination

▼

Stage 3—Strategy implemention, evaluation and adjustment

Step 7—Implement and coordinate marketing and service mix

Step 8—Coordinate marketing function (feedback, evaluation)

CHAPTER OBJECTIVES

Chapter 17 summarises the important concepts introduced throughout this book. It does so by reviewing the role of the control function in coordinating and implementing the selected marketing strategies. Three forms of control are introduced—feed forward, concurrent and feedback—and their role is discussed in relation to the key measures used to determine the success of the sport-marketing program. A short section reviewing careers in sport marketing is also included in this chapter.

After studying this chapter you should be able to:

1. Understand the importance of control in the marketing function.
2. Identify the three types of control.
3. Identify the primary measures of success.
4. Comprehend the relationship between measures of success and the control process.
5. Recognise the importance of coordinating and implementing marketing strategies.
6. Identify possible career options in sport marketing.

HEADLINE STORY

Volleyball digs in

> Spikes, digs and kills will be rampant throughout the country 17–25 June. Thanks to the week-long 'Volley across America', volleyball enthusiasts will have the opportunity to participate in a wide-reaching grassroots promotion, designed to help increase the interest in the game and build participation...As part of the year-long celebration of the sport's centennial birthday, spearheaded by the SGMA Volleyball Council, 'Volley across America' will open with a range of participatory activities to be held on The Mall in Washington DC. It will include the set-up of volleyball courts on the city's grassy expanse, and free clinics featuring some of the country's top volleyball players. (Pesky 1995: 22)

Volleyball's need to 'dig in' brings us to the last theme of this book: coordinating and implementing marketing strategies. The book has considered the marketing mix and thus all the variables that the sport marketer can manipulate to ensure that a sport is able to identify and sustain a competitive advantage. Volleyball's decision to implement a year-long promotion campaign in association with its centennial birthday is an example of a range of marketing and promotion mix variables combining to form a marketing strategy. How these strategies are implemented is part of the management aspect of marketing.

This chapter reviews the range of functions necessary to implement strategies. It examines some of the control mechanisms available to the marketer to ensure that performance targets are met, and considers some of the more relevant measures used to gauge success in sport. Inherent in these measures is the question of game design and its contribution to the marketing process. Also, the place and importance of sponsorship are discussed in the context of overall strategy determination. Finally, the chapter revisits the question of sport-marketing planning, noting the importance of integrating all the components of the marketing mix in one overall strategy. Given that the strategy determination process is the job of the sport marketer, it is important to review this role in sporting organisations. As part of this analysis, careers in sport marketing will be examined.

Controlling the sport marketing function

Boyd and Walker (1990: 865) note that the control process 'consists essentially of setting standards, specifying and obtaining feedback data, evaluating it, and taking corrective action'. Setting standards is part of the marketing planning process discussed in chapter 2. Marketing objectives established during this process will have identified the standards to be achieved. In sporting organisations these objectives and standards differ from those of organisations solely concerned with profit and providing dividends to shareholders.

Sport is unique in this regard as there are often broader goals than simply maximising profits, as was discussed in chapter 6. For example, in the dispute between the Australian Rugby League (ARL) and Superleague, the judge noted that the ARL board was 'motivated in large part by considerations other than the pursuit of profit. It is concerned with the preservation and enhancement of the traditions of the game.' (Burchett 1996: 65)

Recognition of these broader considerations does not in any way lessen the importance of marketing sport. In fact quite the opposite, as sport, like most non-profit entities, often does not have access to financial resources to the same extent as for-profit entities. Sporting organisations rely on the ability of marketing programs to raise the revenue required to run the club, association or league. Several consistent themes have emerged during this book alluding to the main measures of success in sporting organisations. Most of them are directly aligned to elements of the marketing mix. Establishing and benchmarking performance standards represent the first step towards controlling the marketing program.

Types of control

There are three types of organisational control:

- feed forward;
- concurrent; and
- feedback.

Feed forward control takes place before production and operations begin and commences during the strategic sport-marketing planning process (SSMPP). Determining the operating procedures and setting standards for the operation of a facility prior to a season commencing are examples of feed forward control. As part of this review of operational procedures, appropriate staff training will be provided consistent with service quality policies. This form of control ensures all inputs are of the highest quality for optimum spectator enjoyment.

Concurrent control occurs during the sporting fixture or, in other words, while the plans are being carried out. Often in sport this will be a major event or the weekly fixtures in a season. In the sport facility, monitoring the quality of service delivery exemplifies concurrent control. Supervisors will be responsible for checking that staff carry out their jobs in a manner consistent with the organisation's policy. In some cases it is possible to fine-tune the activity as it occurs or to rectify problems immediately, which is an example of concurrent control. Concurrent control can also occur during a major event or a season when monitoring attendances. If these are lower than expected, advertising may need to be intensified or altered, or sales promotions implemented to return the organisation to a satisfactory level of performance. Determining acceptable levels of performance requires the identification of appropriate measures during the strategic sport-marketing planning process.

Feedback control focuses on the final performance measured against the standards or targets foreordained. As a consequence of this feedback, the marketing plan can be reviewed and modified where necessary to ensure that the defined performance standards can be achieved during the next season or event.

Figure 17.1 displays the link between the stages of the control process and the measures typically used to ascertain success in a sporting organisation.

Measures of success

On-field success

On-field success is typically the most obvious and visible measure of success by which to assess the performance of sporting organisations. It is, however, as indicated in chapter 1,

FIGURE 17.1 The control process and measures of success

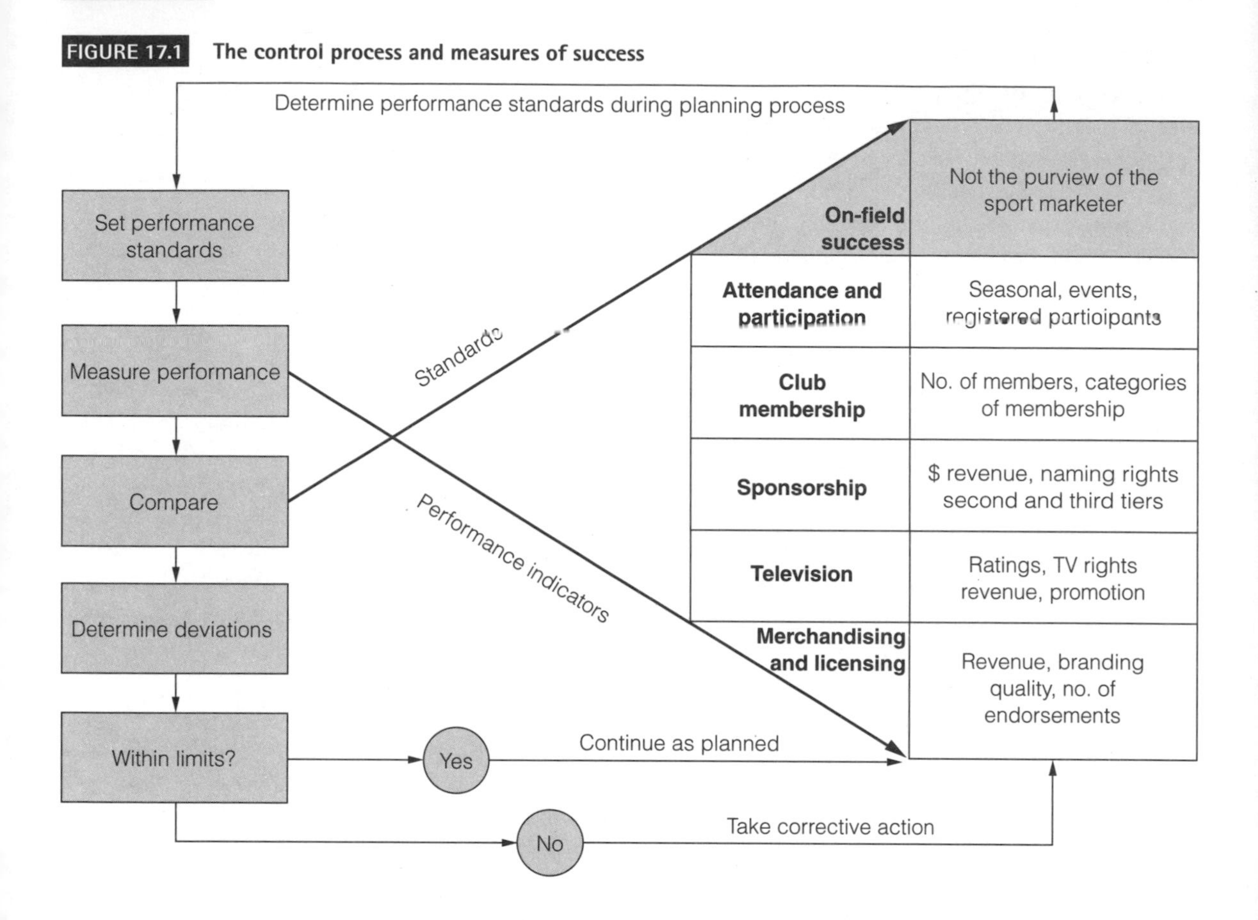

an area over which the sport marketer has little control. Unlike most products, where the marketer has some input into design and packaging, the sport marketer has no control over the quality of the team selected. The selection and development of players are not the purview of the sport marketer. The sport marketer, however, is responsible for promoting the team based on its quality and its star athletes. Elements of this marketing effort will be seen in ticketing and games promotions, advertising, public relations and sponsorship strategies, all discussed in earlier chapters.

It has been stressed in this book that the sport marketer needs to ensure that overpromising is not a feature of the promotion mix. It could be argued, for example, that the head coach of the Australian swimming team at the 1996 Olympic Games overpromised in relation to the success of his athletes. Ultimately, the Australian swimming team performed well, but expectations were so high that the actual performance (in terms of medals) was seen to be relatively poor. What could have been a perfect situation on which to build future marketing strategies turned into an exercise in managing negative public relations.

On-field success, then, is an organisation-wide measure not specific to the efforts of marketing personnel. The derivates, however, of on-field or off-field success are the purview of the sport marketer. These are now discussed.

Attendance and participation

Attendance and participation are two key measures of marketing performance. They are linked, as elite athletes serve as role models for those participating at lower levels of sporting competition. Known as the 'Norman factor' in Australia, or globally as the 'Tiger Woods' factor, the effect that Greg Norman and Tiger Woods have on golf participation and attendance when they visit Australia to play in major golf tournaments is undisputed. Typically, attendances at the event and interest in golf both rise. Increased participation in a sport has the added benefit of contributing to increased attendances, as people's affinity to a sport grows with participation and they are therefore more likely to watch it, either live or on television.

Sporting organisations are therefore concerned with boosting the numbers of registered participants. Strategies designed to ensure participation have been discussed in this book. The introduction of modified rules for juniors has been the main strategy designed to attract juniors to play sport. These modified rules programs become integral parts of marketing strategy as all sports strive to capture a finite group of participants. Registration numbers are important measures of success, in particular of the success of marketing programs.

Attendance also is a frequently cited measure of success for an association, club or league. Elements of the promotion mix, pricing policies, service quality and facility management have been important factors discussed in this book contributing to the likely success of maximising attendances.

Club membership

Club membership is another important measure. As discussed in chapter 9, club members represent heavy attendance on the frequency attendance escalator and are thus an important source of revenue. More importantly, this revenue often comes well before the season, providing much-needed income during a period when no games are conducted to generate weekly revenues. Chapter 9 also highlighted the importance of ensuring loyalty for long-term members. Marketing programs should be designed to reward longevity and minimise defection, or season ticket holders 'falling off' the frequency attendance escalator.

Sponsorship

Sponsorship is another key measure of success in the marketing program. In fact, sponsorship has been considered so important that many sports have developed unidimensional marketing programs aimed at attracting sponsorship revenue. In the long term, this myopic view is detrimental to the sporting organisation for two reasons:

1 It negates the extent to which the sporting organisation can devise a full range of marketing-related benefits that can be provided to the sponsor; and
2 It concentrates the success of the marketing program on one objective.

Concentration on any one objective is potentially poor strategy. Sporting organisations need to diversify their range of marketing strategies to ensure that there is not an overreliance on any one area. For example, if sponsorship income falls well below anticipated projections, the overall success of the organisation will be threatened because no effort has been made to raise revenues by ensuring attendance, attracting members and selling merchandise. As chapters 13 and 14 noted, sponsorship myopia is caused by the capacity of sport to attract sponsors seeking a relatively inexpensive way to promote their products. As some sporting organisations have the capacity to fulfil sponsor objectives easily, this adds to the potential to concentrate solely on sponsorship income at the expense of developing a broad-based marketing program, including all elements of the marketing mix.

Television

The importance of television to the marketing effort has been stressed throughout this book. Television has the capacity to provide significant streams of revenue as well as to act as an important promotion vehicle for sports, even if no television revenue is forthcoming. Therefore, television as a measure of success is very important.

Sport marketers must carefully determine the role of television in their marketing plans. Questions to be answered in relation to setting marketing objectives include: Is the sport capable of attracting television rights revenue? If so, how much? If not, can some coverage be obtained to help promote the sport? Answers to these questions determine the marketing objectives set in relation to television and thus the measures used to assess performance. Chapter 11 conveyed in detail the range of measures used to assess the success of sport programming and the subsequent advertising revenue that these programs can attract. Successful sport marketers need to have an intimate knowledge of the way in which the television business operates to ensure that television revenues or promotions are successfully implemented in the overall marketing strategy.

Television's impact on sport is an important strategic issue for sport marketers. To what extent are sports required to modify their game to make it more attractive to television? Although the need to appease television can be a potential problem, in some instances it has also forced sports to modernise and therefore present a more attractive product. Cricket, as discussed in this book, has been better off for the World Series Cricket revolution in 1977. The introduction of the one-day game, with a variety of new rules better suited to television, has brought an added dimension to playing standards through improved fielding, more creative batting and an array of tactics not seen previously. It is not the purpose of this book to take one view as to whether television's impact on sport in relation to changing the game is either good or bad. Clearly, there are examples of such changes benefiting sport and others working to the detriment of the sport. This is an important issue, and rather than adopt an extreme position either way sport marketers should carefully think through the implications of change. The sport marketer should conduct research, consult past and current players and trial changes, in just the way marketers do when preparing to introduce new products.

Merchandising and licensing

Merchandising and licensing are important marketing objectives. Promotional licensing was the subject of chapter 16, where it was shown that sporting organisations license their logos and trademarks for two reasons:

1 to create awareness of the sport, club or league; and
2 to endorse product lines outside of sport as a means of generating additional revenue.

Revenue from licensing income becomes the main measure in determining the success of such a program. Clearly, this revenue can easily be measured.

Service quality

Another important but less tangible measure is service quality, which has been developed as an ongoing theme through this book. It has been specifically discussed in chapters 5, 7 and 8 as providing the basis for establishing a competitive advantage. It also indirectly affects everything that is concerned with attracting spectators, members and sponsors, contributing to the likelihood of repeat purchase. Strategically, it is significant because it has the capacity to even out the fluctuations in enjoyment governed by winning or losing. An enjoyable night at the basketball, for example, may to some extent offset the disappointment of losing.

This raises the critical question in relation to this intangible area of assessing how much participants and spectators enjoy the sport experience. Equally, this question relates to winning. Clubs, associations and leagues are increasingly realising that their marketing programs should be designed to build loyalty–loyalty that has the capacity to withstand periods of poor on-field performance. The reality of most sporting competitions is that it is in their own interests to ensure that winning is shared by all, and therefore mechanisms will be put in place to even out the competition. Clubs will experience periods during which they are successful and periods when they perform poorly. Success on the field does not guarantee success off the field, but poor on-field performance almost certainly guarantees poor off-field success based on the measures discussed above. Reducing the impact of these periods of poor on-field performance enhances the likelihood of achieving financial stability.

Financial stability

Despite an earlier statement in this chapter that profit is not the sole goal of sporting organisations, it has grown in importance during the past 15 years. Many sporting organisations typified the extreme position, where debt could be freely incurred without considering the consequences. Fortunately, this culture is changing, reinforcing the importance of control in the implementation of marketing activities. Modern sporting organisations more readily understand the balance between on-field success and sound off-field success.

Most of the measures of success discussed in this section contribute to the income-generating potential of the organisation. The ability to reign in costs is the subject of broader texts in the management domain, covering the issue of control in more detail.

Coordinating and implementing marketing strategy

The framework for determining marketing strategy was discussed in chapter 2. Coordination and implementation of this strategy are primarily the responsibility of the marketing department. Kotler et al. (1989: 635) define marketing implementation as 'the process that turns marketing strategies and plans into marketing actions in order to accomplish strategic marketing objectives'. Coordination cannot occur, however, without the support of the entire organisation. Marketing staff are often reliant, for example, on sport operations staff to allow star players to become involved in promotion activities. Typically, these star players are in high demand for such promotion activities, often conflicting with training and playing schedules.

Implementation is primarily about staff management, and in essence deals with the who, what, where and when of the marketing plan. The who, what, where and when activities are the result of the strategies determined, otherwise referred to as the what and why. Implementation is often difficult–more difficult than determining the strategies. It is easy to dream up a range of interesting and creative strategies; however, when it comes to actual implementation it may be found that they are totally unrealistic or impractical. When setting SMART objectives, as discussed in chapter 2, the 'R' for realistic is of paramount importance. Ultimately, it is the staff and their expertise that determine the ability of the organisation to coordinate the marketing strategy.

Added to the difficulties of coordinating marketing strategies is the relatively recent introduction of marketing personnel, even marketing departments, to sporting organisations. In fact, in some sporting organisations in Australia, a national development officer or state development officer is responsible for the marketing program, based on his/her responsibility for promoting and encouraging participation. In some sports, specialist sport-marketing staff are now employed. The Australian Cricket Board (ACB), for example, has for some time employed a general manager of marketing, sales manager, events and sponsorship manager, events assistant and sponsorship officer, licensing manager and marketing officer. Careers in sport marketing are beginning to flourish.

Careers in sport marketing

The ACB is indicative of the range of career options emerging in this field. Professional sports in particular offer the greatest range of career options. Marketing staff employed in Australian Football League (AFL) clubs have multiplied markedly during the 1990s and early 2000s. The Port Adelaide Football Club, for example, employed twelve staff in its marketing division in 2001 plus three staff in media and public relations. Jobs covered include a membership and database manager, sponsorship executive, merchandise manager, sales executives and assistants and marketing assistants, media and public relations manager, assistant and communications coordinator. All staff were responsible for the implementation and coordination of all the club's marketing activities. Also, their employment is indicative of the breadth and range of activities undertaken by the club. Sponsorship, media and public relations, sales of merchandise, overseeing licensing and merchandising, and servicing game day functions cover the gamut of marketing mix variables discussed in this book.

Most large sporting organisations now incorporate media relations in their marketing department, or as a related department such as at Port Adelaide. Tennis Australia is one such organisation, with a marketing and media department. The importance of public relations has been stressed throughout this book as a vital function within the marketing mix and should be integrated in, or closely associated with, the activities of the marketing department. Table 17.1 illustrates some of the employment and career prospects emerging in the field in Australia. The jobs shown in Table 17.1 were advertised during 2001 and 2002 in *The Age* and *Weekend Australian*.

Slowly there is evidence that marketing personnel are being employed in a greater variety of sporting organisations. The biggest hurdle to overcome in expanding an organisation's staff expertise has been the view that sport promotes itself and therefore does not require marketing staff. This complacency has been responsible for the slow pace at which sport has embraced the need for marketing expertise. There is evidence of this changing.

TABLE 17.1
Careers in marketing

Job	Organisation
Sales and Marketing Manager	Western Bulldogs
Membership Development Executive	Melbourne Racing Club
Licensing Officer	Australian Cricket Board
Marketing Manager	2002 World Masters Games
Service Officer	Waves Leisure Centre
Event Marketing/PR Coordinator	Country Racing Victoria
Community Services Manager	Links Golf Community
Golf Membership Sales Manager	Links Golf Community
Corporate Communications Manager	Nike Australia
Brand Manager	Adidas
Lifesaving Public Relations & Marketing Manager	The Royal Life Saving Society

Interestingly, the pace of change has become more urgent as sporting organisations realise the capacity of a skilled marketing team's potential to contribute to the full range of revenue-earning possibilities via marketing programs. It is true that in some instances it is necessary to spend money up front to ensure that revenue-earning potential is maximised. Advertising, public relations launches and staff training in terms of service delivery are examples of this. However, they are also the means of communicating with a public increasingly subject to an attractive range of recreation and leisure pursuits capable of detracting from interest in sport. The past decade in particular has seen a rapidly intensifying range of competitive forces within the recreation and leisure industry. In many ways this has been good for sport, as sports have been forced to professionalise their operations and modernise the way they deliver the overall sport package. The overall sport package remains the domain of all staff and board members associated with various sports, but the sport marketer's input to the package is rapidly growing.

Sport-marketing planning revisited

Central to this book has been the role of strategic marketing planning in sporting organisations. Figure 2.1 showed the steps involved in the process. Sport marketers should follow the steps shown until they become familiar with the process. It is possible to vary the steps at times, but in general the process remains unchanged for the different sporting organisations. What does change is the emphasis placed on the importance of various steps in the process. A summary of the strategic sport-marketing plan (SSMP) is shown in Figure 17.2. Sport marketers required to develop an SSMP should use this framework to prepare their plan. This book has provided the added detail to help the sport marketer consider all necessary issues at each stage of the marketing plan.

Stage 1, 'Identification of marketing opportunities', should remain fairly constant. As each organisation prepares to enter a new three- to five-year plan, a renewed analysis of the environment and review of the organisation's capabilities should be undertaken. Importantly, this review should recognise the changing forces driving competition in the sport and recreation industry. This book has already noted changes in the competitive forces confronted by sporting organisations during the past 10–15 years. Decisions taken in regard to the overall analysis of the organisation filter down to the marketing mission and objectives

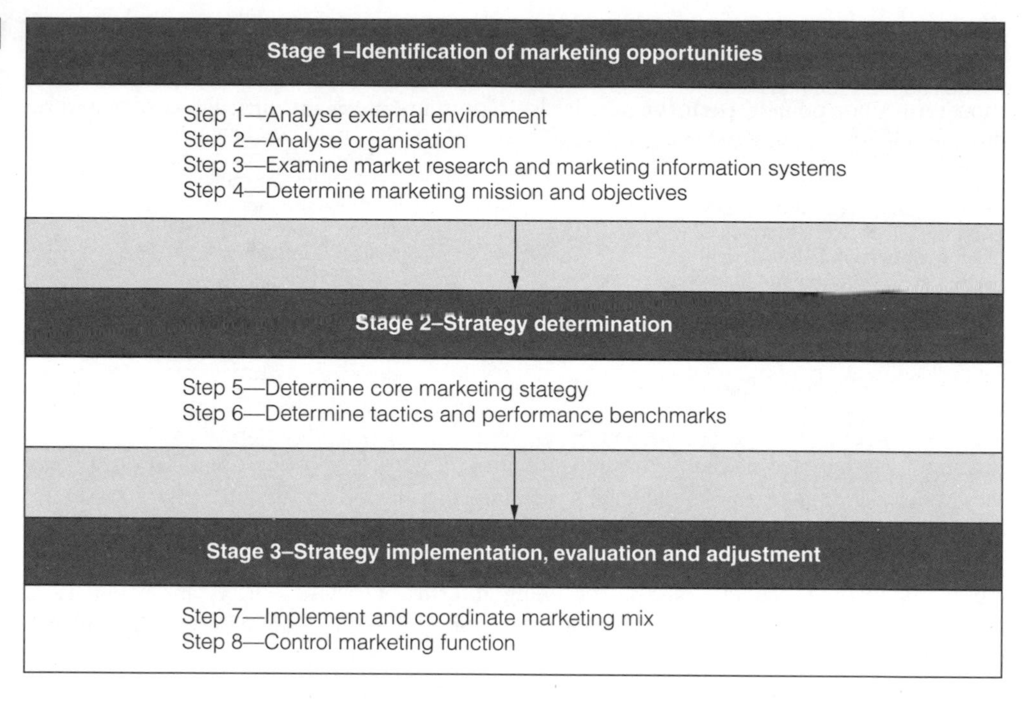

FIGURE 17.2 **Summary of the strategic sport-marketing planning process**

set, to allow marketing activities to contribute to broader organisational goals. Most of these decisions are based on the market research and data available to accurately assess buying patterns and consumer behaviour in general. Understanding consumer behaviour in sport and market research and segmentation were covered in Part I of this book. In general, these stages remain constant components of the SSMPP.

Stage 2, 'Strategy determination', represents the greatest detail provided in this book. This is because it is at this stage of determining the core marketing strategy that the range of marketing mix variables can be varied to suit the circumstances confronting an organisation. The reason for selecting the mix of variables also changes depending on whether a repositioning exercise is required, such as that described for the NBL during this book, or the development of product offerings aimed at specific market segments. Stage 2 also represents the greatest unknown in terms of 'Have we chosen the right core marketing strategy?' There is no correct answer to the question. It can be answered only over time, and even this is subject to the ability of staff to implement marketing plans.

Stage 3, 'Strategy implementation', consists of measuring performance based on standards determined earlier in the process and, where necessary, modifying or altering the way in which the core marketing strategy is implemented. Control, implementation and coordination, as discussed in this last chapter, are crucial to the overall success of the marketing strategy. Implementation, like strategy determination, is an ongoing process. As one season or event rolls into the next, it becomes important for marketing personnel to step back every so often to assess progress and to ensure that strategies are not subject to rapid change based on short-term success. In particular, for seasonal sports it is important that week-by-week winning or losing does not unduly interfere with strategic marketing plans, usually prepared for three to five years. This is one of sport's greatest pitfalls: reacting to short-term poor on-field performance. It also represents the main difficulty confronted by the sport marketer: to market a product over which there is little control.

Implementation is also guided by the assumptions made during the planning process. Because all strategies and action plans are based on these assumptions about the future, they are subject to considerable risk. It is necessary for marketing managers to assess continually the assumption on which strategies were based. It is here that the beginning and end of the planning process meet. In fact, there is never an end, as the cycle continues in a feedback loop that sometimes blurs beginning and end. To some extent this is a good sign. It indicates that once the plan and associated strategies are formulated they are not simply put on the shelf. Plans put into action are subject to contingency planning to correct assumptions that do not prove to be true. Therefore the SSMPP is dynamic, rarely stagnant, and laden with challenges to ensure that the full potential of marketing's contribution to the overall functioning of a sporting organisation is optimised. We wish you well with this challenge.

CASE STUDY

MCG: product, positioning, strategy and the Melbourne Cricket Club—a case for marketing strategy

A world-famous brand and product in its own right, today's Melbourne Cricket Ground (MCG) has marketed itself as 'the people's ground' since it found its present location in 1853, although it is frequently alluded to also as 'the hallowed ground'. An Australian asset, it is Victoria's biggest and most popular stadium, with capacity of 97 000 and a busy schedule. A natural turf arena used one day in four accommodates international cricket, AFL and Australian rules generally, concerts, dinners and other major functions (MCC 2001a).

Its sources of revenue show the breadth of its products and target markets. In round figures, annual income in 1999–2000 was $48.5 million. Members' contributions from the Melbourne Cricket Club (MCC) constituted $19.25 million, corporate entertainment facilities netted above $7.5 million, and the remaining $26.75 million, which amounted to more than half, came from a share of catering, ground advertising and MCG functions income (MCC 2001a: 10). With a downturn in the economy at the micro-level and competition from Telstra Dome (Docklands), fewer concerts and tourism and expendable income in people's pockets in 2000/01, the MCC made a loss, albeit with a trading profit of $21–22m (Clark, pers. comm.).

The MCG is facing challenges from the new Telstra Dome and Telstra Stadium (Sydney), concurrently with sporting codes becoming more important than the stadia themselves in attracting revenue. Broadcasting (including Internet, pay-TV and, in the future, virtual advertising) now provides a substantial part of overall revenue. For example, cricket sponsorship and media rights provided 72% of ACB revenue in 1998/99, and an increasingly independent AFL is gaining more strength in the market and becoming a threat to the MCG's viability. Consequently, the MCG is looking to alliances with stadia like The Gabba in Brisbane and Telstra Stadium Australia in Sydney to strengthen its negotiating power with the AFL (MCG Trust 2000b).

Another complicating factor necessitating stronger alliances for the MCG is the dominance of the government-driven Major Events Corporations (MECs). The Victorian MEC has inadvertently 'driven a divider between the venues and the national sporting organisations (NSOs) who like to initially discuss financial terms with the MECs before linking themselves with a particular venue...' (MCC 2001b: 3). Therefore, it is imperative for the MCC/MCG to maintain a strong alliance with the Victorian MEC.

The role of the MCC

Contributing 40% of MCG revenue, MCC membership fees have wholly financed the construction of all MCG stands with the exception of the Olympic Stand in 1956 and the Great Southern Stand in 1992. At April 2001, the MCG had 51 800 voting members (10% women), 19 700 restricted members (28% women), and a waiting list of more than 172 000, growing annually by 10–12 000 (MCC 2001a: 17–18).

The MCC administered, promoted and stewarded the colony's cricket and football until after the turn of the century when the Victoria Cricket Association (VCA) took over, also introducing Australian football. This was developed by MCC honorary secretary and cricketer T.W. Willis, who wanted to introduce a suitable pastime to keep cricketers fit during winter, avoiding rugby's dangerous tackles on hard Australian grounds by creating a game in which the ball would be in the air more often. A four-member committee produced the nine 'Melbourne Rules' which were the basis of the Australian code in 1857 (MCC 2001a: 12).

The management of the MCG is vested in the MCC by the government-appointed MCG Trust, an Act of Parliament guaranteeing the club's occupation of about 20% of the stadium for its Members' Reserve. MCG staff and management regard 'the people's ground' as crown land, its major stakeholders being 'the people, the Trust and the MCC'. Other important stakeholders include the state government, the Melbourne City Council, which comes under the government-appointed trust, tenant sporting codes, tenant clubs (Richmond, Essendon, Collingwood, Melbourne and, potentially, Carlton), their sponsors and business partners, and the media which is integral to their strategic marketing. They see the MCC's role as (Clark, pers. comm.):

> a private Club with public responsibility to the people's ground...using everything as a way of raising revenue...and servicing the members and those who attend the MCG itself across tourism, MCG Tours, cricket, Pura Cup, one day matches and Test matches, plus non-match day functions such as corporate functions and family days...

Mission and goals

The mission of the MCC in fulfilling its role as ground manager for the Melbourne Cricket Ground is:

- To manage the MCG as the world's best stadium for all people.

For this to be achieved, the club must establish a venue team that will carry out innovative and professional stadium management practices which deliver quality and market-leading services and facilities.

With this in mind, a number of goals have been established that the club must strive to deliver, that:

- the stadium is utilised extensively throughout the year;
- first-class services and facilities are enjoyed by all users;
- a safe and clean environment exists for sportsmen and women, performers and patrons;
- a customer service culture is embedded throughout the organisation; and
- opportunities are taken to maximise the net financial return from all possible sources.

These goals must be achieved in a financially responsible manner and are to be balanced against providing a reasonable financial return for the club and the MCG Trust.

Promoting the MCG as the nation's premier sports venue

Historically entrepreneurial in developing its image as an exciting world-class venue where other colonies and nations competed, the MCG hosted the first inter-colony game of cricket against NSW in 1856 and the first international competition on New Year's Day 1862, the English Captain Stephenson acclaiming the ground better than any in England. The first football match was played between the Melbourne Football Club and the police at the MCG in 1869, followed in the 1880s by more regular games (MCC 2001a: 9–12).

With the biggest membership of any sporting club in Australia, the MCG has been proactive in staging many firsts over more than a century, including international baseball, lacrosse, the Austral Wheel Race, experimental aeroplane flights, the 1956 Olympic Games, state of origin, rugby league, international rugby union, soccer matches and Olympic football. It has provided a local venue for cricket, lacrosse, baseball, tennis, lawn bowls, shooting, hockey and squash (MCC 2001a).

The MCG hosts 80–90 days of cricket and football each year, with about 3.5 million people visiting the ground annually. Visitors include 300 000 cricket fans, 3 million football fans and those attending other events such as concerts, national and international rugby and soccer matches, and guided tours. The most popular fixtures are the limited overs day/night matches that have attracted more than 87 000; Friday night AFL, which attracts more than 40 000; and grand finals which generally attract about 95 000 (MCC 2001a). The new Telstra Dome has taken 30% of the MCG's football market and most concerts since opening.

The city's 'heart and soul'

From 1853 when ladies promenaded and its band rotunda extended on to the ground, the MCG has always promoted itself as 'the city's heart and soul', a multipurpose venue offering social and civic as well as sporting events—hence its hosting of royal pageants, religious conventions and blockbuster concerts from the 1970s onwards. Since the 1956 Olympics it has also focused on corporate facilities and on non-corporate social gatherings such as dinners, entertainment packages, wedding receptions, cocktail parties and guided tours of its heritage attractions, to boost its revenue and prominence (MCC 2001a).

Corporate clients

Centrally located and open nearly every day of the year, the MCG rents out 133 corporate suites (8–20 people), usually on a three-year lease, including 20-person sponsor boxes with full bar and black-tie waiter service, parking and signage space (MCC 2001c), to secure income that is critical to MCG development funding. Corporate packages are tailored to both cricket and football seasons, with virtually all corporate entertainment areas fully utilised on major cricket and football days and match-day facilities open during the week for varied commercial and social groups (MCC 2001a).

Open-air luncheons can accommodate up to 1500 people, and 15 function rooms are equipped with theatre, cocktail and banquet facilities; the Hayden Bunton Room, with the largest capacity, accommodates 350 in the theatre, 400 for cocktails and 320 for banquet/ dinner. Car parking is available on non-match days, conference equipment and services are onhand, clients can use the giant electronic scoreboards, and tours can be scheduled with functions (MCC 2001a).

Tourism

Heritage, tradition, a place in the heart of ordinary Victorians and reasonable costs constitute the MCG's biggest competitive advantage against newcomers like the Telstra Dome. Its tourist market is targeted for profitable expansion as the Australian Gallery of Sport and Olympic Museum seeks to become cost-neutral, and the MCC Pavilion, its famous long room and Cricket Museum, the Australian Cricket Hall of Fame and the library are promoted more aggressively (MCC 2001a). A scathing review breathed new life into the MCG's lacklustre historic features (The Strategy Planning Group 1992), proposing a strategy that will become more important in the future.

The four variables of place

Facility planning and physical evidence have always featured strongly in the management and marketing of the MCG, and 'the people's ground' is a world icon of longer standing than Lords and America's Wrigley Field.

Facility planning

In 1853, the Melbourne Cricket Club (MCC) chose a site offered by Governor La Trobe because 'the situation was not quite as level as desirable yet afforded sufficient slope that without interfering with the game would ensure its always being free from floods…' (MCC 2001a). Since then, it has grown in a fairly ad-hoc way, meeting needs as they arose, largely financed by the MCC, which the Trust has overseen. Each new building has reflected the changing market needs of venues.

The first grandstands, built in 1861 and 1877 for Australia's first international matches, were replaced in 1884 by 'The Grandstand'. This was replaced in 1956 by the Northern (Olympic) Stand, which reflected the widening product base of venues, seated 22 213, and had 504 dining rooms and 1006 corporate boxes. Costing £7000, this was the first MCG building ever partially funded by the government, which contributed £1000.

The Grey Smith Stand of 1906 was replaced by the Western Stand (Ponsford Stand) in

1966. The Harrison and Wardill Stands, built in 1908 and 1912, were replaced by the Southern Stand in 1936/37, again replaced in 1992 by the state-of-the-art Great Southern Stand, jointly funded and costing nearly $150 million. It has a capacity of 44 696 with 1012 corporate suites, 23 food halls and/or self-service bars, seven dining rooms named after sporting heroes and two major bars (MCC 2001a).

With the marketing department closely involved, development of the out-of-date Northern Stand is planned both as a response to the Telstra Dome from 2002–05 and in preparation for the 2006 Commonwealth Games. It will be undertaken in times of more change, competition and global disquiet than ever previously faced by the MCG and is underpinned by a complete review of the MCC's current management structure, emphases, operations and directions, which will see the MCG partially reinventing itself. Cost-cutting measures and sources of extra funding have been calculated to sustain the construction period (MCG Trust 2000a).

Location and accessibility. The MCG is ideally located within 15 minutes' walking distance of the city centre. Two nearby railway stations and tramway and bus links with all suburbs give it excellent drawing radii and travel time for visitors to diverse events, and surrounding parkland accommodates about 6000 vehicles (MCC 2001a). Parking is sometimes a problem, controlled as it is by the Melbourne City Council. Accessibility is a management priority, and while some sections of Members' Reserve are not open to the public when matches are in progress, the Australian Gallery of Sport and Olympic Museum is open on all days but Christmas Day and Good Friday.

Servicescape. Its design accommodating all tangible convenience needs, the MCG's servicescape seeks to provide comfort and ambience as well. With the exception of the unroofed and poorly seated Northern Stand, the facility meets world standards appropriate to its age, a recent survey finding that, despite age and eclectic architecture, ordinary spectators seem to accept the buildings for 'the stories they tell' (MCG Trust, 2000a). There is generous provision for the disabled, revenue-sharing on-line ticketing is being developed with Ticketmaster, and three TAB agencies are an extra convenience.

Multipurpose flexibility, efficient spatial layout and functionality of access and exit are reinforced by comfortable seats, efficient aisles and walkways, well-located food services/bars and accessible, clean restrooms, with horticultural upgrades planned for 2001–02 (MCC 2001b). However, crowded female toilets, 'barely passable, expensive' kiosk food for families and poor drainage in the centre of the arena are cited as needing improvement (MCG Trust 2000a). This is particularly important if the MCG intends to differentiate itself from the more elite Telstra Dome as the less costly 'people's ground' that has good facilities and provides an optimum game of football.

A comprehensive updated disaster plan is in place across the whole venue, with crowd-alert and evacuation procedures clearly documented, regular staff refresher courses and St John Ambulance personnel always on hand. High-quality security sees a fully serviced police station at the ground, well-trained staff complying with various bylaws and regulations, a video crowd-surveillance system that is monitored by police at all major sporting fixtures, three-phase power, an emergency generator, and on-site engineering and technical staff for emergencies (MCC 2001a).

Physical evidence: sport facility design

The ambience of the MCG lies in its setting, internal aesthetics, historical displays and attractive and well-resourced corporate and social facilities. However, its use of technology is exemplary. Having always nurtured a world-class natural turf arena and introduced the world's first night game under lights in 1879, the first sightboard in 1881 and the first deluxe scoreboard in 1882 (MCC 2001a), the MCG was fast to become high-tech in the 20th century.

Natural turf arena. Used one day in four, the MCG is subject to year-round wear and tear unlike any other natural turf surface in the world. Surveyed and configured into today's conventional oval in 1861, it was remodelled in 1956 to international athletics specifications, the red mountain soil used resulting in a clay consistency and poor drainage in the 1980s. In 1992, the arena was completely reconstructed to cope with concerts without damaging the sporting program. A sand-based profile with excellent drainage and load-bearing ability was reinforced with Tasmanian peat moss, sand particles, nylon mesh and a couch base oversown with rye grass, enabling frequent patch-ups with four-metre clods as needed (MCC 2001a).

Special roll-out turf for Olympic 2000 soccer was retained for the football corridor in 2001, and preparation for track and field at the 2006 Games is now being planned (MCC 2001a). With the current loss of 30% of AFL matches to the Telstra Dome, and the burgeoning presence of rugby and soccer at the MCG, it is also planned to reconfigure the arena to better accommodate rectangular field sports (MCG Trust 2000a).

Scoreboards and lighting. Famous for its state-of-the-art manually operated scoreboard in 1903, the MCG upgraded in 1982 to a fully electronic Mitsubishi scoreboard, the large TV screen for replays and action close-ups revolutionising sport at the ground for spectators. This was replaced by an updated model in 1992 and a Sony Jumbo Tron was installed in the Olympic Stand so that almost everyone could see the scoreboards; TV sets were installed in the few blindspots. In 1999 the Mitsubishi board was burnt out, replaced in March 2000 by the world's most advanced LED screen. Both colour boards are controlled from a sophisticated video studio in the Olympic Stand (MCC 2001a).

Lighting towers have become the most influential element of sports promotion. The VCA helped to finance the MCG's $5 million light towers and was the prime mover in staging the first day/night cricket matches in 1985, closely followed by AFL night matches. The lamps on the six MCG towers are computer-aligned to provide ground-level lighting of colour-TV quality and positioned to avoid shadows during daytime. An independent underground source distributed direct from Richmond switchyard (also the supply source for nearby hospitals) virtually eliminates accidental disruption to supply. Any circuit-breaking failure at the switchyard can see power restored, usually within 20 minutes, by an on-call technician. There is also the emergency generator (MCC 2001a).

Physical evidence: promotion material and advertising

The MCC has largely depended on the AFL, which controls and uses the brand name and logo, to do its MCG promotion and bring in AFL-associated revenue. It has not had to optimise its name for either sporting events or exciting non-corporate public events like concerts, tours and pleasant dining except in the short term, because most of its marketing revenue has come from strategic marketing business with valuable contracts for catering, signage, preferred suppliers, naming rights, multimedia, promotional licensing through the MCG/MCC shop, and strong partnerships with sponsors. For example, Carlton United Brewery (CUB) outlets have boosted CUB sales by 5%, and Cadbury chocolate sales have benefited significantly from Cadbury's association with the MCG (Clark, pers. comm.).

Its marketing staff have focused on servicing tenant clubs and corporates (MCG Trust 2000a), its only significant promotion targeting corporate clients, sponsors and contracts. Glossy informational and promotional brochures produced exclusively for members and corporate clients emphasise both 'the people's ground' and 'the hallowed ground' themes, blending historical black-and-white images with highlighted contemporary action shots on a sepia background, and are well targeted considering the revenue gained from the upper end of MCG's market (MCC 2001c, d). Media advertising has focused only on guided tours and information about schedules and transport.

However, the AFL has recently strengthened its marketing position and become, with Telstra Dome, the MCG's 'major competitor for market power' (MCG Trust 2000a: B1). In need of sensitive handling, MCG's current market share is holding, its tenant clubs (including Carlton if it can be secured—also negotiating with Telstra Dome), currently having more drawing power than Telstra Dome teams (Clark, pers. comm.).

With Telstra Dome targeting a more elite and commercial market, it is important that the MCG as 'the people's ground' refocuses attention on its 'bread-and-butter' spectators—particularly families, work and social groups looking for a good time out. Current strategies are to emphasise the ground's history, traditions and the Australian Gallery of Sport, and its sporting pedigree for international events including the 2006 Commonwealth Games (MCG Trust 2000a). It has also begun a strategic marketing program for major events other than AFL and cricket, focusing on summer, when ground utilisation is comparatively low and weather conditions are conducive to an open-air stadium (MCG Trust 2000a).

Members are being nurtured, and new promotion programs are targeted at:

- *the media*, through briefing, lunches and interviews with local and national print, TV and radio, journalists and commentators;
- *decision makers*, including State and local politicians, other sports bodies, sporting companies, promoters and heritage groups, plus any public speaking opportunities; and
- *tenants*, to arrange promotional opportunities such as open days and family days, when families and tours have maximum possible access and use of the playing surface (MCG Trust 2000a B1–B2).

Special projects include promotion of the new Northern Stand and the 2006 Commonwealth Games, background briefings to key journalists, appointment of high-profile sporting personalities, nostalgia days, and a competition with media/sponsors for the ten most memorable events at the MCG. A comprehensive long-term strategy is targeted at stakeholders, and a new advertising campaign is imminent (MCG Trust 2000a).

More strategic promotion is underway with media/broadcasting, the Internet, virtual advertising and digital television being investigated, and the website currently being upgraded for electronic merchandising, ticketing, ground promotion, and interaction with content sites.

Special attention is being given to leverage the MCG brand into the e-commerce market. Its MCG brand is far more recognisable internationally than 'AFL' or 'ACB', and its national 'trophy value', if promoted, should enhance the commercial value of major contracts it is able to lease when they come up for renewal (e.g. advertising, catering, ticketing, merchandising and supplier rights) (MCG Trust 2000a).

The MCG is currently considering going after segments like 'theatre-goers and the uncommitted' (Clark, pers. comm.). A downturn in concerts, plus promoters' preference for Telstra Dome's retractable roof, make theatre-goers a difficult choice unless pre-theatre dinner packages and transport can be arranged or on-ground MCG theatres can stage plays, intimate concerts and films. Similarly, inroads into the 'uncommitted' will take active television, radio and magazine advertising that is more engaging than in the past, to remind Victorians that the MCG offers special dining, entertainment and tours that can be tailored to any group's wants, as well as world-class sporting events.

A lot of hopes are being pinned on the new Northern Stand, which will equal Telstra Dome's state-of-the-art plushness and technology, will keep costs down once operating, and is expected to increase profits for the MCG and its suppliers with promotions. The grandstand, better corporate suites, larger seating, better toilets, entrance and eating facilities, better view of events, patrons being close to the sideline, more space, attractive glass areas and environment to the field, and MCG's rigorous approach to service quality, are all viewed as bringing spin-offs that will revitalise the ground (Clark, pers. comm.).

Process and people

The MCG deals with a highly complex marketing channel, which demands flexible yet tightly detailed process and building alliances with other stadia. Its 'sport servuction' model is highly effective, with blueprints tailoring planning, and delivering the same high level of service to different audiences, groups and capacities, despite the inevitable trade-offs that occur with mass audiences (Clark, pers. comm.).

In addition to longer running competitions, such as Olympic Football, the MCG's Events and Facilities Department routinely manages the diverse requirements for day, evening and day/night fixtures, which attract crowds of 97 000 over periods of 3–8 hours. High levels of flexibility and skill in the smooth management of crowd arrival peaks and the easing of admission and seating pressure points are demonstrated in these events (MCC 2001a).

Tangibles and reliability are uppermost considerations in planning and preparation, where managers focus sharply on the provision of all practical amenities for stadium hirers, optimum customer service, spectator comfort, ease of access and egress, and quality catering and cleaning, treating every potential customer experience as 'a moment of truth'. They bring all of this together well, the most telling comment on the detail invested coming from Clark (pers. comm.):

> The general public only sees what appears to be a seamless operation. People don't know the behind the scenes work that needs to go on to make the MCG events streamlined...as for example, getting Mathew Lloyd off the ground in 5 minutes instead of 20 minutes last year when he kicked 100 goals in one season...

An ethos of continuous improvement sees constant refinement of systems and processes, a benchmarking manual detailing minimum standards developed in 2000, (MCG Trust 2000a), and endorsement as an accredited quality assurance provider targeted in 2001 (MCC 2001b).

Ever since the early 1990s, customer service and 'moments of truth' have been paramount, '...all staff trained in the doctrines of how to operate/work at the MCG...'. With over half the revenue depending on outsourced hospitality and cleaning workers, and careful selection of thousands of casual front-line staff not always possible in these circumstances, training in quality operations (tangibles, reliability, competence, security and access) and people skills (responsiveness, courtesy, credibility, communication and understanding the customer) is critical. Quality assurance accreditation should ensure this and it would not be unreasonable for the MCC to require its employees to become quality-accredited themselves. The training currently undertaken has been reinforced by ongoing communication in assessing people and ongoing performance reviews (Clark, pers. comm.).

Conclusion

In the past few years the MCG has faced competition for the first time in its history. Although it anticipated a loss of market share with the establishment of Telstra Dome and Telstra Stadium, it seems not to have imagined that sporting codes could become more important than the stadia themselves in attracting revenue, nor the speed with which the AFL would gain such strong negotiating power and become a competitor. Perhaps the MCC mindset and culture could not conceive that the AFL saw its destiny, if not its history, as completely separate from the MCG, despite its continuing need for the venue.

Add to this its slowness to move into online ticketing, the lack of an early proactive strategy to utilise the Internet, pay-TV, virtual advertising and digital TV, and insufficient early attention to developing agreements on how broadcasting revenue would be shared to ensure all parties' continuing viability, and the MCG seems to have been temporarily overtaken by changes that caught it largely unawares. It has set its focus on strengthening its marketing as 'the people's ground', put in place rigorous plans to address the broadcasting issues, form alliances and sustain itself during its building program, and it now undertakes a SWOT analysis of Telstra Dome's progress every six months.

Now that it is learning to be as 'hungry' as its competitors, the MCG may never be the same again, but it will retain its status and recover reasonable and perhaps improved revenue, once it completes its building, realises the efficiency savings and better contracts it has targeted, and identifies new market segments to tap.

Questions

1 What advantages would a club such as the MCC gain from undertaking the strategic sport-marketing planning process (SSMPP)?
2 Is there evidence of marketing strategy in terms of the club's management of the ground?
3 Describe the significance of the use of the slogan 'the people's ground'. What are its marketing implications?

4 What is the significance of the four variables of place, in terms of a marketing strategy for the MCG?
5 What other marketing mix variables are important? Why? Discuss how marketing mix variables can be used and 'mixed' to underpin a marketing strategy for the MCG.

This case was originally prepared by Ted Cousens, as part of his studies towards the Master of Business (Sport Management). Case study reprinted by permission of author.

Bibliography

Anderson, L.K. and Sollenberger, H.M. (1992). *Managerial Accounting*, 8th edn, South-Western Publishing, Cincinnati, OH.

Ansoff, H.I. (1957). 'Strategies for diversification', *Harvard Business Review*, September-October, pp. 113-24.

ANZ McCaughan (1993). 'Broadcasting bounces back: A financial evaluation of Australian commercial metropolitan television', Part 1, *Industry Overview*, ANZ McCaughan, Melbourne.

Armstrong, C.P. and Sambamurthy, V. (1999). 'Information technology assimilation in firms: The influence of senior leadership and IT infrastructures', *Information Systems Research*, 10 (4), pp. 304–27.

Armstrong, K. (2001). 'Black women's participation in sport and fitness: Implications for sport marketing', *Sport Marketing Quarterly*, 10 (1), pp. 9–18.

Australian Bureau of Statistics (1996). *Sports Attendance, March 1995*, AGPS, Canberra.

——(2000). *Sports Attendance, December*, AGPS, Canberra.

——(2000a). *Participation in Sport and Physical Activities, Australia*, AGPS, Canberra.

——(2000b). *Australians Less Active*, AGPS, Canberra.

Australian Football League (AFL) (1994). *AFL Strategic Plan 1994*, Melbourne.

——(1995). *AFL 99th Annual Report–1995*, Melbourne.

Australian Sports Commission (2002). *2002–2005 Strategic Plan*, ASC, ACT.

Baghdikian, E. (1996). 'Building the sports organisation's merchandise licensing program: the appropriateness, significance, and considerations', *Sport Marketing Quarterly*, 5 (1), pp. 35–41.

Baker, M. (2000). *Marketing Strategy and Management*, 3rd edn, Macmillan Business, London.

Beikoff, K. (2002). 'Packaged to sell', *The Advertiser*, 5 June, p. 116.

Belch, G.E. and Belch, M.A. (1998). *Introduction to Advertising and Promotion: An Integrated Marketing Communications Perspective*, 4th edn, Irwin, Homewood, IL.

——(2001). *Advertising and Promotion: An Integrated Marketing Communications Perspective*, 5th edn, McGraw-Hill/Irwin, New York.

Beydemuller, K. and Fiedler, M. (2001). 'The Schumacher effect', *Germany 2001*, SportBusiness Group, September, p. 29.

Bishop, B. (1998). *Strategic Marketing for the Digital Age*, NTC Contemporary Publishing Group, Chicago.

Bitner, M.J. (1992). 'Servicescapes: the impact of physical surrounding on customers and employees', *Journal of Marketing*, 56 (2), pp. 57–71.

Bitner, M.J., Booms, B.H. and Tetreault, M.S. (1990). 'The service encounter: Diagnosing favorable and unfavorable incidents', *Journal of Marketing*, 54, pp. 71–84.

Boon, G. (1999). *Deloitte & Touche annual review of football finance* (1997-1998 season), Deloitte & Touche, Manchester.

——(2001). *Deloitte & Touche annual review of football finance* (1999-2000 season), Deloitte & Touche, Manchester.

Boyd, H.W. and Walker, O.C. (1990). *Marketing Management: A Strategic Approach*, Irwin, Homewood, IL.
Boyd, H.W., Walker, O.C and Larréché, J.C. (1995). *Marketing Management*, Irwin, Sydney.
Boyle, R. and Haynes, R. (2000). *Power Play: Sport, the Media and Popular Culture*, Pearson Education, Harlow.
Branch, D. (1992). 'Rethinking sport's product position and program concept', *Sport Marketing Quarterly*, 1 (2), pp. 21-7.
Britcher, C. (2001). 'Kirch's world cup web cops', *SportBusiness International*, 64, p. 16.
Brooks, C.M. (1998). 'Sport/exercise identity theory and participation marketing: Theory formation and theoretical justification', *Sport Marketing Quarterly*, 7(1), pp. 38-47
Brown, M. (1992). 'The big gamble', *The Age*, Green Guide, 14 February, pp. 1-2.
——(1993). 'NBL rethinks its strategy as crowds fall', *Sunday Age*, Sports Extra, 27 June, p. 6.
Bryden-Brown, S. (2001). 'OzTAM figures to get no respect', *The Australian*, 5 March, p. 3.
Burchett, J. (1996). *News Limited v Australian Rugby League Limited and Others*, NG 197 of 1995, Federal Court of Australia, Sydney.
Business Review Weekly (2001). 'Ratings war gets serious', p. 16.
Buzzard, K. (1992). *Electronic Media Ratings: Turning Dollars into Sense*, Focal Press, Boston, MA.
Campbell, D. (2001). 'Is the people's game going back to its roots?', *SportBusiness International*, October, p. 22.
Carroll, J. (2002). 'In awe of a Tiger out in the Open', *The Age*, January, p. 1/8.
Chase, R.B. and Stewart, D.M. (1994). 'Make your service fail-safe', *Sloan Management Review*, Spring, pp. 35-44.
Chernatony, de L. and McDonald, M.H.B. (1992). *Creating Powerful Brands*, Butterworth/Heinemann, Oxford.
Cheverton, P. (2000). *Key Marketing Skills*, Koran Page, London.
Church, R. (2000). *Sport on the Internet*, Screen Digest.
Churches, D. (1994). 'Sydney 2000', *Panstadia International*, 2 (2), pp. 10-14.
Churchill, G.A., Jr. and Surprenant, C. (1982). 'An investigation into the determinants of customer satisfaction', *Journal of Marketing Research*, 19, 491-504.
Cialdini, R.B., Borden, R.J., Thorne, A., Walker, M.R., Freeman, S. and Sloan, L.R. (1976). 'Basking in reflected glory: Three (football) field studies', *Journal of Personality and Social Psychology*, 34, pp. 366-75.
Clark, J. (2001). Marketing Manager of the Melbourne Cricket Ground (MCG), 13 September, personal communications.
Clarke, R. (2002). 'Wearing out the opposition', *SportBusiness International*, pp. 26-7.
Cockington, J. (2002). 'Speed freaks', *The Sydney Morning Herald*, Metropolitan, 5 January, p. 5.
Collins, J. (2002). 'Athens opts for old fashioned values', *The SportsVine*, 4 (5), p. 8.
Connolly, R. (1995). 'Oakley denies AFL code acts as censor', *The Age*, Sunday 12 March, p. 5, Melbourne.
Cousens, L. and Slack, T. (1996). 'Using sport sponsorship to penetrate local markets: the case of the fast food industry', *Journal of Sport Management*, 10 (2), pp. 169-87.
Coyne, K.P. (1986). 'Sustainable competitive advantage–what it is, what it isn't', *Business Horizons*, January-February, pp. 54-61.
Cravens, D.W. (1994). *Strategic Marketing*, 4th edn, Irwin, IL.
Dampney, J. (2002). 'NBL's rocky road–teams tighten belts'. *The Daily Telegraph*, Saturday, 22 June, p. 101.
Darby, J. (2002). 'Rocky Mountain High', *The Herald Sun* (Melbourne).
Dauncey, H. and Hare, G. (2000). 'World Cup France '98 metaphors, meanings and values', *International Review for the Sociology of Sport*, 35 (3), pp. 331-47.
Delpy L. and Bosetti, H.A. (1998). 'Sport management and marketing via the World Wide Web', *Sport Marketing Quarterly*, 7 (1), pp. 21-7.

Denham, G. (1995a). 'Dons to act on Long racism complaints', *The Age*, Monday 1 May, p. 1.
——(1995b). 'Lewis supports fines for racial abuse', *The Age*, Saturday 11 March, p. 36.
Dennis, A. (2002) 'Gay Games showing the critics a racy pair of heels', *The Sydney Morning Herald,* 16 April, p. 3.
Department of Industry, Science and Resources/Australian Services Network (DISR), (2000). *The Australian Service Sector Review 2000*, vol. 1. Commonwealth of Australia: Author.
DeSensi, J.T. and Rosenberg, D. (1996). *Ethics in Sport Management*, Fitness Information Technology, Morgantown, WV.
DeVito, J.A. (1999). *Essentials of Human Communication*, 3rd edn, Addison Wesley Longman, New York.
Dietz-Uhler, B. and Harrick, E.A. (2000). 'Sex differences in sport fan behaviour and reasons for being a sport fan', *Journal of Sport Behavior*, 23 (3), pp. 219-31.
Eccles, J. (2002). 'It's big, beautiful and a touch shambolic', *The Canberra Times*, 14 September, p. 11.
El Sawy, O.A., Malhotra, A., Gosain, S. and Young, K.M. (1999). 'IT-intensive value innovation in the electronic economy: Insights from marshall industries', *MIS Quarterly*, 23 (3), pp. 305-35.
Evans, J.R. and Berman, B. (1987). *Marketing*, Macmillan, New York.
Farber, B. and Wycoff, J. (1991). 'Customer service: Evolution and revolution', *Sales and Marketing Management*, May, pp. 44-51.
Fink, J., Trail, G. and Anderson, D. (2002). 'Environmental factors associated with spectator attendance and sport consumption behavior: Gender and team differences', *Sport Marketing Quarterly*, 11 (1), pp. 8-19.
Friedman, W. (2000). 'Hockey comeback tied to engaging its core audience', *Advertising Age*, 71 (9), p. 40.
——(2002). 'Super Bowl ads sell super early', *Advertising Age*, 73 (23), pp. 3, 66.
Funk, D. and James, J. (2001). 'The psychological continuum model: A conceptual framework for understanding and individual's psychological connection to sport', *Sport Management Review*, 4 (2), pp. 119-50.
Funk, D., Haugtvedt, C. and Howard, D. (2000). 'Contemporary attitude theory in sport: Theoretical considerations and implications', *Sport Management Review*, 3 (2), pp. 125-44.
Funk, D., Mahony, D. and Ridinger, L. (2002). 'Characterizing consumer motivation as individual difference factors: Augmenting the sport interest inventory (SII) to explain level of spectator support', *Sport Marketing Quarterly*, 11 (1), pp. 33-43.
Gaudron, M. (2002). 'Sydney builds on Olympic success', *SportBusiness International*, February, pp. 37-8.
Gellatly, A. (2001). 'Online gambling: The buzz becomes a roar', Online gambling special, *SportBusiness International*, August, p. 7.
George, W. and Berry, L. (1981). 'Guidelines for advertising services', *Business Horizons*, 24 (4), pp. 52-6.
Gerlis, S. (2001). 'Gambling on online future', *SportBusiness International*, September, p. 35.
Gillis, R. (2002). 'Being Nick Faldo', *SportBusiness International*, March, pp. 24-5.
——(2002). 'Delivering on the deal', *SportBusiness International*, March, pp. 58-9.
Gladden, J., Milne, G.R. and Sutton, W. (1998). 'A conceptual framework for assessing brand equity in Division I college athletics', *Journal of Sport Management*, 12 (1), pp. 1-19.
Glendinning, M. (1999). 'Mapping out the future of sports licensing', *Sport Business*, September, p. 10.
Griswold, D. (1995). in *The Practice of Public Relations*, F. P. Seitel (ed.), Prentice-Hall, Englewood Cliffs, NJ.
Gritsi, S. (2000). 'Volunteer attrition at the Olympic Games: the case of Sydney 2000 Olympic Games,' unpublished Master of Management in Sport Management Project, UTS, Sydney.
Grönroos, C. (1990). *Service Management and Marketing*, Lexington Books, MA.

GTV Nine Network (2002). 'Australian Grand Prix 2002', *Wide World of Sports*, Nine Network.
Haigh, G. (1993). *The Cricket War: The Inside Story of Kerry Packer's World Series Cricket*, The Text Publishing Company, Melbourne.
Halbish, G. (1995). 'Developing professional sporting leagues', keynote address to the Sport Management and Marketing Conference, Sydney, August.
Hancock, S. (2001). 'Feyenoord gearing up for change', *SportBusiness International*, October, p. 42.
Hansen, F. and Scotwin, L. (1995). 'An experimental inquiry into sponsoring: what effects can be measured?', in *Advertising, Sponsorship and Promotions: Understanding and Measuring the Effectiveness of Commercial Communication*, ESOMAR, Amsterdam, pp. 65-82.
Harvard Business Review on Knowledge Management (1998), Harvard Business School Press, Boston.
Hawkins, D.I., Best, R.J. and Coney, K.A. (1992). *Consumer Behavior–Implications for Marketing Strategy*, Irwin, Boston, MA.
Hay, D. (1996). 'Jordan plays the money game', *Sunday Age*, 26 May, p. 18.
Helitzer, M. (1996). *The Dream Job: Sports Publicity, Promotion and Marketing*, 2nd edn, University Sports Press, Athens, OH.
Henderson, I. (1996). 'AFL kicks a goal on marketing strategy', *The Australian*, 23 July, p. 5.
Hickman, B. (2002). 'To get interactive, viewers must box clever', *The Australian*, 3 May, p. 6.
Hirons, M. (2002). 'Nice lookin' result among sponsorship swirl', Sweeney Sports Media Release, Friday, 15 March.
Hirsley, M. (1998). 'ABC, ESPN Gobble rest of NFL rights: networks pay $17.6 billion for 8 years', *Chicago Tribune*, 14 January, p. 1.
Hoffman, K.D. and Bateson, J.E.G. (1997). *Essentials of Services Marketing*, The Dryden Press, Orlando, FL.
Howard, D.R. (1999). 'The changing fanscape for big-league sports: Implications for sport managers', *Journal of Sport Management*, 13 (78-91), p. 89.
Huggins, M.H. (1992). 'Marketing research: a must for every sport organisation', *Sport Marketing Quarterly*, 1 (1), pp. 37-40.
Hunt, K., Bristol, T. and Bashaw R.E. (1999). 'A conceptual approach to classifying sports fans', *Journal of Services Marketing*, 13 (6), pp. 439-52.
Hyman, M. (2000). 'Masters of anti-sports marketing', *Business Week*, 17 April, p. 14.
International Olympic Committee (1996b). 'Marketing matters', *The Olympic Marketing Newsletter*, 8, Spring, Lausanne.
——(2002a). [electronic version] Sydney. 1997-2000 Games of the Olympiad. Facts and Figures. Retrieved 28 June 2002, from http://multimedia.olympic.org/pdf/en_report_180.pdf.
——(2002b). 'Marketing matters', *The Olympic Newsletter*, 21 June, Lausanne.
Irwin, R.L. and Stotlar, D.K. (1993). 'Operational protocol analysis of sport and collegiate licensing programs', *Sport Marketing Quarterly*, 2 (1), pp. 7-16.
Irwin, R.L., Sutton, W.A. and McCarthy, L.M. (2002). *Sport Promotion and Sales Management*, Human Kinetics, Champaign, IL.
Jarratt, P. (1988). 'A nation of Norms', *The Bulletin*, 4 October, pp. 56-8/92.
Jefkins, F. (1994). *Public Relations Techniques*, Butterworth/Heinemann, Oxford.
Jones, T.O. and Sasser, W.E. Jr. (1995). 'Why satisfied customers defect', *Harvard Business Review*, 73, pp. 88-99.
Judson, B. and Kelly, K. (1999). *Hyperwars - Eleven Strategies for Survival and Profit in the Era of Online Business*, Scribner, New York.
Kahn, R. (1972). *The Boys of Summer*, Harper & Row, New York.
Kates, S. (1998). 'Consumer research and sport marketing: Starting the conversation between two different academic discourses', *Sport Marketing Quarterly*, 7 (2), pp. 24-31.
Kim, D. and Kim, S.Y. (1995). 'QUESC: An instrument for assessing the service quality of sport centers in Korea', *Journal of Sport Management*, 9, pp. 208-20.

Klattell, D.A. and Marcus, N. (1988). *Sports for Sale*, Oxford University Press, New York.

Kleinman, M. (2001). 'Marketing to build up British sport', *Marketing*, 26 July, p. 19.

Kotler, P. and Andreasen, A.R. (1991). *Strategic Marketing for Nonprofit Organisations*, Prentice-Hall, Englewood Cliffs, NJ.

Kotler, P., Chandler, P., Gibbs, R. and McColl, R. (1989). *Marketing in Australia*, 2nd edn, Prentice-Hall, Englewood Cliffs, NJ.

Kotler, P., Chandler, P.C., Brown, L. and Adam, S. (1994). *Marketing: Australia and New Zealand*, 3rd edn, Prentice-Hall, Englewood Cliffs, NJ.

Langeard, E., Bateson, J., Lovelock, C. and Figlier, P. (1981). *Services Marketing: New Insights from Consumers and Managers*, Report no. 81-104, Marketing Science Institute, Cambridge, MA.

Lans, M.S. (1995). 'Sports team logos are big business', *Marketing News*, 29 (12), 5 June, p. 6.

Lapidus, R.S. and Pinkerton, L. (1995). 'Customer complaint situations: An equity theory perspective', *Psychology & Marketing*, 12, pp. 105-22.

Lawrence, M. (1995). 'High stakes keep growing and there can only be one winner', *The Age*, 8 April, p. 17.

Lee, J.A. (1996). 'Sites for sore eyes', *The Bulletin*, 7 May, p. 86.

Legg, D. and Baker, J. (1987). Chapter in *Add Value to Your Service*, C. Surprenant (ed.), American Marketing Association, Chicago, pp. 163-8.

Linnell, S. (1991). 'How Channel Seven scored the rights to TV football', *The Age*, 25 September, p. 3/29.

Linnell, S. (1995a). 'Magpies threaten legal action over Monkhorst', *The Age*, Thursday 4 May, p.36.

Linnell, S. (1995b). 'Two AFL race cases kept confidential', *The Age*, Wednesday 4 October, p. 42.

Lloyd, D.C. and Clancy, K.J. (1991). 'CPMs versus CPMIs: implications for media planning', *Journal of Advertising Research*, August/September, pp. 34-43.

Lovelock, C.H. (1991). Services Marketing, 2nd edn, Prentice-Hall, Englewood Cliffs, NJ.

Lovelock, C.H., Patterson, P.G. and Walker, R.H. (2001). *Services Marketing: An Asia-Pacific Perspective*, Pearson Education, Sydney.

Lyons Jr., R. and Jackson Jr., E.N. (2001). 'Factors that influence African American gen-Xers to purchase Nikes', *Sport Marketing Quarterly*, 10 (2), pp. 96-101.

M2 PressWIRE (2002). 'Di3: Sky Gamestar invests in interactive TV software for World Cup 2002', *M2 Communications*, 16 May.

McCarthy, J.E. and Perreault, W.D. (1990). *Basic Marketing*, 10th edn, Irwin, Homewood, IL.

McCarthy, L. (1998). 'Marketing sport to Hispanic consumers', *Sport Marketing Quarterly*, 7 (4), pp. 19-24.

McDonald, M.A., Sutton, W.A. and Milne, G.R. (1995). 'TEAMQUAL: Measuring service quality in professional team sports', *Sport Marketing Quarterly*, 4, pp. 9-15.

McGeoch, R. and Korporaal, G. (1994). *The Bid: How Australia Won the 2000 Games*, William Heinemann, Melbourne.

McGuire, M. (2002). 'On the ball–Why advertisers keep sponsoring sport: Sport's fevered pitch', *The Australian*, 22 February, PM01.

Macnow, G. (1990). 'A winning game plan', *Nation's Business*, March, pp. 82-4.

Madourou, A. (2000). 'The impact of special/hallmark events on the host community', unpublished Master of Management in Sport Management Project, UTS, Sydney.

Madrigal, R. (1995). 'Cognitive and affective determinants of fan satisfaction with sporting event attendance', *Journal of Leisure Research*, 27, pp. 205-27.

Mahony, D., Nakazawa, M., Funk, D., James, J. and Gladden, J. (2002). 'Motivational factors influencing the behavior of J. League Spectators', *Sport Management Review*, 5 (1), pp. 1-24.

Marketing News (1988). 'Clients now insist that their ads actually sell products', collegiate edn, January, p. 3.

Martin, C. (1997). *The digital estate–Strategies for competing, surviving, and thriving in an Internetworked world*, U.S.A., Mcgraw-Hill.
Martin, C.L. (1990). 'The employee/customer interface: An empirical investigation of employee behaviors and customer perceptions', *Journal of Sport Management*, 4, pp. 1-20.
Matthews, B. (2002). 'More courses for new mecca', *The Herald Sun* (Melbourne), 31 July, p. 75.
MCC (2001a). MCG Information Kit.
——(2001b). MCG Venue Operating Plan–draft 13 July 2001.
——(2001c). Brochure and Order Form, Test Cricket and One Day International Schedule.
——(2001d). Promotional Brochure, 'MCG–The People's Ground'.
MCG Trust (2000a). MCG Trust Business Plan 2000 to 2004.
——(2000b). MCG Trust Complimentary Business Plan 2000-01.
Meade, A. (2001). 'Outsider to test TV ratings agencies', *The Australian*, 20 March, p. 8.
Menary, S. (2001). 'Clubs profit from good groundwork', *Football Business International*, December, pp. 44-6.
Mermigas, D. (2002). 'NBA passes over to Disney and AOL', *Electronic Media*, 21 (4), p. 6.
Miller, J.A. (1977). 'Studying satisfaction, modifying models, eliciting expectations, posing problems, and making meaningful measurements', in conference conducted by Marketing Science Institute with support of National Science Foundation: *Conceptualization and Measurement of Consumer Satisfaction and Dissatisfaction*, H.K. Hunt (ed.), Marketing Science Institute, Cambridge, MA, pp. 72-91.
Minchin, L. (2002). 'If it's on television, it must be more sport', *The Sunday Age*, 16 June, p. 9.
Mithen, A. (1995). 'Clubs face $50,000 penalty for racial abuse', *The Age*, Friday 30 June, p. 1.
Mithen, A. and Smith, P. (1995). 'Clubs to be given names on racial abuse list', *The Age*, Thursday 18 May, p. 36.
Moore, D., Allport, S. and Kelly, A. (1995). 'The inaugural Cathay Pacific Australian PGA Par 3 Golf Championship Report', commissioned research report, Sydney.
Morgan Poll (2001). *The Bulletin*, 119 (6264), 6 March, p. 20.
Mullin, B.J. (1980). 'Sport management: the nature and utility of the concept', *Arena Review*, 3 (4), pp. 1-11.
——(1985). 'Characteristics of sport marketing', in *Successful Sport Management*, G. Lewis and H. Appenzellar (eds), Michie Co., Charlottesville, VA, pp. 101-23.
——(1985). 'Internal marketing–a more effective way to sell sport', in *Successful Sport Management*, G. Lewis and H. Appenzellar (eds), Michie Co., Charlottesville, VA.
Mullin, B.J., Hardy, S. and Sutton, W.A. (2000). *Sport Marketing*, 2nd edn, Human Kinetics, Champaign, IL.
Naidoo, U. and Gardiner, S. (2002). 'Preventing ambush–innovative ideas from Salt Lake City 2002', *SportBusiness International*, March, p. 62.
Nakra, P. (1991). 'Zapping nonsense: should television media planners lose sleep over it?', *International Journal of Advertising*, 10, pp. 217-22.
National Basketball League (1994). *Chief Executive Annual Report*, NBL, Melbourne.
——(1995). *Chief Executive Annual Report*, NBL, Melbourne.
——(2000). *Chief Executive Annual report*, NBL, Melbourne.
Naughton, J. (1992). 'Marketing Michael: the making of a commercial superstar', *Washington Post Magazine*, 9 February, pp. 11-29.
Nowell, M. (1995). 'The women's golf market: an overview of spectators and participants', *Sport Marketing Quarterly*, 4 (2), pp. 39-41.
O'Hara, B. and Weese, W.J. (1994). 'Advertising theory applied to the intramural–recreation sports environment', *Sport Marketing Quarterly*, 3 (1), pp. 9-14.
O'Riordan, B. (2002). 'Sport sponsorship on the road to recovery', *Financial Review*, 20 May, p. 48.
Oakley, R. (1996). 'Racism: new rule', *Football Record*, Round 13, June 30-2 July, pp. 3-9.
Oldfield, S. (1995). 'Long's abuse claim to test code of conduct', *The Age*, Sunday 28 April, p. 1.

Oliver, R.L. (1993). 'A conceptual model of service quality and service satisfaction: Compatible goals, different concepts', in *Advances in Services Marketing and Management*, vol. 2, T.A. Swartz, D.E. Bowen and S.W. Brown (eds), JAI Press, Greenwich, CT, pp. 65-85.

——(1997). *Satisfaction: A Behavioral Perspective on the Consumer*. McGraw-Hill, Singapore.

Otway, G. (2002). 'Promoters breathless as Woods beats cut', *Weekend Australian*, 12/13 January, p. 43.

OzTAM (2001). 'Comparison of OzTAM and ACNielsen TV ratings services', Press release: Author, 22 May.

——(2002a). 'Enter the discovery guide', Sydney: Author.

——(2002b). Top 20 programs 2 June to 8 June 2002. [electronic version] Retrieved on 20 July, <www.oztam.com.au/weeklydata/datafiles.html>.

Parasuraman, A., Zeithaml, V.A. and Berry, L.L. (1985). 'A conceptual model of service quality and its implications for future research', *Journal of Marketing*, 49, Fall, pp. 41-50.

Parasuraman, A., Zeithaml, V.A. and Berry, L.L. (1988). 'SERVQUAL: A multiple-item scale for measuring consumer perceptions of service quality', *Journal of Retailing*, 64, pp. 12-37.

Patterson, P.G. (1993). 'Expectations and product performance as determinants of satisfaction for a high-involvement purchase', *Psychology and Marketing*, 10, pp. 449-65.

Peek, A. (1998). Personal interview held at the offices of the Australian Football League, Brunton Ave, Melbourne, Monday 5 October.

Pesky, G. (1995). 'SGMA council serves up week long volley across America', *Sporting Goods Business*, 28 (4), p. 22.

Peterson, R.A. and Wilson, W.R. (1992). 'Measuring customer satisfaction: Fact and artifact', *Journal of the Academy of Marketing Science*, 20 (1), pp. 61-71.

Porter, M. (1980). *Competitive Strategy*, Free Press, New York.

——(1985), *Competitive Advantage: Creating and sustaining superior performance*, The Free Press, New York.

Quick, S. (1998). Fan Survey Report to NSWRU, unpublished technical report.

Quick, S. (1999). Fan Survey Report to NSWRU, unpublished technical report.

Raghunathan, B. and Raghunathan, T.S. (1994). 'Adaptation of a planning system success model to information systems planning', *Information Systems Research*, 5 (3), pp. 326-40.

Rhoden, W.C. (1993). 'High stakes: low sense of values', *New York Times*, 21 July, p. B11.

Richards, C. (1995). 'Schools to join fight against racism in sport', *The Age*, Friday 19 May, p. 5.

Ries, A. and Trout, J. (1986). *Positioning: The Battle for Your Mind*, Warner Books, New York.

Roberts, K. (2002). 'Visa playing its cards right', *SportBusiness International*, February, pp. 22-3.

Sandler, D.M. and Shani, D. (1989). 'Olympic sponsorship vs. "ambush" marketing: who gets the gold?', *Journal of Advertising Research*, August/September, pp. 9-14.

Schaaf, P. (1995). *Sports Marketing: It's Not Just a Game Anymore*, Prometheus Books, Amherst, NY.

Schulze, J. (2001). 'New ratings system shakes the networks', *The Age*, 12 February, p. 3.

Seitel, F.P. (1995). *The Practice of Public Relations*, Prentice-Hall, Englewood Cliffs, NJ.

Sherman, A.J. (1991). *Franchising and Licensing: Two Ways to Build Your Business*, American Management Association, New York.

Shilbury, D. (1989). 'Characteristics of sport marketing: developing trends', *ACHPER National Journal*, Autumn, pp. 21-4.

——(1991). 'Marketing scores with game plan for sports', *Marketing*, July, pp. 18-22.

——(1994). 'Delivering quality service in professional sport', *Sport Marketing Quarterly*, 3 (1), pp. 29-35.

——(1994). 'Ticketing strategy in the Australian National Basketball League', *Sport Marketing Quarterly*, 3 (1), pp. 17-22.

Shoebridge, N. (1996). 'The sprint to Atlanta becomes a marathon to Sydney', *Business Review Weekly*, 29 April, p. 75.

Shoham, A. and Kahle, L.R. (1996). 'Spectators, viewers, readers: communication and consumption in sport marketing', *Sport Marketing Quarterly*, 5 (1), pp. 11–19.

Simeon, R. (1999). 'Evaluating domestic and international web-site strategies', *Internet Research: Electronic Networking Applications and Policy*, 9 (4), pp. 297–308.

Sleight, S. (1989). *Sponsorship: What Is It and How to Use It*, McGraw-Hill, Sydney.

Smith, A. and Stewart, B. (1999). *Sports Management: A Guide to Professional Practice*, Allen & Unwin, Sydney.

Smith, G. (1996a). 'A strategy to sell the Swans', *The Age*, 6 June, p. B6.

——(1996b). 'Swans kick goals with marketing research', *Marketing*, June, Niche, Melbourne.

Smith, P. (1995a). 'AFL is out of step in attempt to solve race row', *The Age*, Monday 8 May, p. 1.

——(1995b). 'AFL a bold and significant leader against racism', *The Age*, Saturday 1 July, p.55, Melbourne.

Sofios, S. (2002). 'They displayed the spirit of Sydney and we thank them', *The Daily Telegraph*, 16 September, p. 19.

Spolestra, J. (1991). *How to Sell the Last Seat in the House*, vol. 1, SRO Partners, Portland, OR.

Sport and Recreation Victoria (2000). *Sport and Recreation Business Information Series*, No. 3. p. 1.

SportBusiness (2000). 'Sportfacs', April, p. 58.

SportBusiness International (2002). 'Content to strike new sponsorship deals', March, p. 46.

Standing, C. (2000). *Internet Commerce Development*, Artech House, Boston.

Stanton, W.J., Miller, K.E. and Layton, R. (1995). *Fundamentals of Marketing*, 3rd edn, McGraw-Hill, Sydney.

Stapleton, R. (1995). 'Michael Long's true colours', *Inside Sport*, no. 43, July.

Stensholt, J. (2002). 'Rugby's dream run', *Business Review Weekly*, 4–10 April, pp. 70-3.

Stotlar, D. (1993). *Successful Sport Marketing*, Brown & Benchmark, Dubuque, IA.

——(1995). 'Sports grill demographics and marketing implications', *Sport Marketing Quarterly*, 3 (3), pp. 9–16.

Strategy Planning Group (1992). *Towards the Millennium: Building a Strategic Vision for the MCC*, Melbourne Cricket Club, Melbourne.

Sutherland, M. (1993). *Advertising and the Mind of the Consumer*, Allen & Unwin, Sydney.

Sutton, W.A. and Parrett, I. (1992). 'Marketing the core product in professional team sports in the United States', *Sport Marketing Quarterly*, 1 (2), pp. 7–19.

Swan, J.E. and Trawick, I.F. (1980). 'Satisfaction related to predictive vs desired expectations', in Fourth Annual Conference on Consumer Satisfaction, Dissatisfaction and Complaining Behavior (1979): *Refining Concepts and Measures of Consumer Satisfaction and Complaining Behavior*, H.K. Hunt and R.L. Day (eds), Indiana University, Bloomington, IN, pp. 7–12.

Swan, J.E., Trawick, I.F. and Carroll, M.G. (1982). 'Satisfaction related to predictive, desired expectations: A field study', in Fifth Annual Conference on Consumer Satisfaction, Dissatisfaction and Complaining Behavior (1980): *New Findings on Consumer Satisfaction and Complaining*, R.L. Day and H.K. Hunt (eds), Indiana University, Bloomington, IN, pp. 11–14.

The Sydney Morning Herald (2002). 'Reebok's Cup spend won't runneth over', 11 February, p. 25.

Taylor, L. (1984). 'The marketing and sponsorship of sport in Australia', *Sports Coach*, 8 (2), pp. 12–14.

Team Marketing Report (2001). 'Team Marketing Report's NBA Fan Cost Index 2000-2001', *Team Marketing Report Inc.*, Chicago, IL.

Tennis Australia (2001). The perfect match for Australia: Tennis Australia strategic plan, 2002–2004, Melbourne, Author.

Teutsch, D. (2002). 'All you need is gloves', *The Sun-Herald*, 29 September, p. 52.

Thamnopoulos, I. (2000). 'Ticketing the Sydney 200 Olympic Games: Marketing and operational aspects in Olympic marketing', *unpublished Master of Management in Sport Management Project*, UTS, Sydney.

Timms, D. (2002). 'Plenty to crow about', *Herald Sun*, 19 April, p. 108.

Todreas, T.M. (1999). *Value Creation and Branding in Television's Digital Age. Quorum Books*, Westport, CT.
Turner, P. and Shilbury, D. (1997). 'Sport on television: a study of the Australian Football League television rights', *Sport Marketing Quarterly*, 6 (3), pp. 55-62.
USA Today (1994). 'TV pays the way', 21 October.
Van Leeuwen, L. (2001). 'Determinants of customer satisfaction with the season ticket service of professional sport clubs', unpublished doctoral dissertation, University of Technology, Sydney.
Veeck, B. and Linn, E. (1962). *Veeck–as in Wreck*, New American Library, New York.
——(2002) 'Hitting an all-time low', *The Sydney Morning Herald*, 10 July, p. 35.
Wakefield, K.L. and Blodgett, J.G. (1994). 'The importance of servicescapes in leisure service settings', *Journal of Services Marketing*, 8 (3), pp. 66-76.
Wakefield, K.L., and Blodgett, J.G. (1996). 'The effect of the servicescape on customers' behavioral intentions in leisure service settings'. *Journal of Services Marketing*, 10 (6), pp. 45-61.
Wakefield, K.L., Blodgett, J.G., and Sloan, H.J. (1996). Measurement and management of the sportscape, *Journal of Sport Management*, 10 (1), pp. 15-31.
Wakefield, K.L., and Sloan, H.J. (1995). 'The effects of team loyalty and selected stadium factors on spectator attendance', *Journal of Sport Management*, 9 (2), pp. 153-72.
Wallace, T. (2002). 'Expanding the branding', *Football Business International*, March, pp. 31-2.
Walmsley, D. (2001). 'Is the rights party over?', *Sport Business International*, November, p. 26.
Warren, I. and Tsaousis, S. (1997). 'Racism and the law in Australian Rules Football: A critical analysis', *Sporting Traditions*, 14 (1).
Westerbeek, H.M. (2000). 'Is sponsorship retention dependent on the geographic location of the sport facility?', *Journal of Marketing Communications*, 6 (2), pp. 53-68.
Westerbeek, H.M. and Smith, A. (2001). 'Understanding the criteria for a winning bid strategy', *The Future for Host Cities*, SportBusiness Group, p. 24.
——(2002). 'Location dependency and sport sponsors: a factor analytic study', *Sport Marketing Quarterly*, 11 (3), pp. 151-61.
——(2003). *Sport Business in the Global Marketplace*, Palgrave Macmillan, London.
Westerbeek, H.M. and Turner, P. (1996). 'Market power of sport organisations: an Australian case study', *Conference Proceedings: 4th International Conference on Sport Management (EASM)*, Montpellier, France.
Westland, J.C. and Clark, T.H.K. (2000). *Global Electronic Commerce: Theory and Case Studies*, The MIT Press, London.
Whyte, J. (2001). 'Adelaide's wheel of fortune', *Australian Financial Review*, 20 January, p. 9.
Wilkof, N.J. (1995). *Trade Mark Licensing*, Sweet & Maxwell, London.
Wilmoth, P. (2001). 'TV ratings systems favors the young', *The Age*, 23 May p. 2.
Wilmshurst, J. (1993). *Below-the Line Promotion*, Butterworth/Heinemann, Oxford.
Wilner, B. (2000). 'Internet leading NFL development', *Sport Business*, August, p. 28.
——(2001a). 'Tiger helps PGA paw $870m TV deal', *SportBusiness International*, September, p. 18.
——(2001b). 'Back in the high life again', *SportBusiness International*, November, p. 15.
Zbar, J.D. (2002). 'Ball's bounce goes ESPN, TNT's way'. *Advertising Age*, 73 (23), p. S12.
Zeithaml, V.A., Parasuraman, A. and Berry, L. (1985). 'Problems and strategies in services marketing', *Journal of Marketing*, 49, Spring, pp. 33-46.
——(1990). *Delivering Service Quality: Balancing Customer Perceptions and Expectations*, Free Press, New York.
Zhang, J.J., Pease, D.G., Lam, T.C., Bellerive, L.M., Pham, U.L., Williamson, D.P., Lee, J.T. andWall, K.A. (2001). 'Sociomotivational factors affecting attendance at minor league hockey games', *Sport Marketing Quarterly*, 10 (1), pp. 43-56.

Index